GUN CONTROL

A Documentary and Reference Guide

Robert J. Spitzer

Greenwood Press

Westport, Connecticut • London

10/09

Library of Congress Cataloging-in-Publication Data

Spitzer, Robert J., 1953–
    Gun control : a documentary and reference guide / Robert J. Spitzer.
        p.   cm.
    Includes index.
    ISBN 978–0–313–34566–1 (alk. paper)
    1. Firearms—Law and legislature—United States.   I. Title.
    KF3941.S678 2009
    344.7305'33—dc22   2008037472

British Library Cataloguing in Publication Data is available.

Library of Congress Catalog Card Number: 2008037472
ISBN: 978-0-313-34566-1

First published in 2009

Greenwood Press, 88 Post Road West, Westport, CT 06881
An imprint of Greenwood Publishing Group, Inc.
www.greenwood.com

Printed in the United States of America

The paper used in this book complies with the
Permanent Paper Standard issued by the National
Information Standards Organization (Z39.48–1984).

10 9 8 7 6 5 4 3 2 1

To Tess
At the sound of your voice,
heaven opens its portals to me—

CONTENTS

Contents

READER'S GUIDE TO RELATED DOCUMENTS AND SIDEBARS

Note: Some documents appear in more than one category.

Reader's Guide to Related Documents and Sidebars

FOREWORD

Cross-national comparisons of gun-related mortality rates reveal that something is sorely amiss in the United States. Compared to its peer nations—other industrially developed democracies—the United States has a homicide rate that is six times higher, with two-thirds of its homicides involving firearms; and when gun deaths resulting from homicide, suicide, and accident are taken together, the U.S. rate is almost eight times that of the developed nations of Western Europe, Australia, Canada, Japan, and New Zealand (14.2 per 100,000 people in the United States vs. 1.8 per 100,000 in the other 15 nations; see Krug et al., 1998). A variety of factors coalesce to explain this disparity, including the greater levels of economic inequality and social heterogeneity of the United States compared to its typical peer nation; however, two factors stand out: Relative to its peers, the United States has a huge number of guns, nearly as many guns as there are adults (more than 230,000,000), and it has weak national gun laws.

Contrary to the pronouncements of the National Rifle Association (NRA) and other gun rights organizations that deny a causal relationship between gun prevalence and gun violence, such a relationship does exist, as well as between the strength of gun control laws and levels of gun violence. As demonstrated by Ayres and Donohue (2003), Cook and Ludwig (2000), Duggan (2001), Hemenway (2004), and Lambert (2005), these relationships are complex and require sophisticated statistical analyses to fully tease out. The upshot, however, is that Australia, Canada, Japan, New Zealand, and most European countries have much stricter gun regulations than the United States, and these regulations provide part of the explanation for why their homicide and gun-related death rates are generally so much lower. Most important, these countries require that guns are registered, that gun-owners are licensed, and that guns are stored with utmost security. To get a license, a potential gun-owner must typically pass an exam on gun safety. Also required are comprehensive background checks of potential gun purchasers to prevent sales to those with histories of criminality or mental incapacity. Although background checks are required by federally licensed firearms dealers in the United States when selling guns to their customers, sales between private individuals (including those at gun shows and flea markets) are not regulated by federal law, as they are in its peer nations. Moreover, those firearms most often involved in criminal violence—*handguns*—are either outlawed or restricted so severely by the United States' peer nations that ownership is extremely rare. This contrast is reflected in the comparatively high percentage of households with a handgun present in the United States (about 22%) and the relatively tiny percentages elsewhere: 0.1 percent in the United Kingdom, 0.2 percent in the Netherlands, 2 percent in Australia, 2.5 percent in Spain, and 7 percent or less in Belgium, Canada, Finland, France, Norway, and Spain (see Killias 1993). The striking exception in Europe is Switzerland, which has relatively lax gun laws compared to the United States and a relatively high percentage of households where guns are present. Switzerland is the NRA's favorite example of the maxim "guns don't kill, people do" because it has a low murder rate. Gun-control advocates are quick to point out, however, that Switzerland's population is generally better trained than that of the United States in the safe and proper use of firearms, as most adult Swiss men are members of the national militia.

Why is the United States out of step with its peer nations regarding gun control? It is a difficult question to answer. Highly respected political scientist Robert J. Spitzer helps us put together an answer in the present volume. The many historical and contemporary documents he has drawn together allow for the nuanced interpretations of American culture, politics, and history that are required to understand the United States' "exceptionalism" regarding gun ownership and gun rights.

The documentary record reveals that gun ownership was critical to the survival of the colonies and to the waging of their successful war to break away from Great Britain. Indeed, in the seventeenth and eighteenth centuries, a key concern of the colonial and early national governments was to get more arms into the hands of citizens. At the same time, the record shows that the motivation was not the protection of the right of the individual to bear and possess arms but to produce well-armed militias. The record also shows that local and state governments have had no hesitation in imposing gun regulations to maintain order and to prevent overhunting. The Second Amendment, held up today as sacrosanct by gun rights organization in their never-ending resistance to gun control legislation, was not intended to protect the rights of individual gun-owners, nor was it invoked to do this by state and federal courts until June 2008 when the U.S. Supreme Court ruled in favor of Richard Heller in *D.C. v. Heller*. The Supreme Court was sharply divided in its 5–4 vote in favor of Heller, who wanted to keep a handgun in his home for personal protection but was barred by local gun laws—and thus the motivation for his lawsuit. In writing for the five-judge majority, however, Justice Antonin Scalia emphasized that "nothing in our opinion should be taken to cast doubt on longstanding gun control laws, including prohibitions on the possession of firearms by felons and the mentally ill, or laws forbidding the carrying of firearms in sensitive places such as schools and government buildings, or laws imposing conditions and qualifications on the commercial sale of firearms." In this sense, the *Heller* decision coheres with both state and federal courts' consistency in upholding the right of the government to regulate the purchase, possession, transfer, and use of firearms. More generally, there is little fear in the legal community that the ruling will negate other forms of gun control other than the relatively few local laws banning the possession of guns normally considered legal—sporting rifles and shotguns, as well as handguns that hold a small number of rounds.

In sum, Professor Spitzer has provided the serious student of gun control the raw materials, both in the documents he includes and in the keen analyses that he has written to accompany them, to grasp not only where we now stand regarding gun control, but why. These documents and analysis also hold the potential for better grasping how the United States can produce even greater reductions in gun violence.

Gregg Lee Carter
Bryant University Smithfield,
Rhode Island, July 2008

REFERENCES

Ayres, Ian, and John D. Donohue III. 2003. "Shooting Down the More Guns, Less Crime Hypothesis." *Stanford Law Review* 55:1193–1312.

Cook, Philip J., and Jens Ludwig. 2000. *Gun Violence: The Real Cost.* New York: Oxford University Press.

Duggan, Mark. 2001. "More Guns More Crime." *Journal of Political Economy* 99:1086–1114.

Hemenway, David. 2004. *Private Guns, Public Health.* Ann Arbor: University of Michigan Press.

Killias, Martin. 1993. "International Correlations between Gun Ownership and Rates of Homicide and Suicide." *Canadian Medical Association Journal* 148:1721–1725.

Krug, E. G., K. E. Powell, and L. L. Dahlberg. 1998. "Firearm-Related Deaths in the United States and 35 Other High- and Upper-Middle-Income Countries." *International Journal of Epidemiology* 27:214–221.

Lambert, Tim. 2005. *Do More Guns Cause Less Crime?* http://timlambert.org/guns/lott/ Accessed June 10, 2008.

PREFACE

The purpose of this book is to bring together a wide variety of documents, organized both by chronology and subject, in order to provide the reader with a fuller understanding of the history, evolution, scope, and consequences of the issue of gun control. The great emphasis on documents in this book is especially important for this subject matter because it allows the reader to examine these sources firsthand instead of relying on someone else's account of what these documents say. This proves to be of particular value to the reader because so much of the writing and commentary on the contentious gun issue centers on what the nation's founders did and said, on laws, court cases, and other documents that may or may not be described accurately in public writings on the issue.

Chapter 1 begins with founding-era documents up to the formulation and debate concerning the adoption of the modern Constitution. Chapter 2 picks up with the Bill of Rights, centering on the Second Amendment and the right to bear arms enshrined in that amendment, focusing in particular on the critically important debate in the First Congress, followed by the federal government's efforts to effectuate national defense and effective militia service. This chapter also includes early state gun regulations, some of which read very much like contemporary gun laws. Chapter 3 excerpts early, and often neglected, Supreme Court rulings on the meaning of the Second Amendment from the nineteenth century. State court decisions pertaining to gun regulations and rights are examined in chapter 4, and chapter 5 examines twentieth century Supreme Court cases on the Second Amendment and militias, and concludes with the most recent—and significant—high court ruling from 2008 (which is of course in the twenty-first century), *D.C. v. Heller*. Chapter 6 turns to lower federal court rulings, Chapter 7 examines modern federal gun laws, and Chapter 8 provides the texts of state right-to-bear-arms-type provisions, along with party platform excerpts pertaining to gun issues.

The style of document presentation is uniform throughout this book. Each document is introduced by an outline giving the name of the document to follow, the document's date, its location, and a brief summary of its significance. The document is then reprinted, sometimes in edited form (a necessary step given the sheer length of some of the documents), and then followed by an analysis section that summarizes its significance, context, and consequences. Further readings are then offered for the reader seeking more information. Each chapter also includes "Did You Know?" sidebars that highlight some bit of history or related side issue pertinent to the chapter topics. At the back of this book, the reader will find a listing of gun control resources, including Web sites and a bibliography of books on the gun issue. The reader should also note that writing and stylistic habits and conventions have changed over time, and matters like punctuation, capitalization, and seemingly arcane word use often do not follow modern writing conventions, especially in legal documents and documents pre-dating the twentieth century. These apparent quirks are generally maintained for the sake of accuracy. The gun issue has been, and will continue to be, one of the nation's most controversial and intractable policy issues. The documents and sources presented here offer a way for the reader to judge the contemporary debate in the light of those decisions and actions that have brought the nation to this point.

ACKNOWLEDGMENTS

I would like to thank Greenwood Press for the opportunity to contribute to their Reference Guide Series, and especially to editors Alicia Merritt and Kaitlin Ciarmiello. This is the second time I have had the pleasure of working with Alicia, and I value her skill, experience, and professionalism. Kaitlin has also been a pleasure to work with, and I thank her for her good efforts, as well as those of Mary Cotofan. At Cortland, I extend thanks as well to my colleague Christopher Latimer and department manager Deb Dintino. I reserve special gratitude to my research assistant, then-SUNY Cortland student Joe Agovino. Joe's work was prodigious, complete, and prompt. He pulled together numerous documents from sources with which he was formerly unacquainted and helped me with related technical matters. He did a great job. And aside from his important contribution to this work, Joe's many undergraduate accomplishments at Cortland exemplify the value-added nature of a SUNY education. He is one of our institution's many (but among its most gratifying) success stories.

This work drew from many resources to compile the documents and information found in this book. I am grateful for support from SUNY Cortland, and especially its digital imaging specialist, Dawn Van Hall, who did a superb job providing the firearms photographs found in this book, and in preparing for publication those photos she did not take. The gun photographs were made possible thanks to the courtesy of the Cortland City Police Department, and I am especially grateful for the cooperation and assistance of Cortland's men and women in blue, including City Police Chief James Nichols, Lt. Paul Sandy, and Officer J. A. Aiken. The other pictures in this book appear in the public domain courtesy of the National Archives and Records Administration, the Library of Congress, the Lyndon Baines Johnson Library, and the U.S. Army. One other resource merits particular note: the Second Amendment Center at the John Glenn Institute for Public Service and Public Policy at The Ohio State University. The Center, headed by noted historian Saul Cornell, brings together information and sources related to historical gun issues found nowhere else. It offers a valuable resource for researchers, and I recommend its use to all interested in this subject.

As always, I happily acknowledge Mellissa, Aaron, and Olivia; Shannon, Scott, Alexis, Luke, and Cassandra Jane. Gary, Gail, Skye, Jinny, and above all Teresa, to whom this book, and everything worth anything to me, is dedicated.

INTRODUCTION

It is a truism of American politics that some issues seem to invite a consistent and protracted degree of political conflict. It should come as no surprise to the reader that gun control is such an issue.

Modern gun control efforts date back about a century, when two types of events consistently associated with the call for stricter gun laws—crime and assassination—prompted New York State to enact the Sullivan law in 1911. In the 1920s and early 1930s, prohibition and the rise of gangster violence shocked and outraged the nation. That phenomenon, plus an unsuccessful attempt to assassinate newly elected President Franklin D. Roosevelt—the assassin missed his target and instead killed Chicago Mayor Anton Cermak, who had the misfortune of sharing the dais with Roosevelt that day in 1933—yielded the first set of modern national gun laws. In the 1960s, spiraling urban disorder, the spread of crime, and successful assassination attempts against a sitting president (John F. Kennedy), the nation's most prominent civil rights leader (Martin Luther King, Jr.), and a presidential aspirant (Robert F. Kennedy) paved the way for new national gun control measures. In the late 1980s and early 1990s, rising crime and horrific mass shootings spurred new national gun measures. Yet earlier in the 1980s and again in the first decade of the twenty-first century, the national government moved in the opposite direction by reducing gun regulations and, in one instance, actually providing special legal protections for the gun industry.

Despite this well-known narrative, gun controls did not begin with the dawn of the twentieth century. In fact, gun laws are as old as the country itself. Just as the earliest European settlers brought guns with them to the new continent, so too did they impose an array of gun restrictions and regulations. First in the colonies, then as states, laws were enacted to regulate who could and could not own guns, and when and how they were to be carried and used. Other laws actually required gun ownership and carrying as an indispensable means to provide for the common defense. And in America's nineteenth century "Wild West," local laws restricting gun carrying and use were typically enacted as soon as local governments were established; in fact, the enactment of such laws was sometimes a key reason for the incorporation of local communities. Ironically, and contrary to legend, gun laws did more to settle the West than did guns.

If the intersection of gun laws, gun use, and gun history in America reveal anything, it is that the private and the public have always been intertwined. Americans owned guns for their own purposes (although historians continue to debate how extensive gun ownership and use actually was from colonial times to the pre–Civil War era), but the most important reason for gun ownership was collective self-protection—to protect the colonies from Native Americans, from European military might projected into the Western hemisphere, and to divorce ourselves from our colonial founders, the British. In its early years of existence, America not only couldn't afford, but scarcely trusted, standing armies; and in a land as vast as ours, citizen militias were the nation's bulwark for defense. Yet they were a mostly shoddy, incompetent, and inept bulwark, and it is no small testament to American fortitude—or perhaps luck—that the country survived.

In this book, the reader has a chance to examine a plethora of documents that tell much about the intersection of private gun habits with public gun policies. As a document-based reference work, the materials presented here cover four broad categories: constitutional provisions; colonial, state, and federal laws (what is called "statutory" law); state and federal court cases (judge-made law); and various letters and other assorted documents that inform the meaning of the first three. These documents enhance our understanding of citizens' gun practices both as individuals and as militia-members, and of broader rights, chiefly examined under the "right to bear arms" referenced in the Second Amendment of the Bill of Rights, a subject that receives great attention here.

FOUNDING DOCUMENTS AND GUN RIGHTS (CHAPTER 1)

The first chapter begins with colonial-era documents that reference some precursor to what became the Second Amendment's right to bear arms. Most agree that the wording that found its way into the American Bill of Rights of 1791 began in the British Bill of Rights from the previous century, although there is no direct evidence that the British proviso was a basis for the American version. Wording from the Virginia Bill of Rights did, indisputably, help shape the federal Bill of Rights. As all these documents say, the right to bear arms described citizens' obligations to serve their state and/or country in militia service at a time when (1) militias were America's primary defense from hostile forces; (2) these forces were, at best, uneven in their reliability (commanding General George Washington had far harsher words); and (3) militia-eligible citizens were not just encouraged, but required to have and keep arms in preparation for militia service. When the young America adopted its new Constitution of 1787 after pushing aside the ineffectual Articles of Confederation, it brought formerly state-controlled militias squarely under federal control. This was a seismic shift in the balance of power away from the formerly dominant state governments, and lay at the core of arguably the greatest political dispute of the day.

THE BILL OF RIGHTS, THE SECOND AMENDMENT, AND EARLY LAWS (CHAPTER 2)

Chapter 2 offers a series of documents that provide the best direct evidence regarding the intent and meaning of the Second Amendment. All of these sources link the bearing of arms with the functioning of American militias. Debate over the amendment centered on squarely military matters, such as whether wording allowing militia-eligible men with religious objections to military service should be included. No one in any debate or text argued or suggested that the Second Amendment's right to bear arms protected an individual right to own "arms" for personal self-defense, hunting, or other purposes not related to the "well regulated militia" referenced in the first part of the Second Amendment. In fact, some early laws gave to state governments the power to confiscate guns from citizens who refused to swear allegiance to the new government. Other early laws imposed harsh penalties on those who violated local hunting regulations. Here as with other gun measures, laws regulating hunting practices were not new to the twentieth century, but existed even before the time of the ratification of the Constitution.

EARLY SUPREME COURT RULINGS ON GUN LAWS AND RIGHTS (CHAPTER 3)

The Supreme Court first heard cases involving the Second Amendment in the post–Civil War era of the nineteenth century. Several principles arose from these cases—principles that still apply to the meaning of the right to bear arms. The high court held that the Second Amendment was not "incorporated," meaning that it applied only to the federal government, and not to the states. Until the very end of the nineteenth century, none of the Bill of Rights was "incorporated" or applied to the states (the process, referred to as "incorporation," eventually occurred because of the Fourteenth Amendment's guarantee that states could not deprive persons within their borders of equal protection and due process). Up to the present time, most of the Bill of Rights has been applied to the states, but not all. Among portions not incorporated (as of the date of this publication) is the Second Amendment. In addition, the court concluded that the states cannot prevent citizens from performing their service to militias, that control over military activities is the exclusive province of the government, that citizens cannot create their own militias outside of government control, and that the Second Amendment pertains to militia matters.

EARLY STATE COURT RULINGS ON GUN REGULATIONS AND RIGHTS (CHAPTER 4)

Throughout the nineteenth century, dozens of state court rulings were handed down that offered some perspectives on both the federal Constitution's right to bear arms, on similar state constitutional provisions, and on how state regulations pertained to either or both. Bearing in mind the principle that state courts exist to interpret state, not federal law, some of these decisions do shed light on how such provisions were viewed. In general, state courts upheld state gun laws and other related restrictions. When they offered opinions about the meaning of the federal right to bear arms, it was always as a right related to citizen service in a government-regulated militia. And when interpreting often more broadly written state right to bear arms-type provisions, the state courts weighted public safety and militia service concerns as the most important values.

TWENTIETH CENTURY SUPREME COURT CASES (CHAPTER 5)

Supreme Court case law in the twentieth century spoke again to the meaning of the Second Amendment and also addressed the definition, evolution, and role of the modern militias, now known as the National Guard. The most important Second Amendment case of the era, *U.S. v. Miller*, again viewed the amendment as a militia-based right, an interpretation echoed in subsequent cases. Yet in 2008 (a twenty-first century case, of course), the Supreme Court redefined the meaning of the Second Amendment in the important *Heller* case, interpreting the amendment as protecting an individual right, aside from militia service (overturning in fact, although not in law, the *Miller* case). In addition, the high court ratified the century-long trend toward greater federal government control (and less state control) over the former militias. With court approval, the old-style general militias, encompassing all males from the ages of 18 to 45, were essentially deactivated; the old-style volunteer or select militias (which behaved more like professional military units) became the National Guards.

LOWER FEDERAL COURT RULINGS ON THE SECOND AMENDMENT (CHAPTER 6)

Beginning in 1942, nearly 50 lower federal court rulings have been handed down that offer interpretation on the Second Amendment. Using the Supreme Court's 1939 *Miller* case as the key interpretive guide, all of those court decisions (with two exceptions) viewed the amendment as a collective or militia-based right that pertained to citizen service in a government-organized and regulated militia, consistently turning aside claims that the amendment provides a personal or individual right for citizens to own guns, even upholding, in one instance, a local law barring handgun possession. In 2001, however, a federal court ruled for the first time in the *Emerson* case that the Second Amendment did, in fact, protect a personal or individual right—although in that case, the federal court's ruling was of no help to the man who sought protection under the Second Amendment. Then in 2007, another federal court accepted the individualist view (saying that the Second Amendment protected an individual right to own guns for such purposes as self-defense and hunting but also pertaining to militia service as well), but this time used it to overturn the District of Columbia's handgun ban. That case, *Parker v. D.C.*, is not reprinted here because the ruling was appealed to the Supreme Court as *D.C. v. Heller*. That ruling appears in Chapter 5.

militia-eligible men with religious objections to military service should be included. No one in any debate or text argued or suggested that the Second Amendment's right to bear arms protected an individual right to own "arms" for personal self-defense, hunting, or other purposes not related to the "well regulated militia" referenced in the first part of the Second Amendment. In fact, some early laws gave to state governments the power to confiscate guns from citizens who refused to swear allegiance to the new government. Other early laws imposed harsh penalties on those who violated local hunting regulations. Here as with other gun measures, laws regulating hunting practices were not new to the twentieth century, but existed even before the time of the ratification of the Constitution.

EARLY SUPREME COURT RULINGS ON GUN LAWS AND RIGHTS (CHAPTER 3)

The Supreme Court first heard cases involving the Second Amendment in the post–Civil War era of the nineteenth century. Several principles arose from these cases—principles that still apply to the meaning of the right to bear arms. The high court held that the Second Amendment was not "incorporated," meaning that it applied only to the federal government, and not to the states. Until the very end of the nineteenth century, none of the Bill of Rights was "incorporated" or applied to the states (the process, referred to as "incorporation," eventually occurred because of the Fourteenth Amendment's guarantee that states could not deprive persons within their borders of equal protection and due process). Up to the present time, most of the Bill of Rights has been applied to the states, but not all. Among portions not incorporated (as of the date of this publication) is the Second Amendment. In addition, the court concluded that the states cannot prevent citizens from performing their service to militias, that control over military activities is the exclusive province of the government, that citizens cannot create their own militias outside of government control, and that the Second Amendment pertains to militia matters.

EARLY STATE COURT RULINGS ON GUN REGULATIONS AND RIGHTS (CHAPTER 4)

Throughout the nineteenth century, dozens of state court rulings were handed down that offered some perspectives on both the federal Constitution's right to bear arms, on similar state constitutional provisions, and on how state regulations pertained to either or both. Bearing in mind the principle that state courts exist to interpret state, not federal law, some of these decisions do shed light on how such provisions were viewed. In general, state courts upheld state gun laws and other related restrictions. When they offered opinions about the meaning of the federal right to bear arms, it was always as a right related to citizen service in a government-regulated militia. And when interpreting often more broadly written state right to bear arms-type provisions, the state courts weighted public safety and militia service concerns as the most important values.

1

FOUNDING DOCUMENTS
AND GUN RIGHTS

The British Bill of Rights, 1689

- **Document:** The British Bill of Rights, also known as the Declaration of Rights; subtitled, "An Act Declaring the Rights and Liberties of the Subject and Settling the Succession of the Crown"
- **Date:** 1689
- **Where:** London, England
- **Significance:** This is the first document that expressly references citizen arms-bearing in the context of a statement regarding rights and liberties.

DOCUMENT

Whereas the late King James the Second, by the assistance of divers evil counsellors, judges and ministers employed by him, did endeavour to subvert and extirpate the Protestant religion and the laws and liberties of this kingdom. . . . By causing several good subjects being Protestants to be disarmed at the same time when papists were both armed and employed contrary to law. . . .

That the subjects which are Protestants may have arms for their defence suitable to their conditions and as allowed by law. . . .

SOURCE: http://www.yale.edu/lawweb/avalon/england.htm

ANALYSIS

For 13 years in the mid-seventeenth century, professional military forces under the control of Oliver Cromwell ruled England. During this period, the country was ruled by military force. After Cromwell's overthrow, monarchy was restored under Charles II, who was succeeded by James II. James was a devout Catholic, however, and he attempted to transform Britain into a Catholic nation, referred to as promoting "papism," by barring Protestants from top civilian and military posts, and appointing Catholics. Contrary to existing law, James tried to disarm Protestants in this mostly Protestant country. James's oppressive policies on behalf of Catholicism, including a swelling Catholic-led army that might overwhelm local Protestant militias controlled by the landed gentry, eventually led to his overthrow and replacement by William of Orange and Mary II, an event dubbed the Glorious Revolution of 1688.

Thereafter, Parliament enacted the British Bill of Rights, a document that detailed James's many abuses, including his effort to disarm the Protestant militias, and then stipulating the protection of various rights. The right to arms quoted in this document was consistent with a wide variety of government restrictions on gun ownership imposed by the British government extending back more than a century before this time. As would be true of the early American militias, militia members were often obliged to provide their own weapons instead of being armed by the government. This provision from the British Bill of Rights is often cited as the forerunner of the Second Amendment's "right to bear arms" provision that later appeared in the American Bill of Rights, although there is no direct evidence of such a link.

FURTHER READING

Macaulay, Thomas Babington. *The History of England from the Accession of James II.* 5 vols. New York: T. Y. Crowell, 1879.

Malcolm, Joyce Lee. *To Keep and Bear Arms.* Cambridge, MA: Harvard University Press, 1994.

Schwoerer, Lois. "To Hold and Bear Arms: The English Perspective." *Chicago-Kent Law Review* 76 (2000): 27–60.

The Virginia Bill of Rights, 1776

- *Document:* The Virginia Bill of Rights, also called the Virginia Declaration of Rights
- *Date:* June 12, 1776
- *Where:* Williamsburg, Virginia
- *Significance:* This important early statement of rights includes wording presaging that appearing in the Bill of Rights.

DOCUMENT

A DECLARATION OF RIGHTS *made by the representatives of the good people of Virginia, assembled in full and free Convention; which rights do pertain to them, and their posterity, as the basis and foundation of government.*

(1) That all men are by nature equally free and independent, and have certain inherent rights, of which, when they enter into a state of society, they cannot, by any compact, deprive or divest their posterity; namely, the enjoyment of life and liberty, with the means of acquiring and possessing property, and pursuing and obtaining happiness and safety.

(2) That all power is vested in, and consequently derived from, the people; that magistrates are their trustees and servants, and at all times amenable to them.

(3) That government is, or ought to be, instituted for the common benefit, protection, and security, of the people, nation, or community; of all the various modes and forms of government that is best, which is capable of producing the greatest degree of happiness and safety, and is most effectually secured against the danger of maladministration; and that whenever any government shall be found inadequate or contrary to these purposes, a majority of

the community hath an indubitable, unalienable, and indefeasible right, to reform, alter, or abolish it, in such manner as shall be judged most conducive to the publick weal. . . .

(13) That a well regulated militia, composed of the body of the people, trained to arms, is the proper, natural, and safe defence of a free state; that standing armies, in time of peace, should be avoided, as dangerous to liberty; and that, in all cases, the military should be under strict subordination to, and governed by, the civil power.

SOURCE: http://www.constitution.org/bor/vir_bor.htm

ANALYSIS

The Virginia Bill of Rights was formulated by George Mason and adopted by the Virginia Convention of Delegates. It proclaimed a series of fundamental rights, including liberty, equality, the right of the accused to confront their accusers, freedom of the press, freedom of religion, and a prohibition against excessive bails. Mason drew from previous documents, including the British Bill of Rights. The Virginia document's sweeping explication of rights served as a model for subsequent early documents, including the Declaration of Independence. Item 13 quoted here underscored the great store placed in militias as the mainstay of military defense. Even though militias were part-time soldiers who lacked the training, skill, and equipment of professional armies, they were popular in the country because Americans believed that standing armies posed a threat to hard-won liberties—a threat often realized in European history. Not only did the Continental Congress and colonial governments lack the resources to form and fund a standing army, they could scarcely even afford to arm the militias; thus, the burden for obtaining weapons and other equipment for military exigencies fell to militia-eligible men. Bitter experience showed that men rarely possessed firearms or other weapons usable for military purposes.

FURTHER READING

Rossiter, Clinton. *Seedtime of the Republic*. New York: Harcourt, Brace, and World, 1953.

Snow, Donald M., and Dennis M. Drew. *From Lexington to Desert Storm*. Armonk, NY: M. E. Sharpe, 1994.

Wood, Gordon S. *The Creation of the American Republic, 1776–1787*. Chapel Hill: University of North Carolina Press, 1998.

The Declaration of Independence, 1776

- **Document:** The Declaration of Independence
- **Date:** July 4, 1776
- **Where:** Philadelphia, Pennsylvania
- **Significance:** The Declaration of Independence was the document in which the American colonies explained to the world why they wished to sever ties with Great Britain and become an independent nation. Its eloquence and idealistic expression have been widely admired around the world.

DOCUMENT

When in the Course of human events it becomes necessary for one people to dissolve the political bands which have connected them with another and to assume among the powers of the earth, the separate and equal station to which the Laws of Nature and of Nature's God entitle them, a decent respect to the opinions of mankind requires that they should declare the causes which impel them to the separation. . . .

He has kept among us, in times of peace, Standing Armies without the Consent of our legislatures.

He has affected to render the Military independent of and superior to the Civil Power. . . .

For quartering large bodies of armed troops among us:

For protecting them, by a mock Trial from punishment for any Murders which they should commit on the Inhabitants of these States. . . .

He is at this time transporting large Armies of foreign Mercenaries to compleat the works of death, desolation, and tyranny, already begun with circumstances of Cruelty

& Perfidy scarcely paralleled in the most barbarous ages, and totally unworthy the Head of a civilized nation. . . .

SOURCE: http://www.ushistory.org/declaration/document/index.htm

"Washington Receiving a Salute on the Field of Trenton." Copy of print by William Holl after John Faed, published ca. 1860s. National Archives and Records Administration.

ANALYSIS

The lengthy laundry list of grievances expressed in the Declaration of Independence against the British government (the reference to "He" at the start of many of its sentences refers to King George III) included abuses by the British army (the "standing army" mentioned in the document), such as ignoring local laws, intimidating the local populations, and using paid mercenaries to enforce British rule. All of these practices fed American mistrust of professional, standing armies, for not only did they hold themselves above the law, but their actions supported American fears that standing armies would overthrow civilian governments and deprive people of their liberties, as had often happened in European history. This fear of standing armies led young America to rely mostly on militias during and after the Revolutionary War, but though politically popular, militias were too often unreliable or ineffective on the battlefield.

FURTHER READING

Armitage, David. *The Declaration of Independence: A Global History.* Cambridge, MA: Harvard University Press, 2007.

Ferling, John. *Almost a Miracle: The American Victory in the War of Independence.* New York: Oxford University Press, 2007.

Letter from General George Washington to the Continental Congress

- **Document:** Letter from George Washington to the President of Congress
- **Date:** September 24, 1776
- **Where:** Harlem, New York
- **Significance:** Washington's desperate plea for help to the Congress underscored the generally critical military situation and the many problems caused by the colonial militias.

DOCUMENT

To the President of Congress,

Colonel Morris's, on the Heights of Harlem,
September 24, 1776.

Sir: From the hours allotted to Sleep, I will borrow a few Moments to convey my thoughts on sundry important matters to Congress. I shall offer them, with that sincerity which ought to characterize a man of candour; and with the freedom which may be used in giving useful information, without incurring the imputation of presumption.

We are now as it were, upon the eve of another dissolution of our Army; the remembrance of the difficulties which happened upon that occasion last year, the consequences which might have followed the change, if proper advantages had been taken by the Enemy; added to a knowledge of the present temper and Situation of the Troops, reflect but a very gloomy prospect upon the appearance of things now, and satisfie me, beyond the possibility of doubt, that unless some speedy, and effectual measures are adopted by Congress, our cause will be lost. . . .

To place any dependance upon Militia, is, assuredly, resting upon a broken staff. Men just dragged from the tender Scenes of domestick life; unaccustomed to the din of Arms; totally unacquainted with every kind of Military skill, which being followed by a want of confidence in themselves, when opposed to Troops regulary train'd, disciplined, and appointed, superior in knowledge, and superior in Arms, makes them timid, and ready to fly from their own shadows. Besides, the sudden change in their manner of living, (particularly in the lodging) brings on sickness in many; impatience in all, and such an unconquerable desire of returning to their respective homes that it not only produces shameful, and scandalous Desertions among themselves, but infuses the like spirit in others. Again, Men accustomed to unbounded freedom, and no controul, cannot brook the Restraint which is indispensably necessary to the good order and Government of an Army; without which, licentiousness, and every kind of disorder triumphantly reign. To bring Men to a proper degree of Subordination, is not the work of a day, a Month or even a year; and unhappily for us, and the cause we are Engaged in, the little discipline I have been labouring to establish in the Army under my immediate Command, is in a manner done away by having such a mixture of Troops as have been called together within these few Months.

Relaxed, and unfit, as our Rules and Regulations of War are, for the Government of an Army, the Militia (those properly so called, for of these we have two sorts, the Six Months Men and those sent in as a temporary aid) do not think themselves subject to 'em, and therefore take liberties, which the Soldier is punished for; this creates jealousy; jealousy begets dissatisfaction, and these by degrees ripen into Mutiny; keeping the whole Army in a confused, and disordered State; rendering the time of those who wish to see regularity and good Order prevail more unhappy than Words can describe. Besides this, such repeated changes take place, that all arrangement is set at nought, and the constant fluctuation of things, deranges every plan, as fast as adopted. These Sir, Congress may be assured, are but a small part of the Inconveniences which might be enumerated and attributed to Militia; but there is one that merits particular attention, and that is the expence. Certain I am, that it would be cheaper to keep 50, or 100,000 Men in constant pay than to depend upon half the number, and supply the other half occasionally by Militia. The time the latter is in pay before and after they are in Camp, assembling and Marching; the waste of Ammunition; the consumption of Stores, which in spite of every Resolution, and requisition of Congress they must be furnished with, or sent home, added to other incidental expences consequent upon their coming, and conduct in Camp, surpasses all Idea, and destroys every kind of regularity and economy which you could establish among fixed and Settled Troops; and will, in my opinion prove (if the scheme is adhered to) the Ruin of our Cause.

The Jealousies of a standing Army, and the Evils to be apprehended from one, are remote; and in my judgment, situated and circumstanced as we are, not at all to be dreaded; but the consequence of wanting one, according to my Ideas, formed from the present view of things, is certain, and inevitable Ruin; for if I was called upon to declare upon Oath, whether the Militia have been most serviceable or hurtful upon the whole; I should subscribe to the latter. . . .

SOURCE: http://www.let.rug.nl/usa/P/gw1/writings/brf/recrui.htm

ANALYSIS

Named commander-in-chief of American forces during the Revolutionary War, George Washington faced an array of daunting problems in attempting to defeat the British Army, generally considered the finest fighting force in the world in the eighteenth century. Although in public Washington praised his forces, he complained bitterly in private correspondence to Congress about his desperate military situation, a situation made nearly impossible by his need to rely on colonial militias. Part-time citizen soldier militias were popular in the country, just as standing armies aroused suspicion; yet Washington's bitter experiences with the militias pushed the uprising against the British to the brink of failure. The militiamen lacked training, discipline, and every military skill, including knowledge of firearms. They got drunk, fought, consumed limited supplies, and too often fled from camp or battle. As Washington opined in his letter, amateur militia units were simply no match for a professional army, and he urged Congress to appropriate money to increase the number of professional soldiers instead of relying on militias from the colonies. Congress did not oblige him. Ultimately, of course, America did win its independence, thanks to Washington's willingness to abandon traditional military tactics, the tenacity of the core group of soldiers who composed the Continental Army and who maintained the force's continuity as militia groups came and went, the sheer size of American forces (more than 400,000 men participated during the course of the war), British difficulties related to distance and supply, the assistance of the French, and the American "home court" advantage.

FURTHER READING

Jensen, Merrill. *The New Nation*. New York: Vintage, 1965.

Mahon, John K. *The American Militia: Decade of Decision, 1789–1800*. Gainesville: University of Florida Press, 1960.

Shy, John. *A People Numerous and Armed*. Ann Arbor: University of Michigan Press, 1990.

The U.S. Constitution of 1787 Pertaining to Militias

- *Document:* U.S. Constitution of 1787
- *Date:* completed September 17, 1787
- *Where:* Philadelphia, Pennsylvania
- *Significance:* The modern Constitution is the cornerstone of the modern American legal and political system, including the enshrinement of the militia system and the right to bear arms.

DOCUMENT

Article I, Section. 8.

The Congress shall have Power To lay and collect Taxes, Duties, Imposts and Excises, to pay the Debts and provide for the common Defence and general Welfare of the United States; but all Duties, Imposts and Excises shall be uniform throughout the United States . . .

To declare War, grant Letters of Marque and Reprisal, and make Rules concerning Captures on Land and Water;

To raise and support Armies, but no Appropriation of Money to that Use shall be for a longer Term than two Years;

To provide and maintain a Navy;

To make Rules for the Government and Regulation of the land and naval Forces;

To provide for calling forth the Militia to execute the Laws of the Union, suppress Insurrections and repel Invasions;

To provide for organizing, arming, and disciplining, the Militia, and for governing such Part of them as may be employed in the Service of the United States, reserving to the States respectively, the Appointment of the Officers, and the Authority of training the Militia according to the discipline prescribed by Congress. . . .

Article II, Section. 2.

The President shall be Commander in Chief of the Army and Navy of the United States, and of the Militia of the several States, when called into the actual Service of the United States. . . .

SOURCE: www.archives.gov

ANALYSIS

The Constitution drawn up in Philadelphia during the summer of 1787 represented a sharp break with the country's first constitution, the Articles of Confederation. Rejecting the weak national government that had served the country so poorly in the late 1770s and early 1780s, the new document gave vast new powers to the national government, including the power to establish a professional standing army, as well as control over militias, which formerly had been under the exclusive control of the states. Congress would now have the power to call forth or activate the militias, as well as to organize, arm, and regulate them. The only power over militias given to the states was to appoint militia officers and to train them; yet even that training was subject to congressional control.

This major shift in power to the new federal government met with alarm in the states, which were accustomed to handling military threats, whether from Native Americans, European powers, or other states, on their own. Southern states were particularly concerned because they relied on their local militias to suppress slave rebellions. They now had good reason to fear that a national government dominated by northern states hostile to slavery might decline to provide military assistance at such times.

These concerns might have held sway in 1787 were it not for the realization that a weak central government was inadequate not only to effectively run the new country but to provide a proper defense for the country. While retaining the option of calling up the militias to meet military emergencies, the Constitution's founders knew that a professional military force was central to the nation's survival on this hostile continent. And they hoped that civilian control of the military, through Congress and the president, would keep in check any temptation on the part of the military to overthrow the government.

DID YOU KNOW?

Federalists versus Antifederalists

The first great divide in American politics was between Federalists, who favored adoption of the new Constitution, and Antifederalists who opposed the document. Antifederalists opposed the new Constitution for many reasons, but they were generally united in their belief that the federal government it created would be too powerful, and that the states would, in turn, lose too much power. Three main areas of disagreement included representation, tyranny, and governmental power.

The Antifederalists believed that the best representative government was that closest to the people, meaning state and local governments, whereas the Federalists believed that some distance between the people and the government would provide a better balance between popular preferences and the considered judgment of the leaders. The two opposing sides both feared tyranny, but of different sorts. The Antifederalists worried that the government would become more aristocratic or elitist and would therefore pay little heed to public preferences. The Federalists feared a different kind of tyranny—the tyranny of the majority, meaning that they feared a numerical majority would run roughshod over the rights of others and, in the words of James Madison, "trample on the rules of justice." As for governmental power, the Antifederalists wanted national government power to be carefully specified and limited, and wanted a Bill of Rights included to limit the government's power over the states and its citizens. Federalists wanted the national government to have broader powers, with those powers controlled by checks and balances rather than by keeping the national government weak.

FURTHER READING

Bogus, Carl T. "The Hidden History of the Second Amendment." *U.C. Davis Law Review* 31(Winter 1998): 309–408.

Peltason, J. W., and Sue Davis. *Corwin and Peltason's Understanding the Constitution*. New York: Harcourt, 2000.

Spitzer, Robert J. *The Right to Bear Arms: Rights and Liberties Under the Law*. Santa Barbara, CA: ABC-CLIO, 2001.

The Federalist Papers

- *Document:* Federalist Papers, Numbers 24, 25, 28, 29, 46
- *Date:* late 1787 and early 1788
- *Where:* first published in New York newspapers
- *Significance:* The Federalist Papers, composed of 85 essays, numbered consecutively, sought to persuade the country to adopt the new Constitution by explaining and defending its provisions. The papers reprinted here discuss in detail concerns related to federal versus state power in relation to militias and standing armies.

DOCUMENT

Federalist #24: The Powers Necessary to Common Defense Further Considered for the Independent Journal

To THE powers proposed to be conferred upon the federal government, in respect to the creation and direction of the national forces, I have met with but one specific objection, which, if I understand it right, is this, that proper provision has not been made against the existence of standing armies in time of peace; an objection which, I shall now endeavor to show, rests on weak and unsubstantial foundations.

It has indeed been brought forward in the most vague and general form, supported only by bold assertions, without the appearance of argument; without even the sanction of theoretical opinions; in contradiction to the practice of other free nations, and to the general sense of America, as expressed in most of the existing constitutions. The propriety of this remark will appear, the moment it is recollected that the objection under consideration turns upon a supposed necessity of restraining the LEGISLATIVE authority of the nation, in the article of military establishments; a principle unheard of, except in one or two of our State constitutions, and rejected in all the rest.

A stranger to our politics, who was to read our newspapers at the present juncture, without having previously inspected the plan reported by the convention, would be naturally led to one of two conclusions: either that it contained a positive injunction, that standing armies should be kept up in time of peace; or that it vested in the EXECUTIVE the whole power of levying troops, without subjecting his discretion, in any shape, to the control of the legislature.

If he came afterwards to peruse the plan itself, he would be surprised to discover, that neither the one nor the other was the case; that the whole power of raising armies was lodged in the LEGISLATURE, not in the EXECUTIVE; that this legislature was to be a popular body, consisting of the representatives of the people periodically elected; and that instead of the provision he had supposed in favor of standing armies, there was to be found, in respect to this object, an important qualification even of the legislative discretion, in that clause which forbids the appropriation of money for the support of an army for any longer period than two years a precaution which, upon a nearer view of it, will appear to be a great and real security against the keeping up of troops without evident necessity.

Disappointed in his first surmise, the person I have supposed would be apt to pursue his conjectures a little further. He would naturally say to himself, it is impossible that all this vehement and pathetic declamation can be without some colorable pretext. It must needs be that this people, so jealous of their liberties, have, in all the preceding models of the constitutions which they have established, inserted the most precise and rigid precautions on this point, the omission of which, in the new plan, has given birth to all this apprehension and clamor.

If, under this impression, he proceeded to pass in review the several State constitutions, how great would be his disappointment to find that TWO ONLY of them contained an interdiction of standing armies in time of peace; that the other eleven had either observed a profound silence on the subject, or had in express terms admitted the right of the Legislature to authorize their existence.

Still, however he would be persuaded that there must be some plausible foundation for the cry raised on this head. He would never be able to imagine, while any source of information remained unexplored, that it was nothing more than an experiment upon the public credulity, dictated either by a deliberate intention to deceive, or by the overflowings of a zeal too intemperate to be ingenuous. It would probably occur to him, that he would be likely to find the precautions he was in search of in the primitive compact between the States. Here, at length, he would expect to meet with a solution of the enigma. No doubt, he would observe to himself, the existing Confederation must contain the most explicit provisions against military establishments in time of peace; and a departure from this model, in a favorite point, has occasioned the discontent which appears to influence these political champions.

If he should now apply himself to a careful and critical survey of the articles of Confederation, his astonishment would not only be increased, but would acquire a mixture of indignation, at the unexpected discovery, that these articles, instead of containing the prohibition he looked for, and though they had, with jealous circumspection, restricted the authority of the State legislatures in this particular, had not imposed a single restraint on that of the United States. If he happened to be a man of quick sensibility, or ardent temper, he could now no longer refrain from regarding these clamors as the dishonest artifices of a sinister and unprincipled opposition to a plan which ought at least to receive a fair and candid examination from all sincere lovers of their country! How else, he would say, could the authors of them have been tempted to vent such loud censures upon that plan, about a point in which it seems to have conformed itself to the general sense of America as declared in its different forms of government, and in which it has even superadded a new and powerful guard unknown to any of them? If, on the contrary, he happened to be a man of calm and dispassionate feelings, he would indulge a sigh for the frailty of human nature, and would lament, that in a matter so interesting to the happiness of millions, the true merits of the question should be perplexed and entangled by expedients so unfriendly to an impartial and right determination. Even such a man could hardly forbear remarking, that a conduct of this kind has too much the appearance of an intention to mislead the people by alarming their passions, rather than to convince them by arguments addressed to their understandings.

But however little this objection may be countenanced, even by precedents among ourselves, it may be satisfactory to take a nearer view of its intrinsic merits. From a close examination it will appear that restraints upon the discretion of the legislature in respect to military establishments in time of peace, would be improper to be imposed, and if imposed, from the necessities of society, would be unlikely to be observed.

Though a wide ocean separates the United States from Europe, yet there are various considerations that warn us against an excess of confidence or security. On one side of us, and stretching far into our rear, are growing settlements subject to the dominion of Britain. On the other side, and extending to meet the British settlements, are colonies and establishments subject to the dominion of Spain. This situation and the vicinity of the West India Islands, belonging to these two powers create between them, in respect to their American possessions and in relation to us, a common interest. The savage tribes on our Western frontier ought to be regarded as our natural enemies, their natural allies, because they have most to fear from us, and most to hope from them. The improvements in the art of navigation have, as to the facility of communication, rendered distant nations, in a great measure, neighbors. Britain and Spain are among the principal maritime powers of Europe. A future concert of views between these nations ought not to be regarded as improbable. The increasing remoteness of consanguinity is every day diminishing the force of the family compact between France and Spain. And politicians have ever with great reason considered the ties of blood as feeble and precarious links of political connection. These circumstances combined, admonish us not to be too sanguine in considering ourselves as entirely out of the reach of danger.

Previous to the Revolution, and ever since the peace, there has been a constant necessity for keeping small garrisons on our Western frontier. No person can doubt that these will continue to be indispensable, if it should only be against the ravages and depredations of the Indians. These garrisons must either be furnished by occasional detachments from the militia, or by permanent corps in the pay of the government. The first is impracticable; and if practicable, would be pernicious. The militia would not long, if at all, submit to be dragged from their occupations and families to perform that most disagreeable duty in times of profound peace. And if they could be prevailed upon or compelled to do it, the increased expense of a frequent rotation of service, and the loss of labor and disconcertion of the industrious pursuits of individuals, would form conclusive objections to the scheme. It would be as burdensome and injurious to the public as ruinous to private citizens. The latter resource of permanent corps in the pay of the government amounts to a standing army in time of peace; a small one, indeed, but not the less real for being small. Here is a simple view of the subject that shows us at once the impropriety of a constitutional interdiction of such establishments, and the necessity of leaving the matter to the discretion and prudence of the legislature.

In proportion to our increase in strength, it is probable, nay, it may be said certain, that Britain and Spain would augment their military establishments in our neighborhood. If we should not be willing to be exposed, in a naked and defenseless condition, to their insults and encroachments, we should find it expedient to increase our frontier garrisons in some ratio to the force by which our Western settlements might be annoyed. There are, and will be, particular posts, the possession of which will include the command of large districts of territory, and facilitate future invasions of the remainder. It may be added that some of those posts will be keys to the trade with the Indian nations. Can any man think it would be wise to leave such posts in a situation to be at any instant seized by one or the other of two neighboring and formidable powers? To act this part would be to desert all the usual maxims of prudence and policy.

If we mean to be a commercial people, or even to be secure on our Atlantic side, we must endeavor, as soon as possible, to have a navy. To this purpose there must be dock-yards and arsenals; and for the defense of these, fortifications, and probably garrisons. When a nation has become so powerful by sea that it can protect its dock-yards by its fleets, this supersedes the necessity of garrisons for that purpose; but where naval establishments are in their infancy, moderate garrisons will, in all likelihood, be found an indispensable security against descents for the destruction of the arsenals and dock-yards, and sometimes of the fleet itself.

Publius [Alexander Hamilton]

SOURCE: http://www.yale.edu/lawweb/avalon/federal/fed24.htm

Federalist # 25: The Same Subject Continued (The Powers Necessary to the Common Defense Further Considered)

IT MAY perhaps be urged that the objects enumerated in the preceding number ought to be provided for by the State governments, under the direction of the Union. But this would be, in reality, an inversion of the primary principle of our political association, as it would in practice transfer the care of the common defense from the federal head to the individual members: a project oppressive to some States, dangerous to all, and baneful to the Confederacy.

The territories of Britain, Spain, and of the Indian nations in our neighborhood do not border on particular States, but encircle the Union from Maine to Georgia. The danger, though in different degrees, is therefore common. And the means of guarding against it ought, in like manner, to be the objects of common councils and of a common treasury. It happens that some States, from local situation, are more directly exposed. New York is of this class. Upon the plan of separate provisions, New York would have to sustain the whole weight of the establishments requisite to her immediate safety, and to the mediate or ultimate protection of her neighbors. This would neither be equitable as it respected New York nor safe as it respected the other States. Various inconveniences would attend such a system. The States, to whose lot it might fall to support the necessary establishments, would be as little able as willing, for a considerable time to come, to bear the burden of competent provisions. The security of all would thus be subjected to the parsimony, improvidence, or inability of a part. If the resources of such part becoming more abundant and extensive, its provisions should be proportionally enlarged, the other States would quickly take the alarm at seeing the whole military force of the Union in the hands of two or three of its members, and those probably amongst the most powerful. They would each choose to have some counterpoise, and pretenses could easily be contrived. In this situation, military establishments, nourished by mutual jealousy, would be apt to swell beyond their natural or proper size; and being at the separate disposal of the members, they would be engines for the abridgment or demolition of the national authority.

Reasons have been already given to induce a supposition that the State governments will too naturally be prone to a rivalship with that of the Union, the foundation of which will be the love of power; and that in any contest between the federal head and one of its members the people will be most apt to unite with their local government. If, in addition to this immense advantage, the ambition of the members should be stimulated by the separate and independent possession of military forces, it would afford too strong a temptation and too great a facility to them to make enterprises upon, and finally to subvert, the constitutional authority of the Union. On the other hand, the liberty of the people would be less safe in this state of things than in that which left the national forces in the hands of the national government. As far as an army may be considered as a dangerous weapon of power, it had better be in those hands of which the people are most likely to be jealous than in those of which they are least likely to be jealous. For it is a truth, which the experience of ages has attested, that the people are always most in danger when the means of injuring their rights are in the possession of those of whom they entertain the least suspicion.

The framers of the existing Confederation, fully aware of the danger to the Union from the separate possession of military forces by the States, have, in express terms, prohibited them from having either ships or troops, unless with the consent of Congress. The truth is, that the existence of a federal government and military establishments under State authority are not less at variance with each other than a due supply of the federal treasury and the system of quotas and requisitions.

There are other lights besides those already taken notice of, in which the impropriety of restraints on the discretion of the national legislature will be equally manifest. The design of the objection, which has been mentioned, is to preclude standing armies in time of peace, though we have never been informed how far it is designed the prohibition should extend; whether to raising armies as well as to KEEPING THEM UP in a season of tranquillity or not. If it be confined to the latter it will have no precise signification, and it will be ineffectual for the purpose intended. When armies are once raised what shall be denominated "keeping them up," contrary to the sense of the Constitution? What time shall be requisite to ascertain the violation? Shall it be a week, a month, a year? Or shall we say they may be continued as long as the danger which occasioned their being raised continues? This would be to admit that they might be kept up IN TIME OF PEACE, against threatening or impending danger, which would be at once to deviate from the literal meaning of the prohibition, and to introduce an extensive latitude of construction. Who shall judge of the continuance of the danger? This must undoubtedly be submitted to the national government, and the matter would then be brought to this issue, that the national government, to provide against apprehended danger, might in the first instance raise troops, and might afterwards keep them on foot as long as they supposed the peace or safety of the community was in any degree of jeopardy. It is easy to perceive that a discretion so latitudinary as this would afford ample room for eluding the force of the provision.

The supposed utility of a provision of this kind can only be founded on the supposed probability, or at least possibility, of a combination between the executive and the legislative, in some scheme of usurpation. Should this at any time happen, how easy would it be to fabricate pretenses of approaching danger! Indian hostilities, instigated by Spain or Britain, would always be at hand. Provocations to produce the desired appearances might even be given to some foreign power, and appeased again by timely concessions. If we can reasonably presume such a combination to have been formed, and that the enterprise is warranted by a sufficient prospect of success, the army, when once raised, from whatever cause, or on whatever pretext, may be applied to the execution of the project.

If, to obviate this consequence, it should be resolved to extend the prohibition to the RAISING of armies in time of peace, the United States would then exhibit the most extraordinary spectacle which the world has yet seen, that of a nation incapacitated by its Constitution to prepare for defense, before it was actually invaded. As the ceremony of a formal denunciation of war has of late fallen into disuse, the presence of an enemy within our territories must be waited for, as the legal warrant to the government to begin its levies of men for the protection of the State. We must receive the blow, before we could even prepare to return it. All that kind of policy by which nations anticipate distant danger, and meet the gathering storm, must be abstained from, as contrary to the genuine maxims of a free government. We must expose our property and liberty to the mercy of foreign invaders, and invite them by our weakness to seize the naked and defenseless prey, because we are afraid that rulers, created by our choice, dependent on our will, might endanger that liberty, by an abuse of the means necessary to its preservation.

Here I expect we shall be told that the militia of the country is its natural bulwark, and would be at all times equal to the national defense. This doctrine, in substance, had like to have lost us our independence. It cost millions to the United States that might have been saved. The facts which, from our own experience, forbid a reliance of this kind, are too recent to permit us to be the dupes of such a suggestion. The steady operations of war against a regular and disciplined army can only be successfully conducted by a force of the same kind. Considerations of economy, not less than of stability and vigor, confirm this position. The American militia, in the course of the late war, have, by their valor on numerous occasions, erected eternal monuments to their fame; but the bravest of them feel and know that the liberty of their country could not have been established by their efforts alone, however great and valuable they were. War, like most other things, is a science to be acquired and perfected by diligence, by perseverance, by time, and by practice.

All violent policy, as it is contrary to the natural and experienced course of human affairs, defeats itself. Pennsylvania, at this instant, affords an example of the truth of this remark. The Bill of Rights of that State declares that standing armies are dangerous to liberty, and ought not to be kept up in time of peace. Pennsylvania, nevertheless, in a time of profound peace, from the existence of partial disorders in one or two of her counties, has resolved to raise a body of troops; and in all probability will keep them up as long as there is any appearance of danger to the public peace. The conduct of Massachusetts affords a lesson on the same subject, though on different ground. That State (without waiting for the sanction of Congress, as the articles of the Confederation require) was compelled to raise troops to quell a domestic insurrection, and still keeps a corps in pay to prevent a revival of the spirit of revolt. The particular constitution of Massachusetts opposed no obstacle to the measure; but the instance is still of use to instruct us that cases are likely to occur under our government, as well as under those of other nations, which will sometimes render a military force in time of peace essential to the security of the society, and that it is therefore improper in this respect to control the legislative discretion. It also teaches us, in its application to the United States, how little the rights of a feeble government are likely to be respected, even by its own constituents. And it teaches us, in addition to the rest, how unequal parchment provisions are to a struggle with public necessity.

It was a fundamental maxim of the Lacedaemonian commonwealth, that the post of admiral should not be conferred twice on the same person. The Peloponnesian confederates, having suffered a severe defeat at sea from the Athenians, demanded Lysander, who had before served with success in that capacity, to command the combined fleets. The Lacedaemonians, to gratify their allies, and yet preserve the semblance of an adherence to their ancient institutions, had recourse to the flimsy subterfuge of investing Lysander with the real power of admiral, under the nominal title of vice-admiral. This instance is selected from among a multitude that might be cited to confirm the truth already advanced and illustrated by domestic examples; which is, that nations pay little regard to rules and maxims calculated in their very nature to run counter to the necessities of society. Wise politicians will be cautious about fettering the government with restrictions that cannot be observed, because they know that every breach of the fundamental laws, though dictated by necessity, impairs that sacred reverence which ought to be maintained in the breast of rulers towards the constitution of a country, and forms a precedent for other breaches where the same plea of necessity does not exist at all, or is less urgent and palpable.

Publius [Alexander Hamilton]

SOURCE: http://www.yale.edu/lawweb/avalon/federal/fed25.htm

Federalist #28: The Same Subject Continued (The Idea of Restraining the Legislative Authority in Regard to the Common Defense Considered)

THAT there may happen cases in which the national government may be necessitated to resort to force, cannot be denied. Our own experience has corroborated the lessons taught by the examples of other nations; that emergencies of this sort will sometimes arise in all societies, however constituted; that seditions and insurrections are, unhappily, maladies as inseparable from the body politic as tumors and eruptions from the natural body; that the idea of governing at all times by the simple force of law (which we have been told is the only admissible principle of republican government), has no place but in the reveries of those political doctors whose sagacity disdains the admonitions of experimental instruction.

Should such emergencies at any time happen under the national government, there could be no remedy but force. The means to be employed must be proportioned to the extent of the mischief. If it should be a slight commotion in a small part of a State, the militia of the residue would be adequate to its suppression; and the national presumption is that they would be ready to do their duty. An insurrection, whatever may be its immediate cause, eventually endangers all government. Regard to the public peace, if not to the rights of the Union, would engage the citizens to whom the contagion had not communicated itself to oppose the insurgents; and if the general government should be found in practice conducive to the prosperity and felicity of the people, it were irrational to believe that they would be disinclined to its support.

If, on the contrary, the insurrection should pervade a whole State, or a principal part of it, the employment of a different kind of force might become unavoidable. It appears that Massachusetts found it necessary to raise troops for repressing the disorders within that State; that Pennsylvania, from the mere apprehension of commotions among a part of her citizens, has thought proper to have recourse to the same measure. Suppose the State of New York had been inclined to re-establish her lost jurisdiction over the inhabitants of Vermont, could she have hoped for success in such an enterprise from the efforts of the militia alone? Would she not have been compelled to raise and to maintain a more regular force for the execution of her design? If it must then be admitted that the necessity of recurring to a force different from the militia, in cases of this extraordinary nature, is applicable to the State governments themselves, why should the possibility, that the national government might be under a like necessity, in similar extremities, be made an objection to its existence? Is it not surprising that men who declare an attachment to the Union in the abstract, should urge as an objection to the proposed Constitution what applies with tenfold weight to the plan for which they contend; and what, as far as it has any foundation in truth, is an inevitable consequence of civil society upon an enlarged scale? Who would not prefer that possibility to the unceasing agitations and frequent revolutions which are the continual scourges of petty republics?

Let us pursue this examination in another light. Suppose, in lieu of one general system, two, or three, or even four Confederacies were to be formed, would not the same difficulty oppose itself to the operations of either of these Confederacies? Would not each of them be exposed to the same casualties; and when these happened, be obliged to have recourse to the same expedients for upholding its authority which are objected to in a government for all the States? Would the militia, in this supposition, be more ready or more able to support the federal authority than in the case of a general union? All candid and intelligent men must, upon due consideration, acknowledge that the principle of the objection is equally applicable to either of the two cases; and that whether we have one government for all the States, or different governments for different parcels of them, or even if there should be an entire separation of the States, there might sometimes be a necessity to make use of a force constituted differently from the militia, to preserve the peace of the community and to maintain the just authority of the laws against those violent invasions of them which amount to insurrections and rebellions.

Independent of all other reasonings upon the subject, it is a full answer to those who require a more peremptory provision against military establishments in time of peace, to say that the whole power of the proposed government is to be in the hands of the representatives of the people. This is the essential, and, after all, only efficacious security for the rights and privileges of the people, which is attainable in civil society.

If the representatives of the people betray their constituents, there is then no resource left but in the exertion of that original right of self-defense which is paramount to all positive forms of government, and which against the usurpations of the national rulers, may be exerted with infinitely better prospect of success than against those of the rulers of an individual state. In a single state, if the persons intrusted with supreme power become usurpers, the different parcels, subdivisions, or districts of which it consists, having no distinct government in each, can take no regular measures for defense. The citizens must rush tumultuously to arms, without concert, without system, without resource; except in their courage and despair. The usurpers, clothed with the forms of legal authority, can too often crush the opposition in embryo. The smaller the extent of the territory, the more difficult will it be for the people to form a regular or systematic plan of opposition, and the more easy will it be to defeat their early efforts. Intelligence can be more speedily obtained of their preparations and movements, and the military force in the possession of the usurpers can be more rapidly directed against the part where the opposition has begun. In this situation there must be a peculiar coincidence of circumstances to insure success to the popular resistance.

The obstacles to usurpation and the facilities of resistance increase with the increased extent of the state, provided the citizens understand their rights and are disposed to defend them. The natural strength of the people in a large community, in proportion to the artificial strength of the government, is greater than in a small, and of course more competent to a struggle with the attempts of the government to establish a tyranny. But in a confederacy the people, without exaggeration, may be said to be entirely the masters of their own fate. Power being almost always the rival of power, the general government will at all times stand ready to check the usurpations of the state governments, and these will have the same disposition towards the general government. The people, by throwing themselves into either scale, will infallibly make it preponderate. If their rights are invaded by either, they can make use of the other as the instrument of redress. How wise will it be in them by cherishing the union to preserve to themselves an advantage which can never be too highly prized!

It may safely be received as an axiom in our political system, that the State governments will, in all possible contingencies, afford complete security against invasions of the public liberty by the national authority. Projects of usurpation cannot be masked under pretenses so likely to escape the penetration of select bodies of men, as of the people at large. The legislatures will have better means of information. They can discover the danger at a distance; and possessing all the organs of civil power, and the confidence of the people, they can at once adopt a regular plan of opposition, in which they can combine all the resources of the community. They can readily communicate with each other in the different States, and unite their common forces for the protection of their common liberty.

The great extent of the country is a further security. We have already experienced its utility against the attacks of a foreign power. And it would have precisely the same effect against the enterprises of ambitious rulers in the national councils. If the federal army should be able to quell the resistance of one State, the distant States would have it in their power to make head with fresh forces. The advantages obtained in one place must be abandoned to subdue the opposition in others; and the moment the part which had been reduced to submission was left to itself, its efforts would be renewed, and its resistance revive.

We should recollect that the extent of the military force must, at all events, be regulated by the resources of the country. For a long time to come, it will not be possible to maintain a large army; and as the means of doing this increase, the population and natural strength of the community will proportionably increase. When will the time arrive that the federal government can raise and maintain an army capable of erecting a despotism over the great body of the people of an immense empire, who are in a situation, through the medium of their State governments, to take measures for their own defense, with all the celerity, regularity, and system of independent nations? The apprehension may be considered as a disease, for which there can be found no cure in the resources of argument and reasoning.

Publius [Alexander Hamilton]

SOURCE: http://www.yale.edu/lawweb/avalon/federal/fed28.htm

THE

FEDERALIST:

A COLLECTION

OF

E S S A Y S,

WRITTEN IN FAVOUR OF THE

NEW CONSTITUTION,

AS AGREED UPON BY THE FEDERAL CONVENTION,
SEPTEMBER 17, 1787.

IN TWO VOLUMES.

VOL. I.

NEW-YORK:

PRINTED AND SOLD BY J. AND A. McLEAN,
No. 41, HANOVER-SQUARE.
M, DCC, LXXXVIII.

Cover page from *The Federalist,* 1788.

Federalist #29: Concerning the Militia

THE power of regulating the militia, and of commanding its services in times of insurrection and invasion are natural incidents to the duties of superintending the common defense, and of watching over the internal peace of the Confederacy.

It requires no skill in the science of war to discern that uniformity in the organization and discipline of the militia would be attended with the most beneficial effects, whenever they were called into service for the public defense. It would enable them to discharge the duties of the camp and of the field with mutual intelligence and concert an advantage of peculiar moment in the operations of an army; and it would fit them much sooner to acquire the degree of proficiency in military functions which would be essential to their usefulness. This desirable uniformity can only be accomplished by confiding the regulation of the militia to the direction of the national authority. It is, therefore, with the most evident propriety, that the plan of the convention proposes to empower the Union "to provide for organizing, arming, and disciplining the militia, and for governing such part of them as may be employed in the service of the United States, RESERVING TO THE STATES RESPECTIVELY THE APPOINTMENT OF THE OFFICERS, AND THE AUTHORITY OF TRAINING THE MILITIA ACCORDING TO THE DISCIPLINE PRESCRIBED BY CONGRESS.

Of the different grounds which have been taken in opposition to the plan of the convention, there is none that was so little to have been expected, or is so untenable in itself, as the one from which this particular provision has been attacked. If a well-regulated militia be the most natural defense of a free country, it ought certainly to be under the regulation and at the disposal of that body which is constituted the guardian of the national security. If standing armies are dangerous to liberty, an efficacious power over the militia, in the body to whose care the protection of the State is committed, ought, as far as possible, to take away the inducement and the pretext to such unfriendly institutions. If the federal government can command the aid of the militia in those emergencies which call for the military arm in support of the civil magistrate, it can the better dispense with the employment of a different kind of force. If it cannot avail itself of the former, it will be obliged to recur to the latter. To render an army unnecessary, will be a more certain method of preventing its existence than a thousand prohibitions upon paper. . . .

By a curious refinement upon the spirit of republican jealousy, we are even taught to apprehend danger from the militia itself, in the hands of the federal government. It is observed that select corps may be formed, composed of the young and ardent, who may be rendered subservient to the views of arbitrary power. What plan for the regulation of the militia may be pursued by the national government, is impossible to be foreseen. But so far from viewing the matter in the same light with those who object to select corps as dangerous, were the Constitution ratified, and were I to deliver my sentiments to a member of the federal legislature from this State on the subject of a militia establishment, I should hold to him, in substance, the following discourse:

"The project of disciplining all the militia of the United States is as futile as it would be injurious, if it were capable of being carried into execution. A tolerable expertness in military movements is a business that requires time and practice. It is not a day, or even a week, that will suffice for the attainment of it. To oblige the great body of the yeomanry, and of the other classes of the citizens, to be under arms for the purpose of going through military exercises and evolutions, as often as might be necessary to acquire the degree of perfection which would entitle them to the character of a well-regulated militia, would be a real grievance to the people, and a serious public inconvenience and loss. It would form an annual deduction from the productive labor of the country, to an amount which, calculating upon the present numbers of the people, would not fall far short of the whole expense of the civil establishments of all the States. To attempt a thing which would abridge the mass of labor and industry to so considerable an extent, would be unwise: and the experiment, if made, could not succeed, because it would not long be endured. Little more can reasonably be aimed at, with respect to the people at large, than to have them properly armed and equipped; and in order to see that this be not neglected, it will be necessary to assemble them once or twice in the course of a year.

"But though the scheme of disciplining the whole nation must be abandoned as mischievous or impracticable; yet it is a matter of the utmost importance that a well-digested plan should, as soon as possible, be adopted for the proper establishment of the militia. The attention of the government ought particularly to be directed to the formation of a select corps of moderate extent, upon such principles as will really fit them for service in case of need. By thus circumscribing the plan, it will be possible to have an excellent body of well-trained militia, ready to take the field whenever the defense of the State shall require it. This will not only lessen the call for military establishments, but if circumstances should at any time oblige the government to form an army of any magnitude that army can never be formidable to the liberties of the people while there is a large body of citizens, little, if at all, inferior to them in discipline and the use of arms, who stand ready to defend their own rights and those of their fellow-citizens. This appears to me the only substitute that can be devised for a standing army, and the best possible security against it, if it should exist."

Thus differently from the adversaries of the proposed Constitution should I reason on the same subject, deducing arguments of safety from the very sources which they represent as fraught with danger and perdition. But how the national legislature may reason on the point, is a thing which neither they nor I can foresee.

There is something so far-fetched and so extravagant in the idea of danger to liberty from the militia, that one is at a loss whether to treat it with gravity or with raillery; whether to consider it as a mere trial of skill, like the paradoxes of rhetoricians; as a disingenuous artifice to instil prejudices at any price; or as the serious offspring of political fanaticism. Where in the name of common-sense, are our fears to end if we may not trust our sons, our brothers, our neighbors, our fellow-citizens? What shadow of danger can there be from men who are daily mingling with the rest of their countrymen and who participate with them in the same feelings, sentiments, habits and interests? What reasonable cause of apprehension can be inferred from a power in the Union to prescribe regulations for the militia, and to command its services when necessary, while the particular States are to have the SOLE AND EXCLUSIVE APPOINTMENT OF THE OFFICERS? If it were possible seriously to indulge a jealousy of the militia upon any conceivable establishment under the federal government, the circumstance of the officers being in the appointment of the States ought at once to extinguish it. There can be no doubt that this circumstance will always secure to them a preponderating influence over the militia.

In reading many of the publications against the Constitution, a man is apt to imagine that he is perusing some ill-written tale or romance, which instead of natural and agreeable images, exhibits to the mind nothing but frightful and distorted shapes "Gorgons, hydras, and chimeras dire"; discoloring and disfiguring whatever it represents, and transforming everything it touches into a monster.

A sample of this is to be observed in the exaggerated and improbable suggestions which have taken place respecting the power of calling for the services of the militia. That of New Hampshire is to be marched to Georgia, of Georgia to New Hampshire, of New York to Kentucky, and of Kentucky to Lake Champlain. Nay, the debts due to the French and Dutch are to be paid in militiamen instead of Louis d'ors and ducats. At one moment there is to be a large army to lay prostrate the liberties of the people; at another moment the militia of Virginia are to be dragged from their homes five or six hundred miles, to tame the republican contumacy of Massachusetts; and that of Massachusetts is to be transported an equal distance to subdue the refractory haughtiness of the aristocratic Virginians. Do the persons who rave at this rate imagine that their art or their eloquence can impose any conceits or absurdities upon the people of America for infallible truths?

If there should be an army to be made use of as the engine of despotism, what need of the militia? If there should be no army, whither would the militia, irritated by being called upon to undertake a distant and hopeless expedition, for the purpose of riveting the chains of slavery upon a part of their countrymen, direct their course, but to the seat of the tyrants, who had meditated so foolish as well as so wicked a project, to crush them in their imagined intrenchments of power, and to make them an example of the just vengeance of an abused and incensed people? Is this the way in which usurpers stride to dominion over a numerous and enlightened nation? Do they begin by exciting the detestation of the very instruments of their intended usurpations? Do they usually commence their career by wanton and disgustful acts of power, calculated to answer no end, but to draw upon themselves universal hatred and execration? Are suppositions of this sort the sober admonitions of discerning patriots to a discerning people? Or are they the inflammatory ravings of incendiaries or distempered enthusiasts? If we were even to suppose the national rulers actuated by the most ungovernable ambition, it is impossible to believe that they would employ such preposterous means to accomplish their designs.

In times of insurrection, or invasion, it would be natural and proper that the militia of a neighboring State should be marched into another, to resist a common enemy, or to guard the republic against the violence of faction or sedition. This was frequently the case, in respect to the first object, in the course of the late war; and this mutual succor is, indeed, a principal end of our political association. If the power of affording it be placed under the direction of the Union, there will be no danger of a supine and listless inattention to the dangers of a neighbor, till its near approach had superadded the incitements of self-preservation to the too feeble impulses of duty and sympathy.

Publius [Alexander Hamilton]

SOURCE: http://www.yale.edu/lawweb/avalon/federal/fed29.htm

Federalist #46: The Influence of the State and Federal Governments Compared

. . . The only refuge left for those who prophesy the downfall of the State governments is the visionary supposition that the federal government may previously accumulate a military force for the projects of ambition. The reasonings contained in these papers must have been employed to little purpose indeed, if it could be necessary now to disprove the reality of this danger. That the people and the States should, for a sufficient period of time, elect an uninterrupted succession of men ready to betray both; that the traitors should, throughout this period, uniformly and systematically pursue some fixed plan for the extension of the military establishment; that the governments and the people of the States should silently and patiently behold the gathering storm, and continue to supply the materials, until it should be prepared to burst on their own heads, must appear to every one more like the incoherent dreams of a delirious jealousy, or the misjudged exaggerations of a counterfeit zeal, than like the sober apprehensions of genuine patriotism.

Extravagant as the supposition is, let it however be made. Let a regular army, fully equal to the resources of the country, be formed; and let it be entirely at the devotion of the federal government; still it would not be going too far to say, that the State governments, with the people on their side, would be able to repel the danger. The highest number to which, according to the best computation, a standing army can be carried in any country, does not exceed one hundredth part of the whole number of souls; or one twenty-fifth part of the number able to bear arms. This proportion would not yield, in the United States, an army of more than twenty-five or thirty thousand men. To these would be opposed a militia amounting to near half a million of citizens with arms in their hands, officered by men chosen from among themselves, fighting for their common liberties, and united and conducted by governments possessing their affections and confidence. It may well be doubted, whether a militia thus circumstanced could ever be conquered by such a proportion of regular troops. Those who are best acquainted with the last successful resistance of this country against the British arms, will be most inclined to deny the possibility of it. Besides the advantage of being armed, which the Americans possess over the people of almost every other nation, the existence of subordinate governments, to which the people are attached, and by which the militia officers are appointed, forms a barrier against the enterprises of ambition, more insurmountable than any which a simple government of any form can admit of. Notwithstanding the military establishments in the several kingdoms of Europe, which are carried as far as the public resources will bear, the governments are afraid to trust the people with arms. And it is not certain, that with this aid alone they would not be able to shake off their yokes. But were the people to possess the additional advantages of local governments chosen by themselves, who could collect the national will and direct the national force, and of officers appointed out of the militia, by these governments, and attached both to them and to the militia, it may be affirmed with the greatest assurance, that the throne of every tyranny in Europe would be speedily overturned in spite of the legions which surround it.

Let us not insult the free and gallant citizens of America with the suspicion that they would be less able to defend the rights of which they would be in actual possession, than the debased subjects of arbitrary power would be to rescue theirs from the hands of their oppressors. Let us rather no longer insult them with the supposition that they can ever reduce themselves to the necessity of making the experiment, by a blind and tame submission to the long train of insidious measures which must precede and produce it. The argument under the present head may be put into a very concise form, which appears altogether conclusive. Either the mode in which the federal government is to be constructed will render it sufficiently dependent on the people, or it will not. On the first supposition, it will be restrained by that dependence from forming schemes obnoxious to their constituents. On the other supposition, it will not possess the confidence of the people, and its schemes of usurpation will be easily defeated by the State governments, who will be supported by the people. On summing up the considerations stated in this and the last paper, they seem to amount to the most convincing evidence, that the powers proposed to be lodged in the federal government are as little formidable to those reserved to the individual States, as they are indispensably necessary to accomplish the purposes of the Union; and that all those alarms which have been sounded, of a meditated and consequential annihilation of the State governments, must, on the most favorable interpretation, be ascribed to the chimerical fears of the authors of them.

Publius [James Madison]

SOURCE: http://www.yale.edu/lawweb/avalon/federal/fed46.htm

ANALYSIS

Federalist Papers 24, 25, 28, 29, and 46 all deal with critically important government controversies that swirled around the new Constitution, including federalism, meaning the balance of power between the new proposed national government and the states; the pressing military threats facing the country from every side; the necessity of maintaining a standing army, even in peacetime; and the problems and limitations of militias. Paper 24 confronts directly one of the biggest objections raised to the new Constitution: that the federal government would now have the ability to raise and maintain a standing army, even if the country was not in the middle of a war, as well as to organize and control militias.

Under the country's previous constitution, the Articles of Confederation, the national government had no power to maintain a standing army, and the militias were organized and controlled by the states. Author Alexander Hamilton argued strongly that the country needed to maintain a standing army to guard its frontiers and deter possible military aggression (such as from Britain and Spain), and that militias were simply not up to the task of bearing the main burden of national defense. Militias, after all, were part-time soldiers who lacked training, expertise, and experience in matters of war; and it would be extraordinarily difficult to organize and deploy them, he argued, especially when the country was not actually in the middle of a war. And, he emphasized, the fact that Congress had control over these military forces meant that these elective officials, as the people's elected representatives, could effectively maintain control over these forces and prevent them from usurping the liberties of the people.

In Paper 25, Hamilton continued his argument, noting that the state governments could and should not be trusted to bear the brunt of responsibility for national defense, as had been true before this time. He again addressed the concern of many in the country that the maintenance of a standing army in peacetime posed a threat to the country's freedoms and democratic institutions by arguing that any effort to prevent an American peacetime army would result in America becoming "a nation incapacitated by its Constitution to prepare for defense before it was actually invaded." The Constitution's critics argued that, instead of a standing army, the militias could be mobilized rapidly to meet military threats. Hamilton's retort was sharp. Such an idea nearly lost the country its independence in the previous decade, he said, and that experience was "too recent to permit us to be dupes of such a suggestion." The only way to successfully confront the professional military force of another country, he said, is with our own professional force. "War, like most other things, is a science to be acquired and perfected by diligence, by perseverance, by time, and by practice." Amateur militias may be a useful, even necessary, military supplement, but they are no substitute for military professionals.

In Paper 28, Hamilton describes limited-scale problems that militias could effectively address, such as law enforcement in local communities, and then returns to his larger theme that an American standing army is indispensable for American security. Further, he reminds the reader that federal government power would be checked by state power, and that this would be an additional basis for preserving liberty. In any case, the country's limited resources of the time mean that it would be a long time before the federal government could acquire the resources necessary to establish a standing army of any size.

Paper 29 defends putting control of the militias in the hands of Congress, arguing that the best way to defend a free country is to make sure that the country's government has that control. Any effort to provide extensive training for the entire general militia (meaning all men capable of serving between the ages of 18 and 45) of the country would simply be unfeasible. It would be feasible, Hamilton then says, to provide systematic training for "select corps," a synonym for select or volunteer militias. These militias, which functioned in the country since the 1600s, represented a small subset of all militias, but were different from the general militias in that the select militias sought more training, were more loyal to their units, and acquired more equipment and other accoutrements of war. These select militias, Hamilton argues, could fill other military needs in addition to the standing army (the select militias survive to the present when they became the National Guard by act of Congress in 1903; see Chapter 7).

Paper 46, written by James Madison, addresses the federal-state power balance question as it pertained to military matters. The federal government should be allowed to establish a standing army without fear that it might somehow be used to destroy state power. After all, Madison argues, the states have a huge advantage: the federal government could create an army of perhaps 25,000–30,000 soldiers, but the number of militia-eligible men in the 13 states easily amounted to a half-million men. Thus by sheer numbers, the states had nothing to fear from a standing army controlled by the national government. And unlike European nations where the governments did not trust their people to have guns, America's web of state and local governments could draw on their armed local populations to "collect the national will and direct the national force," including appointing militia officers from America's grassroots. Thus federalism would exert necessary checks on any temptation by the national government, through a national army, to seize power from the states or deprive its people of its hard-won freedoms.

FURTHER READING

Hamilton, Alexander, James Madison, and John Jay. *The Federalist Papers*. New York: New American Library, 1961.

DID YOU KNOW?

The Federalist Papers: The Eighteenth-Century Equivalent of TV Ads

When the Constitution's founders concluded their deliberations in Philadelphia on September 17, 1787, they knew they faced a daunting task in trying to get the new document ratified by at least 9 of the 13 states. To counter the criticisms of those opposing the new document and help persuade the country to accept the new Constitution, three supporters—Alexander Hamilton, James Madison, and John Jay—wrote a series of essays initially published in New York newspapers in 1787 and 1788 to explain and defend the document. Hamilton was the only New Yorker to sign the document; Madison, from Virginia, was considered the "father" of the new Constitution; New Yorker Jay had not attended the convention, but was a widely respected diplomat and jurist. In all, the three wrote 85 such essays, later published together and numbered consecutively. All were written under the pseudonym "Publius" to hide the authors' identities (a common practice at the time for political essays). The essays are considered a brilliant exegesis on the meaning of the Constitution and are widely read today to shed light on the document and its principles.

Proposed Constitutional Amendments from State Ratifying Conventions

- *Document:* Proposed Constitutional Amendments related to the bearing of arms from New Hampshire, Virginia, New York, and North Carolina
- *Date:* 1788
- *Where:* New Hampshire, Virginia, New York, North Carolina
- *Significance:* Concerns from several states about the federal government's sweeping new powers over militias and armies caused several states to propose amendments to the new Constitution to include assurances that the states would still retain the right to form and maintain their own militias, as had been the case under the old Articles of Confederation.

DOCUMENT

New Hampshire—TENTH, That no standing Army shall be Kept up in time of Peace unless with the consent of three fourths of the Members of each branch of Congress, nor shall Soldiers in Time of Peace be Quartered upon private Houses without the consent of the Owners . . . TWELFTH Congress shall never disarm any Citizen unless such as are or have been in Actual Rebellion.

Virginia—SEVENTEENTH, That the people have a right to keep and bear arms; that a well regulated Militia composed of the body of the people trained to arms is the proper, natural and safe defence of a free State. That standing armies in time of peace are dangerous to liberty, and therefore ought to be avoided, as far as the circumstances and protection of the Community will admit; and that in all cases the military should be under strict subordination to and governed by the Civil power. EIGHTEENTH, That no Soldier in time of peace ought to be quartered in any house without the consent of the owner, and in time of war in such manner only as the laws direct. NINETEENTH, That any person religiously scrupulous of bearing arms ought to be exempted upon payment of an equivalent to employ another to bear arms in his stead . . . [amendments proposed to the body of the Constitution]. . . . NINTH, that no standing army or regular troops shall be raised or kept up in time of peace, without the consent of two thirds of the members present in both houses. TENTH, That no soldier shall be inlisted for any longer term than four years, except in time of war, and then for no longer term than the continuance of the war. ELEVENTH, That each State respectively shall have the power to provide for organizing, arming and disciplining its own Militia, whensoever Congress shall omit or neglect to provide for the same. That the Militia shall not be subject to Martial Law, except when in actual service in time of war, invasion, or rebellion; and when not in the actual service of the United States, shall be subject only to such fines, penalties and punishments as shall be directed or inflicted by the laws of its own State.

New York—That the People have a right to keep and bear Arms; that a well regulated Militia, including the body of the People capable of bearing Arms, is the proper, natural and safe defence of a free State; that the Militia should not be subject to Martial Law, except in time of War Rebellion or Insurrection. That standing Armies in time of Peace are dangerous to Liberty, and ought not to be kept up, except in Cases of necessity; and that at all times, the Military should be under strict Subordination to the Civil Power. That in time of Peace no Soldier ought to be quartered in any House without the consent of the Owner, and in time of War only by the civil Magistrate in such manner as the Laws may direct . . . that the Militia of any State shall not be compelled to serve without the limits of the State for a longer term than six weeks, without the Consent of the Legislature thereof.

North Carolina—That the people have a right to keep and bear arms; that a well regulated militia, composed of the body of the people, trained to arms, is the proper, natural, and safe defence of a free state; that standing armies, in time of peace, are dangerous to liberty, and therefore ought to be avoided, as far as the circumstances and protection of the community will admit; and that, in all cases, the military should be under strict subordination to, and governed by, the civil power.

SOURCE: http://www.constitution.org/mil/militia_debate_1789.htm

---

ANALYSIS

The U.S. Constitution is today considered a masterpiece of work, its architects are revered, and its place in history assured. Yet the document was met with great skepticism when it was circulated to the country in 1787 and 1788, in large measure because it proposed giving the new national government vast and sweeping new powers—powers that had formerly belonged to the states under the previous governing document, the Articles of Confederation. These concerns eventually led to the adoption of a Bill of Rights, which was added to the document in 1791. Much of the impetus for the inclusion of these added protections came from the state conventions convened to ratify the new document, where Antifederalists expressed two sets of concerns: that the new Constitution tipped the balance of governmental power too much in favor of the new national government, and that stronger guarantees to protect personal liberties needed to be inserted. Chief among the new powers to be given to Congress in the new national government was the power to form a standing army, and also control over militias. This enhanced federal power over the American military prompted proposed amendments from several states. The Constitution's defenders—Federalists—argued that the failings of the national government under the Articles showed that the new government needed greater powers, and that there was no need to attach a separate list of protected liberties, as Americans were protected by state bills of rights, and that such a list might actually harm rights because it would inevitably leave off some rights, which might then be subject to usurpation.

Four states—New Hampshire, Virginia, New York, and North Carolina—proposed that the new Constitution include stricter controls over standing armies; that militia-eligible citizens retain the right to bear arms, but that those who had religious objections to military service (such as Quakers) be allowed to opt out of military service (what today is referred to as "conscientious objector" status); and that states retain the ability to form their own militias. Much of the wording quoted in this passage bears close resemblance to that debated and eventually adopted by the First Congress in 1789, including the Second Amendment's right to bear arms, and the Third Amendment's bar against the quartering of troops in people's homes in peacetime.

FURTHER READING

Farrand, Max. *The Records of the Federal Convention of 1787*. New Haven, CT: Yale University Press, 1966.

Kaminski, John P., and Gaspare J. Saladino, eds. *The Documentary History of the Ratification of the Constitution*. Madison, WI: State Historical Society of Wisconsin, 1981.

2

THE BILL OF RIGHTS,
THE SECOND AMENDMENT,
AND EARLY LAWS

Versions of the Second Amendment

- *Document:* versions of the Second Amendment
- *Date:* June–September 1789
- *Where:* New York City, New York
- *Significance:* The changes in wording of what eventually became the Second Amendment discussed in the First Congress, from its time of introduction on June 8 to its approval by the Senate on September 9, 1789, reflected military concerns related to who would compose the militias, the purpose they would serve, and whether express provision should be made for allowing militia-eligible men to opt out of military service for reasons of religious belief.

DOCUMENT

Proposal by James Madison in the House of Representatives, June 8, 1789:

Fourthly. That in article 1st, section 9, between clauses 3 and 4 [of the Constitution], be inserted these clauses, to wit, . . .

The right of the people to keep and bear arms shall not be infringed; a well armed, and well regulated militia being the best security of a free country: but no person religiously scrupulous of bearing arms, shall be compelled to render military service in person.

House Committee Report, July 28, 1789:

A well regulated militia, composed of the body of the people, being the best security of a free State, the right of the people to keep and bear arms shall not be infringed, but no person religiously scrupulous shall be compelled to bear arms.

Resolution Passed by House of Representatives, August 24, 1789:

ARTICLE THE FIFTH. A well regulated militia, composed of the body of the People, being the best security of a free State, the right of the People to keep and bear arms, shall not be infringed, but no one religiously scrupulous of bearing arms, shall be compelled to render military service in person.

On September 4, the Senate agreed to amend Article 5 to read as follows: A well regulated militia, being the best security of a free state, the right of the people to keep and bear arms, shall not be infringed.

On September 9, the Senate replaced "the best" with "necessary to the." On the same day, the Senate disagreed to a motion to insert "for the common defence" after "bear arms." This article was renumbered as Article 4.

Amendment II

A well regulated Militia, being necessary to the security of a free State, the right of the people to keep and bear Arms, shall not be infringed.

SOURCE: http://www.constitution.org/mil/militia_debate_1789.htm

---

ANALYSIS

When the idea of including a Bill of Rights in the Constitution was raised during the First Congress, the plan suggested by James Madison was to integrate the wording directly into the text of the document. That proposal was discarded in favor of listing the rights separately, as amendments, appended to the end of the document. Madison was forced to accept this method of inclusion in order to win essential Federalist support for the Bill of Rights in the House of Representatives. As Representative George Clymer said, "I wish Sir that the Constitution may forever remain in its original form, as a monument of the wisdom and patriotism of those who framed it."

The list of rights and protections that eventually became the Bill of Rights was closely modeled on those of the Virginia Declaration of Rights (see Chapter 1), authored mostly by George Mason. Even so, what eventually became the 10 amendments composing the Bill of Rights began as more than 200 separate amendments suggested by the states. That list was boiled down to about a hundred, and finally became 12 amendments sent to the states for ratification. (Two of these failed to win ratification. One pertained to apportionment of representation. The other, barring Congress from raising its own pay until after an election, was eventually added to the Constitution as the Twenty-seventh Amendment in 1992.)

As the several versions of the Second Amendment show, relatively few changes were made from introduction to final enactment. The most significant change was the elimination of the phrase that "no person religiously scrupulous shall be compelled to bear arms." This provision would have expressly allowed men whose religious beliefs barred them from fighting, such as Quakers, the ability to opt out without penalty. Even in the modern era, at times when military service has been required by the

DID YOU KNOW?

Militias versus Armies

American military forces during the Revolution and the early Federal period consisted of two parts: the militias and a small standing army. Both served as military bulwarks, but these two types of fighting forces were quite different. Militia members consisted of men roughly between the ages of 18 and 45 who functioned as part-time soldiers. That is, they retained their full-time occupations from civilian life, but would leave those occupations for short periods of militia service or training. They were, therefore, part-time "citizen soldiers" who lacked the training, skill, and experience of professional soldiers. Further, militia members were required to acquire their own weapons and other accessories, and were covered only partially by military law. In this way, the government could avoid bearing the cost of arming the militias (think of it as the eighteenth-century equivalent of an "unfunded mandate," where the government establishes requirements, but the cost is borne by someone other than the government).

Professional armies, by comparison, were usually composed of volunteers who served for fixed periods of time—usually several years—and for whom military service was their full-time occupation. As paid full-timers, they received extensive training, acquired more battlefield experience, were armed and equipped by the government, and were subject to full military discipline. The heavy American reliance on militias in its early years reflected the government's limited financial resources, limited power, and general suspicion of large standing armies. Eventually, the military weaknesses of militias forced the government to abandon them, in favor of a military draft that enrolled men into the regular army.

government (most recently during the Vietnam era), allowance is made for men to avoid military service based on their religious beliefs (getting what is now called "conscientious objector" status). The phrase was deleted from the amendment not to eliminate such exemptions, but to minimize the number of such claims that might be made if such a protection remained in the amendment. Even without the inclusion of such language, government leaders knew from painful experience that there had been persistent problems in getting enough men to serve in the country's military forces, and this problem persisted, ultimately leading to government reliance on the military draft.

The text of the Second Amendment has given rise to some controversy. The reference in the first half of the sentence to a "well regulated militia" evokes no little confusion because the old-style militias that were the mainstay of America's military preparedness are no longer a part of U.S. military organization. From the twentieth century to the present, large-scale emergencies requiring the expansion of the American military are met by instituting the military draft, where young men are placed into the country's professional military forces instead of calling up the militias. Additional confusion arises when those who refer to this amendment quote only the second part of the sentence referring to "the right of the people to keep and bear arms" not being "infringed." When this second part of the sentence is quoted by itself, it seems to be saying that the Second Amendment protects an unlimited right of Americans to own guns for any or every legal purpose. But obviously, the two halves of the sentence—well regulated militias and the right to keep and bear arms—are directly linked to each other, as the full sentence says, and as debate from the First Congress, discussed in the next section, shows.

FURTHER READING

Cogan, Neil H., ed. *The Complete Bill of Rights*. New York: Oxford University Press, 1997.
Veit, Helen E., Kenneth R. Bowling, and Charlene Bangs Bickford, eds. *Creating the Bill of Rights*. Baltimore, MD: The Johns Hopkins University Press, 1991.

Debate on Militias and the Right to Keep and Bear Arms, House of Representatives

- *Document:* Congressional debates about the right to bear arms provision of the Bill of Rights.
- *Date:* August 17 and 20, 1789
- *Where:* New York City, New York
- *Significance:* Congressional debate reveals the prominence of military concerns in the First Congress as it debated the addition of amendments to the newly adopted Constitution (Senate debates were secret, and no official notes or records were kept).

DOCUMENT

The Congressional Register, August 17, 1789

The house went into a committee of the whole, on the subject of amendments. The 3rd clause of the 4th proposition in the report was taken into consideration, being as follows; "A well regulated militia, composed of the body of the people, being the best security of a free state; the right of the people to keep and bear arms shall not be infringed, but no person, religiously scrupulous, shall be compelled to bear arms."

Mr. Gerry—This declaration of rights, I take it, is intended to secure the people against the mal-administration of the government; if we could suppose that in all cases the rights of the people would be attended to, the occasion for guards of this kind would be removed. Now, I am apprehensive, sir, that this clause would give an opportunity to the people in power to destroy the constitution itself. They can declare who are those religiously scrupulous, and prevent them from bearing arms. What, sir, is the use of a militia? It is to prevent the establishment of a standing army, the bane of liberty. Now it must be evident, that under this provision, together with their other powers, congress could take such measures with respect to a militia, as make a standing army necessary. Whenever governments mean to invade the rights and liberties of the people, they always attempt to destroy the militia, in order to raise an army upon their ruins. This was actually done by Great Britain at the commencement of the late revolution. They used every means in their power to prevent the establishment of an effective militia to the eastward. The assembly of Massachusetts, seeing the rapid progress that administration were making, to divest them of their inherent privileges, endeavored to counteract them by the organization of the militia, but they were always defeated by the influence of the crown.

Mr. Seney—Wished to know what question there was before the committee, in order to ascertain the point upon which the gentleman was speaking?

Mr. Gerry—Replied, that he meant to make a motion, as he disapproved of the words as they stood. He then proceeded, No attempts that they made, were successful, until they engaged in the struggle which emancipated them at once from their thralldom. Now, if we give a discretionary power to exclude those from militia duty who have religious scruples, we may as well make no provision on this head; for this reason he wished the words to be altered so as to be confined to persons belonging to a religious sect, scrupulous of bearing arms.

Mr. Jackson—Did not expect that all the people of the United States would turn Quakers or Moravians, consequently one part would have to defend the other, in case of invasion; now this, in his opinion, was unjust, unless the constitution secured an equivalent, for this reason he moved to amend the clause, by inserting at the end of it "upon paying an equivalent to be established by law."

Mr. Smith, (of S.C.)—Enquired what were the words used by the conventions respecting this amendment; if the gentleman would conform to what was proposed by Virginia and Carolina, he would second him: He thought they were to be excused provided they found a substitute.

Mr. Jackson—Was willing to accommodate; he thought the expression was, "No one, religiously scrupulous of bearing arms, shall be compelled to render military service in person, upon paying an equivalent."

Mr. Sherman—Conceived it difficult to modify the clause and make it better. It is well-known that those who are religiously scrupulous of bearing arms, are equally scrupulous of getting substitutes or paying an equivalent; many of them would rather die than do either one or the other—but he did not see an absolute necessity for a clause of this kind. We do not live under an arbitrary government, said he, and the states respectively will have the government of the militia, unless when called into actual service; beside, it would not do to alter it so as to exclude the whole of any sect, because there are men amongst the quakers who will turn out, notwithstanding the religious principles of this society, and defend the cause of their country. Certainly it will be improper to prevent the exercise of such favorable dispositions, at least while it is the practice of nations to determine their contests by the slaughter of their citizens and subjects.

Mr. Vining—Hoped the clause would be suffered to remain as it stood, because he saw no use in it if it as amended so as to compel a man to find a substitute, which, with respect to the government, was the same as if the person himself turned out to fight.

Mr. Stone—Enquired what the words "Religiously scrupulous" had reference to, was it of bearing arms? If it was, it ought so to be expressed.

Mr. Benson—Moved to have the words "But no person religiously scrupulous shall be compelled to bear arms" struck out. He would always leave it to the benevolence of the legislature—for, modify it, said he, as you please, it will be impossible to express it in such a manner as to clear it from ambiguity. No man can claim this indulgence of right. It may be a religious persuasion, but it is no natural right, and therefore ought to be left to the discretion of the government. If this stands part of the constitution, it will be a question before the judiciary, on every regulation you make with respect to the organization of the militia, whether it comports with this declaration or not? It is extremely injudicious to intermix matters of doubt with fundamentals. I have no reason to believe but the legislature will always possess humanity enough to indulge this class of citizens in a matter they are so desirous of, but they ought to be left to their discretion.

The motion for striking out the whole clause being seconded, was put, and decided in the negative, 22 members voting for it, and 24 against it.

Mr. Gerry—Objected to the first part of the clause, on account of the uncertainty with which it is expressed: a well-regulated militia being the best security of a free state, admitted an idea that a standing army was a secondary one. It ought to read "a well regulated militia, trained to arms," in which case it would become the duty of the government to provide this security, and furnish a greater certainty of its being done.

Mr. Gerry's motion not being seconded, the question was put on the clause as reported, which being adopted.

Mr. Burke—Proposed to add to the clause just agreed to, an amendment to the following effect: "A standing army of regular troops in time of peace, is dangerous to public liberty, and such shall not be raised or kept up in time of peace but from necessity, and for the security of the people, nor then without the consent of two-thirds of the members present of both houses, and in all cases the military shall be subordinate to the civil authority." This being seconded.

Mr. Vining—Asked whether this was to be considered as an addition to the last clause, or an amendment by itself? If the former, he would remind the gentleman the clause was decided; if the latter, it was improper to introduce new matter, as the house had referred the report specially to the committee of the whole.

Mr. Burke—Feared that what with being trammelled in rules, and the apparent disposition of the committee, he should not be able to get them to consider any amendment; he submitted to such proceeding because he could not help himself.

Mr. Hartley—Thought the amendment in order, and was ready to give his opinion of it. He hoped the people of America would always be satisfied with having a majority to govern. He never wished to see two-thirds or three-fourths required, because it might put it in the power of a small minority to govern the whole union.

The question on mr. Burke's motion was put, and lost by a majority of 13.

The Congressional Register, August 20, 1789

Mr. SCOTT objected to the clause in the sixth amendment, "No person religiously scrupulous shall be compelled to bear arms." He said, if this becomes part of the constitution, we can neither call upon such persons for services nor a n equivalent; it is attended with still further difficulties, for you can never depend upon your militia. This will lead to the violation of another article in the constitution, which secures to the people the right of keeping arms, as in this case you must have recourse to a standing army. I conceive it is a matter of legislative right altogether. I know there are many sects religiously scrupulous in this respect: I am not for abridging them of any indulgence by law; my design is to guard against those who are of no religion. It is said that religion is on the decline; if this is the case, it is an argument in my favour; for when the time comes that there is no religion, persons will more generally have recourse to these pretexts to get excused.

Mr. BOUDINOT said that the provision in the clause or something like it appeared to be necessary. What dependence can be placed in men who are conscientious in this respect? Or what justice can there be in compelling them to bear arms, when, if they are honest men, they would rather die than use them. He then adverted to several instances of oppression in the case which occurred during the [revolutionary] war. In forming a militia we ought to calculate for an effectual defence, and not compel characters of this description to bear arms. I wish that in establishing this government we may be careful to let every person know that we will not interfere with any person's particular religious profession. If we strike out this clause, we shall lead such persons to conclude that we mean to compel them to bear arms.

Mr. VINING and Mr. JACKSON spoke upon the question. The words 'in person' were added after the word 'arms', and the amendment was adopted.

SOURCE: http://www.constitution.org/mil/militia_debate_1789.htm

---

ANALYSIS

The debates in the First Congress provide the most direct evidence regarding the intentions and meaning of what eventually became the Second Amendment. The reference in an early version of the amendment to the militia "composed of the body of the people" has raised questions about who was being referenced. When the phrase "the body of the people" is taken by itself, it suggests the entire population of the country. Yet it was inserted as an operational definition of militia: "A well regulated militia, composed of the body of the people" certainly did not include elderly men, for example, or those with physical infirmities that prevented them from serving in the militia. Thus, while militia service was an important civic right or civic responsibility, it was different from some of the other rights expressed in the Bill of Rights, such as free speech or freedom of assembly, which were not limited to subgroups of the population based on traits like physical fitness or age (leaving aside those adults who were not granted full rights earlier in the country's history, including women and African Americans).

The debate in the First Congress also confronted the longstanding fear of standing armies. The new Constitution gave Congress control over both, but many in Congress, such as Elbridge Gerry, wanted the country to maintain a strong and active militia to serve as a potential counterbalance to a standing army. The subject that prompted the most debate, however, was whether to include an express exemption from military service for those who had religious objections to military service (those "religiously scrupulous"). One lingering question pertained to whether those seeking such an exemption should be able to opt out only "upon paying an equivalent," meaning that they could pay a sum of money to the government if they wished to avoid service. The proposal to include such language was defeated, but such a practice was actually used in the North during the Civil War, where anyone with the means could buy his way out of military service, regardless of religious beliefs. That practice spawned fierce resentment in the country and helped precipitate the draft riots of 1863.

Finally, as the debate transcripts show, all of the debate regarding the Second Amendment pertained to military matters and militia service. No one in the congressional debate ever said, or suggested, that the Second Amendment provided a personal or individual right for citizens to own or carry guns (for purposes such as hunting or personal self-protection). Gun ownership among early American militia-eligible men was indeed important, but only to the extent that it pertained to the country's ability to deploy a militia. Gun ownership has a long and honorable tradition in America, dating back to its colonial origins. The country's militia past is part of that history, but the right that found its way into the Bill of Rights was about the defense needs of states and the country as a whole, not about individual civilians wishing to own guns for personal reasons.

FURTHER READING

Cogan, Neil H., ed. *The Complete Bill of Rights*. New York: Oxford University Press, 1997.

Cornell, Saul. *A Well-Regulated Militia: The Founding Fathers and the Origins of Gun Control in America*. New York: Oxford University Press, 2006.

Spitzer, Robert J. "Lost and Found: Researching the Second Amendment." *Chicago-Kent Law Review* 76(2000): 349–401.

Veit, Helen E., Kenneth R. Bowling, and Charlene Bangs Bickford, eds. *Creating the Bill of Rights*. Baltimore, MD: The Johns Hopkins University Press, 1991.

Controlling Militias

- *Document:* The Calling Forth Act of 1792
- *Date:* May 2, 1792
- *Where:* Philadelphia, Pennsylvania
- *Significance:* This law resolved simmering controversy over control of militias.

DOCUMENT

The Calling Forth Act of 1792, 1 U.S. Stat. 264

Chap. XXVIII—An Act to provide for calling forth the Militia to execute the laws of the Union, suppress insurrections and repel invasions.

SECTION 1. Be it enacted by the Senate and House of Representatives of the United States of America in Congress assembled, That whenever the United States shall be invaded, or be in imminent danger of invasion from any foreign nation or Indian tribe, it shall be lawful for the President of the United States, to call forth such number of the militia of the state or states most convenient to the place of danger or scene of action, as he may judge necessary to repel such invasion, and to issue his orders for that purpose, to such officer or officers of the militia as he shall think proper; and in case of an insurrection in any state, against the government thereof, it shall be lawful for the President of the United States, on application of the legislature of such state, or of the executive (when the legislature cannot be convened) to call forth such number of the militia of any other state or states, as may be applied for, or as he may judge sufficient to suppress such insurrection.

SEC. 2. And be it further enacted, That whenever the laws of the United States shall be opposed, or the execution thereof obstructed, in any state, by combinations too powerful to be suppressed by the ordinary course of judicial proceedings, or by the powers vested in the marshals by this act, the same being notified to the President of the United States, by an associate justice or the district judge, it shall be lawful for the President of the United States to call forth the militia of such state to suppress such combinations, and to cause the laws to be duly executed. And if the militia of a state, where such combinations may happen, shall refuse, or be insufficient to suppress the same, it shall be lawful for the President, if the legislature of the United States be not in session, to call forth and employ such numbers of the militia of any other state or states most convenient thereto, as may be necessary, and the use of militia, so to be called forth, may be continued, if necessary, until the expiration of thirty days after the commencement of the ensuing session.

SEC. 3. Provided always, and be it further enacted, That whenever it may be necessary, in the judgment of the President, to use the military force hereby directed to be called forth, the President shall forthwith, and previous thereto, by proclamation, command such insurgents to disperse, and retire peaceably to their respective abodes, within a limited time.

SEC. 4. And be it further enacted, That the militia employed in the service of the United States, shall receive the same pay and allowances, as the troops of the United States, who may be in service at the same time, or who were last in service, and shall be subject to the same rules and articles of war: And that no officer, non-commissioned officer or private of the militia shall be compelled to serve more than three months in any one year, nor more than in due rotation with every other able-bodied man of the same rank in the battalion to which they belong.

SEC. 5. And be it further enacted, That every officer, non-commissioned officer or private of the militia, who shall fail to obey the orders of the President of the United States in any of the cases before recited, shall forfeit a sum not exceeding one year's pay, and not less than one month's pay, to be determined and adjudged by a court martial; and such officer shall, moreover, be liable to be cashiered by sentence of a court martial: and such non-commissioned officers and privates shall be liable to be imprisoned by a like sentence, on failure of payment of the fines adjudged against them, for the space of one calendar month for every five dollars of such fine.

SEC. 6. And be it further enacted, That courts martial for the trial of militia shall be composed of militia officers only.

SEC. 7. And be it further enacted, That all fines to be assessed, as aforesaid, shall be certified by the presiding officer of the court martial before whom the same shall be assessed, to the marshal of the district, in which the delinquent shall reside, or to one of his deputies; and also to the supervisor of the revenue of the same district, who shall record the said certificate in a book to be kept for that purpose. The said marshal or his deputy shall forthwith proceed to levy the said fines with costs, by distress and sale of the goods and chattels of the delinquent, which costs and the manner of proceeding, with respect to the sale of the goods distrained, shall be agreeable to the laws of the state, in which the same shall be, in other cases of distress; and where any non-commissioned officer or private shall be adjudged to suffer imprisonment, there being no goods or chattels to be found, whereof to levy the said fines, the marshal of the district or his deputy may commit such delinquent to gaol, during the term, for which he shall be so adjudged to imprisonment, or until the fine shall be paid, in the same manner as other persons condemned to fine and imprisonment at the suit of the United States, may be committed.

SEC. 8. And be it further enacted, That the marshals and their deputies shall pay all such fines by them levied to the supervisor of the revenue, in the district in which they are collected, within two months after they shall have received the same, deducting therefrom five per centum, as a compensation for their trouble; and in case of failure, the same shall be recoverable by action of debt or information in any court of the United States, of the district, in which such fines shall be levied, having cognizance thereof, to be sued for, prosecuted and recovered, in the name of the supervisor of the district, with interest and costs.

SEC. 9. And be further enacted, That the marshals of the several districts and their deputies, shall have the same powers in executing the laws of the United States, as sheriffs and their deputies in the several states have by law, in executing the laws of their respective states.

SEC. 10. And be it further enacted, That this act shall continue and be in force, for and during the term of two years, and from thence to the end of the next session of Congress thereafter, and no longer.

APPROVED, May 2, 1792.

SOURCE: http://www.constitution.org/mil/mil_act_1792.htm

DID YOU KNOW?

How Many Guns Were There in Early America?

A sharp and protracted debate among historians and others has swirled around the question of how common guns actually were in early America. Without question, gun ownership became more common by the 1850s because of improved gun manufacturing techniques and materials (led by entrepreneurs such as Samuel Colt). Gun ownership increased dramatically after the Civil War, as millions of returning veterans now acquainted with the use and care of guns were allowed to keep their weapons or sought to acquire them.

Before this period, however, the historical and technological record mostly supports the idea that, from the colonial period up through the early 1800s, gun ownership was uncommon, if not rare, among the general population. Three types of information support this conclusion. First, military records show consistently that militia recruits (the subcategory of the population most likely to own guns) throughout this period were mostly unacquainted with the use and care of firearms. Second, militias throughout the country were consistently underarmed, a fact that prompted much concern in both military and political circles. And third, firearms during this period were expensive (they were either handmade in America or imported from Europe), were made of materials (mostly iron) that rusted and deteriorated rapidly (even with regular care and maintenance), and were complicated and cumbersome to operate. In 1804, for example, Secretary of War Henry Dearborn conducted a nationwide census of arms owned both publicly and privately, which concluded that about 45 percent of militiamen (men ages 18 to 45) in the country had arms (including guns, working and nonworking, and other military weaponry, like sabers).

Source: *American State Papers: Documents, Legislative and Executive, of the Congress of the United States, Class V: Military Affairs,* 7 vols. (Washington, D.C.: Gales and Seaton, 1789–1838).

ANALYSIS

The Calling Forth Act represented the culmination of three years of political wrangling over how to implement congressional authority over militias. The compromise was for Congress to delegate this power to the president, leaving him a relatively free hand in the case of invasion, but circumscribing this power some in the case of domestic insurrection, when the president needed to seek approval from a federal judge. It also invited the states to request militia help from the federal government in times of need, yet also made clear that the federal government could act against one or more states "whenever the laws of the United States shall be opposed, or the execution thereof obstructed." The larger objective was to balance federal and state power by making sure that the national government could act decisively, yet also to address Antifederalist fears of an overly strong national government. The Second

Amendment's assurance to the states that they would be able to form and maintain their own militias would not, this act said, absolve them of national connections, needs, or obligations. Any state that refused to call forth or commit its militias in appropriate circumstances could expect to find other state militias sent to its soil. Although this initial law included a time limit of two years, subsequent legislation was enacted to confirm and extend federal power over the militias, notably in 1795 and 1807.

FURTHER READING

Coakley, Robert W. *The Role of Federal Military Forces in Domestic Disorders, 1789–1878.* Darby, PA: DIANE Publishing, 1996.

Higginbotham, Don. "The Federalized Militia Debate." *William and Mary Quarterly* 55(January 1998): 39–57.

The Federal Government Attempts to Get Militia-Eligible Men to Be Prepared for Militia Service

- *Document:* The Uniform Militia Act of 1792
- *Date:* May 8, 1792
- *Where:* Philadelphia, Pennsylvania
- *Significance:* This law attempted to require militia-eligible men to be armed and prepared for militia service.

DOCUMENT

The Uniform Militia Act of 1792, 1 U.S. Stat. 271

CHAP. XXXIII—An Act more effectually to provide for the National Defence by establishing an Uniform Militia throughout the United States.

SECTION I. Be it enacted by the Senate and House of Representatives of the United States of America in Congress assembled, That each and every free able-bodied white male citizen of the respective states, resident therein, who is or shall be of the age of eighteen years, and under the age of forty-five years (except as is herein after excepted) shall severally and respectively be enrolled in the militia by the captain or commanding officer of the company, within whose bounds such citizen shall reside, and that within twelve months after the passing of this act. And it shall at all times hereafter be the duty of every such captain or commanding officer of a company to enrol every such citizen, as aforesaid, and also those who shall, from time to time, arrive at the age of eighteen years, or being of the age of eighteen years and under the age of forty-five years (except as before excepted) shall come to reside within his bounds; and shall without delay notify such citizen of the said enrolment, by a proper non-commissioned officer of the company, by whom such notice may be proved. That every citizen so enrolled and notified, shall, within six months thereafter, provide himself with a good musket or firelock, a sufficient bayonet and belt, two spare flints, and a knapsack, a pouch with a box therein to contain not less than twenty four cartridges, suited to the bore of his musket or firelock, each cartridge to contain a proper quantity of powder and ball: or with a good rifle, knapsack, shot-pouch and powder-horn, twenty balls suited to the bore of his rifle, and a quarter of a pound of powder; and shall appear, so armed, accoutred and provided, when called out to exercise, or into service, except, that when called out on company days to exercise only, he may appear without a knapsack. That the commissioned officers shall severally be armed with a sword or hanger and espontoon, and that from and after five years from the passing of this act, all muskets for arming the militia as herein required, shall be of bores sufficient for balls of the eighteenth part of a pound. And every citizen so enrolled, and providing himself with the arms, ammunition and accoutrements required as aforesaid, shall hold the same exempted from all suits, distresses, executions or sales, for debt or for the payment of taxes.

SEC. 2. And be it further enacted, That the Vice President of the United States; the officers judicial and executive of the government of the United States; the members of both Houses of Congress, and their respective officers; all custom-house officers with their clerks; all post officers, and stage drivers, who are employed in the care and conveyance of the mail of the post-office of the United States; all ferrymen employed at any ferry on the post road; all inspectors of exports; all pilots; all mariners actually employed in the sea service of any citizen or merchant within the United States; and all persons who now are or may hereafter be exempted by the laws of the respective states, shall be, and are hereby exempted from militia duty, notwithstanding their being above the age of eighteen, and under the age of forty-five years.

SEC. 3. And be it further enacted, That within one year after the passing of this act, the militia of the respective states shall be arranged into divisions, brigades, regiments, battalions and companies, as the legislature of each state shall direct; and each division, brigade and regiment, shall be numbered at the formation thereof; and a record made of such numbers in the adjutant-general's office in the state; and when in the field, or in service in the state, each division, brigade and regiment shall respectively take rank according to their numbers, reckoning the first or lowest number highest in rank. That if the same be convenient, each brigade shall consist of four regiments; each regiment of two battalions; each battalion of five companies; each company of sixty-four privates. That the said militia shall be officered by the respective states, as follows: To each division, one major-general and two aids-de-camp, with the rank of major; to each brigade, one brigadier-general, with one brigade inspector, to serve also as brigade-major, with the rank of a major; to each regiment, one lieutenant-colonel commandant; and to each battalion one major; to each company one captain, one lieutenant, one ensign, four sergeants, four corporals, one drummer and one fifer or bugler. That there shall be a regimental staff, to consist of one adjutant and one quartermaster, to rank as lieutenants; one paymaster; one surgeon, and one surgeon's mate; one sergeant-major; one drum-major, and one fife-major.

SEC. 4. And be it further enacted, That out of the militia enrolled, as is herein directed, there shall be formed for each battalion at least one company of grenadiers, light infantry or riflemen; and that to each division there shall be at least one company of artillery, and one troop of horse: there shall be to each company of artillery, one captain, two lieutenants, four sergeants, four corporals, six gunners, six bombadiers, one drummer, and one fifer. The officers to be armed with a sword or hanger, a fusee, bayonet and belt, with a cartridge-box to contain twelve cartridges; and each private or matross shall furnish himself with all the equipments of a private in the infantry, until proper ordnance and field artillery is provided. There shall be to each troop of horse, one captain, two lieutenants, one cornet, four sergeants, four corporals, one saddler, one farrier, and one trumpeter. The commissioned officers to furnish themselves with good horses of at least fourteen hands and an half high, and to be armed with a sword and pair of pistols, the holsters of which to be covered with bearskin caps. Each dragoon to furnish himself with a serviceable horse, at least fourteen hands and a half high, a good saddle, bridle, mailpillion and valise, holsters, and a breast-plate and crupper, a pair of boots and spurs, a pair of pistols, a sabre, and a cartouche-box, to contain twelve cartridges for pistols. That each company of artillery and troop of horse shall be formed of volunteers from the brigade, at the discretion of the commander-in-chief of the state, not exceeding one company of each to a regiment, nor more in number than one eleventh part of the infantry, and shall be uniformly clothed in regimentals, to be furnished at their own expense; the colour and fashion to be determined by the brigadier commanding the brigade to which they belong.

SEC. 5. And be it further enacted, That each battalion and regiment shall be provided with the state and regimental colours by the field officers, and each company with a drum and fife, or bugle-horn, by the commissioned officers of the company, in such manner as the legislature of the respective states shall direct.

SEC. 6. And be it further enacted, That there shall be an adjutant-general appointed in each state, whose duty it shall be to distribute all orders from the commander-in-chief of the state to the several corps; to attend all public reviews when the commander-in-chief of the state shall review the militia, or any part thereof; to obey all orders from him relative to carrying into execution and perfecting the system of military discipline established by this act; to furnish blank forms of different returns that may be required, and to explain the principles on which they should be made; to receive from the several officers of the different corps throughout the state, returns of the militia under their command, reporting the actual situation of their arms, accoutrements, and ammunition, their delinquencies, and every other thing which relates to the general advancement of good order and discipline: all which the several officers of the divisions, brigades, regiments, and battalions, are hereby required to make in the usual manner, so that the said adjutant-general may be duly furnished therewith: from all which returns he shall make proper abstracts, and lay the same annually before the commander-in-chief of the state.

SEC. 7. And be it further enacted, That the rules of discipline, approved and established by Congress in their resolution of the twenty-ninth of March, one thousand seven hundred and seventy-nine, shall be the rules of discipline to be observed by the militia throughout the United States, except such deviations from the said rules as may be rendered necessary by the requisitions of this act, or by some other unavoidable circumstances. It shall be the duty of the commanding officer at every muster, whether by battalion, regiment, or single company, to cause the militia to be exercised and trained agreeably to the said rules of discipline.

SEC. 8. And be it further enacted, That all commissioned officers shall take rank according to the date of their commissions; and when two of the same grade bear an equal date, then their rank to be determined by lot, to be drawn by them before the commanding officer of the brigade, regiment, battalion, company, or detachment.

SEC. 9. And be it further enacted, That if any person, whether officer or soldier, belonging to the militia of any state, and called out into the service of the United States, be wounded or disabled while in actual service, he shall be taken care of and provided for at the public expense.

SEC. 10. And be it further enacted, That it shall be the duty of the brigade-inspector to attend the regimental and battalion meetings of the militia composing their several brigades, during the time of their being under arms, to inspect their arms, ammunition, and accoutrements; superintend their exercise and manoeuvres, and introduce the system of military discipline before described throughout the brigade, agreeable to law, and such orders as they shall from time to time receive from the commander-in-chief of the state; to make returns to the adjutant-general of the state, at least once in every year, of the militia of the brigade to which he belongs, reporting therein the actual situation of the arms, accoutrements, and ammunition of the several corps, and every other thing which, in his judgment, may relate to their government and the general advancement of good order and military discipline; and the adjutant-general shall make a return of all the militia of the state to the commander-in-chief of the said state, and a duplicate of the same to the President of the United States.

And whereas sundry corps of artillery, cavalry, and infantry now exist in several of the said states, which by the laws, customs, or usages thereof have not been incorporated with, or subject to the general regulations of the militia:

SEC. 11. Be it further enacted, That such corps retain their accustomed privileges, subject, nevertheless, to all other duties required by this act, in like manner with the other militia.

APPROVED, May 8, 1792.

SOURCE: http://www.constitution.org/mil/mil_act_1792.htm

ANALYSIS

The Uniform Militia Act, passed by Congress one year after the adoption of the Bill of Rights, reveals in considerable detail what the country's leaders meant by the concept of militia at a time when it was still considered to be the backbone of the American military. Congress required the militias to be organized according to military principles; membership was limited not only to white males, but to those between 18 and 45 who were fit for service, underscoring the fact that white males over the age of 45 and the infirm were excluded from militias, even though they were eligible to exercise other rights and freedoms; they were to provide their own arms and other military accessories (since neither the states nor the national government could be relied on to provide weapons and the like); and the militias were to be put to any use specified by the government. Thus militias were not to be privately formed or operated, nor were they to be used against the government (except by the federal government against a state in rebellion or chaos), as some modern commentators have suggested. Notice in particular in Section I of the law the very detailed list of items that militia-eligible men were required to obtain, at their own expense, including a musket, a bayonet, spare flints (these made the necessary spark to ignite the gun powder to fire the gun), a knapsack, 24 cartridges and more. For all of this, however, the act included no penalties against states or men who did not comply—another compromise owing to continued tensions between Federalists and Antifederalists—and the terms of this act, along with similar state enactments, were largely ignored.

This law reflects the reality of the American military at the time the Second Amendment was written. The amendment's reference to "the right of the people to keep and bear arms" harkened to the requirements described in this law, where militiamen had to provide their own weapons, as had been true up until this time. Preventing men from doing so would have been tantamount to disarming the nation's militias, which were still the backbone of American military defense. The nature of America's military defense gradually changed in the nineteenth century, however. By the time of the Civil War (1861–1865), Union army soldiers were armed, equipped, and uniformed by the federal government. In the twentieth century, the idea that soldiers needed to obtain and bring to military service their own weaponry had become a quaint historical oddity. In addition, national military emergencies were met

Battle of Lexington, April 19, 1775. Copy of print by John Baker, 1882. National Archives and Records Administration.

by drafting young men into the professional army (or by aggressively soliciting volunteers), not by forming separate militia units. Both the Calling Forth Act and the Uniform Militia Act also demonstrate how Congress participates in the process of interpreting the Constitution, as both of these acts represent congressional efforts to specify the nature and purposes of the militias discussed in the Constitution and the Second Amendment.

FURTHER READING

Cornell, Saul, ed. *Whose Right to Bear Arms Did the Second Amendment Protect?* New York: Bedford/St. Martin's, 2000.

Cress, Lawrence D. Citizens in Arms: *The Army and the Militia in American Society to the War of 1812.* Chapel Hill: University of North Carolina Press, 1982.

Shy, John. *A People Numerous and Armed.* Ann Arbor: University of Michigan Press, 1990.

Early Gun Control Law from Pennsylvania Taking Guns from Those Who Refuse Military Service

- *Document:* An Ordinance Respecting the Arms of Non-Associators
- *Date:* July 19, 1776
- *Where:* Pennsylvania
- *Significance:* This is a stark example of a strict early gun law that called for gun confiscation.

DOCUMENT

Chapter 729

An Ordinance Respecting the Arms of Non-Associators

Whereas the non-associators in this state have either refused or neglected to deliver up their arms according to the resolves of the honorable Continental Congress and the assembly of Pennsylvania, and effectual measures have not been taken to carry the said resolves into execution:

[Section I] Be it therefore ordained by the authority of this Convention, That the colonel or next officer in command of every battalion of militia in this state is hereby authorized, empowered and required to collect, receive and take all the arms in his district or township nearest to such officer which are in the hands of non-associators in the most expeditious and effectual manner in his power, and shall give to the owners receipts for such arms, specifying the amount of the appraisement; and such as can be repaired shall with all possible dispatch be rendered fit for service, and the value according to the appraisement of all such arms, together with the repairs and transportation, shall be paid to the officers by the treasurer on the order of the council of safety for the use of the owners and defraying the charges. . . .

[Section III] And it is further ordained, That the colonels aforesaid shall arm the associators with the said arms and keep an account to whom they are delivered and return the same to the council of safety; and every associator shall be answerable for such arms or the value unless lost or destroyed by some unavoidable accident or in actual service. . . .

Passed July 19, 1776.

SOURCE: The Statutes at Large of Pennsylvania

ANALYSIS

This law was one of several enacted in Pennsylvania and in other states around the time of the American Revolution that gave the state government the power to confiscate the guns of "non-associators," referring to citizens who refrained from military service whether because they opposed the Patriot cause or because of religious beliefs that morally bound them to nonviolence, such as Quakers. Thus, disarmament (that is, the legal right of the government to take or "impress arms" of citizens) was not simply to take guns from the hands of Loyalists, but also from any who owned guns but who would not fight, regardless of the reason. In this way, guns were viewed as objects that the government could rightfully confiscate to use for a public purpose. This principle was common in the country's early history, when manifold military threats prompted local governments to, for example, require citizens to keep their guns (along with gun powder and other militarily useful items) in a local storage facility so they could be readily accessed in case of attack.

According to the law, the gun owners were to be given receipts when their guns were taken, noting the estimated value of the weapon. The arms so obtained were then to be given to "associators" (those who supported, and were prepared to fight for, the revolutionary cause) for their use, subject to the control of the local supervising "council of safety." No express provision was made for return of the arms, except in the case of arms that were "not worth repairing." These broken guns were to be "laid by," perhaps to be used for spare parts, and were to be returned to the owners at such time as local leaders thought appropriate.

FURTHER READING

Jensen, Merrill. *The New Nation.* New York: Vintage, 1965.
Wood, Gordon S. *The Creation of the American Republic, 1776–1787.* Chapel Hill: University of North Carolina Press, 1998.

Early Loyalty Oath-Based Gun Control Law from Pennsylvania

- **Document:** An Act Obliging the White Male Inhabitants of this State to Give Assurances of Allegiance
- **Date:** June 13, 1777
- **Where:** Pennsylvania
- **Significance:** Pennsylvania's law confiscated guns from those who refused to take a loyalty oath and also deprived them of other, although not all, rights.

DOCUMENT

Chapter 756

An Act Obliging the Male White Inhabitants of this State to Give Assurances of Allegiance to the Same and for Other Purposes Therein Mentioned

(Section I, P. L.) Whereas by the separation of the thirteen United States from the government of the crown and parliament of Great Britain . . . the good people of this state of Pennsylvania are become free and independent of the said crown and parliament:

(Section II, P. L.) And whereas from sordid and mercenary motives or other causes inconsistent with the happiness of a free and independent people sundry persons have or may yet be induced to withhold their service and allegiance from the commonwealth of Pennsylvania as a free and independent state as declared by Congress:

And whereas sundry other persons in their several capacities have at the risk of their lives and the hazard of their fortunes or both rendered great and eminent service in defense and support of the said independence and may yet continue to do the same, as both those sorts of persons remain at this time mixed in some measure undistinguished from each other, the disaffected deriving undeserved service from the faithful and well affected:

And whereas allegiance and protection are reciprocal, and those who will not bear the former are not nor ought not to be entitled to the benefits of the latter:

Therefore:

[Section I] Be it enacted by the Representatives of the Freemen of the Commonwealth of Pennsylvania in General Assembly met, and by the authority of the same, That all male white inhabitants of this state . . . above the age of eighteen years shall on or before the first day of July next take and subscribe the following oath or affirmation before some one of the justices of the peace of the city or county where they shall respectively inhabit . . . :

I, ... , do swear (or affirm) that I renounce and refuse all allegiance to George the Third, King of Great Britain, his heirs and successors, and that I will be faithful and bear true allegiance to the commonwealth of Pennsylvania as a free and independent state, and that I will not at any time do or cause to be done any matter or thing that will be prejudicial or injurious to the freedom and independence thereof, as declared by Congress; and also that I will discover and make known to some one justice of the peace of the said state all treasons or traitorous conspiracies which I now know or hereafter shall know to be formed against this or any of the United States of America. . . .

[Section III] (Section IV P.L.) And be it further enacted by the authority aforesaid, That every person above the age aforesaid refusing or neglecting to take and subscribe the said oath or affirmation shall during the time of such neglect or refusal be incapable of holding any office or place of trust in this state, serving on juries, suing for any debt, electing or being elected, buying, selling or transferring any lands, tenements, or hereditaments, and shall be disarmed by the lieutenant or sub-lieutenants of the city or counties respectively. . . .

Passed June 13, 1777.

SOURCE: The Statutes at Large of Pennsylvania

ANALYSIS

Laws like this one were collectively referred to as The Test Acts. These laws used loyalty oaths to disarm segments of the population. Such loyalty oath provisions were enacted in other states as well. Citizens who refused to take the oath reprinted in the law had their guns taken from them. In addition, they were barred from serving on juries or holding public office, although they could exercise other rights, including the right to petition the government, to assemble, and to publish. According to one historian, as much as 40 percent of the citizenry was affected by this law. The Test Acts were not repealed until after the Revolutionary War ended in 1783.

In general, early gun laws fell into two categories: laws that restricted or barred gun ownership, and laws that required gun ownership (such as the Militia Act of 1792 reprinted earlier in this chapter). From the country's earliest beginnings in the

1600s, the colonies enacted laws barring guns to Native Americans (selling guns to Indians was punishable by death in Virginia and elsewhere), indentured servants, slaves, people of mixed race, and even non-Protestants. Early laws were also enacted to restrict gun use or carrying in certain circumstances, such as during times of collective drinking or entertainment (in Virginia, for example) because of the likelihood that drunken men would waste ammunition or shoot each other.

Among colonial laws requiring gun ownership were measures enacted to, for example, require white men to carry guns to church, because of the particular concern that Indians would attack on Sundays, normally a day of peace. The militia laws of the 1780s and 1790s also required gun ownership of militia-eligible men, but as discussed earlier, such laws met with, at best, limited success. Southern states in particular shared great concern about the lack of arms and the readiness of militias because of the constant fear of slave rebellions.

FURTHER READING

Bogus, Carl T. "The Hidden History of the Second Amendment." *U.C. Davis Law Review* (Winter 1998): 309–408.

Cornell, Saul. "Commonplace or Anachronism: The Standard Model, the Second Amendment, and the Problem of History in Contemporary Constitutional Theory." *Constitutional Commentary* 16(Summer 1999): 221–246.

Edel, Wilbur. *Gun Control*. Westport, CT: Praeger, 1995.

Uviller, H. Richard, and William G. Merkel. *The Militia and the Right to Arms*. Durham, NC: Duke University Press.

An Early Tennessee Law Barring the Carrying of Dangerous Weapons

- **Document:** An Act to Prevent the Wearing of Dangerous and Unlawful Weapons
- **Date:** October 19, 1821
- **Where:** Tennessee
- **Significance:** Laws like this one regulating weapons, including but not limited to guns, were common in states and territories.

DOCUMENT

Chapter XIII

An Act to Prevent the Wearing of Dangerous and Unlawful Weapons

Be it enacted by the General Assembly of the State of Tennessee, That from and after the passage of this act, each and every person so degrading himself, by carrying a dirk, sword cane, French knife, Spanish stiletto, belt or pocket pistols, either public or private, shall pay a fine of five dollars for every such offence, which may be recovered by warrant before any Justice of the Peace, in the name of the county and for its use, in which the offence may have been committed; and it shall be the duty of a Justice to issue a warrant on the application on oath of any person applying; and that it shall be the duty of every Judge, Justice of the Peace, Sheriff, Coroner and Constable within this state to see that this act shall have its full effect: *Provided nevertheless,* That nothing herein contained shall affect any person that may carry a knife of any size in a conspicuous manner on the strop of a shot pouch, or any person that may be on a journey to any place out of his county or state.

JAMES FENTRESS, Speaker of the House of Representatives.
W. HALL, Speaker of the Senate, *pro tem*.
October 19, 1821.

SOURCE: Tennessee State Session Laws

ANALYSIS

This 1821 measure enacted in Tennessee states at the outset its disapproval of those who try to carry the weapons named in the law by saying that those caught doing so are "degrading" themselves. Note that the act bars the carrying only of "belt or pocket pistols," not long guns. By singling out handguns for regulation, the law reflects two problems with civilian ownership and carrying of handguns that continue to raise problems up to the present: their concealability and their connection with possible criminal use. Similarly, the law does not bar the carrying of all knives, but only the ones listed, all of which were singled out and barred because they were weapons used for fighting. These types of knives typically had long, thin, tapered, double-edged blades. Note also that the law exempts those knives carried "in a conspicuous manner," meaning not concealed, and also those who were simply passing through the local area.

FURTHER READING

Cornell, Saul. *A Well-Regulated Militia: The Founding Fathers and the Origins of Gun Control in America.* New York: Oxford University Press, 2006.

An Early Georgia Law Banning Carrying of Deadly Weapons

- **Document:** Deadly Weapons Act
- **Date:** December 25, 1837
- **Where:** Georgia
- **Significance:** This Georgia state law is another example of states trying to sever the link between dangerous weapons, including, but not limited to, handguns, and crime, by restricting merchants' ability to sell such weapons.

DOCUMENT

Deadly Weapons

AN ACT to guard and protect the citizens of this State, against the unwarrantable and too prevalent use of deadly weapons.

SECTION 1. *Be it enacted by the Senate and House of Representatives of the State of Georgia, in General Assembly met, and it is hereby enacted by the authority of the same,* That from and after the passage of this act, it shall not be lawful for any merchant, or vender of wares or merchandise in this State, or any other person or persons whatsoever, to sell, or offer to sell, or to keep, or have about their person or elsewhere, any of the hereinafter described weapons, to wit: Bowie, or any other kind of knives, manufactured and sold for the purpose of wearing, or carrying the same as arms of offence or defence, pistols, dirks, sword canes, spears, &c., shall also be contemplated in this act, save such pistols as are known and used, as horseman's pistols, &c.

SEC. 2. *And be it further enacted by the authority aforesaid,* That any person or persons within the limits of this State, violating the provisions of this act, except as hereafter excepted, shall, for each and every such offence, be deemed guilty of a high misdemeanor, and upon trial and conviction thereof, shall be fined, in a sum not exceeding five hundred dollars for the first offence, nor less than one hundred dollars at the direction of the Court; and upon a second conviction, and every after conviction of a like offence, in a sum not to exceed one thousand dollars, nor less than five hundred dollars, at the discretion of the Court. . . . *Provided, nevertheless,* that the provisions of this act shall not extend to Sheriffs, Deputy Sheriffs, Marshals, Constables, Overseers or Patrols, in actual discharge of their respective duties, but not otherwise: *Provided, also,* that no person or persons, shall be found guilty of violating the before recited act, who shall openly wear, externally, Bowie Knives, Dirks, Tooth Picks, Spears, and which shall be exposed plainly to view: *And provided, nevertheless,* that the provisions of this act shall not extend to prevent venders, or any other persons who now own and have for sale, any of the aforesaid weapons, before the first day of March next. . . .

Assented to, 25th December 1837.

SOURCE: Laws of Georgia

ANALYSIS

Like the Tennessee law preceding this one, this Georgia law was aimed at staunching the flow of certain types of concealable knives and pistols that were considered fighting and crime-related weapons (a Bowie knife was a large, curved-blade knife named after pioneer outdoorsman Jim Bowie). This law is distinctive because it attacks the problem by barring merchants' sale of such weapons. The law barred pistols as well, except for "horseman's pistols," large pistols normally not carried in a concealed manner. It also provided exemptions for law enforcement (who might give such weapons to deputies or others engaged in law enforcement), and for those who carried such weapons "exposed plainly to view." One can readily see that, even in the nineteenth century, government officials were concerned with protecting public safety, and that their remedy focused on dealers (as so-called rogue gun dealers are today prosecuted for selling guns illegally) to stem the flow of the weapons itemized in the law, just as it sought to bar the concealed carrying of weapons by civilians. The law's larger purpose was plainly to sever the observed link between such weapons and crimes of the day.

FURTHER READING

Carter, Gregg Lee. *The Gun Control Movement.* New York: Twayne, 1997.

An Early Virginia Law Banning Carrying of Deadly Weapons

- **Document:** An Act to Prevent the Carrying of Concealed Weapons
- **Date:** February 2, 1838
- **Where:** Richmond, Virginia
- **Significance:** This early law was typical of laws enacted in states and territories throughout the country that sought to prevent the carrying of dangerous weapons, including, but not limited to, guns.

DOCUMENT

CHAP. 101—An Act to Prevent the Carrying of Concealed Weapons

[Passed February 2, 1838]

1. *Be it enacted by the sgeneral assembly,* That if any person shall hereafter habitually or generally keep or carry about his person any pistol, dirk, bowie knife, or any other weapon of the like kind, from the use of which the death of any person might probably ensue, and the same be hidden or concealed from common observation, and he be thereof convicted, he shall for every such offence forfeit and pay the sum of not less than fifty dollars nor more than five hundred dollars, or be imprisoned in the common jail for a term not less than one month nor more than six months, and in each instance at the discretion of the jury; and a moiety [portion] of the penalty recovered in any prosecution under this act, shall be given to any person who may voluntarily institute the same.

2. *And be it further enacted,* That if any person shall hereafter be examined in any county or corporation court upon a charge of murder or felony, perpetrated by shooting, stabbing, maiming, cutting, or wounding, and it shall

appear that the offence charged was in fact committed by any such weapon as is above mentioned, and that the same was hidden or concealed from or kept out of the view of the person against whom it was used, until within the space of one half hour next preceding the commission of the act, or the infliction of the wound, which shall be charged to have caused the death, or constituted the felony, it shall be the duty of the examining court to state that the fact did so appear from the evidence; and if the court shall discharge or acquit the accused, such discharge or acquittal shall be no bar to an indictment for the same offence in the superior court having jurisdiction thereof, provided the same be found within one year thereafter. And whether the accused shall be by such court sent on for further trial or discharged, it shall be lawful to charge in the indictment that the offence was committed in any of the modes herein before described; and upon the trial it shall be the duty of the jury (if they find the accused not guilty of the murder or felony) to find also whether the act charged was in fact committed by the accused, though not feloniously, and whether the same was committed or done with or by means of any pistol, dirk, bowie knife, or other dangerous weapon, which was concealed from or kept out of the view of the person on or against whom it was used, for the space before mentioned, next preceding such use thereof; and if the jury find that the act was so committed, they shall assess a fine against the accused, and it shall be lawful for the court to pronounce judgment as in cases of misdemeanor. . . .

SOURCE: Virginia State Sessions Law

ANALYSIS

This law criminalized the carrying of concealed weapons, including guns and large knives, as an offense separate from their use in the commission of a crime. The law first criminalizes the concealed carrying of dangerous weapons "habitually or generally," presumably to exclude those who were simply transporting such weapons from one place to another. It then stipulates that if a murder or other felony is committed by anyone carrying such a weapon, the carry charge shall be separately noted and prosecuted, even if the person is found not guilty of the other charge or charges.

The aim of such laws was to reduce lawlessness and mayhem, and, as noted earlier, they were enacted in the states and territories throughout the country in the 1700s and 1800s. In fact, contrary to popular impression, restrictions against the carrying of concealed weapons, laws disarming all those entering cities and towns, and similar restrictions, were a common feature not just in the East, but in the expanding Western frontier. A primary reason for the establishment and incorporation of cities and towns in the nineteenth century West was so that local leaders could then impose bans on gun possession and carrying within town limits, precisely to tamp down lawlessness and shootings, attract settlers, and encourage commerce and economic development.

FURTHER READING

Billington, Ray Allen. *Westward Expansion: A History of the American Frontier.* New York: Macmillan, 1974.

Cornell, Saul. *A Well-Regulated Militia: The Founding Fathers and the Origins of Gun Control in America.* New York: Oxford University Press, 2006.

Kennett, Lee, and James LaVerne Anderson. *The Gun in America.* Westport, CT: Greenwood Press, 1975.

Early Hunting by Firelight Law Sends Those Convicted into the Military

- *Document:* An Act to Prevent Hunting with a Gun by Firelight
- *Date:* 1778
- *Where:* North Carolina
- *Significance:* This law barred a practice that is still illegal today—hunting at night using artificial light.

DOCUMENT

An Act to Prevent Hunting with a Gun by Fire Light, in the Night

I. WHEREAS many Persons under Pretence of Hunting for Deer in the Night, by Fire Light, kill Horses and Cattle, to the Prejudice of the Owners thereof.

II. *BE it therefore Enacted by the General Assembly of the State of North Carolina, and by the Authority of the same,* That if any Person or Persons shall be discovered Hunting in the Woods with a Gun, in the Night Time by Fire Light, such Person or Persons so offending, shall upon due Conviction thereof, by the Proof of One credible Witness, before any Justice of the Peace in the County where the Offence was committed, be compelled to go into the Service of the United States, and there serve as a Continental Soldier, for the Space of Three Years, subject to the same Rules, Regulations and Restrictions, as are prescribed by the Continental Congress, for the Government of the Army; and shall be turned over to the Army in the same Manner as is directed by an Act passed this Session, for the Encouragement of the Recruiting Services.

III. *PROVIDED nevertheless,* That in Case the said Offender shall immediately procure One able-Bodied and effective Man, to serve in the Continental Army, for the aforesaid Term of Three Years, then the said convicted Person shall be excused, and stand acquitted of the Judgment passed upon him.

IV. *AND be it further Enacted, by the Authority aforesaid,* That if any Slave or Slaves shall be discovered Hunting in the Manner herein before mentioned, such Slave or Slaves shall, upon due Conviction thereof, before any Justice of the Peace for the County in which the Offence was committed, by the Oath of a credible Witness, be sentenced to receive Thirty Nine Lashes on his bare Back; and the Gun or Guns found in the Possession of any Slave so Hunting in the Night aforesaid, shall be forfeited to, and become the Property of the Person or Persons that shall discover and prosecute any Slave or Slaves in Manner aforesaid: And the Owner of the Slave so convicted, shall be fined in the Sum of Five Pounds, to be recovered by Warrant before any Justice of the Peace for the County in which the Offence was committed; to be applied towards defraying the contingent Charges of the said County.

V. *AND be it further Enacted, by the Authority aforesaid,* That this Act shall be and continue for the Term of Five Months, and from thence to the End of the next Session of Assembly, and no longer.

SOURCE: Acts of North-Carolina, 1778

ANALYSIS

This North Carolina law from 1778 is interesting for several reasons. First, it barred a practice that is still illegal in most places under most circumstances: hunting at night by artificial light. In the modern era, such hunting would occur with automobile headlights or searchlights. Its prohibition is usually justified on the grounds that deer and other animals freeze when caught in bright lights at night, rendering the hunting process unsportsmanlike. In addition, it is more difficult to see where a gunshot might travel at nighttime, owing to limited visibility, thereby increasing risk.

The penalty stipulated in the North Carolina law is severe: the offending person is sent to serve as a Continental soldier for three years, although the convicted person could avoid military service if he could find someone to take his place. (This law was enacted in 1778, in the middle of the Revolutionary War, when American forces were desperate for manpower.) In addition, if a slave was caught under the terms of this law, he or she was to be given 39 lashes on a bare back, the gun or guns used were to be given to the person who witnessed the incident, and the slave's owner was fined five pounds.

DID YOU KNOW?

The Not-So-Wild West

The commonplace Hollywood image of a nineteenth-century, gun-filled American West typified by shootouts, duels, and rampant gunplay bears little resemblance to reality. Yes, guns were present in the Old West, but their prevalence and role have been wildly exaggerated thanks to newspaper articles and pulp novels of the time, and later, countless movies and television programs. In fact, the six-shooter and rifle played a relatively small role in westward settlement.

As many historians of the American West have noted, even in the most violence-prone western towns, gunplay and lawlessness were only briefly tolerated. In the most violent towns of the old West, including Abilene, Caldwell, Dodge City, Ellsworth, and Wichita, a total of 45 killings were recorded from 1870–1885. Of those, only 6 were from six-shooters, and 16 were by police. In Dodge City's most deadly year, 1878, five persons were killed. In Deadwood, South Dakota's deadliest year, four people were killed. In Tombstone, Arizona's worst year (the home of the famed shootout at the OK Corral), five were killed. And the western-style shootouts endlessly dramatized in books and movies were, in the words of historian Ray Allen Billington, literally "unheard of." Numerous studies of the most famous (or infamous) Western outlaws have shown that they were few in number and were mostly unknown until writers glorified, exaggerated, or even invented the misdeeds for which they later became famous. Most of the shooting and dying in the old West occurred between Native Americans and the U.S. Cavalry.

Source: Ray Allen Billington, *Westward Expansion: A History of the American Frontier.* New York: Macmillan, 1974.

Contrary to popular impression, hunting regulations were common even in the eighteenth century, both as game-conserving measures and to protect safety and property. Finally, the law said it would lapse after five months. The North Carolina legislature subsequently enacted a new version of this law.

FURTHER READING

Cornell, Saul. *A Well-Regulated Militia: The Founding Fathers and the Origins of Gun Control in America.* New York: Oxford University Press, 2006. http://www.secondamendment center.org/digital_archive.asp

Another Early Hunting Regulation

- **Document:** An ACT to prevent the destruction of wild fowl in the counties of Accomack and Fairfax.
- **Date:** April 9, 1839
- **Where:** Virginia
- **Significance:** Laws regulating improper hunting practices were also common among the states.

DOCUMENT

CHAP. 80—An ACT to prevent the destruction of wild fowl in the counties of Accomack and Fairfax

(Passed April 9, 1839.)

(1) *Be it enacted by the general assembly,* That no person whatsoever shall at any time shoot or kill wild fowl in the waters of, or within the jurisdiction of the counties of Accomack and Fairfax, by or with the aid of skiffs, and any person being convicted of a violation of this act before any justice of the peace of said county of Accomack, shall forthwith surrender his gun and skiff to the said justice, who shall cause the same to be sold; one half of the proceeds thereof shall go to the commonwealth for the use of the literary fund, and the other half to the informer.

(2) *Be it further enacted,* That if any person other than an actual inhabitant and resident of this commonwealth, shall violate the prohibition of this act, and being thereof convicted, he or she so offending shall for every such offence be subject to the same penalties, mode of proceeding and recovery as prescribed in the second and third sections of the act, entitled, "an act to prevent the destruction of oysters and terrapins in certain waters of

this commonwealth," passed March the twenty-fifth, eighteen hundred and thirty-seven: *Provided,* That nothing in this act contained shall prevent the owners of marshes from using skiffs while hunting in them.

(3) This act shall be in force from and after the passing thereof.

SOURCE: Virginia State Session Laws

ANALYSIS

This law barred hunting of "wild fowl" with guns from skiffs (small, flat-bottomed boats that could maneuver in shallow waters) in two counties in Virginia. The penalty for violating this law was stiff: persons so convicted were forced to give up both their gun and their boat, which were in turn sold, with the proceeds divided between the state and the "informer" who reported the crime. The law exempted those who chose to so hunt on their own marsh land.

Hunters and sportspeople today must abide by state and local laws that regulate when, where, how, and under what circumstances hunting may occur. Here again, however, such laws are by no means new. In 1778, for example, North Carolina passed a law barring hunting by firelight (just as hunters today are barred from hunting at night with searchlights or car headlights). Laws protecting the hunting of endangered or protected species (such as certain birds) and deer hunting regulations, for example, were common in the eighteenth and nineteenth centuries. The state of Virginia showed no reluctance about confiscating the gun of a hunter who violated this hunting restriction.

FURTHER READING

Hollon, W. Eugene. *Frontier Violence.* New York: Oxford University Press, 1974.
Kerasote, Ted. *Bloodties: Nature, Culture, and the Hunt.* New York: Random House, 1993.
    http://www.secondamendmentcenter.org/digital_archive.asp

3

EARLY SUPREME COURT RULINGS ON GUN LAWS AND RIGHTS

The Supreme Court's First Examination of the Second Amendment

- **Document:** Supreme Court case of *U.S. v. Cruikshank*
- **Date:** December 27, 1876
- **Where:** Washington, D.C.
- **Significance:** Although it received only brief examination, this Supreme Court case is the high court's first explication of the meaning of the Second Amendment and also its affirmation that this amendment, plus the rest of the Bill of Rights, applies only to the national government, not to the states.

DOCUMENT

U.S. v. Cruikshank, 92 U.S. 542 (1876)

Argued March 30, 31, April 1, 1875. Decided March 27, 1876.

MR. CHIEF JUSTICE WAITE delivered the opinion of the court.

This case comes here with a certificate by the judges of the Circuit Court for the District of Louisiana that they were divided in opinion upon a question which occurred at the hearing. It presents for our consideration an indictment containing sixteen counts, divided into two series of eight counts each, based upon sect. 6 of the Enforcement Act of May 31, 1870. That section is as follows:—

'That if two or more persons shall band or conspire together, or go in disguise upon the public highway, or upon the premises of another, with intent to violate any provision of this act, or to injure, oppress, threaten, or intimidate any citizen, with intent to prevent or hinder his free exercise and enjoyment of any right or privilege granted or secured to him by the constitution or laws of the United States, or because of his having exercised the same, such persons shall be held guilty of felony, and, on conviction thereof, shall be fined or imprisoned, or both, at the discretion of the court, the fine not to exceed $5,000, and the imprisonment not to exceed ten years; and shall, moreover, be thereafter ineligible to, and disabled from holding, any office or place of honor, profit, or trust created by the constitution or laws of the United States.' 16 Stat. 141.

The question certified arose upon a motion in arrest of judgment after a verdict of guilty generally upon the whole sixteen counts, and is stated to be, whether 'the said sixteen counts of said indictment are severally good and sufficient in law, and contain charges of criminal matter indictable under the laws of the United States.'

The general charge in the first eight counts is that of 'banding,' and in the second eight, that of 'conspiring' together to injure, oppress, threaten, and intimidate Levi Nelson and Alexander Tillman, citizens of the United States, of African descent and persons of color, with the intent thereby to hinder and prevent them in their free exercise and enjoyment of rights and privileges 'granted and secured' to them 'in common with all other good citizens of the United States by the constitution and laws of the United States.'

The offences provided for by the statute in question do not consist in the mere 'banding' or 'conspiring' of two or more persons together, but in their banding or conspiring with the intent, or for any of the purposes, specified. To bring this case under the operation of the statute, therefore, it must appear that the right, the enjoyment of which the conspirators intended to hinder or prevent, was one granted or secured by the constitution or laws of the United States. If it does not so appear, the criminal matter charged has not been made indictable by any act of Congress.

We have in our political system a government of the United States and a government of each of the several States. Each one of these governments is distinct from the others, and each has citizens of its own who owe it allegiance, and whose rights, within its jurisdiction, it must protect. The same person may be at the same time a citizen of the United States and a citizen of a State, but his rights of citizenship under one of these governments will be different from those he has under the other. . . .

Citizens are the members of the political community to which they belong. They are the people who compose the community, and who, in their associated capacity, have established or submitted themselves to the dominion of a government for the promotion of their general welfare and the protection of their individual as well as their collective rights. In the formation of a government, the people may confer upon it such powers as they choose. The government, when so formed, may, and when called upon should, exercise all the powers it has for the protection of the rights of its citizens and the people within its jurisdiction; but it can exercise no other. The duty of a government to afford protection is limited always by the power it possesses for that purpose.

Experience made the fact known to the people of the United States that they required a national government for national purposes. The separate governments of the separate States, bound together by the articles of confederation alone, were not sufficient for the promotion of the general welfare of the people in respect to foreign nations, or for their complete protection as citizens of the confederated States. For this reason, the people of the United States, 'in order to form a more perfect union, establish justice, insure domestic tranquillity, provide for the common defence, promote the general welfare, and secure the blessings of liberty' to themselves and their posterity (Const. Preamble), ordained and established the government of the United States, and defined its powers by a constitution, which they adopted as its fundamental law, and made its rule of action.

The government thus established and defined is to some extent a government of the States in their political capacity. It is also, for certain purposes, a government of the people. Its powers are limited in number, but not in degree. Within the scope of its powers, as enumerated and defined, it is supreme and above the States; but beyond, it has no existence. It was erected for special purposes, and endowed with all the powers necessary for its own preservation and the accomplishment of the ends its people had in view. It can neither grant nor secure to its citizens any right or privilege not expressly or by implication placed under its jurisdiction.

The people of the United States resident within any State are subject to two governments: one State, and the other National; but there need be no conflict between the two. The powers which one possesses, the other does not. They are established for different purposes, and have separate jurisdictions. Together they make one whole, and furnish the people of the United States with a complete government, ample for the protection of all their rights at home and abroad. True, it may sometimes happen that a person is amenable to both jurisdictions for one and the same act. Thus, if a marshal of the United States is unlawfully resisted while executing the process of the courts within a State, and the resistance is accompanied by an assault on the officer, the sovereignty of the United States is violated by the resistance, and that of the State by the breach of peace, in the assault. So, too, if one passes counterfeited coin of the United States within a State, it may be an offence against the United States and the State: the United States, because it discredits the coin; and the State, because of the fraud upon him to whom it is passed. This does not, however, necessarily imply that the two governments possess powers in common, or bring them into conflict with each other. It is the natural consequence of a citizenship which owes allegiance to two sovereignties, and claims protection from both. The citizen cannot complain, because he has voluntarily submitted himself to such a form of government. He owes allegiance to the two departments, so to speak, and within their respective spheres must pay the penalties which each exacts for disobedience to its laws. In return, he can demand protection from each within its own jurisdiction.

The government of the United States is one of delegated powers alone. Its authority is defined and limited by the Constitution. All powers not granted to it by that instrument are reserved to the States or the people. No rights can be acquired under the constitution or laws of the United States, except such as the government of the United States has the authority to grant or secure. All that cannot be so granted or secured are left under the protection of the States.

We now proceed to an examination of the indictment, to ascertain whether the several rights, which it is alleged the defendants intended to interfere with, are such as had been in law and in fact granted or secured by the constitution or laws of the United States.

The first and ninth counts state the intent of the defendants to have been to hinder and prevent the citizens named in the free exercise and enjoyment of their 'lawful right and privilege to peaceably assemble together with each other and with other citizens of the United States for a peaceful and lawful purpose.' The right of the people peaceably to assemble for lawful purposes existed long before the adoption of the Constitution of the United States. In fact, it is, and always has been, one of the attributes of citizenship under a free government. It 'derives its source,' to use the language of Chief Justice Marshall, in *Gibbons v. Ogden*, 9 Wheat. 211, 'from those laws whose authority is acknowledged by civilized man throughout the world.' It is found wherever civilization exists. It was not, therefore, a right granted to the people by the Constitution. The government of the United States when established found it in existence, with the obligation on the part of the States to afford it protection. As no direct power over it was granted to Congress, it remains, according to the ruling in *Gibbons v. Ogden*, id. 203, subject to State jurisdiction. Only such existing rights were committed by the people to the protection of Congress as came within the general scope of the authority granted to the national government.

The first amendment to the Constitution prohibits Congress from abridging 'the right of the people to assemble and to petition the government for a redress of grievances.' This, like the other amendments proposed and adopted at the same time, was not intended to limit the powers of the State governments in respect to their own citizens, but to operate upon the National government alone. . . . It is now too late to question the correctness of this construction. As was said by the late Chief Justice, in *Twitchell v. The Commonwealth*, 7 Wall. 325, 'the scope and application of these amendments are no longer subjects of discussion here.' They left the authority of the States just where they found it, and added nothing to the already existing powers of the United States.

The particular amendment now under consideration assumes the existence of the right of the people to assemble for lawful purposes, and protects it against encroachment by Congress. The right was not created by the amendment; neither was its continuance guaranteed, except as against congressional interference. For their protection in its enjoyment, therefore, the people must look to the States. The power for that purpose was originally placed there, and it has never been surrendered to the United States.

The right of the people peaceably to assemble for the purpose of petitioning Congress for a redress of grievances, or for any thing else connected with the powers or the duties of the national government, is an attribute of national citizenship, and, as such, under the protection of, and guaranteed by, the United States. The very idea of a government, republican in form, implies a right on the part of its citizens to meet peaceably for consultation in respect to public affairs and to petition for a redress of grievances. If it had been alleged in these counts that the object of the defendants was to prevent a meeting for such a purpose, the case would have been within the statute, and within the scope of the sovereignty of the United States. Such, however, is not the case. The offence, as stated in the indictment, will be made out, if it be shown that the object of the conspiracy was to prevent a meeting for any lawful purpose whatever.

The second and tenth counts are equally defective. The right there specified is that of 'bearing arms for a lawful purpose.' This is not a right granted by the Constitution. Neither is it in any manner dependent upon that instrument for its existence. The second amendment declares that it shall not be infringed; but this, as has been seen, means no more than that it shall not be infringed by Congress. This is one of the amendments that has no other effect than to restrict the powers of the national government, leaving the people to look for their protection against any violation by their fellow-citizens of the rights it recognizes, to what is called, in *The City of New York v. Miln*, 11 Pet. 139, the 'powers which relate to merely municipal legislation, or what was, perhaps, more properly called internal police,' 'not surrendered or restrained' by the Constitution of the United States.

The third and eleventh counts are even more objectionable. They charge the intent to have been to deprive the citizens named, they being in Louisiana, 'of their respective several lives and liberty of person without due process of law.' This is nothing else than alleging a conspiracy to falsely imprison or murder citizens of the United States, being within the territorial jurisdiction of the State of Louisiana. The rights of life and personal liberty are natural rights of man. 'To secure these rights,' says the Declaration of Independence, 'governments are instituted among men, deriving their just powers from the consent of the governed.' The very highest duty of the States, when they entered into the Union under the Constitution, was to protect all persons within their boundaries in the enjoyment of these 'unalienable rights with which they were endowed by their Creator.' Sovereignty, for this purpose, rests alone with the States. It is no more the duty or within the power of the United States to punish for a conspiracy to falsely imprison or murder within a State, than it would be to punish for false imprisonment or murder itself.

The fourteenth amendment prohibits a State from depriving any person of life, liberty, or property, without due process of law; but this adds nothing to the rights of one citizen as against another. It simply furnishes an additional guaranty against any encroachment by the States upon the fundamental rights which belong to every citizen as a member of society. As was said by Mr. Justice Johnson, in *Bank of Columbia v. Okely*, 4 Wheat. 244, it secures 'the individual from the arbitrary exercise of the powers of government, unrestrained by the established principles of private rights and distributive justice.' These counts in the indictment do not call for the exercise of any of the powers conferred by this provision in the amendment.

The fourth and twelfth counts charge the intent to have been to prevent and hinder the citizens named, who were of African descent and persons of color, in 'the free exercise and enjoyment of their several right and privilege to the full and equal benefit of all laws and proceedings, then and there, before that time, enacted or ordained by the said State of Louisiana and by the United States; and then and there, at that time, being in force in the said State and District of Louisiana aforesaid, for the security of their respective persons and property, then and there, at that time enjoyed at and within said State and District of Louisiana by white persons, being citizens of said State of Louisiana and the United States, for the protection of the persons and property of said white citizens.' There is no allegation that this was done because of the race or color of the persons conspired against. When stripped of its verbiage, the case as presented amounts to nothing more than that the defendants conspired to prevent certain citizens of the United States, being within the State of Louisiana, from enjoying the equal protection of the laws of the State and of the United States.

The fourteenth amendment prohibits a State from denying to any person within its jurisdiction the equal protection of the laws; but this provision does not, any more than the one which precedes it, and which we have just considered, add any thing to the rights which one citizen has under the Constitution against another. The equality of the rights of citizens is a principle of republicanism. Every republican government is in duty bound to protect all its citizens in the enjoyment of this principle, if within its power. That duty was originally assumed by the States; and it still remains there. The only obligation resting upon the United States is to see that the States do not deny the right. This the amendment guarantees, but no more. The power of the national government is limited to the enforcement of this guaranty.

No question arises under the Civil Rights Act of April 9, 1866 (14 Stat. 27), which is intended for the protection of citizens of the United States in the enjoyment of certain rights, without discrimination on account of race, color, or previous condition of servitude, because, as has already been stated, it is nowhere alleged in these counts that the wrong contemplated against the rights of these citizens was on account of their race or color.

Another objection is made to these counts, that they are too vague and uncertain. This will be considered hereafter, in connection with the same objection to other counts.

The sixth and fourteenth counts state the intent of the defendants to have been to hinder and prevent the citizens named, being of African descent, and colored, 'in the free exercise and enjoyment of their several and respective right and privilege to vote at any election to be thereafter by law had and held by the people in and of the said State of Louisiana, or by the people of and in the parish of Grant aforesaid.' In *Minor v. Happersett*, 21 Wall. 178, we decided that the Constitution of the United States has not conferred the right of suffrage upon any one, and that the United States have no voters of their own creation in the States. In *United States v. Reese et al.*, supra, p. 214, we hold that the fifteenth amendment has invested the citizens of the United States with a new constitutional right, which is, exemption from discrimination in the exercise of the elective franchise on account of race, color, or previous condition of servitude. From this it appears that the right of suffrage is not a necessary attribute of national citizenship; but that exemption from discrimination in the exercise of that right on account of race, &c., is. The right to vote in the States comes from the States; but the right of exemption from the prohibited discrimination comes from the United States. The first has not been granted or secured by the Constitution of the United States; but the last has been.

Inasmuch, therefore, as it does not appear in these counts that the intent of the defendants was to prevent these parties from exercising their right to vote on account of their race, &c., it does not appear that it was their intent to interfere with any right granted or secured by the constitution or laws of the United States. We may suspect that race was the cause of the hostility; but it is not so averred. This is material to a description of the substance of the offence, and cannot be supplied by implication. Every thing essential must be charged positively, and not inferentially. The defect here is not in form, but in substance.

The seventh and fifteenth counts are no better than the sixth and fourteenth. The intent here charged is to put the parties named in great fear of bodily harm, and to injure and oppress them, because, being and having been in all things qualified, they had voted 'at an election before that time had and held according to law by the people of the said State of Louisiana, in said State, to wit, on the fourth day of

November, A.D. 1872, and at divers other elections by the people of the State, also before that time had and held according to law.' There is nothing to show that the elections voted at were any other than State elections, or that the conspiracy was formed on account of the race of the parties against whom the conspirators were to act. The charge as made is really of nothing more than a conspiracy to commit a breach of the peace within a State. Certainly it will not be claimed that the United States have the power or are required to do mere police duly in the States. If a State cannot protect itself against domestic violence, the United States may, upon the call of the executive, when the legislature cannot be convened, lend their assistance for that purpose. This is a guaranty of the Constitution (art. 4, sect. 4); but it applies to no case like this.

We are, therefore, of the opinion that the first, second, third, fourth, sixth, seventh, ninth, tenth, eleventh, twelfth, fourteenth, and fifteenth counts do not contain charges of a criminal nature made indictable under the laws of the United States, and that consequently they are not good and sufficient in law. They do not show that it was the intent of the defendants, by their conspiracy, to hinder or prevent the enjoyment of any right granted or secured by the Constitution.

We come now to consider the fifth and thirteenth and the eighth and sixteenth counts, which may be brought together for that purpose. The intent charged in the fifth and thirteenth is 'to hinder and prevent the parties in their respective free exercise and enjoyment of the rights, privileges, immunities, and protection granted and secured to them respectively as citizens of the United States, and as citizens of said State of Louisiana,' 'for the reason that they, . . . being then and there citizens of said State and of the United States, were persons of African descent and race, and persons of color, and not white citizens thereof'; and in the eighth and sixteenth, to hinder and prevent them 'in their several and respective free exercise and enjoyment of every, each, all, and singular the several rights and privileges granted and secured to them by the constitution and laws of the United States.' The same general statement of the rights to be interfered with is found in the fifth and thirteenth counts.

According to the view we take of these counts, the question is not whether it is enough, in general, to describe a statutory offence in the language of the statute, but whether the offence has here been described at all. The statute provides for the punishment of those who conspire 'to injure, oppress, threaten, or intimidate any citizen, with intent to prevent or hinder his free exercise and enjoyment of any right or privilege granted or secured to him by the constitution or laws of the United States.' These counts in the indictment charge, in substance, that the intent in this case was to hinder and prevent these citizens in the free exercise and enjoyment of 'every, each, all, and singular' the rights granted them by the Constitution, &c. There is no specification of any particular right. The language is broad enough to cover all.

In criminal cases, prosecuted under the laws of the United States, the accused has the constitutional right 'to be informed of the nature and cause of the accusation.' Amend. VI. In *United States v. Mills*, 7 Pet. 142, this was construed to mean, that the indictment must set forth the offence 'with clearness and all necessary certainty, to apprise the accused of the crime with which he stands charged;' and in *United States v. Cook*, 17 Wall. 174, that 'every ingredient of which the offence is composed must be accurately and clearly alleged.' It is an elementary principle of criminal pleading, that where the definition of an offence, whether it be at common law or by statute, 'includes generic terms, it is not sufficient that the indictment shall charge the offence in the same generic terms as in the definition; but it must state the species—it must descend to particulars. 1 Arch. Cr. Pr. and Pl., 291. The object of the indictment is, first, to furnish the accused with such a description of the charge against him as will enable him to make his defence, and avail himself of his conviction or acquittal for protection against a further prosecution for the same cause; and, second, to inform the court of the facts alleged, so that it may decide whether they are sufficient in law to support a conviction, if one should be had. For this, facts are to be stated, not conclusions of law alone. A crime is made up of acts and intent; and these must be set forth in the indictment, with reasonable particularity of time, place, and circumstances.

It is a crime to steal goods and chattels; but an indictment would be bad that did not specify with some degree of certainty the articles stolen. This, because the accused must be advised of the essential particulars of the charge against him, and the court must be able to decide whether the property taken was such as was the subject of larceny. So, too, it is in some States a crime for two or more persons to conspire to cheat and defraud another out of his property; but it has been held that an indictment for such an offence must contain allegations setting forth the means proposed to be used to accomplish the purpose. This, because, to make such a purpose criminal, the conspiracy must be to cheat and defraud in a mode made criminal by statute; and as all cheating and defrauding has not been made criminal, it is necessary for the indictment to state the means proposed, in order that the court may see that they are in fact illegal. . . . In Maine, it is an offence for two or more to conspire with the intent unlawfully and wickedly to commit any crime punishable by imprisonment in the State prison (*State v. Roberts*); but we think it will hardly be claimed that an indictment would be good under this statute, which charges the object of the conspiracy to have been 'unlawfully and wickedly to commit each, every, all, and singular the crimes punishable by imprisonment in the State prison.' All crimes are not so punishable. Whether a particular crime be such a one or not, is a question of law. The accused has, therefore, the right to have a specification of the charge against him in this respect, in order that he may decide whether he should present his defence by motion to quash, demurrer, or plea; and the court, that it may determine whether the facts will sustain the indictment. So here, the crime is made to consist in the unlawful combination with an intent to prevent the enjoyment of any right granted or secured by the Constitution, &c. All rights are not so granted or secured. Whether one is so or not is a question of law, to be decided by the court, not the prosecutor. Therefore, the indictment should state the particulars, to inform the court as well as the accused. It must be made to appear-that is to say, appears from the indictment, without going further-that the acts charged will, if proved, support a conviction for the offence alleged.

But it is needless to pursue the argument further. The conclusion is irresistible, that these counts are too vague and general. They lack the certainty and precision required by the established rules of criminal pleading. It follows that they are not good and sufficient in law. They are so defective that no judgment of conviction should be pronounced upon them.

The order of the Circuit Court arresting the judgment upon the verdict is, therefore, affirmed; and the cause remanded, with instructions to discharge the defendants.

22 caliber Arminius revolver. Photo by Dawn Van Hall.

DID YOU KNOW?

The Colfax Massacre

One of the worst massacres of African Americans in the post-Civil War South occurred in Louisiana on Easter Sunday in 1873. The previous year's bitter elections resulted in a fierce dispute between the North-backed Republicans, who were supported by freed blacks, and the white-backed Democrats. Both groups claimed victory. In an effort to protect themselves from attacks and harassment by white groups like the White League and the Ku Klux Klan, blacks had been organized into militia units and armed by the federal government. In Louisiana's Grant Parish (named after Union General Ulysses S. Grant), both Democrats and Republicans claimed election victory. When the state's governor declared local Republicans the electoral winners, a group of black men entered the Colfax courthouse to claim it for the victors.

After a fruitless effort to end what quickly became an armed standoff between blacks inside the building and a larger force of whites outside, shots were exchanged. Two whites were killed. The enraged whites set fire to the building and shot those who tried to escape. The official death toll concluded that more than 100 blacks were killed that day, although estimates ran as high as 280. The few whites who were tried were eventually cleared of charges as the result of the Supreme Court's ruling in *U.S. v. Cruikshank.*

MR. JUSTICE CLIFFORD dissenting. . . .

SOURCE: http://caselaw.lp.findlaw.com/cgi-bin/getcase.pl?court=us&vol=92&invol=542

ANALYSIS

Tensions ran high between African Americans and whites in the American South after the Civil War, and violent confrontations often occurred between former slaves and whites who could not accept the free status of these former slaves. The Federal government even helped blacks by arming and organizing them as "black militias." The *Cruikshank* case arose because of one of the bloodiest episodes of white violence visited against blacks, the Colfax massacre. In the aftermath of the disputed election of 1872, the white-supported Democratic sheriff told the incumbent Republican sheriff that he intended to take over the Colfax, Louisiana courthouse with the backing of a Ku Klux Klan white paramilitary force. The Republican sheriff summoned the local Negro militia to resist the white takeover, but that force was overmatched by white reinforcements. After a failed effort to negotiate a settlement, the whites burned the courthouse and shot fleeing blacks, over a hundred of whom were killed.

The *Cruikshank* case was the only prosecution stemming from the massacre. Among the several charges leveled against the defendants were that they violated a federal civil rights law and various other federal rights of the blacks, including the Second Amendment's right to bear arms. A lower court upheld the convictions, but the Supreme Court reversed the lower court, noting among other things the Second Amendment's militia basis, and that this amendment, along with the rest of the Bill of Rights, did not apply to the states. Although much of the Bill of Rights has since been applied to the states through the process of incorporation, the Second Amendment has not. This case also reveals much of how the court defined federalism and dual citizenship in the era before the incorporation process began.

FURTHER READING

Goldman, Robert M. *Reconstruction and Black Suffrage: Losing the Vote in* Reese *and* Cruik-shank. Lawrence: University Press of Kansas, 2001.

Uviller, H. Richard, and William G. Merkel. *The Militia and the Right to Arms, or, How the Second Amendment Fell Silent*. Durham, NC: Duke University Press, 2002.

The Supreme Court Affirms the Militia Basis of the Second Amendment and Says "No" to Private Militias

- *Document:* Supreme Court case of *Presser v. Illinois*
- *Date:* January 4, 1886
- *Where:* Washington, D.C.
- *Significance:* This case clearly establishes the militia-based understanding of the Second Amendment, and it squarely rejects any right of citizens to form their own private militias.

DOCUMENT

Presser v. State of Illinois, 116 U.S. 252 (1886)

Mr. Justice Woods delivered the opinion of the court:

Herman Presser, the plaintiff in error, was indicted on September 24, 1879, in the criminal court of Cook county, Illinois, for a violation of the following sections of article 11 of the Military Code of that state (Act May 28, 1879; Laws 1876, 192):

"Sec. 5. It shall not be lawful for any body of men whatever, other than the regular organized volunteer militia of this state, and the troops of the United States, to associate themselves together as a military company or organization, or to drill or parade with arms in any city or town of this state, without the license of the governor thereof, which license may at any time be revoked: and provided, further, that students in educational institutions, where military science is a part of the course of instruction, may, with the consent of the governor, drill and parade with arms in public, under the superintendence of their instructors, and may take part in any regimental or brigade encampment, under command of their military instructor; and while so encamped shall be governed by the provisions of this act. They shall be entitled only to transportation and subsistence, and shall report and be subject to the commandant of such encampment: Provided, that nothing herein contained shall be construed so as to prevent benevolent or social organizations from wearing swords.

Sec. 6. Whoever offends against the provisions of the preceding section, or belongs to, or parades with, any such unauthorized body of men with arms, shall be punished by a fine not exceeding the sum of ten dollars, ($10,) or by imprisonment in the common jail for a term not exceeding six months, or both."

The indictment charged in substance that Presser, on September 24, 1879, in the county of Cook, in the state of Illinois, "did unlawfully belong to, and did parade and drill in the city of Chicago with, an unauthorized body of men with arms, who had associated themselves together as a military company and organization, without having a license from the governor, and not being a part of, or belonging to, 'the regular organized volunteer militia' of the state of Illinois, or the troops of the United States."

A motion to quash the indictment was overruled. Presser then pleaded not guilty, and, both parties having waived a jury, the case was tried by the court, which found Presser guilty and sentenced him to pay a fine of $10.

The bill of exceptions taken upon the trial set out all the evidence, from which it appeared that Presser was 31 years old, a citizen of the United States and of the state of Illinois, and a voter; that he belonged to a society called the *Lehr und Wehr Verein*, a corporation organized April 16, 1875, in due form, under chapter 32, Revised Statutes of Illinois, called the General Incorporation Laws of Illinois, "for the purpose," as expressed by its certificate of association, "of improving the mental and bodily condition of its members so as to qualify them for the duties of citizens of a republic. Its members shall, therefore, obtain, in the meetings of the association, a knowledge of our laws and political economy, and shall also be instructed in military and gymnastic exercises;" that Presser, in December, 1879, marched at the head of said company, about 400 in number, in the streets of the city of Chicago, he riding on horseback and in command; that the company was armed with rifles, and Presser with a cavalry sword; that the company had no license from the Governor of Illinois to drill or parade as a part of the militia of the state, and was not a part of the regular organized militia of the state, nor a part of troops of the United States, and had no organization under the militia law of the United States. The evidence showed no other facts. Exceptions were reserved to the ruling of the court upon the motion to quash the indictment, to the finding of guilty, and to the judgment thereon. The case was taken to the Supreme Court of Illinois, where the judgment was affirmed. Thereupon Presser brought the present writ of error for a review of the judgment of affirmance.

The position of the plaintiff in error in this court was that the entire statute under which he was convicted was invalid and void because its enactment was the exercise of a power by the legislature of Illinois forbidden to the states by the Constitution of the United States. The clauses of the Constitution of the United States referred to in the assignments of error were as follows:

Article 1, 8. "The Congress shall have power . . . to raise and support armies; . . . to provide for calling forth the militia to execute the laws of the Union, suppress insurrections, and repel invasions; to provide for organizing, arming, and disciplining the militia, and for governing such part of them as may be employed in the service of the United States, reserving to the states, respectively, the appointment of the officers, and the authority of training the militia, according to the discipline prescribed by congress; . . . to make all laws which shall be necessary and proper, for carrying into execution the foregoing powers," etc.

Article 1, 10. "No state shall, without the consent of congress, keep troops . . . in time of peace."

Art. 2 of Amendments. "A well regulated militia being necessary to the security of a free State, the right of the people to keep and bear arms shall not be infringed."

The plaintiff in error also contended that the enactment of the fifth and sixth sections of article 11 of the Military Code was forbidden by subdivision 3 of section 9 of article 1, which declares "no bill of attainder or ex post facto law shall be passed," and by article 14 of Amendments, which provides that "no state shall make or enforce any law which shall abridge the privileges or immunities of citizens of the United States, nor shall any state deprive any person of life, liberty, or property without due process of law."

The first contention of counsel for plaintiff in error is that the Congress of the United States having, by virtue of the provisions of article 1 of section 8, above quoted, passed the act of May 8, 1792, entitled "An Act More Effectually to Provide for the National Defense by Establishing an Uniform Militia Throughout the United States," (1 St. 271,) the act of February 28, 1795, "To Provide for Calling Forth the Militia to Execute the Laws of the Union, Suppress Insurrections, and Repel Invasions," (1 St. 424,) and the Act of July 22, 1861, "To Authorize the Employment of Volunteers to Aid in Enforcing the Laws and Protecting Public Property," (12 St. 268,) and other subsequent Acts, now forming "Title 16, The Militia," of the Revised Statutes of the United States, the legislature of Illinois had no power to pass the act approved May 28, 1879, "To Provide for the Organization of the State Militia, entitled the Military Code of Illinois," under the provisions of which (sections 5 and 6 of article 11) the plaintiff in error was indicted.

The argument in support of this contention is, that the power of organizing, arming, and disciplining the militia being confided by the Constitution to Congress, when it acts upon the subject, and passes a law to carry into effect the constitutional provision, such action excludes the power of legislation by the state on the same subject.

It is further argued that the whole scope and object of the Military Code of Illinois is in conflict with that of the law of Congress. It is said that the object of the act of Congress is to provide for organizing, arming, and disciplining all the able-bodied male citizens of the states, respectively, between certain ages, that they may be ready at all times to respond to the call of the nation to enforce its laws, suppress insurrection, and repel invasion, and thereby avoid the necessity for maintaining a large standing army, with which liberty can never be safe, and that, on the other hand, the effect if not object of the Illinois statute is to prevent such organizing, arming, and disciplining of the militia.

The plaintiff in error insists that the Act of Congress requires absolutely all able-bodied citizens of the state, between certain ages, to be enrolled in the militia; that the Act of Illinois makes the enrollment dependent on the necessity for the use of troops to execute the laws and suppress insurrections, and then leaves it discretionary with the governor by proclamation to require such enrollment; that the Act of Congress requires the entire enrolled militia of the state, with a few exemptions made by it and which may be made by state laws, to be formed into companies, battalions, regiments, brigades, and divisions; that every man shall be armed and supplied with ammunition; provides a system of discipline and field exercises for companies, regiments, etc., and subjects the entire militia of the state to the call of the president to enforce the laws, suppress insurrection, or repel invasion, and provides for the punishment of the militia officers and men who refuse obedience to his orders. On the other hand, it is said that the state law makes it unlawful for any of its able-bodied citizens, except 8,000, called the Illinois National Guard, to associate themselves together as a military company, or to drill or parade with arms without the license of the Governor, and declares that no military company shall leave the state with arms and equipments without his consent; that even the 8,000 men styled the Illinois National Guard are not enrolled or organized as required by the Act of Congress, nor are they subject to the call of the President, but they constitute a military force sworn to serve in the military service of the state, to obey the orders of the Governor, and not to leave the state without his consent; and that, if the state act is valid, the national act providing for organizing, arming, and disciplining the militia is of no force in the state of Illinois, for the Illinois act, so far from being in harmony with the act of Congress, is an insurmountable obstacle to its execution.

We have not found it necessary to consider or decide the question thus raised as to the validity of the entire Military Code of Illinois, for, in our opinion, the sections under which the plaintiff in error was convicted may be valid, even if the other sections of the act were invalid. For it is a settled rule "that statutes that are constitutional in part only will be upheld so far as they are not in conflict with the Constitution, provided the allowed and prohibited parts are separable." *Packet Co. v. Keokuk*, 95 U.S. 80; Penniman's Case, *103 U.S. 714*, 717; *Unity v. Burrage*, Id. 459. See, also, Trade-Mark Cases, *100 U.S. 82.*

We are of opinion that this rule is applicable in this case. The first two sections of article 1 of the Military Code provide that all able bodied male citizens of the state between the ages of 18 and 45 years, except those exempted, shall be subject to military duty, and be designated the "Illinois State Militia," and declare how they shall be enrolled and under what circumstances. The residue of the Code, except the two sections on which the indictment against the plaintiff in error is based, provides for a volunteer active militia, to consist of not more than 8,000 officers and men, declares how it shall be enlisted and brigaded, and the term of service of its officers and men; provides for brigade generals and their staffs, for the organization of the requisite battalions and companies and the election of company officers; provides for inspections, parades, and encampments, arms and armories, rifle practice, and courts-martial; provides for the pay of the officers and men, for medical service, regimental bands, books of instructions and maps; contains provisions for levying and collecting a military fund by taxation, and directs how it shall be expended; and appropriates $25,000 out of the treasury, in advance of the collection of the military fund, to be used for the purposes specified in the Military Code.

It is plain from this statement of the substance of the Military Code that the two sections upon which the indictment against the plaintiff in error is based may be separated from the residue of the Code, and stand upon their own independent provisions. These sections might have been left out of the Military Code and put in an act by themselves, and the act thus constituted and the residue of the Military Code would have been coherent and sensible acts. If it be conceded that the entire Military Code, except these sections, is unconstitutional and invalid, for the reasons stated by the plaintiff in error, these sections are separable, and, put in an act by themselves, could not be considered as forbidden by the clauses of the Constitution having reference to the militia, or to the clause forbidding the states, without the consent of Congress, to keep troops in time of peace. There is no such connection between the sections which prohibit any body of men, other than the organized militia of the state and the troops of the United States, from associating as a military company and drilling with arms in any city or town of the state, and the sections which provide for the enrollment and organization of the state militia, as makes it impossible to declare one, without declaring both, invalid.

This view disposes of the objection to the judgment of the Supreme Court of Illinois, which judgment was in effect that the legislation on which the indictment is based is not invalid by reason of the provisions of the Constitution of the United States which vest Congress with power to raise and support armies, and to provide for calling out, organizing, arming, and disciplining the militia, and governing such part of them as may be employed in the service of the United States, and that provision which declares that "no state shall, without the consent of Congress, . . . keep troops . . . in time of peace."

We are next to inquire whether the fifth and sixth sections of article 11 of the Military Code are in violation of the other provisions of the Constitution of the United States relied on by the plaintiff in error. The first of these is the Second Amendment, which declares: "A well regulated militia being necessary to the security of a free State, the right of the people to keep and bear arms shall not be infringed."

We think it clear that the sections under consideration, which only forbid bodies of men to associate together as military organizations, or to drill or parade with arms in cities and towns unless authorized by law, do not infringe the right of the people to keep and bear arms. But a conclusive answer to the contention that this amendment prohibits the legislation in question lies in the fact that the amendment is a limitation only upon the power of Congress and the national government, and not upon that of the states. It was so held by this court in the case of *U.S. v. Cruikshank, 92 U.S. 542, 553,* in which the Chief Justice, in delivering the judgment of the court, said that the right of the people to keep and bear arms "is not a right granted by the Constitution. Neither is it in any manner dependent upon that instrument for its existence. The Second Amendment declares that it shall not be infringed, but this, as has been seen, means no more than that it shall not be infringed by Congress. This is one of the amendments that has no other effect than to restrict the powers of the national government, leaving the people to look for their protection against any violation by their fellow-citizens of the rights it recognizes to what is called in *City of New York v. Miln,* 11 Pet. the 'powers which relate to merely municipal legislation, or what was perhaps more properly called internal police,' 'not surrendered or restrained' by the Constitution of the United States." . . .

It is undoubtedly true that all citizens capable of bearing arms constitute the reserved military force or reserve militia of the United States as well as of the states, and, in view of this prerogative of the general government, as well as of its general powers, the states cannot, even laying the constitutional provision in question out of view, prohibit the people from keeping and bearing arms, so as to deprive the United States of their rightful resource for maintaining the public security, and disable the people from performing their duty to the general government. But, as already stated, we think it clear that the sections under consideration do not have this effect.

The plaintiff in error next insists that the sections of the Military Code of Illinois, under which he was indicted, are an invasion of that clause of the first section of the Fourteenth Amendment to the Constitution of the United States which declares: "No state shall make or enforce any law which shall abridge the privileges or immunities of citizens of the United States."

It is only the privileges and immunities of citizens of the United States that the clause relied on was intended to protect. A state may pass laws to regulate the privileges and immunities of its own citizens, provided that in so doing it does not abridge their privileges and immunities as citizens of the United States. The inquiry is therefore pertinent: What privilege or immunity of a citizen of the United States is abridged by sections 5 and 6 of article 11 of the Military Code of Illinois?

The plaintiff in error was not a member of the organized volunteer militia of the State of Illinois, nor did he belong to the troops of the United States or to any organization under the militia law of the United States. On the contrary, the fact that he did not belong to the organized militia or the troops of the United States was an ingredient in the offense for which he was convicted and sentenced. The question is, therefore: Had he a right as a citizen of the United States, in disobedience of the state law, to associate with others as a military company, and to drill and parade with arms in the towns and cities of the state? . . .

We have not been referred to any statute of the United States which confers upon the plaintiff in error the privilege which he asserts. The only clause in the Constitution which, upon any pretense, could be said to have any relation whatever to his right to associate with others as a military company, is found in the First Amendment, which declares that "Congress shall make no laws . . . abridging . . . the right of the people peaceably to assemble and to petition the government for a redress of grievances." This is a right which it was held in *U.S. v. Cruikshank*, above cited, was an attribute of national citizenship, and, as such, under the protection of, and guaranteed by, the United States. But it was held in the same case that the right peaceably to assemble was not protected by the clause referred to, unless the purpose of the assembly was to petition the government for a redress of grievances.

The right voluntarily to associate together as a military company or organization, or to drill or parade with arms, without, and independent of, an act of Congress or law of the state authorizing the same, is not an attribute of national citizenship. Military organization and military drill and parade under arms are subjects especially under the control of the government of every country. They cannot be claimed as a right independent of law. Under our political system they are subject to the regulation and control of the state and federal governments, acting in due regard to their respective prerogatives and powers. The Constitution and laws of the United States will be searched in vain for any support to the view that these rights are privileges and immunities of citizens of the United States independent of some specific legislation on the subject.

It cannot be successfully questioned that the state governments, unless restrained by their own constitutions, have the power to regulate or prohibit associations and meetings of the people, except in the case of peaceable assemblies to perform the duties or exercise the privileges of citizens of the United States, and have also the power to control and regulate the organization, drilling, and parading of military bodies and associations, except when such bodies or associations, are authorized by the militia laws of the United States. The exercise of this power by the states is necessary to the public peace, safety, and good order. To deny the power would be to deny the right of the state to disperse assemblages organized for sedition and treason, and the right to suppress armed mobs bent on riot and rapine. . . .

The argument of the plaintiff in error that the legislation mentioned deprives him of either life, liberty, or property without due process of law, or that it is a bill of attainder or ex post facto law, is so clearly untenable as to require no discussion.

It is next contended by the plaintiff in error that sections 5 and 6 of article 11 of the Military Code, under which he was indicted, are in conflict with the acts of Congress for the organization of the militia. But this position is based on what seems to us to be an unwarranted construction of the sections referred to. It is clear that their object was to forbid voluntary military associations, unauthorized by law, from organizing or drilling and parading with arms in the cities or towns of the state, and not to interfere with the organization, arming and drilling of the militia under the authority of the acts of Congress. If the object and effect of the sections were in irreconcilable conflict with the acts of Congress, they would of course be invalid. But it is a rule of construction that a statute must be interpreted so as, if possible, to make it consistent with the Constitution and the paramount law. . . . If we yielded to this contention of the plaintiff in error, we should render the sections invalid by giving them a strained construction, which would make them antagonistic to the law of Congress. We cannot attribute to the legislature, unless compelled to do so by its plain words, a purpose to pass an act in conflict with an act of Congress on a subject over which Congress is given authority by the constitution of the United States. We are, therefore, of opinion that, fairly construed, the sections of the Military Code referred to do not conflict with the laws of Congress on the subject of the militia.

The plaintiff in error further insists that the organization of the *Lehr und Wehr Verein* as a corporate body, under the general corporation law of the state of Illinois, was in effect a license from the Governor, within the meaning of section 5 of article 11 of the Military Code, and that such corporate body fell within the exception of the same section "of students in educational institutions where military science is a part of the course of instruction." In respect to these points we have to say that they present no federal question. It is not, therefore, our province to consider or decide them. . . .

All the federal questions presented by the record were rightly decided by the Supreme Court of Illinois. Judgment affirmed.

SOURCE: http://caselaw.lp.findlaw.com/scripts/getcase.pl?navby=case&court=us&vol=116 &page=252

ANALYSIS

In 1876, the Supreme Court for the first time addressed the meaning of the Second Amendment in the case of *U.S. v. Cruikshank*. Although it devoted only a few paragraphs to the subject, it did establish two principles: that laws may be properly enacted to restrict or regulate the carrying of weapons, including firearms; and that the Second Amendment does not apply to the states (that is, is not "incorporated" under the Fourteenth Amendment). Ten years later, in the *Presser* case, the Supreme Court reaffirmed *Cruikshank's* conclusion that the Second Amendment did not apply to the states, a position that the court has maintained from that day to this, even while it has applied most other Bill of Rights freedoms to the states in the meantime. Beyond that, the court discussed at length the meaning of the term *militia* as it appears in the Second Amendment, and in other parts of the Constitution, rejecting the ideas that citizens may lawfully create their own, private militias, or that there is any private citizen right to own or carry weapons under the Second Amendment. Only the government has the power to create militias.

Seal of the Army National Guard. http://www.defenselink.mil/multimedia/web_graphics/natguard/NGARMYb.jpg.

Sometimes the conclusion of the *Presser* court has been misconstrued. For example, some have focused on this phrase from the decision: " . . . the States cannot . . . prohibit the people from keeping and bearing arms. . . . " Taken by itself, the wording seems to embrace an individual right of citizens to have guns, unrelated to militias or the government. Yet the full sentence actually says something very different: " . . . the States cannot . . . prohibit the people from keeping and bearing arms, so as to deprive the United States of their rightful resource for maintaining the public security, and disable the people from performing their duty to the General Government." The full sentence is saying that the people cannot be kept from keeping and bearing arms if it prevents the people from fulfilling their obligation to maintain public security or fulfill their obligations to the government. This meaning was well understood in the eighteenth and nineteenth centuries when the practices and, later, memories of militia-eligible men obtaining their own weapons for militia service were still fresh.

The *Presser* court was also unambiguous in saying that citizens could not form their own private militias (what today are called paramilitary groups), as only the government has authority over military organizations. If this were not the case, the court said, it would "deny the right of the State to disperse assemblages organized for sedition and treason, and the right to suppress armed mobs bent on riot and rapine [pillaging]." In other words, if the government could not maintain sole control over military organization, armed mobs could simply claim such a right for themselves. Note also that this decision made clear that Illinois's militia at the time was its 8,000 member National Guard.

FURTHER READING

Spitzer, Robert J. *The Right to Bear Arms*. Santa Barbara, CA: ABC-ACIO, 2001.

The Supreme Court Affirms
Prior Rulings

- *Document:* Supreme Court case of *Miller v. Texas*
- *Date:* May 14, 1894
- *Where:* Washington, D.C.
- *Significance:* This case continues to support the court's view that the Second Amendment applies only to the national government, and also leaves standing a state law regulating the carrying of concealed weapons.

DOCUMENT

Miller v. Texas, 153 U.S. 535 (1894)

May 14, 1894

This was an indictment against Franklin P. Miller in a court of the state of Texas for murder, on which he was convicted. The conviction was affirmed by the court of criminal appeals (20 S. W. 1103), and a rehearing of the appeal thereto was denied. Defendant brought error. C. A. Culberson, Texas Atty. Gen., for the motion. Jo. Abbott, opposed.

Mr. Justice BROWN, after stating the facts in the foregoing language, delivered the opinion of the court . . .

. . . we think there is no federal question properly presented by the record in this case, and that the writ of error must be dismissed upon that ground. The record exhibits nothing of what took place in the court of original jurisdiction, and begins with the assignment of errors in the court of criminal appeals. In this assignment no claim was made of any ruling of the court below adverse to any constitutional right claimed by the defendant, nor does any such appear in the opinion of the court, which deals only with certain alleged errors relating to the impaneling of the jury, the denial of a continuance, the admission of certain testimony, and certain exceptions taken to the charge of the court. In his motion for a rehearing, however, defendant claimed that the law of the state of Texas forbidding the carrying of weapons, and authorizing the arrest, without warrant, of any person violating such law, under which certain questions arose upon the trial of the case, was in conflict with the second and fourth amendments to the constitution of the United States, one of which provides that the right of the people to keep and bear arms shall not be infringed, and the other of which protects the people against unreasonable searches and seizures. We have examined the record in vain, however, to find where the defendant was denied the benefit of any of these provisions, and, even if he were, it is well settled that the restrictions of these amendments operate only upon the federal power, and have no reference whatever to proceedings in state courts. *Barron v. Baltimore*, 7 Pet. 243; *Fox v. Ohio*, 5 How. 410; *Twitchell v. Com.*, 7 Wall. 321; *The Justices v. Murray*, 9 Wall. 274; *U.S. v. Cruikshank*, 92 U.S. 542, 552; *Spies v. Illinois*, 123 U.S. 131, 8 Sup. Ct. 21.

And if the fourteenth amendment limited the power of the states as to such rights, as pertaining to citizens of the United States, we think it was fatal to this claim that it was not set up in the trial court. In *Spies v. Illinois*, 123 U.S. 131, 180, 8 S. Sup. Ct. 21, objection was made that a certain letter was obtained from the defendant by an unlawful seizure, and the constitutional immunity was set up in the supreme court of Illinois, as well as in this court, but it was not made on the trial in the court of original jurisdiction. It was held, both by the supreme court of Illinois and by this court, that the defense should have proven that the letter was unlawfully seized by the police, and should then have opposed its admission upon the ground that it was obtained by such unlawful seizure. Said the chief justice: 'As the supreme court of the state was reviewing the decision of the trial court, it must appear that the claim was made in that court, because the supreme court was only authorized to review the judgment for errors committed there; and we can do no more. . . . If the right was not set up or claimed in the proper court below, the judgment of the highest court of the state in the action is conclusive, so far as the right of reviews here is concerned.' So in *Texas & P. Ry. Co. v. Southern Pac. Co.*, 137 U.S. 48, 11 Sup. Ct. 10, it was held directly that a privilege or immunity under the constitution of the United States cannot be set up here under Rev. St. 709, when suggested for the first time in a petition for rehearing after judgment. See, also, *Caldwell v. Texas*, 137 U.S. 692, 698, 11 S. Sup. Ct. 224.

There was no other question under the fourteenth amendment to the constitution. As the proceedings were conducted under the ordinary forms of criminal prosecutions, there certainly was no denial of due process of law; nor did the law of the state, to which reference was made, abridge the privileges or immunities of citizens of the United States as such privileges and immunities are defined in the Slaughterhouse Cases, *16 Wall. 36*, and in *Crandall v. Nevada*, 6 Wall. 35, and *Ward v. Maryland*, 12 Wall. 163.

The writ of error is therefore dismissed.

SOURCE: http://caselaw.lp.findlaw.com/scripts/getcase.pl?court=US&vol=153&invol=535

DID YOU KNOW?

Samuel Colt: Marketing Genius

The man whose name became synonymous with guns of the nineteenth century was more than a manufacturing innovator; he was also highly skilled and innovative when it came to the marketing and sale of his guns. Colt was among the first to improve pistol manufacturing by using machine production of his guns, and by using steel, which was more durable and resistant to rusting, compared with iron. Yet he found little in the way of a ready civilian market for his pistols in the 1840s and 1850s, and the American military was uninterested in purchasing his pistols for military use, so he launched an aggressive marketing campaign, mostly in Eastern newspapers, that linked his guns with romanticized visions of westward expansion and settlement (even though Colt lived in the East, where he conceived of his advertising campaign). In addition, recent innovations in metal engraving techniques allowed him to engrave his guns by machine with western scenes that included men shooting Indians, hunting buffalo, and protecting settlers. By the end of the 1850s, Colt was selling many thousands of his guns annually. Ironically, most of these sales were to Easterners, not Western settlers. Service in the Civil War introduced many men to guns, and after the war gun use and ownership spread.

ANALYSIS

A man convicted of murder in Texas filed suit, arguing that the state law prohibiting the carrying of dangerous weapons on the person (of which the man ran afoul in his trial) was a violation of the Second Amendment's right to keep and bear arms, among other rights. The Supreme Court dismissed the man's claim, arguing that his charges were moot because he did not initially raise them in the Texas state courts. It also noted, consistent with *Cruikshank* and *Presser*, that this and other rights pertained only to actions of the federal government, not the states, so there was no basis for the man's rights claim. The court therefore left intact the Texas law barring the carrying of concealed weapons. As discussed in the previous chapter, laws restricting the concealed carrying of weapons, including but not limited to guns, were commonly enforced around the country, even in frontier areas, and they invariably passed muster.

FURTHER READING

Carter, Gregg Lee, ed. *Guns in American Society: An Encyclopedia of History, Politics, Culture, and the Law*, 2 vols. Santa Barbara, CA: ABC-CLIO, 2002.

Laws Restricting the Carrying of Concealed Weapons Are Constitutional

- **Document:** Supreme Court case of *Robertson v. Baldwin*
- **Date:** January 25, 1897
- **Where:** Washington, D.C.
- **Significance:** In a passing comment, the high court affirms that a law regulating the carrying of concealed weapons does not violate the Second Amendment.

DOCUMENT

Robertson v. Baldwin, 165 U.S. 275 (1897)

January 25, 1897

MR. JUSTICE BROWN delivered the opinion of the court. . . .

But we are also of opinion that, even if the contract of a seaman could be considered within the letter of the Thirteenth Amendment, it is not, within its spirit, a case of involuntary servitude. The law is perfectly well settled that the first ten amendments to the Constitution, commonly known as the Bill of Rights, were not intended to lay down any novel principles of government, but simply to embody certain guaranties and immunities which we had inherited from our English ancestors, and which had from time immemorial been subject to certain well-recognized exceptions arising from the necessities of the case. In incorporating these principles into the fundamental law there was no intention of disregarding the exceptions, which continued to be recognized as if they had been formally expressed. Thus, the freedom of speech and of the press (art. 1) does not permit the publication of libels, blasphemous or indecent articles, or other publications injurious to public morals or private reputation; the right of the people to keep and bear arms (art. 2) is not infringed by laws prohibiting the carrying of concealed weapons; the provision that no person shall be twice put in jeopardy (art. 5) does not prevent a second trial, if upon the first trial the jury failed to agree, or if the verdict was set aside upon the defendant's motion, *United States v.Ball*, 163 U.S. 662, 672; nor does the provision of the same article that no one shall be a witness against himself impair his obligation to testify, if a prosecution against him be barred by the lapse of time, a pardon or by statutory enactment. *Brown v.Walker*, 161 U.S. 591, and cases cited. Nor does the provision that an accused person shall be confronted with the witnesses against him prevent the admission of dying declarations, or the depositions of witnesses who have died since the former trial. . . .

SOURCE: http://www.cs.cmu.edu/afs/cs/user/wbardwel/public/nfalist/robertson_v_baldwin.txt

ANALYSIS

Four men signed on as seamen to serve on the ship Arago, but left the vessel when they discovered aspects of their service that they did not wish to fulfill. They were captured and returned to the vessel against their will, where they were charged with disobeying orders and imprisoned. The men refused to resume their shipboard duties. They were charged with refusing to work, but argued that they had been held improperly and that they were being forced into involuntary servitude, in violation of the Thirteenth Amendment (the amendment that barred slavery and "involuntary servitude"). On appeal, the Supreme Court ruled against the claims of the men. In the decision, the court referenced the Bill of Rights, noting various limitations on the rights listed, commenting in passing that a law barring the carrying of concealed weapons did not infringe on the Second Amendment. No footnote accompanied the reference, but it might have been referring to *Miller v. Texas*. *Robertson v. Baldwin* is not a Second Amendment case, but the court's statement of law regarding the legality of concealed carry restrictions buttresses *Miller*, and the idea that such a restriction is compatible with the Second Amendment.

FURTHER READING

Carter, Gregg Lee, ed. *Guns in American Society: An Encyclopedia of History, Politics, Culture, and the Law*, 2 vols. Santa Barbara, CA: ABC-CLIO, 2002.

4

EARLY STATE COURT RULINGS ON GUN REGULATIONS AND RIGHTS

An Early State Court Upholds Gun Rights

- **Document:** Kentucky state court ruling of *Bliss v. Commonwealth*
- **Date:** October 14, 1822
- **Where:** Kentucky
- **Significance:** This state court ruling is a rare instance where a gun regulation is struck down as in violation of a state right-to-bear-arms–type provision.

DOCUMENT

Bliss v. Commonwealth, 2 Littell 90 (Ky. 1822)

OPINION OF THE COURT. OCTOBER 14, 1822.

This was an indictment founded on the act of the legislature of this state, "to prevent persons in this commonwealth from wearing concealed arms."

The act provides, that any person in this commonwealth, who shall hereafter wear a pocket pistol, dirk, large knife, or sword in a cane, concealed as a weapon, unless when traveling on a journey, shall be fined in any sum not less than $100; which may be recovered in any court having jurisdiction of like sums, by action of debt, or on presentment of a grand jury.

The indictment, in the words of the act charges Bliss with having worn concealed as a weapon, a sword in a cane.

Bliss was found guilty of the charge, and a fine of $100 assessed by the jury, and judgment was thereon rendered by the court. To reverse that judgment Bliss appealed to this court.

2. In argument the judgment was assailed by the counsel of Bliss, exclusively on the ground of the act, on which the indictment is founded, being in conflict with the twenty-third section of the tenth article of the constitution of this state.

That section provides, "that the right of the citizens to bear arms in defense of themselves and the state, shall not be questioned."

The provision contained in this section, perhaps, is as well calculated to secure to the citizens the right to bear arms in defence of themselves and the state, as any that could have been adopted by the makers of the constitution. If the right be assailed, immaterial through what medium, whether by an act of the legislature or in any other form, it is equally opposed to the comprehensive import of the section. The legislature is no where expressly mentioned in the section; but the language employed is general, without containing any expressions restricting its import to any particular department of government; and in the twenty-eighth section of the same article of the constitution, it is expressly declared, "that every thing in that article is excepted out of the general powers of government, and shall forever remain inviolate; and that all laws contrary thereto, or contrary to the constitution, shall be void."

It was not, however, contended by the attorney for the commonwealth, that it would be competent for the legislature, by the enactment of any law, to prevent the citizens from bearing arms either in defence of themselves or the state; but a distinction was taken between a law prohibiting the exercise of the right, and a law merely regulating the manner of exercising that right; and whilst the former was admitted to be incompatible with the constitution, it was insisted, that the latter is not so, and under that distinction, and by assigning the act in question a place in the latter description of laws, its consistency with the constitution was attempted to be maintained.

3. That the provisions of the act in question do not import an entire destruction of the right of the citizens to bear arms in defence of themselves and the state, will not be controverted by the court; for though the citizens are forbid wearing weapons concealed in the manner described in the act, they may, nevertheless, bear arms in any other admissible form. But to be in conflict with the constitution, it is not essential that the act should contain a prohibition against bearing arms in every possible form; it is the right to bear arms in defence of the citizens and the state, that is secured by the constitution, and whatever restraint the full and complete exercise of that right, though not an entire destruction of it, is forbidden by the explicit language of the constitution.

If, therefore, the act in question imposes any restraint on the right, immaterial what appellation may be given to the act, whether it be an act regulating the manner of bearing arms or any other, the consequence, in reference to the constitution, is precisely the same, and its collision with that instrument equally obvious.

And can there be entertained a reasonable doubt but the provisions of the act import a restraint on the right of the citizens to bear arms? The court apprehends not. The right existed at the adoption of the constitution; it had then no limits short of the moral power of the citizens to exercise it, and it in fact consisted in nothing else but in the liberty of the citizens to bear arms. Diminish that liberty, therefore, and you necessarily restrain the right; and such is the diminution and restraint, which the act in question most indisputably imports, by prohibiting the citizens wearing weapons in a manner which was lawful to wear them when the constitution was adopted. In truth, the right of the citizens to bear arms, has been as directly assailed by the provisions of the act, as though they were forbid carrying guns on their shoulders, swords in scabbards, or when in conflict with an enemy, were not allowed the use of bayonets; and if the act be consistent with the constitution, it cannot be incompatible with that instrument for the legislature, by successive enactments, to entirely cut off the exercise of the right of the citizens to bear arms. For in principle, there is no difference between a law prohibiting the wearing concealed arms, and a law forbidding the wearing such as are exposed; and if the former be unconstitutional, the latter must be so likewise.

We may possibly be told, that although a law of either description may be enacted consistently with the constitution, it would be incompatible with that instrument to enact laws of both descriptions. But if either, when alone, be consistent with the constitution, which, it may be asked, would be incompatible with that instrument, if both were enacted?

The law first enacted would not be; for, as the argument supposes either may be enacted consistent with the constitution, that which is first enacted must at the time of enactment, be consistent with the constitution; and if then consistent, it cannot become otherwise, by any subsequent act of the legislature. It must, therefore, be the latter act which the argument infers would be incompatible with the constitution.

But suppose the order of enactment were reversed, and instead of being the first, that which was first, had been the last; the argument, to be consistent, should, nevertheless, insist on the last enactment being in conflict with the constitution. So that the absurd consequence would thence follow, of making the same act of the legislature, either consistent with the constitution, or not so, according as it may precede or follow some other enactment of a different import. Besides, by insisting on the previous act producing any effect on the latter, the argument implies that the previous one operates as a partial restraint on the right of the citizens to bear arms, and proceeds on the notion, that by prohibiting the exercise of the residue of right, not affected by the first act, the latter act comes in collision with the constitution. But it should not be forgotten, that it is not only a part of the right that is secured by the constitution; it is the right entire and complete, as it existed at the adoption of the constitution; and if any portion of that right be impaired, immaterial how small the part may be, and immaterial the order of time at which it be done, it is equally forbidden by the constitution.

4. Hence, we infer, that the act upon which the indictment against Bliss is founded, is in conflict with the constitution; and if so, the result is obvious; the result is what the constitution has declared it shall be, that the act is void. . . .

And such is the conviction entertained by a majority of the court, (Judge Mills dissenting,) in relation to the act in question.

The judgment must, consequently, be reversed.

SOURCE: http://www.cs.cmu.edu/afs/cs.cmu.edu/user/wbardwel/public/nfalist/bliss_v_comm onwealth.txt

---

ANALYSIS

This state court ruling from Kentucky provides a rare instance of a state court striking down a gun regulation. Bliss was convicted of carrying a sword cane, in violation of a state law preventing persons "from wearing concealed arms." Such weapons included various knives and pistols, underscoring the point that the term *arms* encompassed both guns and other, specified weapons subject to government regulation. Bliss appealed, arguing that the state law violated the provision in Kentucky's state constitution saying that "the right of the citizens to bear arms in defense of themselves and the state, shall not be questioned."

Note first that no protection was sought by Bliss under the U.S. Constitution's Second Amendment right to bear arms provision, and the Kentucky state court did not rule on, or discuss, the federal provision. Second, the wording in Kentucky's Constitution was broader, as it specifically refers to personal self-defense, and third, that wording is stronger in saying that this right "shall not be questioned," as the court noted (saying that it did not contain "any expressions restricting its import"). The Kentucky court saw no difference, in principle, between a law barring the carrying of concealed weapons and one barring their carrying in an exposed manner, and reasoned that if the second option were constitutional, the first one should be as well. Bliss's conviction was thus overturned.

This ruling is notable for its rarity among state court rulings in the nineteenth and twentieth centuries (a fact noted in decisions appearing later in this chapter). In fact, concealed carry laws were commonly enacted in the states and were consistently upheld, even in states having state constitutional protections as broad as that in Kentucky.

FURTHER READING

Cornell, Saul. *A Well-Regulated Militia: The Founding Fathers and the Origins of Gun Control in America.* New York: Oxford University Press, 2006.

The Second Amendment Protects Citizen Service in Government Militias

- *Document:* Tennessee state court ruling of *Aymette v. State*
- *Date:* December, 1840
- *Where:* Nashville, Tennessee
- *Significance:* This case was the first time an American court examined in detail the legal history, heritage, and meaning of the right to bear arms, concluding that it was military in nature, pertaining to the organization and maintenance of militias.

DOCUMENT

Aymette v. State, 2 Humphreys 154 (Tenn. 1840)

Nashville, December, 1840.

GREEN, J., delivered the opinion of the court.

The plaintiff in error was convicted in the Giles circuit court, for wearing a bowie-knife concealed under his clothes, under the act of 1837–1838, ch. 137, sec. 2, which provides "that, if any person shall wear any bowie-knife, or Arkansas toothpick, or other knife or weapon that shall in form, shape, or size resemble a bowie-knife or Arkansas toothpick, under his clothes, or keep the same concealed about his person, such person shall be guilty of a misdemeanor, and, upon conviction thereof, shall be fined in a sum not less than two hundred dollars, and shall be imprisoned in the county jail not less than three months and not more than six months."

It is now insisted that the above act of the legislature is unconstitutional, and therefore the judgment in this case should have been arrested.

In the 1st article of the constitution of this state, containing a definition of rights, sec. 26, it is declared "that the free white men of this state have a right to keep and bear arms for their common defence."

This declaration, it is insisted, gives to every man the right to arm himself in any manner he may choose, however unusual or dangerous the weapons he may employ, and, thus armed, to appear wherever he may think proper, without molestation or hindrance, and that any law regulating his social conduct, by restraining the use of any weapon or regulating the manner in which it shall be carried, is beyond the legislative competency to enact, and is void.

In order to have a just and precise idea of the meaning of the clause of the constitution under consideration, it will be useful to look at the state of things in the history of our ancestors, and thus comprehend the reason of its introduction into our constitution.

By the [British] act of 22 & 23 Car. II., ch. 25, sec. 3, it is provided that no person who has not lands of the yearly value of 100 pounds, other than the son and heir apparent of an esquire, or other person of higher degree, etc., shall be allowed to keep a gun, etc. By this act, persons of a certain condition in life were allowed to keep arms, while a large proportion of the people were entirely disarmed. But King James II, by his own arbitrary power, and contrary to law, disarmed the Protestant population, and quartered his Catholic soldiers among the people. This, together with other abuses, produced the revolution by which he was compelled to abdicate the throne of England. William and Mary succeeded him, and, in the first year of their reign, Parliament passed an act recapitulating the abuses which existed during the former reign, and declared the existence of certain rights which they insisted upon as their undoubted privileges. Among these abuses they say, in sec. 5, that he had kept a "standing army within the kingdom in time of peace, without the consent of Parliament, and quartered soldiers contrary to law." Sec. 6. "By causing several good subjects, being Protestants, to be disarmed, at the same time when Papists were both armed and employed contrary to law."

In the declaration of rights that follows, sec. 7 declares that "the subjects which are Protestant may have arms for their defence, suitable to their condition and as allowed by law." This declaration, although it asserts the right of the Protestants to have arms, does not extend the privilege beyond the terms provided in the act of Charles II, before referred to. "They may have arms," says the Parliament, "suitable to their condition and as allowed by law." The law, we have seen, only allowed persons of a certain rank to have arms, and consequently this declaration of right had reference to such only. It was in reference to these facts, and to this state of the English law, that the 2d section of the amendments to the constitution of the United States was incorporated into that instrument. It declares that, "a well-regulated militia being necessary to the security of a free state, the right of the people to keep and bear arms shall not be infringed."

In the same view the section under consideration of our own bill of rights was adopted.

The evil that was produced by disarming the people in the time of James II was that the king, by means of a standing army quartered among the people was able to overawe them, and compel them to submit to the most arbitrary, cruel, and illegal measures.

Whereas, if the people had retained their arms, they would have been able, by a just and proper resistance to those oppressive measures, either to have caused the king to respect their rights, or surrender (as he was eventually compelled to do) the government into other hands. No private defence, was contemplated, or would have availed anything. If the subjects had been armed, they could have resisted the payment of excessive fines, or the infliction of illegal and cruel punishments. When, therefore, Parliament says that "subjects which are Protestants may have arms for their defence, suitable to their condition, as allowed by law," it does not mean for private defence, but, being armed, they may as a body rise up to defend their just rights, and compel their rulers to respect the laws. This declaration of right is made in reference to the fact before complained of, that the people had been disarmed, and soldiers had been quartered among them contrary to law. The complaint was against the government. The grievances to which they were thus forced to submit were for the most part of a public character, and could have been redressed only by the people rising up for their common defence, to vindicate their rights.

The section under consideration, in our bill of rights, was adopted in reference to these historical facts, and in this point of view its language is most appropriate and expressive. Its words are, "the free white men of this state have a right to keep and bear arms for their common defence." It, to be sure, asserts the right much more broadly than the statute of William & Mary. For the right there asserted is subject to the disabilities contained in the act of Charles II. There, lords and esquires, and their sons, and persons whose yearly income from land amounted to 100 pounds, were of suitable condition to keep arms. But, with us, every free white man is of suitable condition, and, therefore, every free white man may keep and bear arms. But to keep and bear arms for what? If the history of the subject had left in doubt the object for which the right is secured, the words that are employed must completely remove that doubt. It is declared that they may keep and bear arms for their common defence. The word "common," here used, means, according to Webster: 1. Belonging equally to more than one, or too many indefinitely. 2. Belonging to the public. 3. General. 4. Universal. 5. Public. The object, then, for which the right of keeping, and bearing arms is secured is the right of the public. The free white men may keep arms to protect the public liberty, to keep in awe those who are in power, and to maintain the supremacy of the laws and the constitution. The words "bear arms," too, have reference to their military use, and were not employed to mean wearing them about the person as part of the dress. As the object for which the right to keep and bear arms is secured is of general and public nature, to be exercised by the people in a body, for their common defence, so the arms the right to keep which is secured are such as are usually employed in civilized warfare, and that constitute the ordinary military equipment. If the citizens have these arms in their hands, they are prepared in the best possible manner to repel any encroachments upon their rights by those in authority. They need not, for such a purpose, the use of those weapons which are usually employed in private broils, and which are efficient only in the hands of the robber and the assassin. These weapons would be useless in war. They could not be employed advantageously in the common defence of the citizens.

The right to keep and bear them is not, therefore, secured by the constitution.

A thousand inventions for inflicting death may be imagined which might come under the appellation of an "arm," in the figurative use of that term, and which could by no possibility be rendered effectual in war, or in the least degree aid in the common defence. Would it not be absurd to contend that a constitutional provision securing to the citizens the means of their common defence should be construed to extend to such weapons, although they manifestly would not contribute to that end, merely because, in the hands of an assassin, they might take away life?

The legislature, therefore, have a right to prohibit the wearing or keeping weapons dangerous to the peace and safety of the citizens, and which are not usual in civilized warfare, or would not contribute to the common defence. The right to keep and bear arms for the common defence is a great political right. It respects the citizens, on the one hand, and the rulers on the other. And, although this right must be inviolably preserved, yet it does not follow that the legislature is prohibited altogether from passing laws regulating the manner in which these arms may be employed.

To hold that the legislature could pass no law upon this subject by which to preserve to prepare and protect our citizens from the terror which a wanton and unusual exhibition of arms might produce, or their lives from being endangered by desperadoes with concealed arms, would be to pervert a great political right to the worst of purposes, and to make it a social evil of infinitely a greater extent to society than would result from abandoning the right itself.

Suppose it were to suit the whim of a set of ruffians to enter the theatre in the midst of the performance, with drawn swords, guns, and fixed bayonets, or to enter the church in the same manner, during service, to the terror of the audience, and this were to become habitual; can it be that it would be beyond the power of the legislature to pass laws to remedy such an evil? Surely not. If the use of arms in this way cannot be prohibited, it is in the power of fifty armed ruffians to break up the churches, and all other public assemblages, where they might lawfully come, and there would be no remedy. But we are perfectly satisfied that a remedy might be applied. The convention, in securing the public political right in question, did not intend to take away from the legislature all power of regulating the social relations of the citizens upon this subject. It is true, it is somewhat difficult to draw the precise line where legislation must cease and where the political right begins, but it, is not difficult to state a case where the right of legislation would exist. The citizens have the unqualified right to keep the weapon, it being of the character before described as being intended by this provision. But the right to bear arms is not of that unqualified character. The citizens may bear them for the common defence; but it does not follow that they may be borne by an individual, merely to terrify the people or for purposes of private assassination. And, as the manner in which they are worn and circumstances under which they are carried indicate to every man the purpose of the wearer, the legislature may prohibit such manner of wearing as would never be resorted to by persons engaged in the common defence.

We are aware that the court of appeals of Kentucky, in the case of *Bliss v. The Commonwealth*, 2 Littell, 90, has decided that an act of their legislature, similar to the one now under consideration, is unconstitutional and void. We have great respect for the court, by whom that decision was made, but we cannot concur in their reasoning.

We think the view of the subject which the opinion of the court in that case takes is far too limited for a just construction of the meaning of the clause of the constitution they had under consideration. It is not precisely in the words of our constitution, nevertheless it is of the same general import. The words are, that "the right of the citizens to bear arms in defence of themselves and the state shall not be questioned."

In the former part of this opinion we have recurred to the circumstances under which a similar provision was adopted in England, and have thence deduced the reason of its adoption, and consequently have seen the object in view when the right to keep and bear arms was secured. All these considerations are left out of view in the case referred to, and the court confine themselves entirely to the consideration of the distinction between a law prohibiting the right, and a law merely regulating the manner in which arms may be worn. They say there can be no difference between a law prohibiting the wearing concealed weapons and one prohibiting the wearing them openly.

We think there is a manifest distinction. In the nature of things, if they were not allowed to bear arms openly, they could not bear them in their defence of the state at all. To bear arms in defence of the state is to employ them in war, as arms are usually employed by civilized nations. The arms, consisting of swords, muskets, rifles, etc., must necessarily be borne openly; so that a prohibition to bear them openly would be a denial of the right altogether. And, as in their constitution the right to bear arms in defence of themselves is coupled with the right to bear them in defence of the state, we must understand the expressions as meaning the same thing, and as relating to public, and not private, to the common, and not the individual, defence.

But a prohibition to wear a spear concealed in a cane would in no degree circumscribe the right to bear arms in the defence of the state; for this weapon could in no degree contribute to its defence, and would be worse than useless in an army. And, if, as is above suggested, the wearing arms in defence of the citizens is taken to mean the common defence, the same observations apply.

To make this view of the case still more clear, we may remark that the phrase, "bear arms," is used in the Kentucky constitution as well as in our own, and implies, as has already been suggested, their military use. The 28th section of our bill of rights provides "that no citizen of this state shall be compelled to bear arms provided he will pay in equivalent, to be ascertained by law." Here we know that the phrase has a military sense, and no other; and we must infer that it is used in the same sense in the 26th section, which secures to the citizen the right to bear arms. A man in the pursuit of deer, elk, and buffaloes might carry his rifle every day for forty years, and yet it would never be said of him that he had borne arms; much less could it be said that a private citizen bears arms because he has a dirk or pistol concealed under his clothes, or a spear in a cane. So that, with deference, we think the argument of the court in the case referred to, even upon the question it has debated, is defective and inconclusive. . . .

We think, therefore, that upon either of the grounds assumed in this opinion the legislature had the right to pass the law under which the plaintiff in error was convicted. Let the judgment be affirmed.

SOURCE: http://www.cs.cmu.edu/afs/cs.cmu.edu/user/wbardwel/public/nfalist/aymette_v_state.txt

---

ANALYSIS

A Tennessee man was convicted of carrying a concealed Bowie knife (a large blade knife, named after frontiersman Jim Bowie, which was often used for fighting) in violation of a state law barring the carrying of such concealed weapons. The man appealed his conviction, arguing that the law should be struck down as in violation of the state's right to keep and bear arms provision, which said: "the free white men of this state have a right to keep and bear arms for their common defence." The court rejected the man's appeal. In its decision, the court discussed at great length the origin and genesis of the right to bear arms, dating it to the British tradition and including discussion of the U.S. Constitution's Second Amendment. Based on its analysis, the court concluded emphatically that the right to bear arms referenced in all of these documents was a collective right for local or national defense of the people and the country, not an individual right to personal self-defense (such a right did and does exist in the law, but in criminal law and the common law tradition, not in constitutional law).

Glock Model 22 .40 caliber handgun. Photo by Dawn Van Hall.

Bringing together the British Bill of Rights, the Second Amendment, and the Tennessee provision, the court stated flatly that "No private defence, was contemplated" in that the right to bear arms related "to public, and not private, to the common, and not the individual, defence." The decision therefore made a clear distinction between civilian possession of weapons for citizens' private use as distinct from that referenced in the various government documents by, for example, parsing the phrase "bear arms" as having "reference to their military use." Even if a man went hunting "every day for forty years . . . it would never be said of him that he had borne arms," underscoring the military nature of this phrase. The court concluded that "The right to keep and bear them [arms] is not, therefore, secured by the constitution" because it "is [a right] of general and public nature, to be exercised by the people in a body, for their common defence." In addition to this analysis, the Tennessee court also took issue with the *Bliss* case (see previously), even though it was not bound by a ruling in a different state court, saying "we cannot concur in their reasoning."

This decision was the first detailed explication of the right to bear arms by an American court. Its arguments would find their way into federal case law, including the important 1939 Supreme Court case of *U.S. v. Miller* (see Chapter 5).

FURTHER READING

Spitzer, Robert J. *The Right to Bear Arms: Rights and Liberties Under Law*. Santa Barbara, CA: ABC-CLIO, 2001.

Striking Down a Gun Law That Interfered with Government Militias

- **Document:** Georgia state court ruling of *Nunn v. State*
- **Date:** July, 1846
- **Where:** Americus, Georgia
- **Significance:** In sometimes florid language, this state court decision embraced the militia interpretation of the right to bear arms, and struck down part of a state law that it saw as interfering with the preeminent right of the state and the people to protect itself from military threats.

DOCUMENT

Nunn v. State, 1 Ga. (1 Kel.) 243 (1846)

Americus, July Term, 1846

By the Court.—Lumpkin, Judge. . . .

The act of 1837 was passed to guard and protect the citizens of the State against the unwarrantable and too prevalent use of *deadly weapons*.

Section 1st enacts, "that it shall not be lawful for any merchant or vendor of wares or merchandize in this State, or any other person or persons whatever, to sell, or to offer to sell, or to keep or to have about their persons, or elsewhere, any of the herein-after-described weapons, to wit: Bowie or any other kinds of knives, manufactured and sold for the purpose of wearing or carrying the same as arms of offence or defence; pistols, dirks, sword-canes, spears, &c., shall also be contemplated in this act, save such pistols as are known and used as horseman's pistols," &c.

Section 2d, prescribes the punishment.

Section 3d, makes it the duty of all civil officers to be vigilant in carrying the act into full effect, &c.

Section 4th, disposes of the fines arising under the act, and exempts sheriffs and other officers, therein named, from its provisions while in the actual discharge of their respective duties. It then declares, *that no person or persons shall be found guilty of violating the before-recited act, who shall openly wear, externally, bowie-knives, dirks, tooth-picks, spears, and which shall be exposed plainly* to view. It allows vendors or any other persons to sell any of the aforesaid weapons, which they then owned or had on hand, "till the first day of March next ensuing its date."

There is great vagueness in the wording of this statute. It would seem to have been the intention of the Legislature to make the proviso in the 4th section as broad as the enacting clause in the 1st. But such is not the fact. Pistols and sword-canes are inserted in the 1st, and omitted in the 4th section; and tooth-picks are mentioned for the first time in the proviso, in the 4th section. Were we disposed to criticise language, an ample field is here spread out before us. It might be insisted, and with much plausibility, that even *sheriffs*, and *other officers* therein enumerated, might be convicted for *keeping*, as well as carrying, any of the forbidden weapons, while not in the actual discharge of their respective duties. And yet it is hardly to be supposed, that it was expected of sheriffs, constables, marshals, overseers and patrols, to procure a new supply of arms for each successive service, and *throw them away* when it was accomplished: for they dare not sell or otherwise dispose of them after March, 1838. It is the plain and literal meaning of the act, too, that no person should be found guilty of selling or offering to sell, or keeping or having about their persons, or elsewhere, bowie or any other kind of knives, pistols, dirks, sword-canes, or spears, *who shall openly wear, externally*, bowie-knives, dirks, tooth-picks, and spears, and which shall be exposed plainly to view. But this would be an absurdity too glaring to impute to the wisdom of that body.

What, then, is the obvious purpose of the Assembly, to be deduced from the whole act, deviating a little, as we are at liberty to do, from the literal meaning of its language, and looking to the *subject matter*, to which the words are always supposed to have regard, and the reason and spirit of the act? It *prohibits bowie-knives, dirks, spears, (and it may be, tooth-picks,) from being sold, or secretly kept about the person, or elsewhere; and it forbids, altogether, the use, or sale, or keeping, of sword-canes, and pistols, save such pistols as are known and used as horseman's pistols*, &c. Now, the defendant, Hawkins H. Nunn, was indicted and convicted of a high misdemeanor, "for *having and keeping about his person, and elsewhere, a pistol, the same not being such a pistol as is known and used as a horseman's pistol*."

It is not pretended that he carried his weapon *secretly*, but it is charged as a crime, that he had and kept it about his person, and elsewhere. And this presents for our decision the broad question, is it competent for the Legislature to deny to one of its citizens this privilege? *We think not. . . .*

If this right, "inestimable to freemen," has been guarantied to British subjects, since the abdication and flight of the last of the Stuarts and the ascension of the Prince of Orange, did it not belong to our colonial ancestors in this western hemisphere? Has it been a part of the *English* Constitution ever since the bill of rights and act of settlement? and been forfeited here by the substitution and adoption of our own Constitution? No notion can be more fallacious than this! On the contrary, this is one of the fundamental principles, upon which rests the great fabric of civil liberty, reared by the fathers of the Revolution and of the country. And the Constitution of the United States, in declaring that the right of the people to keep and bear arms, should not be infringed, only reiterated a truth announced a century before, in the act of 1689, "to extend and secure the rights and liberties of English subjects"—whether living 3,000 or 300 miles from the royal palace. And it is worthy of observation, that both charters or compacts look to the same *motive*, for the irrespective enactments. The act of 1 *William and Mary*, declares that it is against law to raise or keep a standing army in the kingdom, in time of peace, without the consent of Parliament, and therefore places arms in the hands of the people; and our Constitution assigns as a reason why this right shall not be interfered with, or in any manner abridged, that the free enjoyment of it will prepare and qualify *a well-regulated militia*, which are necessary to the security of a free State.

I am aware that it has been decided, that this, like other amendments adopted at the same time, is a restriction upon the government of the United States, and does not extend to the individual States. . . . *I am inclined* to the opinion, that the article in question does extend *to all judicial tribunals*, whether constituted by the Congress of the United States or the States individually. The provision is general in its nature and unrestricted in its terms; and the sixth article of the Constitution declares, that that Constitution shall be the supreme law of the land, and the judges in every State shall be bound thereby, any thing in the constitution or laws of any State to the contrary not withstanding. *These general and comprehensive expressions extend the provisions of the Constitution of the United States, to every article which is not confined by the subject matter to the national government, and is equally applicable to the States.* . . .

The language of the second amendment is broad enough to embrace both Federal and State governments—nor is there anything in its terms which restricts its meaning. The preamble which was prefixed to these amendments shows, that they originated in the fear that the powers of the general government were not sufficiently limited. Several of the States, in their act of ratification, recommended that further restrictive clauses should be added. And in the first session of the first Congress, *ten of these* amendments having been agreed to by that body, and afterwards sanctioned by three-fourths of the States, became a part of the Constitution. But admitting all this, does it follow that because the people refused to delegate to the general government the power to take from them the right to keep and bear arms, that they designed to rest it in the State governments? Is this a right reserved to the *States* or to *themselves?* Is it not an inalienable right, which lies at the bottom of every free government? We do not believe that, because the people withheld this arbitrary power of disfranchisement from Congress, they ever intended to confer it on the local legislatures. This right is too dear to be confided to a republican legislature. . . .

In solemnly affirming that a well-regulated militia is necessary to the *security* of a *free State*, and that, in order to train properly that militia, the unlimited right of the *people* to *keep* and *bear* arms shall not be impaired, are not the sovereign people of the State committed by this pledge to preserve this right inviolate? Would they not be recreant to themselves, to free government, and false to their own vow, thus voluntarily taken, to suffer this right to be questioned? If they hesitate or falter, is it not to concede (themselves being judges) that the safety of the States is a matter of indifference?

Such, I apprehend, was never the meaning of the venerated statesman who recommended, nor of the people who adopted, this amendment.

The right of the people peaceably to assemble and petition the government for a redress of grievances; to be secure in their persons, houses, papers, and effects, against unreasonable searches and seizures; in all criminal prosecutions, to be confronted with the witness against them; to be publicly tried by an impartial jury; and to have the assistance of counsel for their defence, *is as perfect under the State as the national legislature, and cannot be violated by either.*

Nor is the *right* involved in this discussion less comprehensive or valuable: "The right of the people to bear arms shall not be infringed." The right of the whole people, old and young, men, women and boys, and not militia only, to keep and bear *arms* of every description, not *such* merely as are used by the *militia*, shall not be *infringed*, curtailed, or broken in upon, in the smallest degree; and all this for the important end to be attained: the rearing up and qualifying a well-regulated militia, so vitally necessary to the security of a free State. Our opinion is, that any law, State or Federal, is repugnant to the Constitution, and void, which contravenes this *right*, originally belonging to our forefathers, trampled under foot by Charles I. and his two wicked sons and successors, reestablished by the revolution of 1688, conveyed to this land of liberty by the colonists, and finally incorporated conspicuously in our own Magna Charta! And Lexington, Concord, Camden, River Raisin, Sandusky, and the laurel-crowned field of New Orleans, plead eloquently for this interpretation! And the acquisition of Texas may be considered the full fruits of this great constitutional right.

We are of the opinion, then, that so far as the act of 1837 seeks to suppress the practice of carrying certain weapons *secretly*, that it is valid, inasmuch as it does not deprive the citizen of his *natural* right of self-defence, or of his constitutional right to keep and bear arms. But that so much of it, as contains a prohibition against bearing arms *openly*, is in conflict with the Constitution, and *void;* and that, as the defendant has been indicted and convicted for carrying a pistol, without charging that it was done in a concealed manner, under that portion of the statute which entirely forbids its use, the judgment of the court below must be reversed, and the proceeding quashed.

SOURCE: http://www.cs.cmu.edu/afs/cs/usr/wbardwel/public/nfalist/nunn_v_state.txt

---

ANALYSIS

A man was convicted under a Georgia law that made it a crime to carry, either concealed or openly, certain weapons, including pistols. He appealed his conviction as a violation of both state and federal "right to bear arms" constitutional protections. Yet the state law in question was not well written, because in listing the weapons that could not be carried in a concealed fashion, it specifically mentioned pistols; but in the list of weapons that could not be carried openly, it omitted pistols (see the text of the law in Chapter 2). No evidence was offered to suggest that the man carried the pistol in a concealed fashion (i.e., "secretly"), and the court expressed its dismay at

DID YOU KNOW?

The Decline of the Militias

Citizen militias were key to early American military defense, but after their abysmal performance in the War of 1812, the government realized that a professional standing army was a better and more reliable basis for national defense. Still, the old-style militias persisted. In cities, towns, and villages around the country, militia "musters" continued to be held throughout the first half of the nineteenth century. Although organized for the purpose of training and practice, such musters were mostly social events where the center of activity was likely a local tavern. Many of militia age (normally defined as able-bodied men from 18–45) never bothered to participate; those who did often did not possess functioning firearms, much less the skill required to demonstrate proficiency; efforts at training and marksmanship were often held up to ridicule by local citizens; drunkenness was too often the order of the day. In fact, several states, including New Hampshire and South Carolina, enacted laws that made it a crime to ridicule or heckle militia units and members. The Civil War effectively ended the pretense that these general militias could play an important role in American defense, but federal law was not changed to reflect this new reality until 1903.

this inconsistency. It overturned the man's conviction and struck down that portion of the 1837 law prohibiting the bearing of arms openly as a flagrant violation of both the federal and state right to bear arms provisions.

The court's sometimes melodramatic justification for doing so was to preserve "the important end to be attained: the rearing up and qualifying a well-regulated militia, so vitally necessary to the security of a free State." Drawing on its analysis of the British and American traditions, this state court, like that of *Aymette*, defined the Second Amendment's right to bear arms as a collective, militia-based right. The Georgia court further noted that militias might indeed make use of the weapons regulated in the state law, and therefore would need to carry these (or other) weapons in the open if called into service. In a somewhat daring assertion, it noted that the maintenance of a free state in a desperate moment might involve not just the enrolled militia, but "the whole people, old and young, men, women and boys." The reference to women is especially interesting, since even today the military service of women is the subject of some controversy.

The Georgia court took one other bold step when it said that, despite its awareness that the U.S. Constitution's Second Amendment did not apply to the states, but only to the federal government, it nevertheless asserted that "the article in question does extend *to all judicial tribunals*." The Supreme Court would not accept this proposition until 1897, and from that year to the present, only some of the Bill of Rights has been applied to the states—but not the Second Amendment.

FURTHER READING

Fisher, Louis, and David Gray Adler. *American Constitutional Law*. Durham, NC: Carolina Academic Press, 2007.
Peltason, J. W., and Sue Davis. *Corwin and Peltason's Understanding the Constitution*. New York: Harcourt, 2000.

The Militia Basis of the Second Amendment Affirmed in State Court

- **Document:** Illinois state court ruling of *Dunne v. People*
- **Date:** 1879
- **Where:** Springfield, Illinois
- **Significance:** The Illinois state court was asked by both litigants to resolve the extent and nature of state and federal power over militias, including the relationship to the right to bear arms.

DOCUMENT

Dunne v. People, 94 Ill. 120 (1879)

Mr. JUSTICE SCOTT delivered the opinion of the Court:

Peter J. Dunne, having been summoned to serve as a juryman in the Criminal Court of Cook county, at the September term, 1879, it was made to appear he was a citizen of Illinois, twenty-two years of age, and that he was an enlisted, active member of the "Illinois National Guard," in Company G, First Regiment, a military company organized and existing under a statute of this State, approved May 28, 1879, and in force July 1, of the same year, entitled "An act to provide for the organization of the State militia, and entitled the Military Code of Illinois" and because of the facts appearing he claimed, under the provisions of the act, which so expressly declares, he was exempt from jury duty, but the court deemed the cause assigned insufficient in law to excuse the juror from service, and notwithstanding the decision of the court he refused to serve in the capacity of a juror, and on account of his contumacy he was fined in the sum of $50.

Acting on the suggestion of counsel, that it is the desire of both parties to obtain the opinion of this court as to the validity of the act of the General Assembly "to provide for the organization of the State militia," approved May 28, 1879, all preliminary considerations as to the manner in which the case comes before the court, and the invalidity of the act under the constitution of the State, will be waived with a view to proceed directly to the question whether the act, or such parts of it as provide for the organization of the active militia of the State, known as the "Illinois National Guard," is void by reason of its repugnancy to the constitution of the United States, and to the laws passed in pursuance thereof. It may be remarked although no point is made that the act in question contravenes any provision of our State constitution it seems to be in entire harmony with that instrument.

Article 12, section 1, constitution of 1870, is, "The militia of the State of Illinois shall consist of all able bodied male persons resident in the State between the ages of eighteen and forty-five, except such persons as now are or hereafter may be exempted by the laws of the United States or of this State." And section 2 of the same article is, "The General, Assembly, in providing for the organization, equipment and discipline of the militia, shall conform as nearly as practicable to the regulations for the government of the armies of the United States." On examination it will be seen the act of the General Assembly under consideration conforms exactly with these constitutional requirements, as will be made to appearing more fully in the sequel of this discussion. . . .

It might be well in this connection to call to mind that "powers not delegated to the United States by the constitution nor prohibited by it to the States, are reserved to the States respectively, or to the people." The power of State governments to legislate concerning the militia, existed and was exercised before the adoption of the constitution of the United States, and as its exercise was not prohibited by that instrument, it is understood to remain with the States, subject only to the paramount authority of acts of Congress enacted in pursuance of the constitution of the United States. The section of the constitution cited does not confer on Congress unlimited power over the militia of the States. It is restricted to specific objects enumerated, and for all other purposes the militia remain as before the formation of the constitution, subject to State authorities. Nor is there any warrant for the proposition that the authority a State may exercise over its own militia is derived from the constitution, of the United States. The States always assumed to control their militia, and, except so far as they have conferred upon the national government exclusive or concurrent authority, the States retain the residue of authority over the militia they previously had and exercised. And no reason exists why a State may not control its own militia within constitutional limitations. Its exercise by the States is simply a means of self-protection.

The States are forbidden to keep "troops" in time of peace, and of what avail is the militia to maintain order and to enforce the laws in the States unless it is organized. "A well-regulated militia" is declared to be "necessary to the security of a free State." The militia is the dormant force upon which both the National and State governments rely "to execute the laws, * * * suppress insurrections and repel invasions." It would seem to be indispensable there should be concurrent control over the militia in both governments within the limitations imposed by the constitution. Accordingly, it is laid down by text writers and courts that the power given to Congress to provide for organizing, arming and disciplining the militia is not exclusive. It is defined to be merely an affirmative power, and not incompatible with the existence of a like power in the States; and hence, the conclusion is, the power of concurrent legislation over the militia exists in the several States with the national government. . . .

The remaining sections of the act, with the exception of those contained in article 11, relate to, organization, arming, drilling and maintaining the "active militia" of the State. The designation "Illinois National Guard," applied to the active militia, is a matter of no consequence, and the act will be construed as though it did not contain those words. That a State may organize such portions of its militia as may be deemed necessary in the execution of its laws and to aid in maintaining domestic tranquility within its borders, is a proposition so nearly self-evident that it need not be elaborated at any great length. " A well regulated militia being necessary to the security of a free State," the States, by an amendment to the constitution have imposed a restriction that Congress shall not infringe the right of the "people to keep and bear arms." The chief executive officer of the State is given power by the constitution to call out the militia "to execute the laws, suppress insurrection and repel invasion." This would be a mere barren grant of power unless the State had power to organize its own militia for its own purposes. Unorganized, the militia would be of no practical aid to the executive in maintaining order and in protecting life and property within the limits of the State. These are duties that devolve on the State, and unless these rights are secured to the citizen, of what worth is the State government? Failing in this respect it would fail in its chief purpose. But what reason is there why a State may not organize its own militia for its own purposes? As we have seen, the State has the power of concurrent legislation with the national government over the militia, when not in the actual service of the United States, within limits quite accurately defined in law as well as in the decisions of courts, both State and federal. Certainly Congress has not exclusive jurisdiction over the militia not actually employed in its service. Congress may, provide for "organizing, arming and disciplining" the militia, but the appointment of officers and the authority to train the militia according to the discipline prescribed by Congress is reserved to the States. There can, therefore, be no efficient organization of the militia when not called into the service of the Union without the cooperative aid of the States. Congress may not deem it necessary to exercise all the authority with which it is clothed by the constitution over the militia. Historically we know there has been no efficient organization, of the militia in this State within the last thirty or forty years. . . .

It is no valid objection to this act of the legislature that it does not require the entire militia of the State to be enrolled as active militia." Counsel do not wish to be understood as claiming that no militia law is valid unless it provides each and every male inhabitant of the specified age should at all times be armed and equipped and engaged in drilling and maneuvering. But the argument made is, that the performance of military service in times of peace can not be legally confined to a select corps consisting of it a limited number of volunteers to the exclusion of all other able-bodied male residents of the State. The argument admits of several conclusive answers that may be shortly stated: 1. It is a matter dependent on the wisdom of Congress whether it will provide for arming and disciplining the entire body of the militia of the United States. 2. The citizen is not entitled under any law, State or Federal, to demand as a matter of right that arms shall be placed in his hands and, 3. It is with the legislative judgment of what number the active militia of the State shall consist, depending on the exigency that makes such organization necessary. . . .

The fifth section contains a clause that makes it unlawful "for any body of men, whatever, other than the regularly organized volunteer militia of this State and the troops the

United States," with an exception in favor of students in educational institutions where military science is taught as a part of the course of instruction, "to associate themselves together as a military company or organization, or to drill or parade with arms in any city or town of this State, without the license of the Governor." We have been referred to no source whence comes the right contend for, to bodies of men organized into military companies under no discipline by the United States or State authorities, "to parade with arms" in any city or public place as their inclination or caprice may prompt them. No such right is conferred by any act of Congress, nor is it insisted this provision of our statute is in conflict with any paramount law of the United States. It is a matter that pertains alone to our domestic polity. The right of the citizen to "bear arms" for the defence of their person and property is not involved, even remotely, in this discussion.

This section has no bearing whatever on that right, whatever it may be, and we will enter upon no discussion of that question. Whether bodies of men with military organizations or otherwise, under no discipline or command by the United States or the State, shall be permitted to "parade with arms" in populous communities is a matter within the regulation and subject to the police power of the State. In matters pertaining to the internal peace and well-being of the State, its police powers are plenary and inalienable. It is a power coextensive with self-protection, and is sometimes termed, and not inaptly, the "law of overruling necessity." Everything necessary for the protection, safety and best interests of the people of the State may be done under this power. Persons and property may be subjected to all reasonable restraints and burdens for the common good. Where mere property interests are involved, this power, like other powers of government, is subject to constitutional limitations; but where the internal peace and health of the people of the State are concerned, the limitations that are said to be upon the exercise of this power are, that such "regulations must have reference to the comfort, safety and welfare of society." It is within the power of the General Assembly to enact laws for the suppression of that which may endanger the public peace, and impose penalties for the infraction of such laws. What will endanger the public security must as a general rule, be left to the wisdom of the legislative department of the government. The provision contained in the fifth section cited was intended by its restraining force to conserve the public peace. That being its object, it is not an unreasonable restraint upon the liberty of the citizens and is within no limitation upon the exercise of the police power of the State.

The judgment will be reversed and the cause remanded.

Judgment reversed.

Mr. JUSTICE MULKEY dissenting.

SOURCE: http://www.cs.cmu.edu/afs/cs.cmu.edu/user/wbardwel/public/nfalist/dunne_v_people.txt

---

ANALYSIS

A man named Dunne refused to serve on a jury because, according to state law, as a member of the Illinois National Guard, he was exempted from jury duty. His refusal to serve nevertheless resulted in a fine, which he appealed to the state court. It ruled that his service under state law was a proper exercise of state power to regulate militias within the rubric of federal laws and the U.S. Constitution concerning militias. The fine levied against the man was overturned. At the request of both parties, the court examined at great length the powers of Illinois regarding the regulation of militias.

In the court's detailed examination of state and federal control over militias, the court referenced the Second Amendment several times, noting that the Second Amendment's wording was designed to reserve to the states their ability to organize and maintain a militia to carry out the purposes of militias listed in Article I, Section 8 of the U.S. Constitution: "to execute the laws . . . suppress insurrections and repel invasions." The federal government and the states had "concurrent power" over militias, said the court, meaning that each level of government possessed the power, just as both the federal government and the states have the power to tax.

The court asked whether the militia law, in order to be valid, must enroll and arm every single militia-eligible male, or whether it could just enroll and arm a "select corps" consisting only of volunteers. Such an arrangement was entirely acceptable, said the court, as "The citizen is not entitled under any law, State or Federal, to demand as a matter of right that arms shall be placed in his hands. . . . It is with the legislative judgment of what number the active militia of the State shall consist. . . ." To drive home the militia-based nature of the Second Amendment and its irrelevance to personal ownership and use of weapons, the court stated flatly that "The right of the citizen to 'bear arms' for the defence of their person and property is not involved, even remotely, in this discussion." In the twentieth century, state control over the militias would be reduced by a succession of federal laws that increased federal control. This rebalancing in favor of the national government would be upheld by the Supreme Court (see subsequent chapters).

> ## DID YOU KNOW?
>
> ### The Fourteenth Amendment and Incorporation
>
> One of three amendments added to the Constitution after the Civil War, the Fourteenth Amendment (added in 1868) made former slaves citizens of the United States. Yet it had another, very important consequence for national rights. Part of the amendment said that states were not to deprive persons of due process or equal protection of the laws. Beginning in 1897, the Supreme Court began to rule, in a series of cases extending up to 1969, that certain rights stipulated in the Bill of Rights now applied to the states, and not just to the federal government. This process of applying parts of the Bill of Rights to the states, called "incorporation," led to a revolution of rights. In 1925, for example, the Supreme Court ruled that states could not violate the First Amendment's protection for free speech (it had formerly applied only to attempts by the federal government to restrict speech). In 1931, it ruled that press freedom applied to the states. By the time of the last incorporation case in 1969, most of the Bill of Rights had been applied to the states. Some portions of the Bill of Rights have not been incorporated, however, including the Second Amendment right to bear arms, the Third Amendment barring the quartering of troops in people's homes during peacetime, the grand jury clause of the Firth Amendment, the Seventh Amendment's right to a jury trial for civil suits, the excessive fines and bails clause of the Eighth Amendment, the Ninth Amendment pertaining to rights not mentioned in the Bill of Rights, and the Tenth Amendment's reservation of powers to the states.

FURTHER READING

Cooper, Jerry. *The Rise of the National Guard*. Lincoln: University of Nebraska Press.

States Viewed the Right to Bear Arms as Militia-Based

- **Document:** Kansas state court ruling of *City of Salina v. Blaksley*
- **Date:** November 11, 1905
- **Where:** Topeka, Kansas
- **Significance:** The Supreme Court of Kansas

DOCUMENT

City of Salina v. Blaksley, 72 Kan. 230, 83 Pac. 619 (1905)

Appeal from District Court, Salina County; R. R. Rees, Judge.

James Blaksley was convicted of carrying a pistol within the city of Salina, and appeals. Affirmed.

David Ritchie, for appellant. R. A. Lovitt, for appellee.

GREENE, J. James Blaksley was convicted in the police court of the city of Salina, a city of the second class, of carrying a revolving pistol within the city while under the influence of intoxicating liquor. He appealed to the district court, where he was again convicted, and this proceeding is prosecuted to reverse the judgment of the latter court.

The question presented is the constitutionality of section 1003 of the General Statutes of 1901, which reads: "The council may prohibit and punish the carrying of firearms or other deadly weapons, concealed or otherwise, and may arrest and imprison, fine or set at work all vagrants and persons found in said city without visible means of support, or some legitimate business."

Section 4 of the [Kansas] Bill of Rights is as follows: "The people have the right to bear arms for their defense and security; but standing armies, in time of peace, are dangerous to liberty, and shall not be tolerated, and the military shall be in strict subordination to the civil power." The contention is that this section of the Bill of

Rights is a constitutional inhibition upon the power of the Legislature to prohibit the individual from having and carrying arms, and that section 1003 of the General Statutes of 1901 is an attempt to deprive him of the right guarantied by the Bill of Rights, and is therefore unconstitutional and void. The power of the Legislature to prohibit or regulate the carrying of deadly weapons has been the subject of much dispute in the courts. The views expressed in the decisions are not uniform, and the reasonings of the different courts vary. It has, however, been generally held that the Legislatures can regulate the mode of carrying deadly weapons, provided they are not such as are ordinarily used in civilized warfare. To this view, there is a notable exception in the early case of *Bliss v. Commonwealth*, 2 Litt. (Ky.) 90, 13 Am. Dec. 251, where it was held, under a constitutional provision similar to ours, that the act of the Legislature prohibiting the carrying of concealed deadly weapons was void, and that the right of the citizen to own and carry arms was protected by the Constitution, and could not be taken away or regulated. While this decision has frequently been referred to by the courts of other states, it has never been followed. The same principle was announced in Idaho in re Brickey, 8 Idaho. 597, 70 Pac. 609, 101 Am. St. Rep. 215, but no reference is made to *Bliss v. Commonwealth*, nor to any other authority in support of the decision. In view of the disagreements in the reasonings of the different courts by which they reached conflicting conclusions, we prefer to treat the question as an original one.

The provision in section 4 of the Bill of Rights "that the people have the right to bear arms for their defense and security" refers to the people as a collective body. It was the safety and security of society that was being considered when this provision was put into our Constitution. It is followed immediately by the declaration that standing armies in time of peace are dangerous to liberty and should not be tolerated, and that "the military shall be in strict subordination to the civil power." It deals exclusively with the military. Individual rights are not considered in this section. The manner in which the people shall exercise this right of bearing arms for the defense and security of the people is found in article 8 of the Constitution, which authorizes the organizing, equipping, and disciplining of the militia, which shall be composed of "able-bodied male citizens between the ages of twenty-one and forty-five years." The militia is essentially the people's army, and their defense and security in time of peace. There are no other provisions made for the military protection and security of the people in time of peace. In the absence of constitutional or legislative authority, no person has the right to assume such duty. In some of the states where it has been held, under similar provisions, that the citizen has the right preserved by the Constitution to carry such arms as are ordinarily used in civilized warfare, it is placed on the ground that it was intended that the people would thereby become accustomed to handling and using such arms, so that in case of an emergency they would be more or less prepared for the duties of a soldier. The weakness of this argument lies in the fact that in nearly every state in the Union there are provisions for organizing and drilling state militia in sufficient numbers to meet any such emergency.

That the provision in question applies only to the right to bear arms as a member of the state militia, or some other military organization provided for by law, is also apparent from the second amendment to the federal Constitution, which says: "A well regulated militia, being necessary to the security of a free state, the right of the people to keep and bear arms shall not be infringed." Here, also, the right of the people to keep and bear arms for their security is preserved, and the manner of bearing them for such purpose is clearly indicated to be as a member of a well-regulated militia, or some other military organization provided for by law. Mr. Bishop, in his work on Statutory Crimes, in treating of this provision, which is found in almost every state Constitution, says, in section 793: "In reason, the keeping and bearing of arms has reference only to war and possibly also to insurrections wherein the forms of war are, as far as practicable observed." *Commonwealth v. Murphy* (Mass.) [166 Mass. *171*,] 44 N.E. 138, 32 L.R.A. 606, strongly supports the position we have taken. The defendant was convicted of being a member of an independent organization which was drilling and parading with guns. The guns, however, had been intentionally made so defective as to be incapable of being discharged. The prosecution was had under a statute which provided that: "No body of men whatsoever, other than the regularly organized corps of the militia [and certain other designated organizations], shall associate themselves together at any time as a company or organization, for drill or parade with fire-arms, or maintain an armory in any city or town of the commonwealth. * * * *"

On the trial the defendant invoked the provisions of the Massachusetts Bill of Rights, "the people have a right to keep and bear arms for the common defense," in support of his contention that he had the right to bear arms. The court said: "This view cannot be supported. The right to keep and bear arms for the common defense does not include the right to associate together as a military organization, or to drill and parade with arms in cities or towns, unless authorized to do so by law. This is a matter affecting the public security, quiet, and good order, and it is within the police power of the legislature to regulate the bearing of arms, so as to forbid such unauthorized drills and parades." The defendant was not a member of an organized militia, nor of any other military organization provided for by law, and was therefore not within the provision of the Bill of Rights, and was not protected by its terms.

The judgment is affirmed. All the Justices concurring.

SOURCE: http://www.guncite.com/court/state/83p619.html

ANALYSIS

A Kansas man, James Blaksley, was convicted in a local court of violating a law restricting the carrying of weapons (the weapon in question was a pistol). He was also under the influence of alcohol at the time. He appealed his conviction, arguing that his rights under the Kansas state Constitution's Bill of Rights (specifically, its "right to bear arms" provision) were being violated.

In its ruling, the state Supreme Court unanimously upheld Blaksley's conviction, saying that the gun law did not violate the state Constitution's right-to-bear-arms provision. The court's decision noted at the outset that, despite some controversy among the states, state legislatures around the country generally have the right to regulate guns and other dangerous weapons. One rare exception, the Kansas high court noted, was the 1822 case of *Bliss v. Commonwealth* (which appears at the start of this chapter), when a state weapons regulation was struck down as in violation of an expansive state right-to-bear-arms–type provision. Yet this decision "has never been followed" according to the Kansas court.

Turning to Section 4 of the state Bill of Rights, the court concluded that the right it protected pertained to "the safety and security of society," not to any individual right. The court then referenced the state Constitution's article 8 describing its militia, concluding that "the provision in question applies only to the right to bear arms as a member of the state militia." It then compared the state protection with the Second Amendment in the U.S. Constitution, which the court said was similarly a right "clearly indicated to be as a member of a well-regulated militia, or some other military organization provided for by law." The court referred to this as a "collective" right, a

Glock Model 22 .40 caliber handgun (unloaded). Photo by Dawn Van Hall.

term that became more common in the twentieth century. While some in the modern era argue that the term *collective* reflected a new idea, its definition makes clear that its militia-based meaning was established when the Second Amendment was written in 1789. Most states of the union followed suit in similar state provisions.

Finally, the Kansas court cited a Massachusetts state court ruling buttressing the definition of the right to bear arms as pertaining only to militia service. In short, the prevailing view emerging from the nineteenth century was that state gun restrictions did not run afoul of either federal or state right-to-bear-arms provisions because that right pertained only to citizen service in a government-organized and regulated militia.

FURTHER READING

Spitzer, Robert J. *The Right to Bear Arms: Rights and Liberties under the Law.* Santa Barbara, CA: ABC-CLIO, 2001.

Privately Organized and Armed Bodies of Men Are Outside the Law

- **Document:** the Washington State court case of *State v. Gohl*
- **Date:** June 5, 1907
- **Where:** Washington State
- **Significance:** This state court decision affirmed that federal and state right to bear arms provisions did not protect private arming, and it noted the prevalence of gun laws among the states.

DOCUMENT

State v. Gohl, 46 Wash. 408 (1907)

OPINION BY: RUDKIN

OPINION: The appellant was convicted of the crime of organizing, maintaining and employing an armed body of men, in violation of Bal. Code, § 7085 (P. C. § 1967), and from the judgment and sentence of the court, the present appeal is prosecuted.

The trial court overruled a demurrer to the information, and upon this ruling the first assignment of error is predicated. The only question raised by the demurrer is the validity of the act under which the information was filed, the appellant contending that it is violative of section 24 of article one of the constitution, which declares that "The right of the individual citizen to bear arms in defense of himself or the state shall not be impaired." A constitutional guaranty of certain rights to the individual citizen does not place such rights entirely beyond the police power of the state. The freedom of speech and of the press guaranteed by the constitution of the United States and the constitutions of the several states has never been construed to carry with it an unbridled license to libel and defame. Nearly all the states have enacted laws prohibiting the carrying of concealed weapons, and the validity of such laws has often been assailed because denying to the citizen the right to bear arms, but we are not aware that such a contention has ever prevailed, except in the courts of the state of Kentucky. Besides, the constitutional provision quoted does not stand alone. It is followed by the express provision that it shall not be "construed as authorizing individuals or corporations to organize, maintain or employ an armed body of men,"—the exact language of the act under which the information was filed. Counsel argue that the act is too sweeping in its terms, that it forbids the organization, maintenance or employment of an armed body of men *for any purpose whatever,* that it exempts no military organization, that high school cadets cannot organize for the purpose of drill, that the sheriff cannot organize a posse, etc. It will be time enough to consider these questions when they arise, but we might suggest at this time that the statute has no application to bodies of men armed by the state or by its authority. We are satisfied that the statute is free from constitutional objection, and the demurrer was properly overruled. . . .

The next assignment is that the court erred in refusing to direct a verdict of acquittal at the close of the state's case. In support of this motion the appellant contends that the proof failed to show that he either organized, maintained or employed the armed body of men in question. For the purposes of this appeal, it may be conceded that he neither organized nor maintained the men; and if the word "employ" in the statute is used in the sense of "to hire"—in other words, if it was incumbent on the state to show that the relation of master and servant existed between the appellant and the armed men—the state has failed in its proof. But is the meaning of the word "employ" thus restricted? The act under which the information was filed recites that the state has provided for and maintains an efficient military and police force, ample for the protection of her citizens in their persons and property, and then proceeds to declare that it shall be unlawful for any person, corporation, or association of persons, or agents of any person, or member, agent or officer of any corporation or association of persons, to organize, maintain or employ an armed body of men in this state for any purpose whatever. Armed bodies of men are a menace to the public, their mere presence is fraught with danger, and the state has wisely reserved to itself the right to organize, maintain and employ them. If we assume that the appellant caused this armed body of men to assemble, and took them down the bay in a launch for the purpose of intimidating the master of the sailing schooner Fearless, and thereby removing a part of the crew from such schooner, as charged in the information and contended for by the state, his act falls clearly within the mischief against which the statute is directed, and in our opinion falls within the prohibition of the statute itself. . . .

We have examined the other errors assigned, but find no reversible error, either in the charge of the court, in the refusal to charge as requested, or in the refusal of a new trial. The evidence before the jury was legally sufficient to sustain their verdict, and finding no prejudicial error in the conduct of the trial, the judgment must be affirmed, and it is so ordered.

ANALYSIS

The Supreme Court of Washington State upheld a state law that barred the organization, maintenance, or employment of an armed body of men, turning aside the appeal of a man convicted under that state law, which he challenged in part on Second Amendment grounds. Addressing rights claims by the defendant related to the Second Amendment, the court noted, first, that constitutional rights are subject to limitations, as for example protections of free speech and free press in the federal Bill of Rights and in state constitutions have "never been construed to carry . . . an unbridled license to libel and defame." Regarding the right to bear arms, the court noted that nearly every state has enacted and upheld laws against carrying concealed weapons, except for Kentucky (a reference to the *Bliss* case discussed earlier in this chapter). The court also found that the state law did not violate the more expansive state right to bear arms provision, which said: "The right of the individual citizen to bear arms in defense of himself or the state shall not be impaired."

FURTHER READING

Cooley, Thomas M. *General Principles of Constitutional Law.* Boston, MA: Little, Brown, 1931.

5

TWENTIETH CENTURY SUPREME COURT CASES

Guns and Non-Citizens

- *Document:* Supreme Court Case of *Patsone v. Pennsylvania*
- *Date:* January 19, 1914
- *Where:* Washington, D.C.
- *Significance:* The court ruled that Pennsylvania's law barring gun ownership (including restricting hunting privileges) to non-citizens was constitutional.

DOCUMENT

Patsone v. Commonwealth of Pennsylvania, 232 U.S. 138 (1914)

Decided January 19, 1914. . . .

Mr. Justice Holmes delivered the opinion of the court.

The plaintiff in error was an unnaturalized foreign born resident of Pennsylvania and was complained of for owning or having in his possession a shot gun, contrary to an *act of May 8, 1909. Laws, 1909, No. 261, p. 466.* This statute makes it unlawful for any unnaturalized foreign born resident to kill any wild bird or animal except in defence of person or property, and 'to that end' makes it unlawful for such foreign born person to own or be possessed of a shot gun or rifle; with a penalty of twenty-five dollars and a forfeiture of the gun or guns. The plaintiff in error was found guilty and was sentenced to pay the above mentioned fine. The judgment was affirmed on successive appeals. He brings the case to this court on the ground that the statute is contrary to the Fourteenth Amendment and also is in contravention of the treaty between the United States and Italy, to which latter country the plaintiff in error belongs.

Under the Fourteenth Amendment the objection is two-fold; unjustifiably depriving the alien of property and discrimination against such aliens as a class. But the former really depends upon the latter, since it hardly can be disputed that if the lawful object, the protection of wild life (*Geer v. Connecticut*, 161 U.S. 519), warrants the discrimination, the means adopted for making it effective also might be adopted. The possession of rifles and shot guns is not necessary for other purposes not within the statute. It is so peculiarly appropriated to the forbidden use that if such a use may be denied to this class, the possession of the instruments desired chiefly for that end also may be. The prohibition does not extend to weapons such as pistols that may be supposed to be needed occasionally for self-defence. . . .

The discrimination undoubtedly presents a more difficult question. But we start with the general consideration that a State may classify with reference to the evil to be prevented, and that if the class discriminated against is or reasonably might be considered to define those from whom the evil mainly is to be feared, it properly may be picked out. A lack of abstract symmetry does not matter. The question is a practical one, dependent upon experience. The demand for symmetry ignores the specific difference that experience is supposed to have shown to mark the class. It is not enough to invalidate the law that others may do the same thing and go unpunished, if, as a matter of fact, it is found that the danger is characteristic of the class named. *Lindsley v. Natural Carbonic Gas Co.*, 220 U.S. 61, 80, 81. The State 'may direct its law against what it deems the evil as it actually exists without covering the whole field of possible abuses.' *Central Lumber Co. v. South Dakota*, 226 U.S. 157, 160. *Rosenthal v. New York*, 226 U.S. 260, 270. *L'Hote v. New Orleans*, 177 U.S. 587. See further *Louisville & Nashville R. R. Co. v. Melton*, 218 U.S. 36. The question therefore narrows itself to whether this court can say that the Legislature of Pennsylvania was not warranted in assuming as its premise for the law that resident unnaturalized aliens were the peculiar source of the evil that it desired to prevent. *Barrett v. Indiana*, 229 U.S. 26, 29.

Obviously the question so stated is one of local experience on which this court ought to be very slow to declare that the state legislature was wrong in its facts. *Adams v. Milwaukee*, 228 U.S. 572, 583. If we might trust popular speech in some States it was right—but it is enough that this court has no such knowledge of local conditions as to be able to say that it was manifestly wrong. See *Trageser v. Gray*, 73 Maryland, 250. *Commonwealth v. Hana*, 195 Massachusetts, 262. . . .

Judgment Affirmed.

The Chief Justice dissents.

SOURCE: http://www.guncite.com/court/fed/sc/232us138.html

ANALYSIS

This case involved the sensitive subject of whether an "unnaturalized foreign-born resident of Pennsylvania"—meaning a person (in this case, an Italian citizen) who was in the United States legally, but who was not an American citizen—could be deprived of a gun for hunting under a state law that barred such possession. The court ruled in favor of the Pennsylvania law, saying that a state has great discretion over such matters, even including a law, like this one, that singled out non-citizens

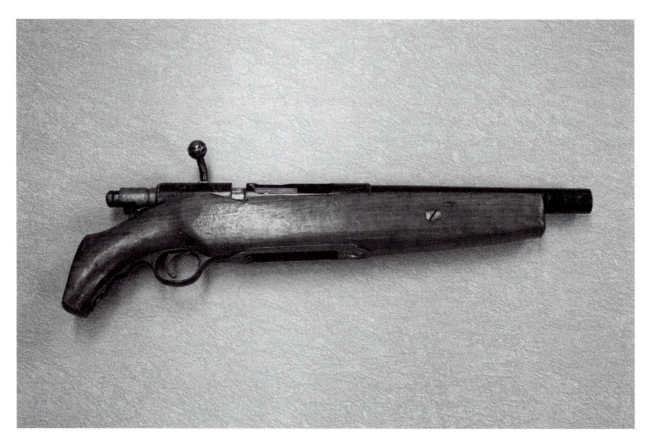

Bolt-action sawed-off Mossberg 16-gauge shotgun. Photo by Dawn Van Hall.

for special restrictions, if, in the state legislature's judgment, such greater restrictions against non-citizens were justifiable. Note that the Second Amendment did not play a part in this case. The Chief Justice of the Supreme Court dissented in the case, but he did not write a dissenting opinion.

FURTHER READING

Edel, Wilbur. *Gun Control*. Westport, CT: Praeger, 1995.

The Second Amendment, the Gangster Era, and Militias

- *Document:* Supreme Court case of *U.S. v. Miller*
- *Date:* May 15, 1939
- *Where:* Washington, D.C.
- *Significance:* The most important Second Amendment case of the twentieth century, the *Miller* case defined the amendment providing a right to bear arms as a militia-based right.

DOCUMENT

United States v. Miller, 307 U.S. 174 (1939)

Argued March 30, 1939.

Decided May 15, 1939.

Appeal from the District Court of the United States for the Western District of Arkansas. Mr. Gordon Dean, of Washington, D.C., for the United States.

No appearance for appellees.

Mr. Justice McREYNOLDS delivered the opinion of the Court.

An indictment in the District Court Western District Arkansas, charged that Jack Miller and Frank Layton "did unlawfully, knowingly, wilfully, and feloniously transport in interstate commerce from the town of Claremore in the State of Oklahoma to the town of Siloam Springs in the State of Arkansas a certain firearm, to-wit, a double barrel 12-gauge Stevens shotgun having a barrel less than 18 inches in length, bearing identification number 76230, said defendants, at the time of so transporting said firearm in interstate commerce as aforesaid, not having registered said firearm as required by Section 1132d of Title 26, United States Code, 26 U.S.C.A. 1132d (Act of June 26, 1934, c. 757, Sec. 5, 48 Stat. 1237), and not having in their possession a stamp-affixed written order for said firearm as provided by Section 1132c, Title 26,

United States Code, 26 U.S.C.A. 1132c (June 26, 1934, c. 757, Sec. 4, 48 Stat. 1237) and the regulations issued under authority of the said Act of Congress known as the 'National Firearms Act' approved June 26, 1934, contrary to the form of the statute in such case made and provided, and against the peace and dignity of the United States." [Footnote 1]

A duly interposed demurrer alleged: The National Firearms Act is not a revenue measure but an attempt to usurp police power reserved to the States, and is therefore unconstitutional. Also, it offends the inhibition of the Second Amendment to the Constitution—"A well regulated Militia, being necessary to the security of a free State, the right of the people to keep and bear Arms, shall not be infringed."

The District Court held that section 11 of the Act violates the Second Amendment. It accordingly sustained the demurrer and quashed the indictment.

The cause is here by direct appeal. Considering *Sonzinsky v. United States* (1937), 300 U.S. 506, 513, and what was ruled in sundry causes arising under the Harrison Narcotic Act [Footnote 2]—*United States v. Jin Fuey Moy* (1916), 241 U.S. 394; *United States v. Doremus* (1919), 249 U.S. 86, 94; *Linder v. United States* (1925), 268 U.S. 5; *Alston v. United States* (1927), 274 U.S. 289; *Nigro v. United States* (1928), 276 U.S. 332—the objection that the Act usurps police power reserved to the States is plainly untenable.

In the absence of any evidence tending to show that possession or use of a "shotgun having a barrel of less than eighteen inches in length" at this time has some reasonable relationship to the preservation or efficiency of a well regulated militia, we cannot say that the Second Amendment guarantees the right to keep and bear such an instrument. Certainly it is not within judicial notice that this weapon is any part of the ordinary military equipment or that its use could contribute to the common defense. . . .

The Constitution as originally adopted granted to the Congress power—"To provide for calling forth the Militia to execute the Laws of the Union, suppress Insurrections and repel Invasions; To provide for organizing, arming, and disciplining, the Militia, and for governing such Part of them as may be employed in the Service of the United States, reserving to the States respectively, the Appointment of the Officers, and the Authority of training the Militia according to the discipline prescribed by Congress." . . . With obvious purpose to assure the continuation and render possible the effectiveness of such forces the declaration and guarantee of the Second Amendment were made. It must be interpreted and applied with that end in view.

The Militia which the States were expected to maintain and train is set in contrast with Troops which they were forbidden to keep without the consent of Congress. The sentiment of the time strongly disfavored standing armies; the common view was that adequate defense of country and laws could be secured through the Militia—civilians primarily, soldiers on occasion.

The signification attributed to the term Militia appears from the debates in the Convention, the history and legislation of Colonies and States, and the writings of approved commentators. These show plainly enough that the Militia comprised all males physically capable of acting in concert for the common defense. "A body of citizens enrolled for military discipline." And further, that ordinarily when called for service these men were expected to appear bearing arms supplied by themselves and of the kind in common use at the time.

Blackstone's Commentaries, Vol. 2, Ch. 13, p. 409 points out "that king Alfred first settled a national militia in this kingdom" and traces the subsequent development and use of such forces.

Adam Smith's Wealth of Nations, Book V. Ch. 1, contains an extended account of the Militia. It is there said: "Men of republican principles have been jealous of a standing army as dangerous to liberty." "In a militia, the character of the labourer, artificer, or tradesman, predominates over that of the soldier: in a standing army, that of the soldier predominates over every other character; and in this distinction seems to consist the essential difference between those two different species of military force."

"The American Colonies In The 17th Century," Osgood, Vol. 1, ch. XIII, affirms in reference to the early system of defense in New England—

"In all the colonies, as in England, the militia system was based on the principle of the assize of arms. This implied the general obligation of all adult male inhabitants to possess arms, and, with certain exceptions, to cooperate in the work of defence." "The possession of arms also implied the possession of ammunition, and the authorities paid quite as much attention to the latter as to the former." "A year later [1632] it was ordered that any single man who had not furnished himself with arms might be put out to service, and this became a permanent part of the legislation of the colony [Massachusetts]."

Also "Clauses intended to insure the possession of arms and ammunition by all who were subject to military service appear in all the important enactments concerning military affairs. Fines were the penalty for delinquency, whether of towns or individuals. According to the usage of the times, the infantry of Massachusetts consisted of pikemen and musketeers. The law, as enacted in 1649 and thereafter, provided that each of the former should be armed with a pike, corselet, head-piece, sword, and knapsack. The musketeer should carry a 'good fixed musket,' not under bastard musket bore, not less than three feet, nine inches, nor more than four feet three inches in length, a priming wire, scourer, and mould, a sword, rest, bandoleers, one pound of powder, twenty bullets, and two fathoms of match. The law also required that two-thirds of each company should be musketeers."

The General Court of Massachusetts, January Session 1784 (Laws and Resolves 1784, c. 55, pp. 140, 142), provided for the organization and government of the Militia. It directed that the Train Band should "contain all able bodied men, from sixteen to forty years of age, and the Alarm List, all other men under sixty years of age, ..." Also, "That every non-commissioned officer and private soldier of the said militia not under the controul of parents, masters or guardians, and being of sufficient ability therefor in the judgment of the Selectmen of the town in which he shall dwell, shall equip himself, and be constantly provided with a good fire arm, &c."

By an Act passed April 4, 1786 (Laws 1786, c. 25), the New York Legislature directed: 'That every able-bodied Male Person, being a Citizen of this State, or of any of the United States, and residing in this State, (except such Persons as are herein after excepted) and who are of the Age of Sixteen, and under the Age of Forty-five Years, shall, by the Captain or commanding Officer of the Beat in which such Citizens shall reside, within four Months after the passing of this Act, be enrolled in the Company of such Beat. . . . That every Citizen so enrolled and notified, shall, within three Months thereafter, provide himself, at his own Expense, with a good Musket or Firelock, a sufficient Bayonet and Belt, a Pouch with a Box therein to contain not less than Twenty-four Cartridges suited to the Bore of his Musket or Firelock, each Cartridge containing a proper Quantity of Powder and Ball, two spare Flints, a Blanket and Knapsack; . . . . "

The General Assembly of Virginia, October, 1785 (12 Hening's Statutes c. 1, p. 9 et seq.), declared: "The defense and safety of the commonwealth depend upon having its citizens properly armed and taught the knowledge of military duty."

It further provided for organization and control of the Militia and directed that "All free male persons between the ages of eighteen and fifty years," with certain exceptions, "shall be inrolled or formed into companies." "There shall be a private muster of every company once in two months."

Also that "Every officer and soldier shall appear at his respective muster-field on the day appointed, by eleven o'clock in the forenoon, armed, equipped, and accoutred, as follows: . . . every non-commissioned officer and private with a good, clean musket carrying an ounce ball, and three feet eight inches long in the barrel, with a good bayonet and iron ramrod well fitted thereto, a cartridge box properly made, to contain and secure twenty cartridges fitted to his musket, a good knapsack and canteen, and moreover, each non-commissioned officer and private shall have at every muster one pound of good powder, and four pounds of lead, including twenty blind cartridges; and each sergeant shall have a pair of moulds fit to cast balls for their respective companies, to be purchased by the commanding officer out of the monies arising on delinquencies. Provided, That the militia of the counties westward of the Blue Ridge, and the counties below adjoining thereto, shall not be obliged to be armed with muskets, but may have good rifles with proper accoutrements, in lieu thereof. And every of the said officers, non-commissioned officers, and privates, shall constantly keep the aforesaid arms, accoutrements, and ammunition, ready to be produced whenever called for by his commanding officer. If any private shall make it appear to the satisfaction of the court hereafter to be appointed for trying delinquencies under this act that he is so poor that he cannot purchase the arms herein required, such court shall cause them to be purchased out of the money arising from delinquents."

Most if not all of the States have adopted provisions touching the right to keep and bear arms. Differences in the language employed in these have naturally led to somewhat variant conclusions concerning the scope of the right guaranteed. But none of them seem to afford any material support for the challenged ruling of the court below.

In the margin some of the more important opinions and comments by writers are cited. [Footnote 3].

We are unable to accept the conclusion of the court below and the challenged judgment must be reversed. The cause will be remanded for further proceedings.

Reversed and remanded.

MR. JUSTICE DOUGLAS took no part in the consideration or decision of this cause.

Footnotes

1. Act of June 26, 1934, c. 757, 48 Stat. 1236–1240, 26 U.S. C. sec. 1132. That for the purposes of this Act—

"(a) The term 'firearm' means a shotgun or rifle having a barrel of less than eighteen inches in length, or any other weapon, except a pistol or revolver, from which a shot is discharged by an explosive if such weapon is capable of being concealed on the person, or a machine gun, and includes a muffler or silencer for any firearm whether or not such firearm is included within the foregoing definition, [The Act of April 10, 1936, c. 169, 49 Stat. 1192 added the words] but does not include any rifle which is within the foregoing provisions solely by reason of the length of its barrel if the caliber of such rifle is .22 or smaller and if its barrel is sixteen inches or more in length.

"Sec. 3. (a) There shall be levied, collected, and paid upon firearms transferred in the continental United States a tax at the rate of $200 for each firearm, such tax to be paid by the transferor, and to be represented by appropriate stamps to be provided by the Commissioner, with the approval of the Secretary; and the stamps herein provided shall be affixed to the order for such firearm, hereinafter provided for. The tax imposed by this section shall be in addition to any import duty imposed on such firearm.

"Sec. 4. (a) It shall be unlawful for any person to transfer a firearm except in pursuance of a written order from the person seeking to obtain such article, on an application form issued in blank in duplicate for that purpose by the Commissioner. Such order shall identify the applicant by such means of identification as may be prescribed by regulations under this Act: Provided, That, if the applicant is an individual, such identification shall include fingerprints and a photograph thereof.

"(c) Every person so transferring a firearm shall set forth in each copy of such order the manufacturer's number or other mark identifying such firearm, and shall forward a copy of such order to the Commissioner. The original thereof with stamps affixed, shall be returned to the applicant.

"(d) No person shall transfer a firearm which has previously been transferred on or after the effective date of this Act, unless such person, in addition to complying with subsection (c), transfers therewith the stamp-affixed order provided for in this section for each transfer, in compliance with such regulations as may be prescribed under this Act for proof of payment of all taxes on such firearms.

"Sec. 5. (a) Within sixty days after the effective date of this Act every person possessing a firearm shall register, with the collector of the district in which he resides, the number or other mark such firearm, together with his name, address, place where is usually kept, and place of business or employment, and, if such person is other than a natural person, the name and home address of an executive officer thereof: Provided, That no person shall be required to register under this section with respect to any firearm acquired after the effective date of, and in conformity with the provisions of, this Act.

"Sec. 6. It shall be unlawful for any person to receive or possess any firearm which has at any time been transferred in violation of section 3 or 4 of this Act.

"Sec. 11. It shall be unlawful for any person who is required to register as provided in section 5 hereof and who shall not have so registered, or any other person who has not in his possession a stamp-affixed order as provided in section 4 hereof, to ship, carry, or deliver any firearm in interstate commerce.

"Sec. 12. The Commissioner, with the approval of the Secretary, shall prescribe such rules and regulations as may be necessary for carrying the provisions of this Act into effect.

"Sec. 14. Any person who violates or fails to comply with any of the requirements of this Act shall, upon conviction, be fined not more than $2,000 or be imprisoned for not more than five years, or both, in the discretion of the court.

"Sec. 16. If any provision of this Act, or the application thereof to any person or circumstance, is held invalid, the remainder of the Act, and the application of such provision to other persons or circumstances, shall not be affected thereby.

"Sec. 18. This Act may be cited as the 'National Firearms Act.'"

2. Act December 17, 1914, c. 1, 38 Stat. 785; February 24, 1919, c. 18, 40 Stat. 1057.

3. Concerning The Militia—*Presser v. Illinois*, 116 U.S. 252; *Robertson v. Baldwin*, 165 U.S. 275; *Fife v. State*, 31 Ark. 455; *Jeffers v. Fair*, 33 Ga. 347; *Salina v. Blaksley*, 72 Kan. 230; 83 P. 619; *People v. Brown*, 253 Mich. 537; 235 N. W. 245; *Aymette v. State*, 2 Humphr. (Tenn.) 154; *State v. Duke*, 42 Texas 455; *State v. Workman*, 35 W. Va. 367; 14 S. E. 9; *Cooley's Constitutional Limitations*, Vol. 1, p. 729; *Story on The Constitution*, 5th Ed., Vol. 2 p. 646; *Encyclopaedia of the Social Sciences*, Vol. X, p. 471, 474.

SOURCE: http://www.cs.cmu.edu/afs/cs/usr/wbardwel/public/nfalist/miller.txt

---

ANALYSIS

Two men, Jack Miller and Frank Layton, were indicted for violating a 1934 federal law that barred transport of a sawed-off shotgun (a weapon modified by gangsters by cutting off part of the barrel to increase a shotgun's lethality) across state lines. The law regulated the interstate transport of such "gangster" weapons as sawed-off shotguns and machine guns by imposing a large tax on their interstate transport. The tax had the desired effect: gun dealers around the country got rid of such weapons. Miller and Layton did not pay the tax, and so were prosecuted under the law. They appealed their indictment through the federal courts, arguing that the law violated their Second Amendment right to keep and bear such a firearm. They also argued that the federal tax power applied to such weapons amounted to an improper attempt by the federal government to usurp the state police power (meaning the power belonging to the states to control criminal conduct).

Reversing a lower federal court ruling, the Supreme Court ruled unanimously against the men, saying that the Second Amendment came in to play only when citizens were serving in a government organized and regulated militia, and that there was no citizen right to keep and bear arms aside from this purpose. The first part of the decision references the Tenth Amendment—the provision of the Bill of Rights that reserves powers to the states—by saying that the 1934 law did not usurp state power. Most of the decision, however, is devoted to a painstaking description of the history of militias, emphasizing that any law-based right to have firearms was always linked to the amendment's "obvious purpose" of ensuring an effective militia as described in Article I, section 8 in the Constitution. (The court also cited the *Cruikshank* and *Presser* cases to buttress its interpretation of the Second Amendment.) Note that Miller and Layton did not send lawyers to represent them before the court, although this did not alter the impact of the court's decision. The text of the 1934 law in question, the National Firearms Act of 1934, is reprinted in footnote 3 of the court's opinion.

Critics of this ruling have argued that the ruling is less than clear, or was at least incomplete in its discussion of the Second Amendment. Some have argued that it can be read to say that ownership of guns that *do* bear some relation to service in a militia (in other words, focusing on the weapon in question rather than whether the individual having the weapon was a member of a militia) would be protected under this ruling (see the 2008 *Heller* decision reprinted in this chapter). The problem with this interpretation, however, is that it would justify citizen ownership of militarily useful "weapons" (a term more expansive than simply "guns") such as machine guns, bazookas, howitzers, and other, even more destructive weapons. Such an interpretation makes no sense, and the court's focus on whether the sawed-off shotgun in question was in the men's possession arose from the text of the 1934 law about which they were adjudicating; that is, their right to have the shotgun would presumably have

President Franklin Delano Roosevelt, 1933. Library of Congress.

been upheld if they had been in the militia, and had been carrying the weapon for that purpose. And as the *Presser* case discussed in Chapter 3 said, citizens may not form their own militias independent of the government.

Both Miller and Layton were known to be habitual criminals. Ironically, Miller was killed in a shootout, probably with another criminal, a month before the court handed down its ruling.

FURTHER READING

Frye, Brian L. "The Peculiar Story of *United States v. Miller*." *N.Y.U. Journal of Law & Liberty* 3(2008): 48–82.

Spitzer, Robert J. "The Second Amendment 'Right to Bear Arms' and the *Emerson* Case," *St. John's Law Review* 77(Winter 2003): 1–27.

The Modern National Guard
Began as Colonial Militias

- *Document:* Supreme Court Case of *Maryland v. U.S.*
- *Date:* May 3, 1965
- *Where:* Washington, D.C.
- *Significance:* This case explicates the modern legal status of the National Guard and its relationship to America's early militias.

DOCUMENT

Maryland v. United States, 381 U.S. 41 (1965)

Decided May 3, 1965. . . .

MR. JUSTICE HARLAN delivered the opinion of the Court.

The question we decide here is whether a civilian employee and military member of the National Guard is an "employee" of the United States for purposes of the Federal Tort Claims Act when his National Guard unit is not in active federal service.

Petitioners' decedents were passengers on a Capital Airlines plane that collided over Maryland with a jet trainer assigned to the Maryland Air National Guard. The only survivor of the accident was the pilot of the trainer, Captain McCoy, and it is not disputed that the collision was caused by his negligence. The estates of the pilot and co-pilot of the Capital plane, and Capital Airlines itself, filed suit against the United States under the Federal Tort Claims Act in the District Court for the District of Columbia, and recovered judgments. The Court of Appeals for the District of Columbia Circuit affirmed. *United States v. Maryland* for the use of Meyer, 116 U.S. App. D.C. 259, 322 F.2d 1009, cert. denied, 375 U.S. 954, motion for leave to file petition for rehearing pending, No. 543, 1963 Term. Meanwhile, petitioners filed a similar suit in the Western District of Pennsylvania, and all parties agreed to proceed solely on the record made in the Meyer case. The District Court rendered judgment for petitioners, but the Court of Appeals for the Third Circuit reversed. 329 F.2d 722. We granted certiorari, 379 U.S. 877, to resolve the conflict between the two Circuits on this single record, and, more broadly, to settle authoritatively the basic question stated at the outset of this opinion which is at the core of other litigation arising out of this same disaster, now pending in a number of courts in different parts of the country. . . .

I

The National Guard is the modern Militia reserved to the States by Art. I. 8, cl. 15, 16, of the Constitution. It has only been in recent years that the National Guard has been an organized force, capable of being assimilated with ease into the regular military establishment of the United States. From the days of the Minutemen of Lexington and Concord until just before World War I, the various militias embodied the concept of a citizen army, but lacked the equipment and training necessary for their use as an integral part of the reserve force of the United States Armed Forces. The passage of the National Defense Act of 1916 materially altered the status of the militias by constituting them as the National Guard. Pursuant to power vested in Congress by the Constitution, the Guard was to be uniformed, equipped, and trained in much the same way as the regular army, subject to federal standards and capable of being "federalized" by units, rather than by drafting individual soldiers. In return, Congress authorized the allocation of federal equipment to the Guard, and provided federal compensation for members of the Guard, supplementing any state emoluments. The Governor, however, remained in charge of the National Guard in each State except when the Guard was called into active federal service; in most instances the Governor administered the Guard through the State Adjutant General, who was required by the Act to report periodically to the National Guard Bureau, a federal organization, on the Guard's reserve status. The basic structure of the 1916 Act has been preserved to the present day.

Section 90 of the National Defense Act authorized the payment of federal funds for the employment by the Guard of civilian "caretakers" to be responsible for the upkeep of federal equipment allocated to the National Guard. This section was later amended to make explicit that employment as a caretaker could be held by officers in the Guard, who would receive a full-time salary as civilian caretakers, and in addition would receive compensation for service as military members of the Guard. The legislative history of these amendments makes clear that the State Adjutant General could appoint officers of the Guard to serve as civilian caretakers, provided only that the appointees met the requirements established by the federal authorities.

II

It is not argued here that military members of the Guard are federal employees, even though they are paid with federal funds and must conform to strict federal requirements in order to satisfy training and promotion standards. Their appointment by state authorities and the immediate control exercised over them by the States make it apparent that military members of the Guard are employees of the States, and so the courts of appeals have uniformly held. Civilian caretakers should not be considered as occupying a different status. Caretakers, like military members of the Guard, are also paid with federal funds and must observe federal requirements in order to maintain their positions. Although they are employed to maintain federal property, it is property for which the States are responsible, and its maintenance is for the purpose of keeping the state militia in a ready status. The National Defense Act of 1916 authorized the allocation of federal property to the National Guard, but provided

> "That as a condition precedent to the issue of any property as provided for by this Act, the State, Territory, or the District of Columbia desiring such issue shall make adequate provision, to the satisfaction of the Secretary of War, for the protection and care of such property. . . . "

The Act also provided that damage or loss of federal property would be charged to the States, unless the Secretary of War determined that the damage or loss was unavoidable. Caretakers appointed under 90 of the Act were thus to perform a state function, the maintenance of federal equipment allocated to the Guard. The caretakers have been termed the "backbone" of the Guard, and are the only personnel on duty with Guard units during the greater part of the year. Like their military counterpart, caretakers are appointed by the State Adjutant General, and are responsible to him in the performance of their daily duties. . . .

In sum, we conclude that the congressional purpose in authorizing the employment by state authorities of civilian caretakers, the administrative practice of the Defense Department in treating caretakers as state employees, the consistent congressional recognition of that status, and the like supervision exercised by the States over both military and civilian personnel of the National Guard, unmistakably lead in combination to the view that civilian as well as military personnel of the Guard are to be treated for the purposes of the Tort Claims Act as employees of the States and not of the Federal Government. This requires a decision that the United States is not liable to petitioners for the negligent conduct of McCoy.

In so holding we are not unmindful that this doubtless leaves those who suffered from this accident without effective legal redress for their losses. It is nevertheless our duty to take the law as we find it, remitting those aggrieved to whatever requirement may be deemed appropriate by Congress, which in affording the administrative remedies, unfortunately not available here, has shown itself not impervious to the moral demands of such distressing situations.

Affirmed.

MR. JUSTICE DOUGLAS dissents.

SOURCE: http://supreme.justia.com/us/381/41/case.html

ANALYSIS

The family of several people who were killed in a mid-air crash between a civilian airliner and a Maryland National Guard training plane filed suit to recover damages for the deaths. The pilot of the training plane was found to be at fault for the crash. The pilot served on active duty with the state National Guard two days a month, but on the day of the crash he was being employed by the Guard in a civilian capacity (the status of "civilian caretaker" referenced in the court's decision). The Supreme Court concluded that the pilot was not acting as an employee of the United States (regardless of whether he was on duty or off duty), despite the national government's control over state National Guard units, and so it was not liable under the Federal Tort Claims Act. The pilot was, instead, functioning as an employee of the Maryland state government.

The case is notable because the decision explains the link between the historic militias and the modern National Guard. Clarifying the all-too-frequent confusion about the relationship between the early militias and the modern National Guard, the decision notes that the militias are indeed "the modern Militia reserved to the States by Art. I. 8, cl. 15, 16, of the Constitution." As discussed earlier in this book, the early militias often lacked in training and equipment; eventually, the states and the federal government stepped in to fill these gaps. This occurred through a series of congressional enactments including the National Defense Act of 1916 (the Militia Act of 1903 was actually the first of this modernizing process). This and other federal laws provided that uniforms, equipment, and training were to be provided by the national government in the manner that the federal government controlled the nation's standing army. The National Guard units, although still state-based, could be "federalized" (i.e., taken over by the national government) if national emergency required. Even so, state governors would remain as heads of state Guard units.

The process of increasing federal control described in this case confirmed the link between the Minutemen of the eighteenth century and modern National Guards; it also completed the shift of power over state militias from state to national authority begun in the late eighteenth century, but uncompleted until the twentieth century. In this way, the federalism balance between the states and the national government eventually came to favor the latter, and that shift was confirmed by the high court in this case.

FURTHER READING

Cooper, Jerry. *The Rise of the National Guard*. Lincoln: University of Nebraska Press, 1997.

Two Justices Address the Politics of Gun Control

- *Document:* Supreme Court case of *Adams v. Williams* (dissenting opinion)
- *Date:* June 12, 1972
- *Where:* Washington, D.C.
- *Significance:* In a dissenting opinion, two Supreme Court justices argue that even strict gun laws do not violate Second Amendment rights, and that the Second Amendment pertains to citizen militia service, not personal rights.

DOCUMENT

Adams v. Williams, 407 U.S. 143 (1972)

Decided June 12, 1972. . . .

Acting on a tip supplied moments earlier by an informant known to him, a police officer asked respondent to open his car door. Respondent lowered the window, and the officer reached into the car and found a loaded handgun (which had not been visible from the outside) in respondent's waistband, precisely where the informant said it would be. Respondent was arrested for unlawful possession of the handgun. A search incident to the arrest disclosed heroin on respondent's person (as the informant had reported), as well as other contraband in the car. Respondent's petition for federal habeas corpus relief was denied by the District Court. The Court of Appeals reversed, holding that the evidence that had been used in the trial resulting in respondent's conviction had been obtained by an unlawful search. Held: As *Terry v. Ohio,* 392 U.S. 1, recognizes, a policeman making a reasonable investigatory stop may conduct a limited protective search for concealed weapons when he has reason to believe that the suspect is armed and dangerous. Here the information from the informant had enough indicia of reliability to justify the officer's forcible stop of petitioner and the protective seizure of the weapon, which afforded reasonable ground for the search incident to the arrest that ensued. . . .

MR. JUSTICE DOUGLAS, with whom MR. JUSTICE MARSHALL concurs, dissenting.

My views have been stated in substance by Judge Friendly, dissenting, in the Court of Appeals. 436 F.2d 30, 35. Connecticut allows its citizens to carry weapons, concealed or otherwise, at will, provided they have a permit. Conn. Gen. Stat. Rev. 29–35, 29–38. Connecticut law gives its police no authority to frisk a person for a permit. Yet the arrest was for illegal possession of a gun. The only basis for that arrest was the informer's tip on the narcotics. Can it be said that a man in possession of narcotics will not have a permit for his gun? Is that why the arrest for possession of a gun in the free-and-easy State of Connecticut becomes constitutional?

The police problem is an acute one not because of the Fourth Amendment, but because of the ease with which anyone can acquire a pistol. A powerful lobby dins into the ears of our citizenry that these gun purchases are constitutional rights protected by the Second Amendment, which reads, "A well regulated Militia, being necessary to the security of a free State, the right of the people to keep and bear Arms, shall not be infringed."

There is under our decisions no reason why stiff state laws governing the purchase and possession of pistols may not be enacted. There is no reason why pistols may not be barred from anyone with a police record. There is no reason why a State may not require a purchaser of a pistol to pass a psychiatric test. There is no reason why all pistols should not be barred to everyone except the police.

The leading case is *United States v. Miller*, 307 U.S. 174, upholding a federal law making criminal the shipment in interstate commerce of a sawed-off shotgun. The law was upheld, there being no evidence that a sawed-off shotgun had "some reasonable relationship to the preservation or efficiency of a well regulated militia." Id., at 178. The Second Amendment, it was held, "must be interpreted and applied" with the view of maintaining a "militia."

> "The Militia which the States were expected to maintain and train is set in contrast with Troops which they were forbidden to keep without the consent of Congress. The sentiment of the time strongly disfavored standing armies; the common view was that adequate defense of country and laws could be secured through the Militia—civilians primarily, soldiers on occasion." Id., at 178–179.

Critics say that proposals like this water down the Second Amendment. Our decisions belie that argument, for the Second Amendment, as noted, was designed to keep alive the militia. But if watering-down is the mood of the day, I would prefer to water down the Second rather than the Fourth Amendment. I share with Judge Friendly a concern that the easy extension of *Terry v. Ohio*, 392 U.S. 1, to "possessory offenses" is a serious intrusion on Fourth Amendment safeguards. "If it is to be extended to the latter at all, this should be only where observation by the officer himself or well authenticated information shows 'that criminal activity may be afoot.'" 436 F.2d, at 39, quoting *Terry v. Ohio*, supra, at 30.

ANALYSIS

This biting excerpt from the Supreme Court case of *Adams v. Williams* differs from other cases presented in this book for two reasons. First, it includes only the dissenting opinion, and not the majority opinion, which had to do with a Fourth Amendment search and seizure question. The law emanating from a court case comes from the majority opinion, not from the minority or dissenting opinion, although dissents can be important as a way to influence future cases. Second, this case did not deal with either gun control or the Second Amendment. Therefore, the reader should understand that what appears here is "dicta," meaning that it is commentary that has no effect on the law. Yet it is notable because it reflected the views of two justices, William O. Douglas and Thurgood Marshall, that the Second Amendment (a subject not otherwise addressed in this case) in their view pertained only to militia service; that the 1939 *Miller* case was central to understanding the meaning of the Second Amendment; that, in their view, the Second Amendment posed no obstacle to gun regulations of any sort, aside from militia activities, and despite the "powerful lobby [that] dins into the ears of our citizenry" insisting that gun controls violated Second Amendment rights (a reference to the National Rifle Association and other gun groups); and that America was awash with too many guns. Coming from two Supreme Court justices, these statements echoed the views of many that sensible gun controls in America were being thwarted by the gun lobby, not the Second Amendment.

FURTHER READING

Kennett, Lee, and James LaVerne Anderson. *The Gun in America*. Westport, CT: Greenwood Press, 1975.

Federal Gun Law Held as Constitutional and a Reasonable Exercise of the Police Power

- *Document:* Supreme Court case of *Lewis v. U.S.*
- *Date:* February 27, 1980
- *Where:* Washington, D.C.
- *Significance:* The Supreme Court approved of the government's right to use its police power to deprive criminals of guns, and stated that the government only needed a "rational basis" to justify such a law.

DOCUMENT

Lewis v. United States, 445 U.S. 55 (1980)

Decided February 27, 1980

MR. JUSTICE BLACKMUN delivered the opinion of the Court.

This case presents the question whether a defendant's extant prior conviction, flawed because he was without counsel, as required by *Gideon v. Wainwright,* 372 U.S. 335 (1963), may constitute the predicate for a subsequent conviction under 1202 (a) (1), as amended, of Title VII of the Omnibus Crime Control and Safe Streets Act of 1968, 18 U.S.C. App. 1202 (a) (1).

I

In 1961, petitioner George Calvin Lewis, Jr., upon his plea of guilty, was convicted in a Florida state court of a felony for breaking and entering with intent to commit a misdemeanor. See Fla. Stat. 810.05 (1961). He served a term of imprisonment. That conviction has never been overturned, nor has petitioner ever received a qualifying pardon or permission from the Secretary of the Treasury to possess a firearm. See 18 U.S.C. App. 1203 (2) and 18 U.S.C. 925 (c).

In January 1977, Lewis, on probable cause, was arrested in Virginia, and later was charged by indictment with having knowingly received and possessed at that time a specified firearm, in violation of 18 U.S.C. App. 1202 (a) (1). He waived a jury and was given a bench trial. It was stipulated that the weapon in question had been shipped in interstate commerce. The Government introduced in evidence an exemplified copy of the judgment and sentence in the 1961 Florida felony proceeding.

Shortly before the trial, petitioner's counsel informed the court that he had been advised that Lewis was not represented by counsel in the 1961 Florida proceeding. He claimed that under *Gideon v. Wainwright*, supra, a violation of 1202 (a) (1) could not be predicated on a prior conviction obtained in violation of petitioner's Sixth and Fourteenth Amendment rights. The court rejected that claim, ruling that the constitutionality of the outstanding Florida conviction was immaterial with respect to petitioner's status under 1202 (a) (1) as a previously convicted felon at the time of his arrest. Petitioner, accordingly, offered no evidence as to whether in fact he had been convicted in 1961 without the aid of counsel. We therefore assume, for present purposes, that he was without counsel at that time.

On appeal, the United States Court of Appeals for the Fourth Circuit, by a divided vote, affirmed. 591 F.2d 978 (1979). It held that a defendant, purely as a defense to a prosecution under 1202 (a) (1), could not attack collaterally an outstanding prior felony conviction, and that the statutory prohibition applied irrespective of whether that prior conviction was subject to collateral attack. The Court of Appeals also rejected Lewis' constitutional argument to the effect that the use of the prior conviction as a predicate for his prosecution under 1202 (a) (1) violated his rights under the Fifth and Sixth Amendments.

Because of conflict among the Courts of Appeals, we granted certiorari. 442 U.S. 939 (1979). . . .

It is not without significance . . . that Title VII, as well as Title IV of the Omnibus Act, was enacted in response to the precipitous rise in political assassinations, riots, and other violent crimes involving firearms, that occurred in this country in the 1960's. See e. g., S. Rep. No. 1097, 90th Cong., 2d Sess., 76–78 (1968); H. R. Rep. No. 1577, 90th Cong., 2d Sess., 7 (1968); S. Rep. No. 1501, 90th Cong., 2d Sess., 22–23 (1968). This Court, accordingly, has observed:

> "The legislative history [of Title VII] in its entirety, while brief, further supports the view that Congress sought to rule broadly—to keep guns out of the hands of those who have demonstrated that 'they may not be trusted to possess a firearm without becoming a threat to society.'" *Scarborough v. United States*, 431 U.S., at 572.

The legislative history, therefore, affords no basis for a loophole, by way of a collateral constitutional challenge, to the broad statutory scheme enacted by Congress. Section 1202 (a) was a sweeping prophylaxis, in simple terms, against misuse of firearms. There is no indication of any intent to require the Government to prove the validity of the predicate conviction.

The very structure of the Omnibus Act's Title IV, enacted simultaneously with Title VII, reinforces this conclusion. Each Title prohibits categories of presumptively dangerous persons from transporting or receiving firearms. See 18 U.S.C. 922 (g) and (h). Actually, with regard to the statutory question at issue here, we detect little significant difference between Title IV and Title VII. Each seeks to keep a firearm away from "any person . . . who has been convicted" of a felony, although the definition of "felony" differs somewhat in the respective statutes. But to limit the scope of 922 (g) (1) and (h) (1) to a validly convicted felon would be at odds with the statutory scheme as a whole. Those sections impose a disability not only on a convicted felon but also on a person under a felony indictment, even if that person subsequently is acquitted of the felony charge. Since the fact of mere indictment is a disabling circumstance, a fortiori the much more significant fact of conviction must deprive the person of a right to a firearm.

Finally, it is important to note that a convicted felon is not without relief. As has been observed above, the Omnibus Act, in 1203 (2) and 925 (c), states that the disability may be removed by a qualifying pardon or the Secretary's consent. Also, petitioner, before obtaining his firearm, could have challenged his prior conviction in an appropriate proceeding in the Florida state courts. . . .

It seems fully apparent to us that the existence of these remedies, two of which are expressly contained in the Omnibus Act itself, suggests that Congress clearly intended that the defendant clear his status before obtaining a firearm, thereby fulfilling Congress' purpose "broadly to keep firearms away from the persons Congress classified as potentially irresponsible and dangerous." *Barrett v. United States*, 423 U.S. 212, 218 (1976). . . .

IV

The firearm regulatory scheme at issue here is consonant with the concept of equal protection embodied in the Due Process Clause of the Fifth Amendment if there is "some 'rational basis' for the statutory distinctions made . . . or . . . they 'have some relevance to the purpose for which the classification is made.'" *Marshall v. United States*, 414 U.S. 417, 422 (1974), quoting from *McGinnis v. Royster*, 410 U.S. 263, 270 (1973), and *Baxstrom v. Herold*, 383 U.S. 107, 111 (1966). See *Vance v. Bradley*, 440 U.S. 93, 97 (1979). [footnote 8]

Section 1202 (a) (1) clearly meets that test. Congress, as its expressed purpose in enacting Title VII reveals, 18 U.S.C. App. 1201, was concerned that the receipt and possession of a firearm by a felon constitutes a threat, among other things, to the continued and effective operation of the Government of the United States. The legislative history of the gun control laws discloses Congress' worry about the easy availability of firearms, especially to those persons who pose a threat to community peace. And Congress focused on the nexus between violent crime and the possession of a firearm by any person with a criminal record. 114 Cong. Rec. 13220 (1968) (remarks of Sen. Tydings); id., at 16298 (remarks of Rep. Pollock). Congress could rationally conclude that any felony conviction, even an allegedly invalid one, is a sufficient basis on which to prohibit the possession of a firearm. See, e. g., *United States v.*

Ransom, 515 F.2d 885, 891–892 (CA5 1975), cert. denied, 424 U.S. 944 (1976). This Court has recognized repeatedly that a legislature constitutionally may prohibit a convicted felon from engaging in activities far more fundamental than the possession of a firearm. See *Richardson v. Ramirez*, 418 U.S. 24 (1974) (disenfranchisement); *De Veau v. Braisted*, 363 U.S. 144 (1960) (proscription against holding office in a waterfront labor organization); *Hawker v. New York*, 170 U.S. 189 (1898) (prohibition against the practice of medicine). . . .

Again, it is important to note that a convicted felon may challenge the validity of a prior conviction, or otherwise remove his disability, before obtaining a firearm. We simply hold today that the firearms prosecution does not open the predicate conviction to a new form of collateral attack. See Note, Prior Convictions and the Gun Control Act of 1968. [445 U.S. 55, 68] 76 Colum. L. Rev. 326, 338–339 (1976). Cf. *Walker v. City of Birmingham*, 388 U.S. 307 (1967).

The judgment of the Court of Appeals is affirmed.

It is so ordered.

Footnotes

[Footnote 8] These legislative restrictions on the use of firearms are neither based upon constitutionally suspect criteria, nor do they trench upon any constitutionally protected liberties. See *United States v. Miller*, 307 U.S. 174, 178 (1939) (the Second Amendment guarantees no right to keep and bear a firearm that does not have "some reasonable relationship to the preservation or efficiency of a well regulated militia"); *United States v. Three Winchester 30–30 Caliber Lever Action Carbines*, 504 F.2d 1288, 1290, n. 5 (CA7 1974); *United States v. Johnson*, 497 F.2d 548 (CA4 1974); *Cody v. United States*, 460 F.2d 34 (CA8), cert. denied, 409 U.S. 1010 (1972) (the latter three cases holding, respectively, that 1202 (a) (1), 922 (g), and 922 (a) (6) do not violate the Second Amendment).

MR. JUSTICE BRENNAN, with whom MR. JUSTICE MARSHALL and MR. JUSTICE POWELL join, dissenting. . . .

SOURCE: http://caselaw.lp.findlaw.com/scripts/getcase.pl?court=US&vol=445&invol=55

ANALYSIS

A man with a felony conviction record was arrested and charged with owning a gun in violation of a provision of a 1968 law, the Omnibus Crime Control and Safe Streets Act, which barred gun possession for anyone who had a prior felony record. The Supreme Court concluded that Congress's intent in passing the 1968 law, enacted partly because of a wave of violence and high-profile political assassinations, was to bar gun ownership to individuals with prior felony records even if the felony conviction in question occurred without benefit of a lawyer (at a time when representation by a lawyer was not required). The court agreed that, unless the conviction was overturned or the man pardoned, he could not legally own a gun.

Depriving such persons of gun ownership was reasonable and justifiable, the high court concluded, as there was a "rational basis" for the rule. This standard is notable because it represents a minimal or easy standard for the government to meet in order to justify a rule or regulation—in this case, a rule barring guns to felons. Note also that in Footnote 8, the decision cites *U.S. v. Miller* (1939) to explain that the gun prohibition does not violate the Second Amendment which, as the footnote says, pertains to "preservation or efficiency of a well regulated militia." The footnote also cites cases in which other courts have concluded that the 1968 law did not violate the Second Amendment.

FURTHER READING

Harcourt, Bernard E., ed. *Guns, Crime, and Punishment in America.* New York: New York University Press, 2003.

Expanded Federal Government Control over the National Guard Is Constitutional

- **Document:** Supreme Court case of *Perpich v. Department of Defense*
- **Date:** June 11, 1990
- **Where:** Washington, D.C.
- **Significance:** Despite shared federal-state control over militias found in the Constitution, Congress has primary control over the disposition and use of the modern militias (i.e., the National Guard).

DOCUMENT

Perpich v. Department of Defense, 496 U.S. 334 (1990)

Decided June 11, 1990

JUSTICE STEVENS delivered the opinion of the Court.

The question presented is whether the Congress may authorize the President to order members of the National Guard to active duty for purposes of training outside the United States during peacetime without either the consent of a State Governor or the declaration of a national emergency.

A gubernatorial consent requirement that had been enacted in 1952 was partially repealed in 1986 by the "Montgomery Amendment," which provides:

"The consent of a Governor described in subsections (b) and (d) may not be withheld (in whole or in part) with regard to active duty outside the United States, its territories, and its possessions, because of any objection to the location, purpose, type, or schedule of such active duty."

In this litigation the Governor of Minnesota and the State of Minnesota (hereinafter collectively referred to as the Governor), challenge the constitutionality of that amendment. The Governor contends that it violates the Militia Clauses of the Constitution.

In his complaint the Governor alleged that pursuant to a state statute the Minnesota National Guard is the organized militia of the State of Minnesota and that pursuant to a federal statute members of that militia "are also members of either the Minnesota unit of the Air National Guard of the United States or the Minnesota unit of the Army National Guard of the United States (hereinafter collectively referred to as the 'National Guard of the United States')." The complaint further alleged that the Montgomery Amendment had prevented the Governor from withholding his consent to a training mission in Central America for certain members of the Minnesota National Guard in January 1987, and prayed for an injunction against the implementation of any similar orders without his consent.

The District Judge rejected the Governor's challenge. He explained that the National Guard consists of "two overlapping, but legally distinct, organizations. Congress, under its constitutional authority to 'raise and support armies' has created the National Guard of the United States, a federal organization comprised of state national guard units and their members." 666 F. Supp. 1319, 1320 (Minn. 1987). The fact that these units also maintain an identity as State National Guards, part of the militia described in Art. I, 8, of the Constitution, does not limit Congress' plenary authority to train the Guard "as it sees fit when the Guard is called to active federal service." Id., at 1324. . . . [T]he Court of Appeals. . . . agreed with the District Court's conclusion that "Congress' army power is plenary and exclusive" and that the State's authority to train the militia did not conflict with congressional power to raise armies for the common defense and to control the training of federal reserve forces. 880 F.2d 11, 17–18 (1989). . . . [W]e conclude that the plain language of Article I of the Constitution, read as whole, requires affirmance of the Court of Appeals' judgment. We believe, however, that a brief description of the evolution of the present statutory scheme will help to explain that holding.

I

Two conflicting themes, developed at the Constitutional Convention and repeated in debates over military policy during the next century, led to a compromise in the text of the Constitution and in later statutory enactments. On the one hand, there was a widespread fear that a national standing Army posed an intolerable threat to individual liberty and to the sovereignty of the separate States, while, on the other hand, there was a recognition of the danger of relying on inadequately trained soldiers as the primary means of providing for the common defense. Thus, Congress was authorized both to raise and support a national Army and also to organize "the Militia."

In the early years of the Republic, Congress did neither. In 1792, it did pass a statute that purported to establish "an Uniform Militia throughout the United States," but its detailed command that every able-bodied male citizen between the ages of 18 and 45 be enrolled therein and equip himself with appropriate weaponry was virtually ignored for more than a century, during which time the militia proved to be a decidedly unreliable fighting force. The statute was finally repealed in 1901. It was in that year that President Theodore Roosevelt declared: "Our militia law is obsolete and worthless." The process of transforming "the National Guard of the several States" into an effective fighting force then began.

The Dick Act divided the class of able-bodied male citizens between 18 and 45 years of age into an "organized militia" to be known as the National Guard of the several States, and the remainder of which was then described as the "reserve militia," and which later statutes have termed the "unorganized militia." The statute created a table of organization for the National Guard conforming to that of the Regular Army, and provided that federal funds and Regular Army instructors should be used to train its members. It is undisputed that Congress was acting pursuant to the Militia Clauses of the Constitution in passing the Dick Act. Moreover, the legislative history of that Act indicates that Congress contemplated that the services of the organized militia would "be rendered only upon the soil of the United States or of its Territories." H. R. Rep. No. 1094, 57th Cong., 1st Sess., 22 (1902). In 1908, however, the statute was amended to provide expressly that the Organized Militia should be available for service "either within or without the territory of the United States."

When the Army made plans to invoke that authority by using National Guard units south of the Mexican border, Attorney General Wickersham expressed the opinion that the Militia Clauses precluded such use outside the Nation's borders. In response to that opinion and to the widening conflict in Europe, in 1916 Congress decided to "federalize" the National Guard. In addition to providing for greater federal control and federal funding of the Guard, the statute required every guardsman to take a dual oath—to support the Nation as well as the States and to obey the President as well as the Governor—and authorized the President to draft members of the Guard into federal service. The statute expressly provided that the Army of the United States should include not only "the Regular Army," but also "the National Guard while in the service of the United States," and that when drafted into federal service by the President, members of the Guard so drafted should "from the date of their draft, stand discharged from the militia, and shall from said date be subject to" the rules and regulations governing the Regular Army. 111, 39 Stat. 211.

During World War I, the President exercised the power to draft members of the National Guard into the Regular Army. That power, as well as the power to compel civilians to render military service, was upheld in the Selective Draft Law Cases, 245 U.S. 366 (1918). Specifically, in those cases, and in *Cox v. Wood*, 247 U.S. 3 (1918), the Court held that the plenary power to raise armies was "not qualified or restricted by the provisions of the militia clause."

The draft of the individual members of the National Guard into the Army during World War I virtually destroyed the Guard as an effective organization. The draft terminated the members' status as militiamen, and the statute did not provide for a restoration of their prewar status as members of the Guard when they were mustered out of the Army. This problem was ultimately remedied by the 1933 amendments to the 1916 Act. Those amendments created the "two overlapping but distinct organizations" described by the District Court—the National Guard of the various States and the National Guard of the United States.

Since 1933 all persons who have enlisted in a State National Guard unit have simultaneously enlisted in the National Guard of the United States. In the latter capacity they became a part of the Enlisted Reserve Corps of the Army, but unless and until ordered to active duty in the Army, they retained their status as members of a separate State Guard unit. Under the 1933 Act, they could be ordered into active service whenever Congress declared a national emergency and authorized the use of troops in excess of those in the Regular Army. . . .

Thus, under the "dual enlistment" provisions of the statute that have been in effect since 1933, a member of the Guard who is ordered to active duty in the federal service is thereby relieved of his or her status in the State Guard for the entire period of federal service.

Until 1952 the statutory authority to order National Guard units to active duty was limited to periods of national emergency. In that year, Congress broadly authorized orders to "active duty or active duty for training" without any emergency requirement, but provided that such orders could not be issued without gubernatorial consent. The National Guard units have under this plan become a sizable portion of the Nation's military forces; for example, "the Army National Guard provides 46 percent of the combat units and 28 percent of the support forces of the Total Army." Apparently gubernatorial consents to training missions were routinely obtained until 1985, when the Governor of California refused to consent to a training mission for 450 members of the California National Guard in Honduras, and the Governor of Maine shortly thereafter refused to consent to a similar mission. Those incidents led to the enactment of the Montgomery Amendment and this litigation ensued.

II

The Governor's attack on the Montgomery Amendment relies in part on the traditional understanding that "the Militia" can only be called forth for three limited purposes that do not encompass either foreign service or nonemergency conditions, and in part on the express language in the second Militia Clause reserving to the States "the Authority of training the Militia." The Governor does not, however, challenge the authority of Congress to create a dual enlistment program. Nor does the Governor claim that membership in a State Guard unit—or any type of state militia—creates any sort of constitutional immunity from being drafted into the Federal Armed Forces. Indeed, it would be ironic to claim such immunity when every member of the Minnesota National Guard has voluntarily enlisted, or accepted a commission as an officer, in the National Guard of the United States and thereby become a member of the Reserve Corps of the Army.

The unchallenged validity of the dual enlistment system means that the members of the National Guard of Minnesota who are ordered into federal service with the National Guard of the United States lose their status as members of the state militia during their period of active duty. If that duty is a training mission, the training is performed by the Army in which the trainee is serving, not by the militia from which the member has been temporarily disassociated. . . .

Notwithstanding the brief periods of federal service, the members of the State Guard unit continue to satisfy this description of a militia. In a sense, all of them now must keep three hats in their closets—a civilian hat, a state militia hat, and an army hat—only one of which is worn at any particular time. When the state militia hat is being worn, the "drilling and other exercises" . . . are performed pursuant to "the Authority of training the Militia according to the discipline prescribed by Congress," but when that hat is replaced by the federal hat, the second Militia Clause is no longer applicable.

This conclusion is unaffected by the fact that prior to 1952 Guard members were traditionally not ordered into active service in peacetime or for duty abroad. That tradition is at least partially the product of political debate and political compromise, but even if the tradition were compelled by the text of the Constitution, its constitutional aspect is related only to service by State Guard personnel who retain their state affiliation during their periods of service. There now exists a wholly different situation, in which the state affiliation is suspended in favor of an entirely federal affiliation during the period of active duty. . . .

Neither the State's basic training responsibility, nor its ability to rely on its own Guard in state emergency situations, is significantly affected. Indeed, if the federal training mission were to interfere with the State Guard's capacity to respond to local emergencies, the Montgomery Amendment would permit the Governor to veto the proposed mission. Moreover, Congress has provided by statute that in addition to its National Guard, a State may provide and maintain at its own expense a defense force that is exempt from being drafted into the Armed Forces of the United States. See 32 U.S.C. 109(c). As long as that provision remains in effect, there is no basis for an argument that the federal statutory scheme deprives Minnesota of any constitutional entitlement to a separate militia of its own.

In light of the Constitution's more general plan for providing for the common defense, the powers allowed to the States by existing statutes are significant. As has already been mentioned, several constitutional provisions commit matters of foreign policy and military affairs to the exclusive control of the National Government. This Court in Tarble's Case, 13 Wall. 397 (1872), had occasion to observe that the constitutional allocation of powers in this realm gave rise to a presumption that federal control over the Armed Forces was exclusive. Were it not for the Militia Clauses, it might be possible to argue on like grounds that the constitutional allocation of powers precluded the formation of organized state militia. The Militia Clauses, however, subordinate any such structural inferences to an express permission while also subjecting state militia to express federal limitations.

We thus conclude that the Montgomery Amendment is not inconsistent with the Militia Clauses. In so doing, we of course do not pass upon the relative virtues of the various political choices that have frequently altered the relationship between the Federal Government and the States in the field of military affairs. This case does not raise any question concerning the wisdom of the gubernatorial veto established in 1952 or of its partial repeal in 1986. We merely hold that because the former was not constitutionally compelled, the Montgomery Amendment is constitutionally valid.

The judgment of the Court of Appeals is affirmed.

It is so ordered.

ANALYSIS

This case involved a direct clash between the governor of Minnesota and the federal government over whether the Minnesota National Guard would be deployed outside of the United States, in time of peace, against the wishes of the governor. In 1985, several state governors challenged an order to send state Guard troops to train in Central America, arguing that, in peacetime, they could prevent their state Guard units from participating. Minnesota's governor, Rudy Perpich, filed suit in federal court against a federal law, the Montgomery Amendment, enacted in 1986 (passed in reaction to governors' refusal to send their Guard units), that prevented governors from withholding their Guard units from federal service. Perpich argued that the federal law violated the U.S. Constitution's militia clauses, which reserve to the states some powers over militias.

The governors' resistance to the federal government's use of state Guard units arose from an ongoing political controversy during Ronald Reagan's presidency. Reagan had been a staunch foe of the leftist regime that had taken control of the Central American nation of Nicaragua. Against American law, Reagan secretly financed the Nicaraguan "Contra" rebels who opposed the governing regime. As part of a show of force, Reagan ordered American military forces, including National Guard units, to participate in training exercises in the region. Administration critics, including some Democratic governors, opposed what they considered to be unnecessary saber-rattling. One product of that controversy was this court case.

In addition, two other factors contributed to this face-off. First, before this time, governors would routinely consent to federal requests for the federalizing of state Guard units. Second, Guard units were not normally called into federal service for foreign deployment in peacetime before this era. During the Vietnam War in the late 1960s and early 1970s, for example, few Guard units were sent to fight in Vietnam. By the time of the Iraq War begun in 2003, Guard units were a mainstay of the American military presence.

Under the National Guards' dual enlistment system, members enlist both with the state Guard unit and the federal Guard. When the latter is ordered to deploy, however, their obligation to their state units is eclipsed by their federal obligation, as the Supreme Court noted in its unanimous decision. The supremacy of the federal government in military matters was already well established, but the militia system, reorganized as the National Guard early in the twentieth century, still included some

DID YOU KNOW?

The NRA Becomes More Political

Throughout most of its history, the nation's largest gun group, the National Rifle Association (NRA) (formed in 1871), had maintained its primary organizational focus on hunting, sporting, and other gun-related activities. Although its leaders had played an important role in shaping national gun legislation from the 1930s through the 1960s, its political agenda traditionally occupied a subordinate role. In 1975, however, the NRA created the Institute for Legislative Action, and appointed a former NRA president, Harlon Carter, to head this politically oriented department. From this position, Carter and his allies pressed the NRA to adopt a more hard-line and more political organizational agenda. But in response, the ruling NRA old guard leaders fired Carter and more than 70 other hard-liners in 1976. Indicative of the old guard leaders' priorities was a plan to build a World Sports Center in Colorado Springs, and to move the NRA's headquarters there, and out of their offices in Washington, D.C. This planned shift away from politics was antithetical to Carter's group, who felt that the NRA needed to become more, not less, political.

At the NRA's annual convention the next year, held in Cincinnati, Carter and his supporters staged a successful organization coup to oust the existing leaders, and Carter was elected to the powerful position of executive vice president. From this point forward, the NRA devoted ever more of its resources to political activities, and became a hard-line organization that opposed all gun control measures (before the 1977 convention, for example, the NRA had supported background checks for handgun purchases). These efforts yielded organizational successes including membership increases, higher visibility, and enactment of less strict gun laws. But the organization also became a more polarizing force in national politics, and it adopted a stridently antigovernment rhetoric that alienated many.

state control over Guard units. Yet the high court concluded that Congress was well within its authority to legislate changes in the federal-state balance of control. In its extensive review of militia history, the court decision chronicled the gradual shift in militia regulations through congressional enactment, beginning with the Uniform Militia Act of 1792 (see Chapter 2) that required militia members to arm themselves, to twentieth-century enactments that greatly increased federal control over the National Guards. This was allowable under Congress's Article I powers. As soon as state Guard units are called into federal service, the court noted, they come under full federal direction. In addition, states retain the power to organize and fund their own supplemental units that are exempt from federal control.

SOURCE: http://caselaw.lp.findlaw.com/cgi-bin/getcase.pl?court=US&vol=496&invol=334

FURTHER READING

Millett, Allan R., and Peter Maslowski. *For the Common Defense: A Military History of the United States of America.* New York: Free Press, 1994.

Congress May Not Require
Local Police to Conduct
Federal Background Checks
for Gun Purchases

- **Document:** Supreme Court case of *Printz v. U.S.*
- **Date:** June 27, 1997
- **Where:** Washington, D.C.
- **Significance:** In a legal challenge to the Brady Law, the Supreme Court struck down required background checks as beyond Congress's powers under the Tenth Amendment.

DOCUMENT

Printz v. U.S., 521 U.S. 898 (1997)

June 27, 1997, Decided

Justice Scalia delivered the opinion of the Court.

The question presented in these cases is whether certain interim provisions of the Brady Handgun Violence Prevention Act, Pub. L. 103–159, 107 Stat. 1536, commanding state and local law enforcement officers to conduct background checks on prospective handgun purchasers and to perform certain related tasks, violate the Constitution.

The Gun Control Act of 1968 (GCA), 18 U.S.C. S. 921 et seq., establishes a detailed federal scheme governing the distribution of firearms. It prohibits firearms dealers from transferring handguns to any person under 21, not resident in the dealer's State, or prohibited by state or local law from purchasing or possessing firearms, S. 922(b). It also forbids possession of a firearm by, and transfer of a firearm to, convicted felons, fugitives from justice, unlawful users of controlled substances, persons adjudicated as mentally defective or committed to mental institutions, aliens unlawfully present in the United States, persons dishonorably discharged from the Armed Forces, persons who have renounced their citizenship, and persons who have been subjected to certain restraining orders or been convicted of a misdemeanor offense involving domestic violence. S. 922(d) and (g).

In 1993, Congress amended the GCA by enacting the Brady Act. The Act requires the Attorney General to establish a national instant background check system by November 30, 1998, Pub. L. 103–159, as amended, Pub. L. 103–322, 103 Stat. 2074, note following 18 U.S.C. S. 922 and immediately puts in place certain interim provisions until that system becomes operative. Under the interim provisions, a firearms dealer who proposes to transfer a handgun must first: (1) receive from the transferee a statement (the Brady Form), S. 922(s)(1)(A) (i)(I), containing the name, address and date of birth of the proposed transferee along with a sworn statement that the transferee is not among any of the classes of prohibited purchasers, S. 922(s)(3); (2) verify the identity of the transferee by examining an identification document, S. 922(s)(1)(A)(i)(II); and (3) provide the "chief law enforcement officer" (CLEO) of the transferee's residence with notice of the contents (and a copy) of the Brady Form, S. 922(s)(1)(A)(i)(III) and (IV). With some exceptions, the dealer must then wait five business days before consummating the sale, unless the CLEO earlier notifies the dealer that he has no reason to believe the transfer would be illegal. S. 922(s)(1)(A)(ii).

The Brady Act creates two significant alternatives to the foregoing scheme. A dealer may sell a handgun immediately if the purchaser possesses a state handgun permit issued after a background check, S. 922(s)(1)(C), or if state law provides for an instant background check, S. 922(s)(1)(D). In States that have not rendered one of these alternatives applicable to all gun purchasers, CLEOs are required to perform certain duties. When a CLEO receives the required notice of a proposed transfer from the firearms dealer, the CLEO must "make a reasonable effort to ascertain within 5 business days whether receipt or possession would be in violation of the law, including research in whatever State and local recordkeeping systems are available and in a national system designated by the Attorney General." S. 922(s)(2). The Act does not require the CLEO to take any particular action if he determines that a pending transaction would be unlawful; he may notify the firearms dealer to that effect, but is not required to do so. If, however, the CLEO notifies a gun dealer that a prospective purchaser is ineligible to receive a handgun, he must, upon request, provide the would-be purchaser with a written statement of the reasons for that determination. S. 922(s)(6)(C). Moreover, if the CLEO does not discover any basis for objecting to the sale, he must destroy any records in his possession relating to the transfer, including his copy of the Brady Form. S. 922(s)(6)(B)(i). Under a separate provision of the GCA, any person who "knowingly violates [the section of the GCA amended by the Brady Act] shall be fined under this title, imprisoned for no more than 1 year, or both." S. 924(a)(5).

Petitioners Jay Printz and Richard Mack, the CLEOs for Ravalli County, Montana, and Graham County, Arizona, respectively, filed separate actions challenging the constitutionality of the Brady Act's interim provisions. In each case, the District Court held that the provision requiring CLEOs to perform background checks was unconstitutional, but concluded that that provision was severable from the remainder of the Act, effectively leaving a voluntary background check system in place. 856 F. Supp. 1372 (Ariz. 1994); 854 F. Supp. 1503 (Mont. 1994). A divided panel of the Court of

Appeals for the Ninth Circuit reversed, finding none of the Brady Act's interim provisions to be unconstitutional. 66 F. 3d 1025 (1995). We granted certiorari. . . .

[I]t is apparent that the Brady Act purports to direct state law enforcement officers to participate, albeit only temporarily, in the administration of a federally enacted regulatory scheme. Regulated firearms dealers are required to forward Brady Forms not to a federal officer or employee, but to the CLEOs, whose obligation to accept those forms is implicit in the duty imposed upon them to make "reasonable efforts" within five days to determine whether the sales reflected in the forms are lawful. While the CLEOs are subjected to no federal requirement that they prevent the sales determined to be unlawful (it is perhaps assumed that their state law duties will require prevention or apprehension), they are empowered to grant, in effect, waivers of the federally prescribed 5 day waiting period for handgun purchases by notifying the gun dealers that they have no reason to believe the transactions would be illegal.

The petitioners here object to being pressed into federal service, and contend that congressional action compelling state officers to execute federal laws is unconstitutional. Because there is no constitutional text speaking to this precise question, the answer to the CLEOs' challenge must be sought in historical understanding and practice, in the structure of the Constitution, and in the jurisprudence of this Court. . . .

The Constitution does not leave to speculation who is to administer the laws enacted by Congress; the President, it says, "shall take Care that the Laws be faithfully executed," Art. II, S. 3, personally and through officers whom he appoints (save for such inferior officers as Congress may authorize to be appointed by the "Courts of Law" or by "the Heads of Departments" who are themselves presidential appointees), Art. II, S. 2. The Brady Act effectively transfers this responsibility to thousands of CLEOs in the 50 States, who are left to implement the program without meaningful Presidential control. . . .

Congress cannot compel the States to enact or enforce a federal regulatory program. Today we hold that Congress cannot circumvent that prohibition by conscripting the State's officers directly. The Federal Government may neither issue directives requiring the States to address particular problems, nor command the States' officers, or those of their political subdivisions, to administer or enforce a federal regulatory program. It matters not whether policymaking is involved, and no case by case weighing of the burdens or benefits is necessary; such commands are fundamentally incompatible with our constitutional system of dual sovereignty. Accordingly, the judgment of the Court of Appeals for the Ninth Circuit is reversed.

It is so ordered. . . .

JUSTICE THOMAS, concurring.

The Court today properly holds that the Brady Act violates the Tenth Amendment in that it compels state law enforcement officers to "administer or enforce a federal regulatory program." See ante, at 25. Although I join the Court's opinion in full, I write separately to emphasize that the Tenth Amendment affirms the undeniable notion that under our Constitution, the Federal Government is one of enumerated, hence limited, powers. See, e.g., *McCulloch v. Maryland*, 4 Wheat. 316, 405 (1819) ("This government is acknowledged by all to be one of enumerated powers"). "[T]hat those limits may not be mistaken, or forgotten, the constitution is written." *Marbury v. Madison*, 1 Cranch 137, 176 (1803). Accordingly, the Federal Government may act only where the Constitution authorizes it to do so. Cf. *New York v. United States, 505 U.S. 144* (1992). . . .

Even if we construe Congress' authority to regulate interstate commerce to encompass those intrastate transactions that "substantially affect" interstate commerce, I question whether Congress can regulate the particular transactions at issue here. The Constitution, in addition to delegating certain enumerated powers to Congress, places whole areas outside the reach of Congress' regulatory authority. The First Amendment, for example, is fittingly celebrated for preventing Congress from "prohibiting the free exercise" of religion or "abridging the freedom of speech." The Second Amendment similarly appears to contain an express limitation on the government's authority. That Amendment provides: "[a] well regulated Militia, being necessary to the security of a free State, the right of the people to keep and bear arms, shall not be infringed." This Court has not had recent occasion to consider the nature of the substantive right safeguarded by the Second Amendment. If, however, the Second Amendment is read to confer a personal right to "keep and bear arms," a colorable argument exists that the Federal Government's regulatory scheme, at least as it pertains to the purely intrastate sale or possession of firearms, runs afoul of that Amendment's protections. As the parties did not raise this argument, however, we need not consider it here. Perhaps, at some future date, this Court will have the opportunity to determine whether Justice Story was correct when he wrote that the right to bear arms "has justly been considered, as the palladium of the liberties of a republic." 3 J. Story, Commentaries S.1890, p. 746 (1833). In the meantime, I join the Court's opinion striking down the challenged provisions of the Brady Act as inconsistent with the Tenth Amendment.

JUSTICE STEVENS, with whom JUSTICE SOUTER, JUSTICE GINSBERG, and JUSTICE BREYER join, dissenting.

When Congress exercises the powers delegated to it by the Constitution, it may impose affirmative obligations on executive and judicial officers of state and local governments as well as ordinary citizens. This conclusion is firmly supported by the text of the Constitution, the early history of the Nation, decisions of this Court, and a correct understanding of the basic structure of the Federal Government. . . .

The Brady Act was passed in response to what Congress described as an "epidemic of gun violence." H. R. Rep. No. 103–344, p. 8 (1993). The Act's legislative history notes that 15,377 Americans were murdered with firearms in 1992, and that 12,489 of these deaths were caused by handguns. Ibid. Congress expressed special concern that "[t]he level of firearm violence in this country is, by far, the highest among developed nations." Ibid. The partial solution contained in the Brady Act, a mandatory background check before a handgun may be purchased, has met with remarkable success. Between 1994 and 1996, approximately 6,600 firearm sales each month to potentially dangerous persons were prevented by Brady Act checks; over 70% of the rejected purchasers were convicted or indicted felons. See U.S. Dept. of Justice, Bureau of Justice Statistics Bulletin, A National Estimate: Presale Firearm Checks 1 (Feb. 1997). Whether or not the evaluation reflected in the enactment of the Brady Act is correct as to the extent of the danger and the efficacy of the legislation, the congressional decision surely warrants more respect than it is accorded in today's unprecedented decision.

The text of the Constitution provides a sufficient basis for a correct disposition of this case.

Article I, S. 8, grants the Congress the power to regulate commerce among the States. Putting to one side the revisionist views expressed by Justice Thomas in his concurring opinion in *United States v. Lopez, 514 U.S. 549, 584* (1995), there can be no question that that provision adequately supports the regulation of commerce in handguns effected by the Brady Act. Moreover, the additional grant of authority in that section of the Constitution "[t]o make all Laws which shall be necessary and proper for carrying into Execution the foregoing Powers" is surely adequate to support the temporary enlistment of local police officers in the process of identifying persons who should not be entrusted with the possession of handguns. In short, the affirmative delegation of power in Article I provides ample authority for the congressional enactment.

Unlike the First Amendment, which prohibits the enactment of a category of laws that would otherwise be authorized by Article I, the Tenth Amendment imposes no restriction on the exercise of delegated powers. Using language that plainly refers only to powers that are "not" delegated to Congress. . . .

The [Tenth] Amendment confirms the principle that the powers of the Federal Government are limited to those affirmatively granted by the Constitution, but it does not purport to limit the scope or the effectiveness of the exercise of powers that are delegated to Congress. . . .

The provision of the Brady Act that crosses the Court's newly defined constitutional threshold is more comparable to a statute requiring local police officers to report the identity of missing children to the Crime Control Center of the Department of Justice than to an offensive federal command to a sovereign state. If Congress believes that such a statute will benefit the people of the Nation, and serve the interests of cooperative federalism better than an enlarged federal bureaucracy, we should respect both its policy judgment and its appraisal of its constitutional power.

Accordingly, I respectfully dissent. . . .

SOURCE: http://caselaw.lp.findlaw.com/scripts/getcase.pl?navby=case&court=us&vol=521&page=898

ANALYSIS

The *Printz* case arose because of a challenge to its constitutionality by those opposed to this new national requirement that all handgun purchases would now be subject to a background check to determine if the prospective buyer had a criminal record or was mentally incompetent. Until this time, requirements varied widely from state to state; some states imposed no background checks at all, but others insisted on detailed checks.

As was true of many important Supreme Court cases in the 1990s and 2000s, the ruling in *Printz* reflected close and sharp divisions between the liberal and conservative justices of the court, as seen in its 5–4 vote split. In fact, this decision produced no less than six different opinions: the majority opinion, written by Justice Antonin Scalia; two concurring opinions; and three dissenting opinions. In striking down the provision of the Brady Law requiring local law enforcement officers to conduct background checks of prospective handgun buyers, the court majority concluded that Congress overstepped its power, concluding that law enforcement activities were primarily a state responsibility, and that Congress therefore could not impose such a requirement on behalf of a federal program. The court majority relied heavily on the Tenth Amendment, which says that "The powers not delegated to the United States by the Constitution, nor prohibited by it to the States, are reserved to the States respectively, or to the people."

The court's four-member minority held a more expansive definition of federal government power, arguing that Congress's power to regulate interstate commerce (a "delegated" power expressly given to Congress in Article I, sec. 8 of the Constitution) gave it ample authority to enlist local police assistance to impose greater control over the sale of handguns, and by extension to curb the illicit trafficking of handguns. Note that only this provision of the Brady Law was struck down. In addition, the basis for the court's action did not extend to any violation of the Second Amendment's right to bear arms. In his concurring opinion, however, Justice Clarence Thomas mentioned the Second Amendment in a passing comment (what is known as "dicta"—a comment in a decision that has no direct bearing on the court's ruling or reasoning) when he said that, even though the Second Amendment was not raised as an issue in the case by lawyers on either side, it could, if interpreted as providing a personal or individual right, have some bearing on laws like the Brady Law. Such side comments are often viewed as an invitation to raise such an issue in the future, and that is just what happened in the 2008 case of *D.C. v. Heller*. In the aftermath of the *Printz* decision, about half the states continued background checks because their state laws already required them. For the other states, the federal government asked local law enforcement to continue the practice voluntarily, and that is what occurred. In 1998, under the terms of the Brady Law, the background check process converted to a computerized instant check system that improved in speed and efficiency after some initial start-up problems. The instant checks now eliminate the need for local law enforcement to do such checks of prospective gun buyers by hand.

FURTHER READING

Spitzer, Robert J. *The Politics of Gun Control*. Washington, D.C.: CQ Press, 2007.

The Supreme Court Creates a New, Personal Right to Own Guns Under the Second Amendment

- *Document:* Supreme Court case of *D.C. v. Heller*
- *Date:* June 26, 2008
- *Where:* Washington, D.C.
- *Significance:* For the first time in American history, a federal court struck down a gun regulation as in violation of the Second Amendment, and ruled, also for the first time, that the Second Amendment protects an individual right to own guns for personal self-defense.

DOCUMENT

District of Columbia v. Heller, 554 U.S. ___ (2008)

Argued March 18, 2008—Decided June 26, 2008

Held:

1. The Second Amendment protects an individual right to possess a firearm unconnected with service in a militia, and to use that arm for traditionally lawful purposes, such as self-defense within the home. Pp. 2–53.
    (a) The Amendment's prefatory clause announces a purpose, but does not limit or expand the scope of the second part, the operative clause. The operative clause's text and history demonstrate that it connotes an individual right to keep and bear arms. Pp. 2–22.
    (b) The prefatory clause comports with the Court's interpretation of the operative clause. The "militia" comprised all males physically capable of acting in concert for the common defense. The Antifederalists feared

that the Federal Government would disarm the people in order to disable this citizens' militia, enabling a politicized standing army or a select militia to rule. The response was to deny Congress power to abridge the ancient right of individuals to keep and bear arms, so that the ideal of a citizens' militia would be preserved. Pp. 22–28.

(c) The Court's interpretation is confirmed by analogous arms-bearing rights in state constitutions that preceded and immediately followed the Second Amendment. Pp. 28–30.

(d) The Second Amendment's drafting history, while of dubious interpretive worth, reveals three state Second Amendment proposals that unequivocally referred to an individual right to bear arms. Pp. 30–32.

(e) Interpretation of the Second Amendment by scholars, courts and legislators, from immediately after its ratification through the late 19th century also supports the Court's conclusion. Pp. 32–47.

(f) None of the Court's precedents forecloses the Court's interpretation. Neither *United States* v. *Cruikshank*, 92 U.S. 542, 553, nor *Presser* v. *Illinois*, 116 U.S. 252, 264–265, refutes the individual-rights interpretation. *United States* v. *Miller*, 307 U.S. 174, does not limit the right to keep and bear arms to militia purposes, but rather limits the type of weapon to which the right applies to those used by the militia, *i.e.*, those in common use for lawful purposes. Pp. 47–54.

2. Like most rights, the Second Amendment right is not unlimited. It is not a right to keep and carry any weapon whatsoever in any manner whatsoever and for whatever purpose: For example, concealed weapons prohibitions have been upheld under the Amendment or state analogues. The Court's opinion should not be taken to cast doubt on longstanding prohibitions on the possession of firearms by felons and the mentally ill, or laws forbidding the carrying of firearms in sensitive places such as schools and government buildings, or laws imposing conditions and qualifications on the commercial sale of arms. *Miller*'s holding that the sorts of weapons protected are those "in common use at the time" finds support in the historical tradition of prohibiting the carrying of dangerous and unusual weapons. Pp. 54–56.

3. The handgun ban and the trigger-lock requirement (as applied to self-defense) violate the Second Amendment. The District's total ban on handgun possession in the home amounts to a prohibition on an entire class of "arms" that Americans overwhelmingly choose for the lawful purpose of self-defense. Under any of the standards of scrutiny the Court has applied to enumerated constitutional rights, this prohibition—in the place where the importance of the lawful defense of self, family, and property is most acute—would fail constitutional muster. Similarly, the requirement that any lawful firearm in the home be disassembled or bound by a trigger lock makes it impossible for citizens to use arms for the core lawful purpose of self-defense and is hence unconstitutional. Because Heller conceded at oral argument that the D.C. licensing law is permissible if it is not enforced arbitrarily and capriciously, the Court assumes that a license will satisfy his prayer for relief and does not address the licensing requirement. Assuming

he is not disqualified from exercising Second Amendment rights, the District must permit Heller to register his handgun and must issue him a license to carry it in the home. Pp. 56–64.

Justice Scalia delivered the opinion of the Court.

We consider whether a District of Columbia prohibition on the possession of usable handguns in the home violates the Second Amendment to the Constitution.

I

The District of Columbia generally prohibits the possession of handguns. It is a crime to carry an unregistered firearm, and the registration of handguns is prohibited. See D.C. Code §§7–2501.01(12), 7–2502.01(a), 7–2502.02(a)(4) (2001). Wholly apart from that prohibition, no person may carry a handgun without a license, but the chief of police may issue licenses for 1-year periods. See §§22–4504(a), 22–4506. District of Columbia law also requires residents to keep their lawfully owned firearms, such as registered long guns, "unloaded and dissembled or bound by a trigger lock or similar device" unless they are located in a place of business or are being used for lawful recreational activities. See §7–2507.02.

Respondent Dick Heller is a D.C. special police officer authorized to carry a handgun while on duty at the Federal Judicial Center. He applied for a registration certificate for a handgun that he wished to keep at home, but the District refused. He thereafter filed a lawsuit in the Federal District Court for the District of Columbia seeking, on Second Amendment grounds, to enjoin the city from enforcing the bar on the registration of handguns, the licensing requirement insofar as it prohibits the carrying of a firearm in the home without a license, and the trigger-lock requirement insofar as it prohibits the use of "functional firearms within the home." App. 59a. The District Court dismissed respondent's complaint, see *Parker v. District of Columbia*, 311 F. Supp. 2d 103, 109 (2004). The Court of Appeals for the District of Columbia Circuit, construing his complaint as seeking the right to render a firearm operable and carry it about his home in that condition only when necessary for self-defense, reversed, see *Parker v. District of Columbia*, 478 F. 3d 370, 401 (2007). It held that the Second Amendment protects an individual right to possess firearms and that the city's total ban on handguns, as well as its requirement that firearms in the home be kept nonfunctional even when necessary for self-defense, violated that right. See *id.*, at 395, 399–401. The Court of Appeals directed the District Court to enter summary judgment for respondent.

We granted certiorari. 552 U.S. ___ (2007).

II

We turn first to the meaning of the Second Amendment.

A

The Second Amendment provides: "A well regulated Militia, being necessary to the security of a free State, the right of the people to keep and bear Arms, shall not be infringed." In interpreting this text, we are guided by the principle that "[t]he Constitution was written to be understood by the voters; its words and phrases were used in their normal and ordinary as distinguished from technical meaning." *United States v. Sprague*, 282 U.S. 716, 731 (1931). . . . Normal meaning may of course include an idiomatic meaning, but it excludes secret or technical meanings that would not have been known to ordinary citizens in the founding generation.

The two sides in this case have set out very different interpretations of the Amendment. Petitioners and today's dissenting Justices believe that it protects only the right to possess and carry a firearm in connection with militia service. . . . Respondent argues that it protects an individual right to possess a firearm unconnected with service in a militia, and to use that arm for traditionally lawful purposes, such as self-defense within the home. . . .

The Second Amendment is naturally divided into two parts: its prefatory clause and its operative clause. The former does not limit the latter grammatically, but rather announces a purpose. The Amendment could be rephrased, "Because a well regulated Militia is necessary to the security of a free State, the right of the people to keep and bear Arms shall not be infringed." . . . Although this structure of the Second Amendment is unique in our Constitution, other legal documents of the founding era, particularly individual-rights provisions of state constitutions, commonly included a prefatory statement of purpose. . . .

Logic demands that there be a link between the stated purpose and the command. The Second Amendment would be nonsensical if it read, "A well regulated Militia, being necessary to the security of a free State, the right of the people to petition for redress of grievances shall not be infringed." That requirement of logical connection may cause a prefatory clause to resolve an ambiguity in the operative clause ("The separation of church and state being an important objective, the teachings of canons shall have no place in our jurisprudence." The preface makes clear that the operative clause refers not to canons of interpretation but to clergymen.) But apart from that clarifying function, a prefatory clause does not limit or expand the scope of the operative clause. . . .

1. Operative Clause.

a. **"Right of the People."** The first salient feature of the operative clause is that it codifies a "right of the people." The unamended Constitution and the Bill of Rights use the phrase "right of the people" two other times, in the First Amendment's Assembly-and-Petition Clause and in the Fourth Amendment's Search-and-Seizure Clause. The Ninth Amendment uses very similar terminology ("The enumeration in the Constitution, of certain rights, shall not be construed to deny or disparage others retained by the people"). All three of these instances unambiguously refer to individual rights, not "collective" rights, or rights that may be exercised only through participation in some corporate body.

Three provisions of the Constitution refer to "the people" in a context other than "rights"—the famous preamble ("We the people"), §2 of Article I (providing that "the people" will choose members of the House), and the Tenth Amendment (providing that those powers not given the Federal Government remain with "the States" or "the people"). Those provisions arguably refer to "the people" acting collectively—but they deal with the exercise or reservation of powers, not rights. Nowhere else in the Constitution does a "right" attributed to "the people" refer to anything other than an individual right.

What is more, in all six other provisions of the Constitution that mention "the people," the term unambiguously refers to all members of the political community, not an unspecified subset. . . .

This contrasts markedly with the phrase "the militia" in the prefatory clause. As we will describe below, the "militia" in colonial America consisted of a subset of "the people"—those who were male, able bodied, and within a certain age range. Reading the Second Amendment as protecting only the right to "keep and bear Arms" in an organized militia therefore fits poorly with the operative clause's description of the holder of that right as "the people."

We start therefore with a strong presumption that the Second Amendment right is exercised individually and belongs to all Americans.

b. **"Keep and bear Arms."** We move now from the holder of the right—"the people"—to the substance of the right: "to keep and bear Arms."

Before addressing the verbs "keep" and "bear," we interpret their object: "Arms." . . . The term was applied, then as now, to weapons that were not specifically designed for military use and were not employed in a military capacity. . . .

Some have made the argument, bordering on the frivolous, that only those arms in existence in the 18th century are protected by the Second Amendment. We do not interpret constitutional rights that way. Just as the First Amendment protects modern forms of communications . . . and the Fourth Amendment applies to modern forms of search . . . the Second Amendment extends, prima facie, to all instruments that constitute bearable arms, even those that were not in existence at the time of the founding.

We turn to the phrases "keep arms" and "bear arms." . . .

The phrase "keep arms" was not prevalent in the written documents of the founding period that we have found, but there are a few examples, all of which favor viewing the right to "keep Arms" as an individual right unconnected with militia service. . . . Petitioners point to militia laws of the founding period that required militia members to "keep" arms in connection with militia service, and they conclude from this that the phrase "keep Arms" has a militia-related connotation. . . . This is rather like saying that, since there are many statutes that authorize aggrieved employees to "file complaints" with federal agencies, the phrase "file complaints" has an employment-related connotation. "Keep arms" was simply a common way of referring to possessing arms, for militiamen *and everyone else*.

At the time of the founding, as now, to "bear" meant to "carry." . . . When used with "arms," however, the term has a meaning that refers to carrying for a particular purpose—confrontation. . . . Although the phrase implies that the carrying of the weapon is for the purpose of "offensive or defensive action," it in no way connotes participation in a structured military organization.

From our review of founding-era sources, we conclude that this natural meaning was also the meaning that "bear arms" had in the 18th century. In numerous instances, "bear arms" was unambiguously used to refer to the carrying of weapons outside of an organized militia. . . .

The phrase "bear Arms" also had at the time of the founding an idiomatic meaning that was significantly different from its natural meaning: "to serve as a soldier, do military service, fight" or "to wage war." See Linguists' Brief 18; *post*, at 11 (*Stevens*, J., dissenting). But it *unequivocally* bore that idiomatic meaning only when followed by the preposition "against," which was in turn followed by the target of the hostilities. . . .

In any event, the meaning of "bear arms" that petitioners and *Justice Stevens* propose is *not even* the (sometimes) idiomatic meaning. Rather, they manufacture a hybrid definition, whereby "bear arms" connotes the actual carrying of arms (and therefore is not really an idiom) but only in the service of an organized militia. No dictionary has ever adopted that definition, and we have been apprised of no source that indicates that it carried that meaning at the time of the founding. But it is easy to see why petitioners and the dissent are driven to the hybrid definition. Giving "bear Arms" its idiomatic meaning would cause the protected right to consist of the right to be a soldier or to wage war—an absurdity that no commentator has ever endorsed. . . .

Petitioners justify their limitation of "bear arms" to the military context by pointing out the unremarkable fact that it was often used in that context—the same mistake they made with respect to "keep arms." It is especially unremarkable that the phrase was often used in a military context in the federal legal sources (such as records of congressional debate) that have been the focus of petitioners' inquiry. Those sources would have had little occasion to use it *except* in discussions about the standing army and the militia. And the phrases used primarily in those military discussions include not only "bear arms" but also "carry arms," "possess arms," and "have arms"—though no one thinks that those *other* phrases also had special military meanings. . . .

Justice Stevens points to a study by *amici* supposedly showing that the phrase "bear arms" was most frequently used in the military context. . . . Of course, as we have said, the fact that the phrase was commonly used in a particular context does not show that it is limited to that context, and, in any event, we have given many sources where the phrase was used in nonmilitary contexts. Moreover, the study's collection appears to include (who knows how many times) the idiomatic phrase "bear arms against," which is irrelevant. The *amici* also dismiss examples such as bear arms . . . for the purpose of killing game'" because those uses are "expressly qualified." . . . That analysis is faulty. A purposive qualifying phrase that contradicts the word or phrase it modifies is unknown this side of the looking glass (except, apparently, in some courses on Linguistics). If "bear arms" means, as we think, simply the carrying of arms, a modifier can limit the purpose of the carriage ("for the purpose of self-defense" or "to make war against the King"). But if "bear arms" means, as the petitioners and the dissent think, the carrying of arms only for military purposes, one simply cannot add "for the purpose of killing game." The right "to carry arms in the militia for the purpose of killing game" is worthy of the mad hatter. Thus, these purposive qualifying phrases positively establish that "to bear arms" is not limited to military use.

Justice Stevens places great weight on James Madison's inclusion of a conscientious-objector clause in his original draft of the Second Amendment: "but no person religiously scrupulous of bearing arms, shall be compelled to render military service in person." Creating the Bill of Rights 12 (H. Veit, K. Bowling, & C. Bickford eds. 1991) (hereinafter Veit). He argues that this clause establishes that the drafters of the Second Amendment intended "bear Arms" to refer only to military service. See *post*, at 26. It is always perilous to derive the meaning of an adopted provision from another provision deleted in the drafting process. In any case, what *Justice Stevens* would conclude from the deleted provision does not follow. It was not meant to exempt from military service those who objected to going to war but had no scruples about personal gunfights. Quakers opposed the use of arms not just for militia service, but for any violent purpose whatsoever—so much so that Quaker frontiersmen were forbidden to use arms to defend their families, even though "[i]n such circumstances the temptation to seize a hunting rifle or knife in self-defense . . . must sometimes have been almost overwhelming." P. Brock, Pacifism in the United States 359 (1968). . . . Thus, the most natural interpretation of Madison's deleted text is that those opposed to carrying weapons for potential violent confrontation would not be "compelled to render military service," in which such carrying would be required.

Finally, *Justice Stevens* suggests that "keep and bear Arms" was some sort of term of art, presumably akin to "hue and cry" or "cease and desist." (This suggestion usefully evades the problem that there is no evidence whatsoever to support a military reading of "keep arms.") *Justice Stevens* believes that the unitary meaning of "keep and bear Arms" is established by the Second Amendment's calling it a "right" (singular) rather than "rights" (plural). . . . There is nothing to this. State constitutions of the founding period routinely grouped multiple (related) guarantees under a singular "right," and the First Amendment protects the "right [singular] of the people peaceably to assemble, and to petition the Government for a redress of grievances." . . . And even if "keep and bear Arms" were a unitary phrase, we find no evidence that it bore a military meaning. Although the phrase was not at all common (which would be unusual for a term of art), we have found instances of its use with a clearly nonmilitary connotation. . . .

    c. **Meaning of the Operative Clause.** Putting all of these textual elements together, we find that they guarantee the individual right to possess and carry weapons in case of confrontation. This meaning is strongly confirmed by the historical background of the Second Amendment. We look to this because it has always been widely understood that the Second Amendment, like the First and Fourth Amendments, codified a *pre-existing* right. The very text of the Second Amendment implicitly recognizes the pre-existence of the right and declares only that it "shall not be infringed." . . .

There seems to us no doubt, on the basis of both text and history, that the Second Amendment conferred an individual right to keep and bear arms. Of course the right was not unlimited, just as the First Amendment's right of free speech was not. . . . Thus, we do not read the Second Amendment to protect the right of citizens to carry arms for *any sort* of confrontation, just as we do not read the First Amendment to protect the right of citizens to speak for *any purpose*. Before turning to limitations upon the individual right, however, we must determine whether the prefatory clause of the Second Amendment comports with our interpretation of the operative clause.

2. Prefatory Clause.

The prefatory clause reads: "A well regulated Militia, being necessary to the security of a free State . . . ."

a. "Well-Regulated Militia." In *United States v. Miller,* 307 U.S. 174, 179 (1939), we explained that "the Militia comprised all males physically capable of acting in concert for the common defense." That definition comports with founding-era sources. . . .

Petitioners take a seemingly narrower view of the militia, stating that "[m]ilitias are the state- and congressionally-regulated military forces described in the Militia Clauses (art. I, §8, cls. 15–16)." . . . Although we agree with petitioners' interpretive assumption that "militia" means the same thing in Article I and the Second Amendment, we believe that petitioners identify the wrong thing, namely, the organized militia. Unlike armies and navies, which Congress is given the power to create ("to raise . . . Armies"; "to provide . . . a Navy," Art. I, §8, cls. 12–13), the militia is assumed by Article I already to be *in existence.* Congress is given the power to "provide for calling forth the militia," §8, cl. 15; and the power not to create, but to "organiz[e]" it—and not to organize "a" militia, which is what one would expect if the militia were to be a federal creation, but to organize "the" militia, connoting a body already in existence, *ibid.,* cl. 16. This is fully consistent with the ordinary definition of the militia as all able-bodied men. From that pool, Congress has plenary power to organize the units that will make up an effective fighting force. That is what Congress did in the first militia Act, which specified that "each and every free able-bodied white male citizen of the respective states, resident therein, who is or shall be of the age of eighteen years, and under the age of forty-five years (except as is herein after excepted) shall severally and respectively be enrolled in the militia." Act of May 8, 1792, 1 Stat. 271. To be sure, Congress need not conscript every able-bodied man into the militia, because nothing in Article I suggests that in exercising its power to organize, discipline, and arm the militia, Congress must focus upon the entire body. Although the militia consists of all able-bodied men, the federally organized militia may consist of a subset of them.

Finally, the adjective "well-regulated" implies nothing more than the imposition of proper discipline and training. . . .

3. Relationship between Prefatory Clause and Operative Clause

We reach the question, then: Does the preface fit with an operative clause that creates an individual right to keep and bear arms? It fits perfectly, once one knows the history that the founding generation knew and that we have described above. . . .

The debate with respect to the right to keep and bear arms, as with other guarantees in the Bill of Rights, was not over whether it was desirable (all agreed that it was) but over whether it needed to be codified in the Constitution. During the 1788 ratification debates, the fear that the federal government would disarm the people in order to impose rule through a standing army or select militia was pervasive in Antifederalist rhetoric. . . .

It is therefore entirely sensible that the Second Amendment's prefatory clause announces the purpose for which the right was codified: to prevent elimination of the militia. The prefatory clause does not suggest that preserving the militia was the only reason Americans valued the ancient right; most undoubtedly thought it even more important for self-defense and hunting. But the threat that the new Federal Government would destroy the citizens' militia by taking away their arms was the reason that right—unlike some other English rights—was codified in a written Constitution. *Justice Breyer's* assertion that individual self-defense is merely a "subsidiary interest" of the right to keep and bear arms, see *post*, at 36, is profoundly mistaken. He bases that assertion solely upon the prologue—but that can only show that self-defense had little to do with the right's *codification;* it was the *central component* of the right itself.

Besides ignoring the historical reality that the Second Amendment was not intended to lay down a "novel principl[e]" but rather codified a right "inherited from our English ancestors," *Robertson v. Baldwin*, 165 U.S. 275, 281 (1897), petitioners' interpretation does not even achieve the narrower purpose that prompted codification of the right. If, as they believe, the Second Amendment right is no more than the right to keep and use weapons as a member of an organized militia, see Brief for Petititioners 8—if, that is, the *organized* militia is the sole institutional beneficiary of the Second Amendment's guarantee—it does not assure the existence of a "citizens' militia" as a safeguard against tyranny. For Congress retains plenary authority to organize the militia, which must include the authority to say who will belong to the organized force. That is why the first Militia Act's requirement that only whites enroll caused States to amend their militia laws to exclude free blacks. . . . Thus, if petitioners are correct, the Second Amendment protects citizens' right to use a gun in an organization from which Congress has plenary authority to exclude them. It guarantees a select militia of the sort the Stuart kings found useful, but not the people's militia that was the concern of the founding generation. . . .

Justice Stevens places overwhelming reliance upon this Court's decision in *United States v. Miller*, 307 U.S. 174 (1939). "[H]undreds of judges," we are told, "have relied on the view of the amendment we endorsed there," *post*, at 2, and "[e]ven if the textual and historical arguments on both side of the issue were evenly balanced, respect for the well-settled views of all of our predecessors on this Court, and for the rule of law itself . . . would prevent most jurists from endorsing such a dramatic upheaval in the law," *post*, at 4. And what is, according to *Justice Stevens*, the holding of *Miller* that demands such obeisance? That the Second Amendment "protects the right to keep and bear arms for certain military purposes, but that it does not curtail the legislature's power to regulate the nonmilitary use and ownership of weapons." *Post*, at 2.

Nothing so clearly demonstrates the weakness of *Justice Stevens'* case. *Miller* did not hold that and cannot possibly be read to have held that. The judgment in the case upheld against a Second Amendment challenge two men's federal convictions for transporting an unregistered short-barreled shotgun in interstate commerce, in violation of the National Firearms Act, 48 Stat. 1236. It is entirely clear that the Court's basis for saying that the Second Amendment did not apply was *not* that the defendants were "bear[ing] arms" not "for . . . military purposes" but for "nonmilitary use," *post*, at 2. Rather, it was that the *type of weapon at issue* was not eligible for Second Amendment protection: "In the absence of any evidence tending to show that the possession or use of a [short-barreled shotgun] at this time has some reasonable relationship to the preservation or efficiency of a well regulated militia, we cannot say that the Second

Amendment guarantees the right to keep and bear *such an instrument*." 307 U.S., at 178 (emphasis added). "Certainly," the Court continued, "it is not within judicial notice that this weapon is any part of the ordinary military equipment or that its use could contribute to the common defense." *Ibid*. Beyond that, the opinion provided no explanation of the content of the right.

This holding is not only consistent with, but positively suggests, that the Second Amendment confers an individual right to keep and bear arms (though only arms that "have some reasonable relationship to the preservation or efficiency of a well regulated militia"). Had the Court believed that the Second Amendment protects only those serving in the militia, it would have been odd to examine the character of the weapon rather than simply note that the two crooks were not militiamen. *Justice Stevens* can say again and again that *Miller* did "not turn on the difference between muskets and sawed-off shotguns, it turned, rather, on the basic difference between the military and nonmilitary use and possession of guns," *post*, at 42–43, but the words of the opinion prove otherwise. The most *Justice Stevens* can plausibly claim for *Miller* is that it declined to decide the nature of the Second Amendment right, despite the Solicitor General's argument (made in the alternative) that the right was collective. . . . *Miller* stands only for the proposition that the Second Amendment right, whatever its nature, extends only to certain types of weapons. . . .

We may as well consider at this point (for we will have to consider eventually) *what* types of weapons *Miller* permits. Read in isolation, *Miller*'s phrase "part of ordinary military equipment" could mean that only those weapons useful in warfare are protected. That would be a startling reading of the opinion, since it would mean that the National Firearms Act's restrictions on machineguns (not challenged in *Miller*) might be unconstitutional, machineguns being useful in warfare in 1939. We think that *Miller*'s "ordinary military equipment" language must be read in tandem with what comes after: "[O]rdinarily when called for [militia] service [able-bodied] men were expected to appear bearing arms supplied by themselves and of the kind in common use at the time." 307 U.S., at 179. The traditional militia was formed from a pool of men bringing arms "in common use at the time" for lawful purposes like self-defense. "In the colonial and revolutionary war era, [small-arms] weapons used by militiamen and weapons used in defense of person and home were one and the same." *State v. Kessler*, 289 Ore. 359, 368, 614 P. 2d 94, 98 (1980) (citing G. Neumann, Swords and Blades of the American Revolution 6–15, 252–254 (1973)). Indeed, that is precisely the way in which the Second Amendment's operative clause furthers the purpose announced in its preface. We therefore read *Miller* to say only that the Second Amendment does not protect those weapons not typically possessed by law-abiding citizens for lawful purposes, such as short-barreled shotguns. That accords with the historical understanding of the scope of the right. . . .

III

Like most rights, the right secured by the Second Amendment is not unlimited. . . . Although we do not undertake an exhaustive historical analysis today of the full scope of the Second Amendment, nothing in our opinion should be taken to cast doubt on longstanding prohibitions on the possession of firearms by felons and the mentally ill, or laws forbidding the carrying of firearms in sensitive places such as schools and government buildings, or laws imposing conditions and qualifications on the commercial sale of arms. . . .

IV

We turn finally to the law at issue here. As we have said, the law totally bans handgun possession in the home. It also requires that any lawful firearm in the home be disassembled or bound by a trigger lock at all times, rendering it inoperable.

As the quotations earlier in this opinion demonstrate, the inherent right of self-defense has been central to the Second Amendment right. The handgun ban amounts to a prohibition of an entire class of "arms" that is overwhelmingly chosen by American society for that lawful purpose. The prohibition extends, moreover, to the home, where the need for defense of self, family, and property is most acute. Under any of the standards of scrutiny that we have applied to enumerated constitutional rights, banning from the home "the most preferred firearm in the nation to 'keep' and use for protection of one's home and family," 478 F. 3d, at 400, would fail constitutional muster. . . .

It is no answer to say, as petitioners do, that it is permissible to ban the possession of handguns so long as the possession of other firearms (*i.e.*, long guns) is allowed. It is enough to note, as we have observed, that the American people have considered the handgun to be the quintessential self-defense weapon. There are many reasons that a citizen may prefer a handgun for home defense: It is easier to store in a location that is readily accessible in an emergency; it cannot easily be redirected or wrestled away by an attacker; it is easier to use for those without the upper-body strength to lift and aim a long gun; it can be pointed at a burglar with one hand while the other hand dials the police. Whatever the reason, handguns are the most popular weapon chosen by Americans for self-defense in the home, and a complete prohibition of their use is invalid.

We must also address the District's requirement (as applied to respondent's handgun) that firearms in the home be rendered and kept inoperable at all times. This makes it impossible for citizens to use them for the core lawful purpose of self-defense and is hence unconstitutional. The District argues that we should interpret this element of the statute to contain an exception for self-defense. See Brief for Petitioners 56–57. But we think that is precluded by the unequivocal text, and by the presence of certain other enumerated exceptions: "Except for law enforcement personnel . . . , each registrant shall keep any firearm in his possession unloaded and disassembled or bound by a trigger lock or similar device unless such firearm is kept at his place of business, or while being used for lawful recreational purposes within the District of Columbia." D.C. Code §7–2507.02. . . .

In sum, we hold that the District's ban on handgun possession in the home violates the Second Amendment, as does its prohibition against rendering any lawful firearm in the home operable for the purpose of immediate self-defense. Assuming that Heller is not disqualified from the exercise of Second Amendment rights, the District must permit him to register his handgun and must issue him a license to carry it in the home.

We are aware of the problem of handgun violence in this country, and we take seriously the concerns raised by the many *amici* who believe that prohibition of handgun ownership is a solution. The Constitution leaves the District of Columbia a variety of tools for combating that problem, including some measures regulating handguns, see *supra*, at 54–55, and n. 26. But the enshrinement of constitutional rights necessarily takes certain policy choices off the table. These include the absolute prohibition of handguns held and used for self-defense in the home. Undoubtedly some think that the Second Amendment is outmoded in a society where our standing army is the pride of our Nation, where well-trained police forces provide personal security, and where gun violence is a serious problem. That is perhaps debatable, but what is not debatable is that it is not the role of this Court to pronounce the Second Amendment extinct.

We affirm the judgment of the Court of Appeals.

It is so ordered. . . .

Justice Stevens, with whom *Justice Souter, Justice Ginsburg,* and *Justice Breyer* join, dissenting.

The question presented by this case is not whether the Second Amendment protects a "collective right" or an "individual right." Surely it protects a right that can be enforced by individuals. But a conclusion that the Second Amendment protects an individual right does not tell us anything about the scope of that right.

Guns are used to hunt, for self-defense, to commit crimes, for sporting activities, and to perform military duties. The Second Amendment plainly does not protect the right to use a gun to rob a bank; it is equally clear that it *does* encompass the right to use weapons for certain military purposes. Whether it also protects the right to possess and use guns for nonmilitary purposes like hunting and personal self-defense is the question presented by this case. The text of the Amendment, its history, and our decision in *United States v. Miller,* 307 U.S. 174 (1939), provide a clear answer to that question.

The Second Amendment was adopted to protect the right of the people of each of the several States to maintain a well-regulated militia. It was a response to concerns raised during the ratification of the Constitution that the power of Congress to disarm the state militias and create a national standing army posed an intolerable threat to the sovereignty of the several States. Neither the text of the Amendment nor the arguments advanced by its proponents evidenced the slightest interest in limiting any legislature's authority to regulate private civilian uses of firearms. Specifically, there is no indication that the Framers of the Amendment intended to enshrine the common-law right of self-defense in the Constitution.

In 1934, Congress enacted the National Firearms Act, the first major federal firearms law. Upholding a conviction under that Act, this Court held that, "[i]n the absence of any evidence tending to show that possession or use of a 'shotgun having a barrel of less than eighteen inches in length' at this time has some reasonable relationship to the preservation or efficiency of a well regulated militia, we cannot say that the Second Amendment guarantees the right to keep and bear such an instrument."

Miller, 307 U.S., at 178. The view of the Amendment we took in *Miller*—that it protects the right to keep and bear arms for certain military purposes, but that it does not curtail the Legislature's power to regulate the nonmilitary use and ownership of weapons—is both the most natural reading of the Amendment's text and the interpretation most faithful to the history of its adoption.

Since our decision in *Miller*, hundreds of judges have relied on the view of the Amendment we endorsed there; we ourselves affirmed it in 1980. See *Lewis v. United States*, 445 U.S. 55, 65–66, n.8 (1980). No new evidence has surfaced since 1980 supporting the view that the Amendment was intended to curtail the power of Congress to regulate civilian use or misuse of weapons. Indeed, a review of the drafting history of the Amendment demonstrates that its Framers *rejected* proposals that would have broadened its coverage to include such uses.

The opinion the Court announces today fails to identify any new evidence supporting the view that the Amendment was intended to limit the power of Congress to regulate civilian uses of weapons. Unable to point to any such evidence, the Court stakes its holding on a strained and unpersuasive reading of the Amendment's text; significantly different provisions in the 1689 English Bill of Rights, and in various 19th-century State Constitutions; postenactment commentary that was available to the Court when it decided *Miller*; and, ultimately, a feeble attempt to distinguish *Miller* that places more emphasis on the Court's decisional process than on the reasoning in the opinion itself.

Even if the textual and historical arguments on both sides of the issue were evenly balanced, respect for the well-settled views of all of our predecessors on this Court, and for the rule of law itself . . . would prevent most jurists from endorsing such a dramatic upheaval in the law. . . .

I

The text of the Second Amendment is brief. It provides: "A well regulated Militia, being necessary to the security of a free State, the right of the people to keep and bear Arms, shall not be infringed."

Three portions of that text merit special focus: the introductory language defining the Amendment's purpose, the class of persons encompassed within its reach, and the unitary nature of the right that it protects.

"A Well Regulated Militia, Being Necessary to the Security of a Free State"

The preamble to the Second Amendment makes three important points. It identifies the preservation of the militia as the Amendment's purpose; it explains that the militia is necessary to the security of a free State; and it recognizes that the militia must be "well regulated." In all three respects it is comparable to provisions in several State Declarations of Rights that were adopted roughly contemporaneously with the Declaration of Independence. Those state provisions highlight the importance members of the founding generation attached to the maintenance of state militias; they also underscore the profound fear shared by many in that era of the dangers posed by standing armies. While the need for state militias has not been a matter of significant public interest for almost two centuries, that fact should not obscure the contemporary concerns that animated the Framers.

The parallels between the Second Amendment and these state declarations, and the Second Amendment's omission of any statement of purpose related to the right to use firearms for hunting or personal self-defense, is especially striking in light of the fact that the Declarations of Rights of Pennsylvania and Vermont *did* expressly protect such civilian uses at the time. . . . It confirms that the Framers' single-minded focus in crafting the constitutional guarantee "to keep and bear arms" was on military uses of firearms, which they viewed in the context of service in state militias.

The preamble thus both sets forth the object of the Amendment and informs the meaning of the remainder of its text. Such text should not be treated as mere surplusage, for "[i]t cannot be presumed that any clause in the constitution is intended to be without effect." *Marbury v. Madison*, 1 Cranch 137, 174 (1803).

The Court today tries to denigrate the importance of this clause of the Amendment by beginning its analysis with the Amendment's operative provision and returning to the preamble merely "to ensure that our reading of the operative clause is consistent with the announced purpose." *Ante*, at 5. That is not how this Court ordinarily reads such texts, and it is not how the preamble would have been viewed at the time the Amendment was adopted. While the Court makes the novel suggestion that it need only find some "logical connection" between the preamble and the operative provision, it does acknowledge that a prefatory clause may resolve an ambiguity in the text. *Ante*, at 4. Without identifying any language in the text that even mentions civilian uses of firearms, the Court proceeds to "find" its preferred reading in what is at best an ambiguous text, and then concludes that its reading is not foreclosed by the preamble. Perhaps the Court's approach to the text is acceptable advocacy, but it is surely an unusual approach for judges to follow.

"The Right of the People"

The centerpiece of the Court's textual argument is its insistence that the words "the people" as used in the Second Amendment must have the same meaning, and protect the same class of individuals, as when they are used in the First and Fourth Amendments. According to the Court, in all three provisions—as well as the Constitution's preamble, section 2 of Article I, and the Tenth Amendment—"the term unambiguously refers to all members of the political community, not an unspecified subset." *Ante*, at 6. But the Court *itself* reads the Second Amendment to protect a "subset" significantly narrower than the class of persons protected by the First and Fourth Amendments; when it finally drills down on the substantive meaning of the Second Amendment, the Court limits the protected class to "law-abiding, responsible citizens," *ante*, at 63. But the class of persons protected by the First and Fourth Amendments is *not* so limited; for even felons (and presumably irresponsible citizens as well) may invoke the protections of those constitutional provisions. The Court offers no way to harmonize its conflicting pronouncements.

The Court also overlooks the significance of the way the Framers used the phrase "the people" in these constitutional provisions. In the First Amendment, no words define the class of individuals entitled to speak, to publish, or to worship; in that

Amendment it is only the right peaceably to assemble, and to petition the Government for a redress of grievances, that is described as a right of "the people." These rights contemplate collective action. While the right peaceably to assemble protects the individual rights of those persons participating in the assembly, its concern is with action engaged in by members of a group, rather than any single individual. Likewise, although the act of petitioning the Government is a right that can be exercised by individuals, it is primarily collective in nature. For if they are to be effective, petitions must involve groups of individuals acting in concert.

Similarly, the words "the people" in the Second Amendment refer back to the object announced in the Amendment's preamble. They remind us that it is the collective action of individuals having a duty to serve in the militia that the text directly protects and, perhaps more importantly, that the ultimate purpose of the Amendment was to protect the States' share of the divided sovereignty created by the Constitution. . . .

"To Keep and Bear Arms"

Although the Court's discussion of these words treats them as two "phrases"—as if they read "to keep" and "to bear"—they describe a unitary right: to possess arms if needed for military purposes and to use them in conjunction with military activities. . . .

The term "bear arms" is a familiar idiom; when used unadorned by any additional words, its meaning is "to serve as a soldier, do military service, fight." 1 Oxford English Dictionary 634 (2d ed. 1989). It is derived from the Latin *arma ferre*, which, translated literally, means "to bear *[ferre]* war equipment *[arma]*." . . . Had the Framers wished to expand the meaning of the phrase "bear arms" to encompass civilian possession and use, they could have done so by the addition of phrases such as "for the defense of themselves," as was done in the Pennsylvania and Vermont Declarations of Rights. The *unmodified* use of "bear arms," by contrast, refers most naturally to a military purpose, as evidenced by its use in literally dozens of contemporary texts. The absence of any reference to civilian uses of weapons tailors the text of the Amendment to the purpose identified in its preamble. But when discussing these words, the Court simply ignores the preamble.

The Court argues that a "qualifying phrase that contradicts the word or phrase it modifies is unknown this side of the looking glass." *Ante*, at 15. But this fundamentally fails to grasp the point. The stand-alone phrase "bear arms" most naturally conveys a military meaning *unless* the addition of a qualifying phrase signals that a different meaning is intended. When, as in this case, there is no such qualifier, the most natural meaning is the military one; and, in the absence of any qualifier, it is all the more appropriate to look to the preamble to confirm the natural meaning of the text. The Court's objection is particularly puzzling in light of its own contention that the addition of the modifier "against" changes the meaning of "bear arms." . . .

The Amendment's use of the term "keep" in no way contradicts the military meaning conveyed by the phrase "bear arms" and the Amendment's preamble. To the contrary, a number of state militia laws in effect at the time of the Second Amendment's drafting used the term "keep" to describe the requirement that militia members store their arms at their homes, ready to be used for service when necessary. . . . "[K]eep and bear arms" thus perfectly describes the responsibilities of a framing-era militia member.

This reading is confirmed by the fact that the clause protects only one right, rather than two. It does not describe a right "to keep arms" and a separate right "to bear arms." Rather, the single right that it does describe is both a duty and a right to have arms available and ready for military service, and to use them for military purposes when necessary. . . .

When each word in the text is given full effect, the Amendment is most naturally read to secure to the people a right to use and possess arms in conjunction with service in a well-regulated militia. So far as appears, no more than that was contemplated by its drafters or is encompassed within its terms. Even if the meaning of the text were genuinely susceptible to more than one interpretation, the burden would remain on those advocating a departure from the purpose identified in the preamble and from settled law to come forward with persuasive new arguments or evidence. The textual analysis offered by respondent and embraced by the Court falls far short of sustaining that heavy burden. And the Court's emphatic reliance on the claim "that the Second Amendment . . . codified a *pre-existing* right," *ante*, at 19, is of course beside the point because the right to keep and bear arms for service in a state militia was also a pre-existing right.

Indeed, not a word in the constitutional text even arguably supports the Court's overwrought and novel description of the Second Amendment as "elevat[ing] above all other interests" "the right of law-abiding, responsible citizens to use arms in defense of hearth and home." *Ante*, at 63. . . .

With all of these sources upon which to draw, it is strikingly significant that Madison's first draft omitted any mention of nonmilitary use or possession of weapons. Rather, his original draft repeated the essence of the two proposed amendments sent by Virginia, combining the substance of the two provisions succinctly into one, which read: "The right of the people to keep and bear arms shall not be infringed; a well armed, and well regulated militia being the best security of a free country; but no person religiously scrupulous of bearing arms, shall be compelled to render military service in person." Cogan 169.

Madison's decision to model the Second Amendment on the distinctly military Virginia proposal is therefore revealing, since it is clear that he considered and rejected formulations that would have unambiguously protected civilian uses of firearms. When Madison prepared his first draft, and when that draft was debated and modified, it is reasonable to assume that all participants in the drafting process were fully aware of the other formulations that would have protected civilian use and possession of weapons and that their choice to craft the Amendment as they did represented a rejection of those alternative formulations.

Madison's initial inclusion of an exemption for conscientious objectors sheds revelatory light on the purpose of the Amendment. It confirms an intent to describe a duty as well as a right, and it unequivocally identifies the military character of both. The objections voiced to the conscientious-objector clause only confirm the central meaning of the text. Although records of the debate in the Senate, which is where the conscientious-objector clause was removed, do not survive, the arguments raised in the House illuminate the perceived problems with the clause: Specifically, there was concern that Congress "can declare who are those religiously scrupulous, and prevent them from bearing arms." The ultimate removal of the clause, therefore, only serves to confirm the purpose of the Amendment—to protect against congressional disarmament, by whatever means, of the States' militias.

The Court also contends that because "Quakers opposed the use of arms not just for militia service, but for any violent purpose whatsoever," *ante,* at 17, the inclusion of a conscientious-objector clause in the original draft of the Amendment does not support the conclusion that the phrase "bear arms" was military in meaning. But that claim cannot be squared with the record. In the proposals cited *supra,* at 21–22, both Virginia and North Carolina included the following language: "That any person religiously scrupulous of bearing arms ought to be exempted, upon payment of an equivalent *to employ another to bear arms in his stead*" (emphasis added).http:// caselaw.lp.findlaw.com/scripts/getcase.pl?court=US&navby=case&vol=000&invol= 07–290—FNdissent1.26 There is no plausible argument that the use of "bear arms" in those provisions was not unequivocally and exclusively military: The State simply does not compel its citizens to carry arms for the purpose of private "confrontation," *ante,* at 10, or for self-defense.

The history of the adoption of the Amendment thus describes an overriding concern about the potential threat to state sovereignty that a federal standing army would pose, and a desire to protect the States' militias as the means by which to guard against that danger. But state militias could not effectively check the prospect of a federal standing army so long as Congress retained the power to disarm them, and so a guarantee against such disarmament was needed. As we explained in *Miller:* "With obvious purpose to assure the continuation and render possible the effectiveness of such forces the declaration and guarantee of the Second Amendment were made. It must be interpreted and applied with that end in view." 307 U.S., at 178. The evidence plainly refutes the claim that the Amendment was motivated by the Framers' fears that Congress might act to regulate any civilian uses of weapons. And even if the historical record were genuinely ambiguous, the burden would remain on the parties advocating a change in the law to introduce facts or arguments "newly ascertained," *Vasquez,* 474 U.S., at 266; the Court is unable to identify any such facts or arguments. . . .

Perhaps in recognition of the weakness of its attempt to distinguish *Miller,* the Court argues in the alternative that *Miller* should be discounted because of its decisional history. It is true that the appellee in *Miller* did not file a brief or make an appearance, although the court below had held that the relevant provision of the National Firearms Act violated the Second Amendment (albeit without any reasoned opinion). But, as our decision in *Marbury v. Madison,* 1 Cranch 137, in which only one side appeared and presented arguments, demonstrates, the absence of adversarial presentation alone is not a basis for refusing to accord *stare decisis* effect to a decision of this Court. . . .

The Court is simply wrong when it intones that *Miller* contained *"not a word"* about the Amendment's history. *Ante,* at 52. The Court plainly looked to history to construe the term "Militia," and, on the best reading of *Miller,* the entire guarantee of the Second Amendment. . . .

The majority cannot seriously believe that the *Miller* Court did not consider any relevant evidence; the majority simply does not approve of the conclusion the *Miller*

Court reached on that evidence. Standing alone, that is insufficient reason to disregard a unanimous opinion of this Court, upon which substantial reliance has been placed by legislators and citizens for nearly 70 years.

V

The Court concludes its opinion by declaring that it is not the proper role of this Court to change the meaning of rights "enshrine[d]" in the Constitution. *Ante,* at 64. But the right the Court announces was not "enshrined" in the Second Amendment by the Framers; it is the product of today's law-changing decision. The majority's exegesis has utterly failed to establish that as a matter of text or history, "the right of law-abiding, responsible citizens to use arms in defense of hearth and home" is "elevate[d] above all other interests" by the Second Amendment. *Ante,* at 64.

Until today, it has been understood that legislatures may regulate the civilian use and misuse of firearms so long as they do not interfere with the preservation of a well-regulated militia. The Court's announcement of a new constitutional right to own and use firearms for private purposes upsets that settled understanding, but leaves for future cases the formidable task of defining the scope of permissible regulations. Today judicial craftsmen have confidently asserted that a policy choice that denies a "law-abiding, responsible citize[n]" the right to keep and use weapons in the home for self-defense is "off the table." *Ante,* at 64. Given the presumption that most citizens are law abiding, and the reality that the need to defend oneself may suddenly arise in a host of locations outside the home, I fear that the District's policy choice may well be just the first of an unknown number of dominoes to be knocked off the table. . . .

The Court properly disclaims any interest in evaluating the wisdom of the specific policy choice challenged in this case, but it fails to pay heed to a far more important policy choice—the choice made by the Framers themselves. The Court would have us believe that over 200 years ago, the Framers made a choice to limit the tools available to elected officials wishing to regulate civilian uses of weapons, and to authorize this Court to use the common-law process of case-by-case judicial lawmaking to define the contours of acceptable gun control policy. Absent compelling evidence that is nowhere to be found in the Court's opinion, I could not possibly conclude that the Framers made such a choice.

For these reasons, I respectfully dissent. . . .

Justice Breyer, with whom *Justice Stevens, Justice Souter,* and *Justice Ginsburg* join, dissenting. . . .

I

The majority's conclusion is wrong for two independent reasons. The first reason is that set forth by *Justice Stevens*—namely, that the Second Amendment protects militia-related, not self-defense-related, interests. These two interests are sometimes intertwined. To assure 18th-century citizens that they could keep arms for militia purposes would necessarily have allowed them to keep arms that they could have used for self-defense as well. But self-defense alone, detached from any militia-related objective, is not the Amendment's concern.

The second independent reason is that the protection the Amendment provides is not absolute. The Amendment permits government to regulate the interests that it serves. Thus, irrespective of what those interests are—whether they do or do not include an independent interest in self-defense—the majority's view cannot be correct unless it can show that the District's regulation is unreasonable or inappropriate in Second Amendment terms. This the majority cannot do.

In respect to the first independent reason, I agree with *Justice Stevens*, and I join his opinion. In this opinion I shall focus upon the second reason. I shall show that the District's law is consistent with the Second Amendment even if that Amendment is interpreted as protecting a wholly separate interest in individual self-defense. That is so because the District's regulation, which focuses upon the presence of handguns in high-crime urban areas, represents a permissible legislative response to a serious, indeed life-threatening, problem. . . .

A

No one doubts the constitutional importance of the statute's basic objective, saving lives. . . . But there is considerable debate about whether the District's statute helps to achieve that objective. I begin by reviewing the statute's tendency to secure that objective from the perspective of (1) the legislature (namely, the Council of the District of Columbia) that enacted the statute in 1976, and (2) a court that seeks to evaluate the Council's decision today.

1

First, consider the facts as the legislature saw them when it adopted the District statute. As stated by the local council committee that recommended its adoption, the major substantive goal of the District's handgun restriction is "to reduce the potentiality for gun-related crimes and gun-related deaths from occurring within the District of Columbia." Hearing and Disposition before the House Committee on the District of Columbia, 94th Cong., 2d Sess., on H. Con. Res. 694, Ser. No. 94–24, p. 25 (1976) (hereinafter DC Rep.). The committee concluded, on the basis of "extensive public hearings" and "lengthy research," that "[t]he easy availability of firearms in the United States has been a major factor contributing to the drastic increase in gun-related violence and crime over the past 40 years." *Id.*, at 24, 25. It reported to the Council "startling statistics," *id.*, at 26, regarding gun-related crime, accidents, and deaths, focusing particularly on the relation between handguns and crime and the proliferation of handguns within the District. See *id.*, at 25–26.

The committee informed the Council that guns were "responsible for 69 deaths in this country each day," for a total of "[a]pproximately 25,000 gun-deaths . . . each year," along with an additional 200,000 gun-related injuries. *Id.*, at 25. Three thousand of these deaths, the report stated, were accidental. *Ibid.* A quarter of the victims in those accidental deaths were children under the age of 14. *Ibid.* And according to the committee, "[f]or every intruder stopped by a homeowner with a firearm, there are 4 gun-related accidents within the home." *Ibid.*

In respect to local crime, the committee observed that there were 285 murders in the District during 1974—a record number. *Id.*, at 26. The committee also stated that, "[c]ontrary to popular opinion on the subject, firearms are more frequently involved in deaths and violence among relatives and friends than in premeditated criminal activities." *Ibid.* Citing an article from the American Journal of Psychiatry, the committee reported that "[m]ost murders are committed by previously law-abiding citizens, in situations where spontaneous violence is generated by anger, passion or intoxication, and where the killer and victim are acquainted." *Ibid.* "Twenty-five percent of these murders," the committee informed the Council, "occur within families." *Ibid.*

The committee report furthermore presented statistics strongly correlating handguns with crime. Of the 285 murders in the District in 1974, 155 were committed with handguns. *Ibid.* This did not appear to be an aberration, as the report revealed that "handguns [had been] used in roughly 54% of all murders" (and 87% of murders of law enforcement officers) nationwide over the preceding several years. *Ibid.* Nor were handguns only linked to murders, as statistics showed that they were used in roughly 60% of robberies and 26% of assaults. *Ibid.* "A crime committed with a pistol," the committee reported, "is 7 times more likely to be lethal than a crime committed with any other weapon." *Id.*, at 25. The committee furthermore presented statistics regarding the availability of handguns in the United States, *ibid.*, and noted that they had "become easy for juveniles to obtain," even despite then-current District laws prohibiting juveniles from possessing them, *id.*, at 26. . . .

The District's special focus on handguns thus reflects the fact that the committee report found them to have a particularly strong link to undesirable activities in the District's exclusively urban environment. See *id.*, at 25–26. The District did not seek to prohibit possession of other sorts of weapons deemed more suitable for an "urban area." See *id.*, at 25. Indeed, an original draft of the bill, and the original committee recommendations, had sought to prohibit registration of shotguns as well as handguns, but the Council as a whole decided to narrow the prohibition. . . .

From 1993 to 1997, there were 180,533 firearm-related deaths in the United States, an average of over 36,000 per year. Dept. of Justice, Bureau of Justice Statistics, M. Zawitz & K. Strom, Firearm Injury and Death from Crime, 1993–97, p. 2 (Oct. 2000), online at http://www.ojp.usdoj.gov/bjs/pub/pdf/fidc9397.pdf (hereinafter Firearm Injury and Death from Crime). Fifty-one percent were suicides, 44% were homicides, 1% were legal interventions, 3% were unintentional accidents, and 1% were of undetermined causes. See *ibid.* Over that same period there were an additional 411,800 nonfatal firearm-related injuries treated in U.S. hospitals, an average of over 82,000 per year. *Ibid.* Of these, 62% resulted from assaults, 17% were unintentional, 6% were suicide attempts, 1% were legal interventions, and 13% were of unknown causes. *Ibid.*

The statistics are particularly striking in respect to children and adolescents. In over one in every eight firearm-related deaths in 1997, the victim was someone under the age of 20. American Academy of Pediatrics, Firearm-Related Injuries Affecting the Pediatric Population, 105 Pediatrics 888 (2000) (hereinafter Firearm-Related Injuries). Firearm-related deaths account for 22.5% of all injury deaths between the ages of 1 and 19. *Ibid.* More male teenagers die from firearms than from all natural causes combined. Dresang, Gun Deaths in Rural and Urban Settings, 14 *J. Am. Bd. Family*

Practice 107 (2001). Persons under 25 accounted for 47% of hospital-treated firearm injuries between June 1, 1992 and May 31, 1993. Firearm-Related Injuries 891.

Handguns are involved in a majority of firearm deaths and injuries in the United States. *Id.*, at 888. From 1993 to 1997, 81% of firearm-homicide victims were killed by handgun. Firearm Injury and Death from Crime 4; see also Dept. of Justice, Bureau of Justice Statistics, C. Perkins, Weapon Use and Violent Crime, p. 8 (Sept. 2003), (Table 10), http://www.ojp.usdoj.gov/bjs/pub/pdf/wuvc01.pdf (statistics indicating roughly the same rate for 1993–2001). In the same period, for the 41% of firearm injuries for which the weapon type is known, 82% of them were from handguns. Firearm Injury and Death From Crime 4. And among children under the age of 20, handguns account for approximately 70% of all unintentional firearm-related injuries and deaths. Firearm-Related Injuries 890. In particular, 70% of all firearm-related teenage suicides in 1996 involved a handgun. *Id.*, at 889; see also Zwerling, Lynch, Burmeister, & Goertz, The Choice of Weapons in Firearm Suicides in Iowa, 83 Am. J. Public Health 1630, 1631 (1993) (Table 1) (handguns used in 36.6% of all firearm suicides in Iowa from 1980–1984 and 43.8% from 1990–1991).

Handguns also appear to be a very popular weapon among criminals. In a 1997 survey of inmates who were armed during the crime for which they were incarcerated, 83.2% of state inmates and 86.7% of federal inmates said that they were armed with a handgun. See Dept. of Justice, Bureau of Justice Statistics, C. Harlow, Firearm Use by Offenders, p. 3 (Nov. 2001), online at http://www.ojp.usdoj.gov/bjs/pub/pdf/fuo.pdf; see also Weapon Use and Violent Crime 2 (Table 2) (statistics indicating that handguns were used in over 84% of nonlethal violent crimes involving firearms from 1993 to 2001). And handguns are not only popular tools for crime, but popular objects of it as well: the FBI received on average over 274,000 reports of stolen guns for each year between 1985 and 1994, and almost 60% of stolen guns are handguns. Dept. of Justice, Bureau of Justice Statistics, M. Zawitz, Guns Used in Crime, p. 3 (July 1995), online at http://www.ojp.usdoj.gov/bjs/pub/pdf/guic.pdf. Department of Justice studies have concluded that stolen handguns in particular are an important source of weapons for both adult and juvenile offenders. *Ibid.*

Statistics further suggest that urban areas, such as the District, have different experiences with gun-related death, injury, and crime, than do less densely populated rural areas. A disproportionate amount of violent and property crimes occur in urban areas, and urban criminals are more likely than other offenders to use a firearm during the commission of a violent crime. . . . Homicide appears to be a much greater issue in urban areas; from 1985 to 1993, for example, "half of all homicides occurred in 63 cities with 16% of the nation's population." Wintemute, The Future of Firearm Violence Prevention, 282 JAMA 475 (1999). One study concluded that although the overall rate of gun death between 1989 and 1999 was roughly the same in urban than rural areas, the urban homicide rate was three times as high; even after adjusting for other variables, it was still twice as high. Branas, Nance, Elliott, Richmond, & Schwab, Urban-Rural Shifts in Intentional Firearm Death, 94 *Am. J. Public Health* 1750, 1752 (2004); see also *ibid.* (noting that rural areas appear to have a higher rate of firearm suicide). And a study of firearm injuries to children and adolescents in Pennsylvania between 1987 and 2000 showed an injury rate in urban counties 10 times higher than in nonurban counties. Nance & Branas, The Rural-Urban Continuum, 156 *Archives of Pediatrics & Adolescent Medicine* 781, 782 (2002).

Finally, the linkage of handguns to firearms deaths and injuries appears to be much stronger in urban than in rural areas. "[S]tudies to date generally support the hypothesis that the greater number of rural gun deaths are from rifles or shotguns, whereas the greater number of urban gun deaths are from handguns." Dresang, *supra*, at 108. And the Pennsylvania study reached a similar conclusion with respect to firearm injuries—they are much more likely to be caused by handguns in urban areas than in rural areas. . . .

For these reasons, I conclude that the District's measure is a proportionate, not a disproportionate, response to the compelling concerns that led the District to adopt it. And, for these reasons as well as the independently sufficient reasons set forth by *Justice Stevens*, I would find the District's measure consistent with the Second Amendment's demands.

With respect, I dissent.

SOURCE: http://laws.findlaw.com/us/000/07–290.html

ANALYSIS

In the early 2000s, several residents of the District of Columbia filed suit against D.C.'s strict no-handgun law. Enacted in 1976 to stem gun crime, the law barred the possession of working handguns, and also required any operable guns to be bound by a trigger lock. In 2007, the Court of Appeals for the D.C. Circuit struck the law down as a violation of the Second Amendment's right to bear arms—the first time in American history that a federal court had struck down a gun law on Second Amendment grounds.

The following year, the Supreme Court upheld the lower court ruling in a 5–4 decision. In one of the most momentous rulings of recent times, the high court ruled for the first time that the amendment protects a right of individuals to own guns for personal purposes such as personal self-defense. The majority decision, authored by Justice Antonin Scalia, admitted that the right was not unlimited, and that some gun regulations would continue to be legal, such as those barring gun sales to felons and the mentally incompetent, and restricting gun carrying into public buildings, for example, but the decision for the first time separated the right stipulated in the amendment from service in a "well-regulated militia" referenced in the first half of the amendment's sentence. Although the ruling did not expressly overturn the 1939 *Miller* ruling (the majority opinion said that their ruling was consistent with the 1939 decision), it offered a judicial view of the amendment that bore little relation to the 1939 opinion.

The majority opinion and the dissenting opinion authored by Justice John Paul Stevens offered dueling interpretations of law and history; the second dissent, authored by Justice Stephen Breyer, emphasized that, whatever the meaning of the amendment, D.C.'s law represented a legitimate effort to address the city's serious gun crime problem. The decision represented a major victory for gun rights organizations, who had long sought such an interpretation of the amendment. While pundits continue to argue about the consequences of the ruling, it had one immediate effect: lawsuits against gun laws all across the country were filed based on this new interpretation of the right to bear arms. And while the ruling applied only to the national government and not to the states (i.e., it was not "incorporated" to apply to the states because D.C. is under federal control), the court left open the possibility that it would incorporate the Second Amendment in a future ruling. Without question, *Heller* would prompt numerous other court challenges.

FURTHER READING

Spitzer, Robert J. "Why History Matters: Saul Cornell's Second Amendment and the Consequences of Law Reviews." *Albany Government Law Review* 1(2008): 312–353.

6

LOWER FEDERAL COURT RULINGS ON THE SECOND AMENDMENT

The Lower Federal Courts Interpret the Supreme Court's View of the Second Amendment as Militia-Based

- **Document:** U.S. Court of Appeals for the Third Circuit case of *U.S. v. Tot*, 131 F.2d 261 (1942); reversed on other grounds, 319 U.S. 463 (1943).
- **Date:** October 28, 1942
- **Where:** Philadelphia, Pennsylvania
- **Significance:** This was the first of many federal court cases that interpreted the Supreme Court's 1939 ruling in *U.S. v. Miller* as providing a militia-based interpretation of the Second Amendment.

DOCUMENT

United States v. Tot, 131 F.2d 261 (3rd Cir. 1942)

Circuit Court of Appeals, Third Circuit
Argued July 7, 1942.
Decided Oct. 28, 1942.
Before MARIS and GOODRICH, Circuit Judges, and BARD, District Judge.
GOODRICH, Circuit Judge.

The defendant, Frank Tot, was convicted and sentenced for violation of the statute known as the Federal Firearms Act, 15 U.S.C.A. section 901 et seq., by which it is made unlawful for any person who has been convicted of a crime of violence "to receive any firearm or ammunition which has been shipped or transported in interstate or foreign commerce * * *." [footnote 1] That defendant had been previously convicted of a crime of violence, as defined in the Act, is undisputed. He was arrested by federal officers at his home in Newark, N. J., on a warrant charging theft of cigarettes from an interstate shipment. A .32 caliber Colt Automatic pistol, was found in his place of residence at the time of the arrest, which took place on September 22,

1938. In this appeal the appellant raises several questions of difficulty and importance concerning the statute cited. Additional facts necessary for presentation of the legal questions involved will be made in connection with the question to which they are relevant.

Search and Seizure

At various stages of the proceedings after his arrest, appellant made timely motions for the suppression and return of the gun and that any evidence pertaining to it, which had been admitted over his objection, be stricken. All of these motions were denied. Their basis was the appellant's contention that the gun had been obtained in violation of his constitutional guarantee, under the Fourth Amendment, against unreasonable searches and seizures.

Since what the Constitution prohibits is unreasonable search and seizure it is inevitable that the courts are confronted with marginal cases and that sometimes the line between what is held reasonable in one case and unreasonable in another becomes faint. Some searches and seizures incident to a lawful arrest are permitted; others are not. The facts presented here however, do not show a case close to the line where our result would be indicated only by a careful analysis and differentiation among authorities by which we are bound. We are not here confronted with the problem of the propriety of the seizure if the officers had found a quantity of cigarettes about the accused's premises and seized them as evidence of his complicity in the crime with which, he was charged in the warrant of arrest. Still less are we concerned with the legality of a seizure of some article of contraband like a package of opium or a container of untaxed alcohol. The only article seized here was the gun. Undoubtedly upon Tot's arrest under a valid warrant, as this was, his person could have been searched and the weapon taken from him. The same privilege to search the place where the arrest is made "in order to find, and seize things connected, with the crime as its fruits * * *, as well as weapons and other things to effect an escape from custody, is not to be doubted." [footnote 4]

The serving of the warrant and the taking of the gun by the officers were practically a contemporaneous transaction. The evidence shows that Tot was asked if he had a gun and that he replied in the affirmative. He stated that it was in the pocket of his coat which was hanging in a wardrobe closet in his bedroom. Whether this conversation took place in the kitchen, where the arresting officers entered, or the adjoining bedroom, is disputed. We think it does not matter. There was also testimony that Tot offered to get the gun himself and that this unusual offer was declined by the officers, one of whom went to the closet, found the coat, removed the gun and took possession thereof. It might well be said that defendant's offer to produce the gun constituted a consent on his part to its taking by the officers. Regardless of this, however, we think it apparent that the seizure in this case is clearly within the rule stated by the Supreme Court as one not to be doubted under which weapons and other things which may be used to effect an escape from custody may be seized without a search warrant upon a lawful arrest.

A general search of the premises was made, however, and the only warrant the officers had was the one for the arrest of the accused. If we assume, solely for the purpose of discussion, however, that the search was wider than constitutional limitations permitted, does this invalidate the arrest and the seizure of the weapon which was otherwise lawful as an incident to the arrest? The analogy at once suggested is the ancient doctrine of trespass *ab initio* [from inception] by which subsequent misconduct of a party entering under license given by law may render the original entry tortious [wrongful]. Even so, however, this doctrine does not invalidate the doing of an act for the accomplishment of which the privilege exists. Nor is it applicable to criminal prosecutions brought by the United States. Our conclusion is that under the facts of this case the defendant may not complain of violation of constitutional rights in the search and seizure of the gun, and the overruling of his various motions, and objections based on this theory were correct.

Meaning of the Statute

Appellant's second contention is that the correct construction of the statute does not include the gun which was in his possession at the time of his arrest. In defining the term: "firearm" the Congressional language states that it "means any weapon, * * * which is designed to expel a projectile * * * by the action of an explosive and a firearm muffler or firearm silencer, or any part or parts of such weapon." [footnote 7]

The pistol here in question was not equipped with a silencer nor is there, according to the testimony of the government's expert, a commercially made silencer for this .32 caliber weapon. It is conceded, however, that a silencer could be made for it and there is evidence of a demonstration of the successful fitting and operation of a made-over .25 silencer on a gun of the same make, model and caliber. The appellant's argument is that the plain words of the statute, in which the conjunctive, "and" is used instead of the disjunctive "or" or a combination of the two, limits the application of the statute to guns which are provided with a silencer, or where one may readily be applied. This being the plain meaning, he says, and the statute a penal one, resort should not be had to extrinsic sources like Treasury Regulations or legislative debates and hearings to give it some other meaning.

If the premise of plain meaning were acceptable, there is something to be said for the suggested conclusion. We do not agree with the appellant's argument about the plain meaning. The statute as a whole indicates an ambitious plan for dealing with firearms in interstate commerce. The very sentence upon which appellant relies shows, in the last phrase, the intent of Congress to deal with the parts as well as the whole. The appellant's interpretation of the language requires the word "and" to be read as "combined with". This, it seems to us, is quite a jump from plain meaning. It is a much narrower construction than we believe Congress meant in view of the statute as a whole and the concluding clause of the sentence referred to.

That Congress had no such narrow limitation in mind is clear from the discussion of the statute prior to its passage. Both the proponents and opponents of the Act thought of its provisions in the broadest terms, applicable to a "gun of any type", "firearms of all kinds", etc. [footnote 8] This reference is not made to put in the statute something which is not there. But, it is a matter for consideration in determining what the scope was of the problem the legislature had in mind. [footnote 9]

There is an additional point of administrative regulation also. Section 903 of the Act relates to licensing of manufacturers of and dealers in firearms and this is committed to the Treasury. Regulations were issued under which the clauses were rearranged and numbered to make explicit the disjunctive relation of the gun and the silencer. [footnote 10] The Congress subsequently amended the definition of ammunition in the very same statute. [footnote 11] The opportunity was then present to modify the firearms definition if the Congress had considered that the administrative officers had carried it beyond it original meaning. We think this is a case where what the Treasury had evidenced as being its understanding of the meaning of the statute, "Congress impliedly confirmed as being correctly interpretative of the legislative intent." [footnote 12] Our conclusion upon this point is that the pistol here in question was within the definition of firearms given in the statute.

The Second Amendment

The Second Amendment to the Constitution of the United States provides: "A well regulated Militia, being necessary to the security of a free State, the right of the people to keep and bear Arms, shall not be infringed."

The appellant's contention is that if the statute under which this prosecution was brought is to be applied to a weapon of the type he had in his possession, then the statute violates the Second Amendment.

It is abundantly clear both from the discussions of this amendment contemporaneous with its proposal and adoption and those of learned writers since [footnote 13] that this amendment, unlike those providing for protection of free speech and freedom of religion, was not adopted with individual rights in mind, but as a protection for the States in the maintenance of their militia organizations against possible encroachments by the federal power. [footnote 14] The experiences in England under James II of an armed royal force quartered upon a defenseless citizenry [footnote 15] was fresh in the minds of the Colonists. They wanted no repetition of that experience in their newly formed government. The almost uniform course of decision in this country, [footnote 16] where provisions similar in language are found in many of the State Constitutions bears out this concept of the constitutional guarantee. A notable instance is the refusal to extend its application to weapons thought incapable of military use.

The contention of the appellant in this case could, we think, be denied without more under the authority of United States v. Miller, 1939, 307 U.S. 174, 59 S. Ct. 816, 83 L.Ed. 1206. This was a prosecution under the National Firearms Act of 1934 and the weapon, the possession of which had occasioned the prosecution of the accused, was a shotgun of less than 18 inch barrel. The Court said that in the absence of evidence tending to show that possession of such a gun at the time has some reasonable relationship to the preservation or efficiency of a well regulated militia, it could not be said that the Second Amendment guarantees the right to keep such an instrument. The appellant here having failed to show such a relationship, the same thing may be said as applied to the pistol found in his possession. It is not material on this point that the 1934 statute was bottomed on the taxing power while the statute in question here was based on a regulation of interstate commerce.

But, further, the same result is definitely indicated on a broader ground and on this we should prefer to rest the matter. Weapon bearing was never treated as anything like an absolute right by the common law. It was regulated by statute as to time and place as far back as the Statute of Northampton in 1328 and on many occasions since. [footnote 17] The decisions under the State Constitutions show the upholding of regulations prohibiting the carrying of concealed weapons, prohibiting persons from going armed in certain public places and other restrictions, in the nature of police regulations, but which do not go so far as substantially to interfere with the public interest protected by the constitutional mandates. [footnote 18] The Federal statute here involved is one of that general type. One could hardly argue seriously that a limitation upon the privilege of possessing weapons was unconstitutional when applied to a mental patient of the maniac type. The same would be true if the possessor were a child of immature years. In the situation at bar Congress has prohibited the receipt of weapons from interstate transactions by persons who have previously, by due process of law, been shown to be aggressors against society. [footnote 19] Such a classification is entirely reasonable and does not infringe upon the preservation of the well regulated militia protected by the Second Amendment. . . .

Constitutionality of the Statutory Presumption

By far the most difficult problem in this case is the constitutionality of a presumption created in section 902(f) [of the Federal Firearms Act]. After declaring it unlawful for any person convicted of a crime of violence to receive any firearm in interstate or foreign commerce, the provision is that the possession of a firearm by such person shall be presumptive evidence that such firearm was received by such person in violation of the chapter. The appellant did not press this point in his main brief or oral argument, though he discusses that portion of the government's argument in his reply brief. Nevertheless, because this is the first time the statute has been before an appellate court for consideration we think that fairness to the accused requires consideration of this problem as well as the other points already discussed.

The obvious offhand response to such presumption in a criminal statute is that it violates the fundamental concept that a man is innocent until proved guilty by putting on him the burden of producing the facts which establish his innocence. Such a sweeping objection comes many years too late. . . . So far as the application to the facts of this case are concerned, we think the considerations show that the presumption is constitutional as applied to an interstate commerce shipment whether the more limited formula of the Turnipseed case or the broader generalization found in the Morrison case is followed. The gun in question certainly had two interstate journeys because it was proved that it was originally shipped from Connecticut to Illinois and it was found in the defendant's possession in New Jersey. Acquisition in New Jersey under the New Jersey law, would not have been easy. New Jersey, in common with many other States, has rather stringent regulations surrounding the transfer of firearms of this type. The tendency is to require such transfers to be open, to make them more difficult and certainly to put obstacles in the way of acquisition by persons of criminal records like that of the defendant.

Furthermore, Congress had, when the Federal Firearms Act was under consideration, evidence dealing with the interstate activity of armed law breakers. In determining the constitutionality of the legislative solution of a problem courts are not to ignore the existence of such facts before legislative bodies even though the evidence of those facts is not part of the record in a particular case. *United States v. Carolene Products Co.*, 1938, 304 U.S. 144, 58 S.Ct. 778, 82 L.Ed. 1234. We think these considerations are sufficient to protect the statute created presumption from the charge of arbitrariness. . . .

The social end sought to be achieved by this legislation, the protection of society against violent men armed with dangerous weapons, all would concede to be fundamental in organized government. The entry of the federal authority in the field to help accomplish this purpose has not been challenged. It has been taken for granted by both sides in the discussion of this case. We also think it may be assumed. In accomplishing the admittedly constitutional object we do not think the means taken by this statute, while stringent, have become so oppressive and arbitrary that we are entitled to say that Congress has exceeded its authority in acting without due process of law.

The judgment is affirmed.

Footnotes

1. 15 U.S.C.A. section 902(f).
4. *Agnello v. United States*, 1925, 269 U.S. 20, 30, 46 S.Ct. 4, 70. L.Ed. 145. The Court states that this privilege exists where the arrest is made for a crime committed in the presence of the arresting officers. The latter requirement merely establishes the lawfulness of an arrest without a warrant, as in the Agnello case. When the arrest in made with a warrant, as here, the requirement is unnecessary, for then, the privilege of search and seizure, being incidental to a lawful arrest is as extensive.
7. 15 U.S.C.A. section 901(3).
8. Hearings before Senate Committee on Commerce on S. 3. 74th Cong., 1st Sess. (1935) 10, 13, 15, 44; Hearings before H. R. Subcommittee of the Committee on Interstate and Foreign Commerce on S. 3, 75th Cong., 1st Sess. (1937) 4, 5, 18. Sen. Rep. No. 997, 74th Cong., 1st Sess. (1935) 1; Sen. Rep. No. 82, 75th Cong. 1st Sess. (1937) 1.
9. It is also noteworthy, that the first two drafts of this section interposed a semicolon between "explosive" and "and." See text as it appears in Senate Hearings, supra at pp. 1, 2 and in 79 Cong. Rec. 11973, 11974 (1935). The semi-colon was absent in the third draft which was sent without further amendment to the House. See H. R. Hearings, supra, at pp. 1–3. The Senate Report on the third draft states that the only change from prior drafts in the bill appears in a section, other than the one under consideration. See Sen. Rep.No. 82, supra, H. R. Hearings, supra, at p. 13. This legislative history indicates that the omission of the semicolon in the final draft was unintentional. With that punctuation mark, it is clear that the statute meant guns with or without silencers as is otherwise apparent from the Hearings, supra.
10. "The term 'firearm' means (1) any weapon, by whatever name known, which is designed to expel a projectile or projectiles by action of an explosive, (2) any part or parts of such weapon, and (3) a firearm muffler or firearm silencer." 26 Code Fed. Regs., 1939 Supp. (1940) section 313—1(b).
11. August 6, 1939, 15 U.S.C.A. section 901(8).
12. *Aluminum Co. of America v. United States*, 3 Cir., 1941, 123 F.2d 615, 620. The Regulation does not, on the facts here, gain authority from its long standing character. It became effective May 1, 1939. The statutory amendment came

in August of the same year. But the subject matter of the statute, and obviously especially the definitional provisions, were before Congress during the dates mentioned.

13. 1 Elliot's Debates on the Federal Constitution (2d Ed. 1901) 371, 372 (Luther Martin's letter to the Maryland Legislature); 4 id. 203 (Lenoir, North Carolina Convention); 5 id. 445 (Sherman of Connecticut at the Federal Convention). Emery, The Constitutional Right to Keep and Bear Arms (1915) 28 Harv. L.Rev. 473; Haight, The Right to Keep and Bear Arms (1941) 2 Bill of Rights Rev. 31; McKenna, The Right to Keep and Bear Arms (1928) 12 Marq. L.Rev. 138.

14. As to the latter, see The Federalist, Nos. XXIV-XXIX and No. XLVI.

15. See *Aymette v. State*, 1840, 2 Humph. 154, 21 Tenn. 154; also law review articles in f.n. 13.

16. See Haight, supra and McKenna, supra.

17. See Emery, supra, at pp. 473, 474.

18. See f.n. 16.

19. The statute is applicable to anyone who has been convicted of a crime of violence which is defined as "murder, manslaughter, rape, mayhem, kidnapping, burglary, housebreaking; assault with intent to kill, commit rape, or rob; assault with a dangerous weapon, or assault with intent to commit any offense punishable by imprisonment for more than one year." section 901(6).

SOURCE: http://www.cs.cmu.edu/afs/cs/user/wbardwel/public/nfalist/us_v_tot.txt

ANALYSIS

Frank Tot was arrested for possessing a handgun, in violation of the Federal Firearms Act of 1938, which made it a crime for anyone convicted of a violent crime to possess a firearm that has been transported across state lines. Tot was convicted, but he appealed, arguing that the police search was improper, and that the federal law violated the Second Amendment, among other things. The Third Circuit court upheld Tot's conviction. Tot appealed to the Supreme Court, which reversed his conviction (and that of another person similarly convicted from another circuit), for reasons unrelated to the search and the Second Amendment. The high court's reversal was based on unresolved ambiguities pertaining to the technical question of whether Tot received possession of the gun before or after July 30, 1938, the date the federal law went into effect.

After discussing the police's search and seizure procedures, which the court upheld, the Third Circuit court dealt with Tot's objection that the handgun in question did not fall within the scope of the 1938 law. Again, the court turned aside those objections. It then dealt with Tot's claim that his Second Amendment rights had been violated by this law. Here, the court stated flatly that, unlike other Bill of Rights protections, the Second Amendment "was not adopted with individual rights in mind, but as a protection for the States in the maintenance of their militia organizations against possible encroachments by the federal power." (Note that some of the footnotes to this case have been kept in where they pertain to sources regarding the Second Amendment.) The court then discusses British and colonial antecedents, and cites the Supreme Court's key 1939 ruling in *U.S. v. Miller* (see Chapter 5) upon which it bases its militia view of the amendment. In several footnotes, this section also cites some law journal articles and cases that explain the Second Amendment as being a militia-based right. (Because this case as it appears here is edited, only those footnotes that pertain to the 1938 law and to the explication of the Second Amendment appear at the end of the case.)

Finally, the court addresses the constitutionality of the 1938 federal law. It concludes that it is a reasonable exercise of government power, aimed at providing fundamental protection to the country's citizens from gun crime. Coming only three years after the Supreme Court's *Miller* decision, this case also reflects the militia-based understanding of the Second Amendment articulated by the high court.

FURTHER READING

Yassky, David. "The Second Amendment: Structure, History, and Constitutional Change," *Michigan Law Review* 99(December 2000): 588–668.

The Militia-Based View of the Second Amendment Applies to U.S. Territories under Federal Control

- **Document:** U.S. Court of Appeals for the First Circuit, case of *Cases v. U.S.*, 131 F.2d 916 (1942), cert. denied sub nom *Velazquez v. U.S.*, 319 U.S. 770 (1943)
- **Date:** November 27, 1942
- **Where:** Boston, Massachusetts
- **Significance:** This federal court denied any personal right to bear arms under the Second Amendment, accepted instead the militia-based view, and supported the applicability of the federal gun control law even though this case technically did not involve interstate commerce.

DOCUMENT

Cases v. United States, 131 F.2d 916 (1st Cir. 1942)

Appeal from the District Court of the United States for Puerto Rico; Cooper, judge.

Jose Cases Velazquez was convicted of violating the Federal Firearms Act, and he appeals.

Affirmed.

Hugh R. Francis, Edgar S. Belaval, and Francis & Belaval, all of San Juan, P. R., for appellant.

Philip F. Herrick, U.S. Atty., Adolfo Valdés, Asst. U.S. Atty., and Francisco Ponsa Feliú, Asst. U.S. Atty., all of San Juan, P. R., for appellee.

Before MAGRUDER, MAHONEY, and WOODBURY, Circuit judges.

WOODBURY, Circuit Judge.

This is an appeal from a judgment of the District Court of the United States for Puerto Rico sentencing the defendant to a term of imprisonment after he had been found guilty by a jury on all four counts of an indictment charging him with violating § 2(e) and (f) of the Federal Firearms Act, 52 Stat. 1250, 15 U.S.C.A. section 901–909, by transporting and receiving a firearm and ammunition. The grounds upon which the defendant bases his appeal are that the statute under which he was indicted is unconstitutional, that the verdict of guilty was contrary to the law and the facts, and that he was denied due process of law by certain rulings of the district court on matters of procedure.

The defendant contends that the Federal Firearms Act is unconstitutional because (a) it is an ex post facto law; (b) it violates the Second Amendment by infringing the right of the people to keep and bear arms; (c) it is an undue extension of the commerce clause; (d) it creates an unreasonable presumption of guilt; and (e) it denies equal protection of the laws. In our view none of these contentions are sound. . . .

The Federal Firearms Act undoubtedly curtails to some extent the right of individuals to keep and bear arms but it does not follow from this as a necessary consequence that it is bad under the Second Amendment which reads "A well regulated Militia, being necessary to the security of a free State, the right of the people to keep and bear Arms, shall not be infringed."

The right to keep and bear arms is not a right conferred upon the people by the federal constitution. Whatever rights in this respect the people may have depend upon local legislation; the only function of the Second Amendment being to prevent the federal government and the federal government only from infringing that right. *United States v. Cruikshank*, 92 U.S. 542, 553, 23 L.Ed. 588; *Presser v. Illinois*, 116 U.S. 252, 265, 6 S.Ct. 580, 29 L.Ed. 615. But the Supreme Court in a dictum in *Robertson v. Baldwin*, 165 U.S. 275, 282, 17 S.Ct. 326, 41 L.Ed. 715, indicated that the limitation imposed upon the federal government by the Second Amendment was not absolute and this dictum received the sanction of the court in the recent case of *United States v. Miller*, 307 U.S. 174, 182, 59 S.Ct. 816, 83 L.Ed. 1206.

In the case last cited the Supreme Court, after discussing the history of militia organizations in the United States, upheld the validity under the Second Amendment of the National Firearms Act of June 26, 1934, 48 Stat. 1236, in so far as it imposed limitations upon the use of a shotgun having a barrel less than eighteen inches long. It stated the reason for its result on page 178 of the opinion in 307 U.S., on page 818 of 59 S.Ct., 83 L.Ed. 1206, as follows: "In the absence of any evidence tending to show that possession or use of a 'shotgun having a barrel of less than eighteen inches in length' at this time has some reasonable relationship to the preservation or efficiency of a well regulated militia, we cannot say that the Second Amendment guarantees the right to keep and bear such an instrument. Certainly it is not within judicial notice that this weapon is any part of the ordinary military equipment or that its use could contribute to the common defense."

Apparently, then, under the Second Amendment, the federal government can limit the keeping and bearing of arms by a single individual as well as by a group of individuals, but it cannot prohibit the possession or use of any weapon which has any reasonable relationship to the preservation or efficiency of a well regulated militia. However, we do not feel that the Supreme Court in this case was attempting to formulate a general rule applicable to all cases. The rule which it laid down was adequate to dispose of the case before it and that we think was as far as the Supreme Court intended to go. At any rate the rule of the Miller case, if intended to be comprehensive and complete would seem to be already outdated, in spite of the fact that it was formulated only three and a half years ago, because of the well known fact that in the so called "Commando Units" some sort of military use seems to have been found for almost any modern lethal weapon. In view of this, if the rule of the Miller case is general and complete, the result would follow that, under present day conditions, the federal government would be empowered only to regulate the possession or use of weapons such as a flintlock musket or a matchlock harquebus. But to hold that the Second Amendment limits the federal government to regulations concerning only weapons which can be classed as antiques or curiosities,—almost any other might bear some reasonable relationship to the preservation or efficiency of a well regulated militia unit of the present day,—is in effect to hold that the limitation of the Second Amendment is absolute. Another objection to the rule of the Miller case as a full and general statement is that according to it Congress would be prevented by the Second Amendment from regulating the possession or use by private persons not present or prospective members of any military unit, of distinctly military arms, such as machine guns, trench mortars, anti-tank or anti-aircraft guns, even though under the circumstances surrounding such possession or use it would be inconceivable that a private person could have any legitimate reason for having such a weapon. It seems to us unlikely that the framers of the Amendment intended any such result. Considering the many variable factors bearing upon the question it seems to us impossible to formulate any general test by which to determine the limits imposed by the Second Amendment but that each case under it, like cases under the due process clause, must be decided on its own facts and the line between what is and what is not a valid federal restriction pricked out by decided cases falling on one side or the other of the line.

We therefore turn to the record in the case at bar. From it it appears that on or about August 27, 1941, the appellant received into his possession and carried away ten rounds of ammunition, and that on the evening of August 30 of the same year he went to Annadale's Beach Club on Isla Verde in the municipality of Carolina, Puerto Rico, equipped with a .38 caliber Colt type revolver of Spanish make which, when some one turned out the lights, he used, apparently not wholly without effect, upon another patron of the place who in some way seems to have incurred his displeasure. While the weapon may be capable of military use, or while at least familiarity with it might be regarded as of value in training a person to use a comparable weapon of military type and caliber, still there is no evidence that the appellant was or ever had been a member of any military organization or that his use of the weapon under the circumstances disclosed was in preparation for a military career. In fact, the only inference possible is that the appellant at the time charged in the indictment was in possession of, transporting, and using the firearm and ammunition purely and simply on a frolic of his own and without any thought or intention of contributing to the efficiency of the well regulated militia which the Second Amendment was designed to foster as necessary to the security of a free state. We are of the view that, as applied to the appellant, the Federal Firearms Act does not conflict with the Second Amendment to the Constitution of the United States.

It is clear that in enacting the Federal Firearms Act Congress was exercising the power conferred upon it by the commerce clause, but it is equally clear that Congress meant to deal comprehensively with the subject and to exert all the power which it had in respect thereto. See *Atlantic Cleansers & Dyers v. United States*, 286 U.S. 427, 434 et seq., 52 S.Ct. 607, 76 L.Ed. 1204; *People of Puerto Rico v. Shell Co.*, 302 U.S. 253, 259, 58 S.Ct. 167, 82 L.Ed. 235. Since its power as we have seen, as to a territory like Puerto Rico is plenary, except as limited by express constitutional restrictions, Congress is not fettered by the commerce clause, Const. art. 1, § 8, cl. 3, in its power to legislate for Puerto Rico. See *Lugo v. Suazo*, 1 Cir., 59 F.2d 386, 390; and *Sancho v. Bacardi Corp.*, 1 Cir., 109 F.2d 57, 62, 63, reversed on another point sub nom, *Bacardi Corp. v. Domenech*, 311 U.S. 150, 61 S.Ct. 219, 85 L.Ed. 98. As far as Puerto Rico is concerned it might, within the limits indicated, make what rules it wished with respect to the use, possession and transportation of firearms on that island, and this we think it did by the technique of definition when, in its attempt to legislate for states and territories alike it defined "interstate or foreign commerce" in § 1(2) of the Act to include commerce "within any Territory or possession or the District of Columbia." That is to say, having much broader powers with respect to territories than it has with respect to states because as to the former it is not limited to the powers conferred by the commerce clause, and having indicated its intention to deal as broadly as it could with respect to the use, possession and transportation of firearms and ammunition in either states or territories, we conclude that Congress not only could but also did make criminal the sort of conduct in which the appellant indulged at Annadale's Beach Club. The question of whether or not Congress would have the power to regulate such conduct if it had occurred in a state is not raised. Since the appellant's argument on this constitutional question assumes that the situation presented is governed by the rules which would be applicable if his acts had been done in a state, it is beside the point and need not be considered. . . .

The judgment of the District Court is affirmed.

SOURCE: http://www.cs.cmu.edu/afs/cs/usr/wbardwel/public/nfalist/cases_v_us.txt

ANALYSIS

A defendant, Jose Cases Velazquez, was convicted of four counts of transporting and possessing a firearm and ammunition in violation of the Federal Firearms Act of 1938. Because the violations occurred in Puerto Rico, a U.S. territory, there was no question of involving interstate commerce, yet the court made clear that the federal law (which criminalized the interstate transport of certain weapons) applied no less to U.S. territories. Coming just three years after the Supreme Court's 1939 *Miller* case, this case noted that the Second Amendment "is not a right conferred upon the people by the federal constitution. . . . the only function of the Second Amendment being to prevent the federal government and the federal government only from infringing that right." It then cited *Cruikshank*, *Presser*, *Robertson*, and the recent *Miller* decision, underscoring the pertinence of this line of cases (see Chapters 3 and 5).

Colt AR15 A3 .223-caliber rifle. Photo by Dawn Van Hall.

This decision directly confronted an ambiguity in *Miller* that has prompted much discussion over the years. *Cases* quoted from *Miller* when it said that the government "cannot prohibit the possession or use of any weapon which has any reasonable relationship to the preservation or efficiency of a well regulated militia." Does this mean that citizens, under this ruling, may possess weapons that *would* be usable by militias or the military? No, said the court; to accept that reading would make no sense, as it would bar regulation of "distinctly military arms, such as machine guns, trench mortars, anti-tank or anti-aircraft guns, even though under the circumstances surrounding such possession or use it would be inconceivable that a private person could have any legitimate reason for having such a weapon." Applying their reasoning to the case at hand, the court said that the defendant acquired the gun in question "without any thought or intention of contributing to the efficiency of the well regulated militia which the Second Amendment was designed to foster as necessary to the security of a free state." And the court upheld the constitutionality of the Federal Firearms Act. Thus, the court accepted the long-accepted militia-based meaning of the Second Amendment, and concluded that it posed no obstacle to federal gun laws.

FURTHER READING

Carter, Gregg Lee, ed. *Guns in American Society*, 2 vols. Santa Barbara, CA: ABC-CLIO, 2003.

Citizens Must Be in Actual Militia Service for the Second Amendment to Apply

- **Document:** U.S. Court of Appeals for the Sixth Circuit, case of *U.S. v. Warin*, 530 F.2d 103 (1976), cert. denied, 426 U.S. 948 (1976)
- **Date:** February 4, 1976
- **Where:** Cincinnati, Ohio
- **Significance:** The right to bear arms under the Second Amendment does not apply to an individual simply because the individual might be eligible for militia service.

DOCUMENT

U.S. v. Warin, 530 F.2d 103 (6th Cir. 1976)

Before PHILLIPS, Chief Judge, and LIVELY and ENGEL, Circuit Judges.

LIVELY, Circuit Judge.

This case requires a determination of whether certain provisions of the National Firearms Act as amended by the Gun Control Act of 1968, 26 U.S.C. § 5801 et seq., are an invalid infringement on the right to keep and bear arms guaranteed by the Second Amendment to the Constitution which provides—

A well regulated Militia, being necessary to the security of a free State, the right of the people to keep and bear Arms, shall not be infringed.

The defendant appeals from his conviction of the charge that he "willfully and knowingly possessed a firearm, that is a 9 mm prototype submachine gun measuring approximately 21 inches overall length, with a barrel length of approximately 7 1/2 inches, which had not been registered to him in the National Firearms Registration and Transfer Record as required by Chapter 53, Title 26, United States Code" in violation of 26 U.S.C. §§ 5861(d) and 5871.

At trial before the court, the following facts were stipulated to be true:

That on or about the 19th day of March, 1974, in the Northern District of Ohio, Western Division, Francis J. Warin willfully and knowingly possessed a firearm, that is, a 9-millimeter prototype submachine gun measuring approximately twenty-one inches overall length, with a barrel length of approximately seven and a half inches, which had not been registered to him in the National Firearms Registration and Transfer Record, . . . that submachine guns are used by the armed forces of the United States, and that submachine guns contribute to the efficient operation of the armed forces of the United States in their function of defending the country. . . . [T]hat the weapon involved in this case is a submachine gun. . . . [T]hat 9-millimeter submachine guns have been used by at least one Special Forces Unit of the Army in the Vietnam, . . . although they are not in general use, 9-millimeter submachine guns have been used by the military forces of the United States on at least one occasion during the Vietnam war. . . . [T]hat submachine guns are part of the military equipment of the United States military—. . . and that firearms of this general type, that is, submachine guns, do bear some relationship, some reasonable relationship, to the preservation or efficiency of the military forces.

The district court found that the defendant, as an adult male resident and citizen of Ohio, is a member of the "sedentary militia" of the State. It was not contended that Warin was a member of the active militia. The court also found that the defendant was an engineer and designer of firearms whose employer develops weapons for the government and—

. . . that the defendant had made the weapon in question, which is indeed a firearm as described in the Act. It is also clear from the evidence that the weapon was of a type which is standard for military use, and fires the ammunition which is in common military use for the weapons used by individual soldiers in combat. The defendant testified that he had designed and built the weapon for the purpose of testing and refining it so that it could be offered to the Government as an improvement on the military weapons presently in use. The weapon was not registered to him as required by law.

These findings are not disputed.

In *United States v. Miller*, 307 U.S. 174, 59 S.Ct. 816, 83 L.Ed. 1206 (1939), the Supreme Court held that the National Firearms Act of 1934 did not violate the Second Amendment. In its opinion the Court stated:

In the absence of any evidence tending to show that possession or use of a "shotgun having a barrel of less than eighteen inches in length" at this time has some reasonable relationship to the preservation or efficiency of a well regulated militia, we cannot say that the Second Amendment guarantees the right to keep and bear such an instrument. Certainly it is not within judicial notice that this weapon is any part of the ordinary military equipment or that its use could contribute to the common defense. Id. at 178, 59 S.Ct. at 818 (citation omitted).

Warin argues that the necessary implication of the quoted language is that a member of the "sedentary militia" may possess any weapon having military capability and that application of 26 U.S.C. § 5861(d) to such a person violates the Second Amendment. We disagree. In *Miller* the Supreme Court did not reach the question of the extent to which a weapon which is "part of the ordinary military equipment" or whose "use could contribute to the common defense" may be regulated. In holding that the absence of evidence placing the weapon involved in the charges against Miller in one of these categories precluded the trial court from quashing the indictment on Second Amendment grounds, the Court did not hold the converse—that the Second Amendment is an absolute prohibition against all regulation of the manufacture, transfer and possession of any instrument capable of being used in military action.

Within a few years after *Miller v. United States* was announced the First Circuit dealt with arguments similar to those made by Warin in the present case. In *Cases v. United States*, 131 F.2d 916 (1st Cir. 1942), cert. denied sub nom., *Velazquez v. United States*, 319 U.S. 770, 63 S.Ct. 1431, 87 L.Ed. 1718 (1943), the court held that the Supreme Court did not intend to formulate a general rule in *Miller*, but merely dealt with the facts of that case. The court of appeals noted the development of new weaponry during the early years of World War II and concluded that it was not the intention of the Supreme Court to hold that the Second Amendment prohibits Congress from regulating any weapons except antiques "such as a flintlock musket or a matchlock harquebus." 131 F.2d at 922. If the logical extension of the defendant's argument for the holding of Miller was inconceivable in 1942, it is completely irrational in this time of nuclear weapons.

Agreeing as we do with the conclusion in *Cases v. United States*, supra, that the Supreme Court did not lay down a general rule in *Miller*, we consider the present case on its own facts and in light of applicable authoritative decisions. It is clear that the Second Amendment guarantees a collective rather than an individual right. In *Stevens v. United States*, 440 F.2d 144, 149 (6th Cir. 1971), this court held, in a case challenging the constitutionality of 18 U.S.C. App. § 1202(a)(1):

Since the Second Amendment right "to keep and bear Arms" applies only to the right of the State to maintain a militia and not to the individual's right to bear arms, there can be no serious claim to any express constitutional right of an individual to possess a firearm.

See also, *United States v. Johnson*, 497 F.2d 548, 550 (4th Cir. 1974); *United States v. Tot*, 131 F.2d 261, 266 (3d Cir. 1942), rev'd on other grounds, 319 U.S. 463, 63 S.Ct. 1241, 87 L.Ed. 1519 (1943).

It is also established that the collective right of the militia is limited to keeping and bearing arms, the possession or use of which "at this time has some reasonable relationship to the preservation or efficiency of a well regulated militia,. . . . " *United States v. Miller*, supra, 307 U.S. at 178, 59 S.Ct. at 818. See also, *United States v. Johnson*, supra; *Cody v. United States*, 460 F.2d 34, 37 (8th Cir.), cert. denied, 409 U.S. 1010, 93 S.Ct. 454, 34 L.Ed.2d 303 (1972).

The fact that the defendant Warin, in common with all adult residents and citizens of Ohio, is subject to enrollment in the militia of the State confers upon him no right to possess the submachine gun in question. By statute the State of Ohio exempts "members of . . . the organized militia of this or any other state, . . . " (emphasis added) from the provision, "No person shall knowingly acquire, have, carry, or use any dangerous ordnance." Ohio Revised Code § 2923.17. "Dangerous ordnance" is defined to include any automatic firearm. O.R.C. § 2923.11. There is no such exemption for members of the "sedentary militia." Furthermore, there is absolutely no evidence that a submachine gun in the hands of an individual "sedentary militia" member would have any, much less a "reasonable relationship to the preservation or efficiency of a well regulated militia." Miller, supra, 307 U.S. at 178, 59 S.Ct. at 818. Thus we conclude that the defendant has no private right to keep and bear arms under the Second Amendment which would bar his prosecution and conviction for violating 26 U.S.C. § 5861(d).

Even where the Second Amendment is applicable, it does not constitute an absolute barrier to the congressional regulation of firearms. After considering several arguments the Third Circuit in *United States v. Tot,* supra, stated that it decided the case on the "broader ground" that "[w]eapon bearing was never treated as anything like an absolute right by the common law. It was regulated by statute as to time and place as far back as the Statute of Northampton in 1328 and on many occasions since." 131 F.2d at 266 (footnote omitted). In *Stevens v. United States,* supra, this court discussed the broad power of Congress in relying on the commerce clause of the Constitution to deal with the changing needs of the nation. 440 F.2d at 150–152. In *United States v. Wilson,* 440 F.2d 1068, 1069 (6th Cir. 1971), we held that—

The congressional history of the National Firearms Act Amendments of 1968 and its predecessor statutes clearly sets out facts sufficient for Congress to have determined that the provisions of 26 U.S.C. § 5801 et seq., as amended in 1968, are within both the taxing power, see *Sonzinsky v. United States,* 300 U.S. 506, 57 S.Ct. 554, 81 L.Ed. 772 (1937), and the commerce power of Congress.

Warin argues that to uphold a tax on firearms transactions by one entitled to Second Amendment protection "would be to sanction a tax on an activity which is constitutionally guaranteed and protected." He cites First Amendment cases such as *Murdock v. Pennsylvania,* 319 U.S. 105, 63 S.Ct. 870, 87 L.Ed. 1292 (1943), for the proposition that a person cannot be compelled to pay a license or tax in order to exercise a privilege granted by the Constitution. First Amendment rights occupy a "preferred position" among those guaranteed by the Bill of Rights, Id. at 115, 63 S.Ct. 870, a position never accorded to Second Amendment rights. Yet even the First Amendment has never been treated as establishing an absolute prohibition against limitations on the rights guaranteed therein. . . .

As the legislative history of the Act under consideration clearly shows, Congress was dealing with problems which threaten the maintenance of public order. There can be no question that an organized society which fails to regulate the importation, manufacture and transfer of the highly sophisticated lethal weapons in existence today does so at its peril. The requirement that no one may possess a submachine gun which is not registered to him in the National Firearms Registration and Transfer Record is a reasonable regulation for the maintenance of public order.

The defendant appears to concede that some regulation of firearms is permitted. He argues that the taxes imposed upon the making and transfer of such weapons are not appropriate revenue measures, but that their imposition constitutes an indirect attempt to suppress the constitutional right to keep arms. Again, this argument assumes that the Second Amendment granted private rights to individuals, a position which we have rejected. Nevertheless it should be noted that the Act imposes no tax or license on the keeping and bearing of arms, the only rights referred to in the Second Amendment. The taxes are imposed on specific transactions involving firearms. Since the Act does not attempt to tax the right to keep and bear arms, its taxing provisions do not, under any set of circumstances, apply to rights protected by the Second Amendment.

The defendant also argues that "certain regulations pertaining to the manufacture of the type of firearm involved here were unconstitutional on Fifth Amendment due process grounds." The defendant was not charged with violating laws pertaining to the manufacture of firearms, but only with possession of an unregistered submachine gun. The Act deals with a number of distinct offenses, and one may not attack his conviction of one of the offenses by questioning the constitutionality of provisions relating to another offense. See *United States v. Black*, 431 F.2d 524, 530 (6th Cir. 1970), cert denied, 402 U.S. 975, 91 S.Ct. 1673, 29 L.Ed.2d 140 (1971). The district court properly declined to consider Warin's due process arguments as a maker of firearms.

We also agree with the disposition by the district court of defendant's contention that the statute under which he was charged and convicted violates the Ninth Amendment to the Constitution. We simply do not conceive of the possession of an unregistered submachine gun as one of those "additional fundamental rights, protected from governmental infringement, which exist alongside those fundamental rights specifically mentioned in the first eight constitutional amendments." *Griswold v. Connecticut*, 381 U.S. 479, 488, 85 S.Ct. 1678, 1684, 14 L.Ed.2d 510 (1965) (concurring opinion of Goldberg, J.).

It would unduly extend this opinion to attempt to deal with every argument made by defendant and amicus curiae, Second Amendment Foundation, all of which are based on the erroneous supposition that the Second Amendment is concerned with the rights of individuals rather than those of the States or that defendant's automatic membership in the "sedentary militia" of Ohio brings him within the reach of its guarantees.

The judgment of the district court is affirmed.

ANALYSIS

Francis Warin was convicted of possessing a gun in violation of the 1968 Gun Control Act. On appeal, the court concluded that even though Warin could have been subject to enrollment in Ohio's state militia (he was not actually a member; the reference to Warin as a member of the "sedentary militia" meant that he was an adult male who could, conceivably, be called up for militia service, even though no such general call-ups had occurred since the nineteenth century), that fact provided no basis for allowing him to own an unregistered submachine gun in violation of law. The court also concluded that the Second Amendment did not give him a right to privately own a gun, referring to "the erroneous supposition that the Second Amendment is concerned with the rights of individuals." And Warin's argument that he was entitled to own a military-style weapon under the Second Amendment because he could be subject to a militia call-up was rejected.

This decision cited the Supreme Court's 1939 *Miller* decision and the lower federal court ruling in *Cases* (see previously) to conclude that "the Second Amendment guarantees a collective rather than an individual right," meaning that the amendment pertains to citizen service in a government militia. It also cited another federal court ruling to emphasize that "there can be no serious claim to any express constitutional right of an individual to possess a firearm" arising from the Second Amendment. Further, the court noted that even when the Second Amendment did apply, it was well understood that gun ownership was and is subject to regulation; that is, it "was never treated as anything like an absolute right by the common law. It was regulated by statute as to time and place as far back as the [British] Statute of Northampton in 1328 and on many occasions since." Finally, the court addressed the matter of public safety and order, saying that "an organized society which fails to regulate the importation, manufacture and transfer of the highly sophisticated lethal weapons in existence today does so at its peril."

FURTHER READING

Bruce, John M., and Clyde Wilcox, eds. *The Changing Politics of Gun Control.* Lanham, MD: Rowman and Littlefield, 1998.

Handgun Ban Judged Constitutional

- **Document:** U.S. Court of Appeals for the Seventh Circuit, case of *Quilici v. Morton Grove*, cert. denied, 464 U.S. 863 (1983)
- **Date:** December 6, 1982
- **Where:** Chicago, Illinois
- **Significance:** A local law barring citizens from possessing handguns in their homes was not in violation of the Second Amendment or other rights.

DOCUMENT

Quilici v. Morton Grove, 695 F.2d 261 (7th Cir., 1982)

Victor D. QUILICI, Robert Stengl, et al., George L. Reichert, and Robert E. Metier, Plaintiffs-Appellants,
VILLAGE OF MORTON GROVE, et al., Defendants-Appellees.
Argued May 28, 1982.
Decided Dec. 6, 1982.
As Amended Dec. 10, 1982.
Rehearing and Rehearing En Banc Denied March 2, 1983.
Before BAUER, WOOD, and COFFEY, Circuit Judges. BAUER, Circuit Judge.

This appeal concerns the constitutionality of the Village of Morton Grove's Ordinance No. 81–11, which prohibits the possession of handguns within the Village's borders. The district court held that the Ordinance was constitutional. We affirm.

I

Victor D. Quilici initially challenged Ordinance No. 81–11 in state court. Morton Grove removed the action to federal court where it was consolidated with two similar actions, one brought by George L. Reichert and Robert E. Metier (collectively Reichert) and one brought by Robert Stengl, Martin Gutenkauf, Alice Gutenkauf, Walter J. Dutchak and Geoffrey Lagonia (collectively Stengi). Plaintiffs alleged that Ordinance No. 81–11 violated article 1, section 22 of the Illinois Constitution and the second, ninth and fourteenth amendments of the United States Constitution. They sought an order declaring the Ordinance unconstitutional and permanently enjoining its enforcement. The parties filed cross motions for summary judgment. The district court granted Morton Grove's motion for summary judgment and denied plaintiffs' motions for summary judgment.

In its opinion, *Quilici v. Village of Morton Grove*, 532 F.Supp. 1169 (N.D.III. 1981), the district court set forth several reasons for upholding the handgun ban's validity under the state and federal constitutions. First, it held that the Ordinance which banned only certain kinds of arms was a valid exercise of Morton Grove's police power and did not conflict with section 22's conditional right to keep and bear arms. Second, relying on *Presser v. Illinois*, 116 U.S. 252 (1886), the court concluded that the second amendment's guarantee of the right to bear arms has not been incorporated into the fourteenth amendment and, therefore, is inapplicable to Morton Grove. Finally, it stated that the ninth amendment does not include the right to possess handguns for self-defense. Appellants contend that the district court incorrectly construed the relevant constitutional provisions, assigning numerous errors based on case law, historical analysis, common law traditions and public policy concerns.

While we recognize that this case raises controversial issues which engender strong emotions, our task is to apply the law as it has been interpreted by the Supreme Court, regardless of whether that Court's interpretation comports with various personal views of what the law should be. We are also aware that we must resolve the controversy without rendering unnecessary constitutional decisions. . . . With these principles in mind we address appellants' contentions.

II

We consider the state constitutional issue first. The Illinois Constitution provides:

Subject only to the police power, the right of the individual citizen to keep and bear arm shall not be infringed. (Ill. Const. art. I, section 22)

The parties agree that the meaning of this section is controlled by the terms "arms" and "police power" but disagree as to the scope of these terms.

Relying on the statutory construction principles that constitutional guarantees should be broadly construed and that constitutional provisions should prevail over conflicting statutory provisions, appellants allege that section 22's guarantee of the right to keep and bear arms prohibits a complete ban of any one kind of arm. They argue that the constitutional history of section 22 establishes that the term "arms" includes those weapons commonly employed for "recreation or the protection of person and property,"

6 Record of Proceedings, Sixth Illinois Constitutional Convention 87 (Proceedings), and contend that handguns have consistently been used for these purposes.

Appellants concede that the phrase "subject to the police power" does not prohibit reasonable regulation of arms. Thus, they admit that laws which require the licensing of guns or which restrict the carrying of concealed weapons or the possession of firearms by minors, convicted felons, and incompetents are valid. However, they maintain that no authority supports interpreting section 22 to permit a ban on the possession of handguns merely because alternative weapons are not also banned. They argue that construing section 22 in this manner would lead to the anomalous situation in which one municipality completely bans handguns while a neighboring municipality completely bans all arms but handguns.

In contrast, Morton Grove alleges that "arms" is a general term which does not include any specific kind of weapon. Relying on section 22's language, which they characterize as clear and explicit, Morton Grove reads section 22 to guarantee the right to keep only some, but not all, arms which are used for "recreation or the protection of person and property." It argues that the Ordinance passes constitutional muster because standard rifles and shotguns are also used for "recreation or the protection of person and property" and Ordinance No. 81–11 does not ban these weapons.

While Morton Grove does not challenge appellants' assertion that "arms" includes handguns, we believe that a discussion of the kind of arms section 22 protects is an appropriate place to begin our analysis. Because we disagree with Morton Grove's assertion that section 22's language is clear and explicit, we turn to the constitutional debates for guidance on the proper construction of arms. . . .

The debates indicate that the category of arms protected by section 22 is not limited to military weapons; the framers also intended to include those arms that "law-abiding persons commonly employ[ed]" for "recreation or the protection of person and property." 6 Proceedings 87. Handguns are undisputedly the type of arms commonly used for "recreation or the protection of person and property."

Our conclusion that the framers intended to include handguns in the class of protected arms is supported by the fact that in discussing the term the Proceedings refer to *People v. Brown*, 253 Mich. 537, 541(42, 235 N.W. 245, 246(47 (1931) and *State v. Duke*, 42 Tex. 455, 458 (1875). Brown defines weapons as those "relied upon . . . for defense or pleasure," including "ordinary guns" and "revolvers." 253 Mich. at 542, 235 N.W. at 247. Duke states that "[t]he arms which every person is secured the right to keep and bear (in defense of himself or the State, subject to legislative regulation), must be such arms as are commonly kept, . . . and are appropriate for . . . self defense, as well as such as are proper for the defense of the State." 42 Tex. at 458. The delegates' statements and reliance on Brown and Duke convinces us that the term *arms* in section 22 includes handguns.

Having determined that section 22 includes handguns within the class of arms protected, we must now determine the extent to which a municipality may exercise its police power to restrict, or even prohibit, the right to keep and bear these arms. The district court concluded that section 22 recognizes only a narrow individual right which is subject to substantial legislative control. It noted that "[t]o the extent that one looks to the convention debate for assistance in reconciling the conflict between the right to arms and the exercise of the police power, the debate clearly supports its narrow construction of the individual right." *Quilici v. Village of Morton Grove*, 532 F.Supp. at 1174. It further noted that while the Proceedings cite some cases holding that the state's police power should be read restrictively, those cases were decided under "distinctly different constitutional provisions" and, thus, have little application to this case. Id. at 1176.

We agree with the district court that the right to keep and bear arms in Illinois is so limited by the police power that a ban on handguns does not violate that right. In reaching this conclusion we find two factors significant. First, section 22's plain language grants only the right to keep and bear arms, not handguns. Second, although the framers intended handguns to be one of the arms conditionally protected under section 22, they also envisioned that local governments might exercise their police power to restrict, or prohibit, the right to keep and bear handguns. For example, Delegate Foster, speaking for the majority, explained:

> It could be argued that, in theory, the legislature now [prior to the adoption of the 1970 Illinois Constitution] has the right to ban all firearms in the state as far as individual citizens owning them is concerned. That is the power which we wanted to restrict(an absolute ban on all firearms. (3 Proceedings 1688)

Delegate Foster then noted that section 22 "would prevent a complete ban on all guns, but there could be a ban on certain categories." Id. at 1693. . . . It is difficult to imagine clearer evidence that section 22 was intended to permit a municipality to ban handguns if it so desired.

Appellants argue that construing section 22 to protect only some unspecified categories of arms, thereby allowing municipalities to exercise their police power to enact dissimilar gun control laws, leads to "untenable" and "absurd" results. Quilici br. at 14. This argument ignores the fact that the Illinois Constitution authorizes local governments to function as home rule units to "exercise any power and perform any function pertaining to its government and affairs". Illinois Const. art. VIII, section 6(a). Home rule government . . . is based on the theory that local governments are in the best position to assess the needs and desires of the community and, thus, can most wisely enact legislation addressing local concerns. . . . Illinois home rule units have expansive powers to govern as they deem proper . . . including the authority to impose greater restrictions on particular rights than those imposed by the state. . . . The only limits on their autonomy are those imposed by the Illinois Constitution . . . or by the Illinois General Assembly exercising its authority to pre-empt home rule in specific instances. Because we have concluded that the Illinois Constitution permits a ban on certain categories of arms, home rule units such as Morton Grove may properly enact different, even inconsistent, arms restrictions. This is precisely the kind of local control envisioned by the new Illinois Constitution.

Appellants concede that municipalities may, under the Illinois Constitution, exercise their police power to enact regulations which prohibit "possession of items legislatively found to be dangerous . . .", Quilici br. at 9. They draw a distinction, however, between the exercise of the police power in general and the exercise of police power with respect to a constitutionally protected right. Indeed, they vehemently insist that a municipality may not exercise its police power to completely prohibit a constitutional guarantee.

We agree that the state may not exercise its police power to violate a positive constitutional mandate . . . but we reiterate that section 22 simply prohibits a[n] absolute ban on all firearms. Since Ordinance No. 81–11 does not prohibit all firearms, it does not prohibit a constitutionally protected right. There is no right under the Illinois Constitution to possess a handgun, nor does the state have an overriding state interest in gun control which requires it to retain exclusive control in order to prevent home rule units from adopting conflicting enactments. . . . Accordingly, Morton Grove may exercise its police power to prohibit handguns even though this prohibition interferes with an individual's liberty or property.

The Illinois Constitution establishes a presumption in favor of municipal home rule. . . . Once a local government identifies a problem and enacts legislation to mitigate or eliminate it, that enactment is presumed valid and may be overturned only if it is unreasonable, clearly arbitrary, and has no foundation in the police power. . . . Thus, it is not the province of this court to pass judgment on the merits of Ordinance No. 81–11; our task is simply to determine whether Ordinance No. 81–11's restrictions are rationally related to its stated goals. . . . As the district court noted, there is at least some empirical evidence that gun control legislation may reduce the number of deaths and accidents caused by handguns. . . . This evidence is sufficient to sustain the conclusion that Ordinance No. 81–11 is neither wholly arbitrary nor completely unsupported by any set of facts. . . . Accordingly, we decline to consider plaintiffs' arguments that Ordinance No. 81–11 will not make Morton Grove a safer, more peaceful place.

We agree with the district court that Ordinance No. 81–11: (1) is properly directed at protecting the safety and health of Morton Grove citizens; (2) is a valid exercise of Morton Grove's police power; and (3) does not violate any of appellants' rights guaranteed by the Illinois Constitution.

III

We next consider whether Ordinance No. 81–11 violates the second amendment to the United States Constitution. While appellants all contend that Ordinance No. 81–11 is invalid under the second amendment, they offer slightly different arguments to substantiate this contention. All argue, however, that the second amendment applies to state and local governments and that the second amendment guarantee of the right to keep and bear arms exists, not only to assist in the common defense, but also to protect the individual. While reluctantly conceding that *Presser v. Illinois*, 116 U.S. 252 (1886), held that the second amendment applied only to action by the federal government they nevertheless assert that *Presser* also held that the right to keep and bear arms is an attribute of national citizenship which is not subject to state restriction. Reichert br. at 36. Finally, apparently responding to the district court's comments that "[p]laintiffs . . . have not suggested that the Morton Grove Ordinance in any way interferes with the ability of the United States to maintain public security . . ." *Quilici v. Village of Morton Grove*, 532 F.Supp. at 1169, Quilici and Reichert argue in this court that the Morton Grove Ordinance interferes with the federal government's ability to maintain public security by preventing individuals from defending themselves and the community from "external or internal armed threats." Quilici br. at 12; Reichert br. at 37-38. These are the same arguments made in the district court. Accordingly, we comment only briefly on the points already fully analyzed in that court's decision.

As we have noted, the parties agree that *Presser* is controlling, but disagree as to what *Presser* held. It is difficult to understand how appellants can assert that *Presser* supports the theory that the second amendment right to keep and bear arms is a fundamental right which the state cannot regulate when the *Presser* decision plainly states that "[t]he Second Amendment declares that it shall not be infringed, but this . . . means no more than that it shall not be infringed by Congress. This is one of the amendments that has no other effect than to restrict the powers of the National government . . ." *Presser v. Illinois*, 116 U.S. 252, 265 (1886). As the district court explained in detail, appellants' claim that *Presser* supports the proposition that the second amendment guarantee of the right to keep and bear arms is not subject to state restriction is based on dicta quoted out of context. *Quilici v. Village of Morton Grove*, 532 F.Supp. at 1181-82. This argument borders on the frivolous and does not warrant any further consideration.

Apparently recognizing the inherent weakness of their reliance on *Presser*, appellants urge three additional arguments to buttress their claim that the second amendment applies to the states. They contend that: (1) *Presser* is no longer good law because later Supreme Court cases incorporating other amendments into the fourteenth amendment have effectively overruled *Presser*, Reichert br. at 52; (2) *Presser* is illogical, Quilici br. at 12; and (3) the entire Bill of Rights has been implicitly incorporated into the fourteenth amendment to apply to the states, Reichert br. at 48-52.

None of these arguments has merit. First, appellants offer no authority, other than their own opinions, to support their arguments that *Presser* is no longer good law or would have been decided differently today. Indeed, the fact that the Supreme Court continues to cite *Presser*, *Malloy v. Hogan*, 378 U.S. 1, 4 n. 2 (1964), leads to the opposite conclusion. Second, regardless of whether appellants agree with the *Presser* analysis, it is the law of the land and we are bound by it. Their assertion that *Presser* is illogical is a policy matter for the Supreme Court to address. Finally, their theory of implicit incorporation is wholly unsupported. The Supreme Court has specifically rejected the proposition that the entire Bill of Rights applies to the states through the fourteenth amendment. . . .

Since we hold that the second amendment does not apply to the states, we need not consider the scope of its guarantee of the right to bear arms. For the sake of completeness, however, and because appellants devote a large portion of their briefs to this issue, we briefly comment on what we believe to be the scope of the second amendment.

The second amendment provides that "A regulated Militia being necessary to the security of a free State, the right of the people to keep and bear Arms, shall not be infringed." U.S. Const. amend. II. Construing this language according to its plain meaning, it seems clear that the right to bear arms is inextricably connected to the preservation of a militia. This is precisely the manner in which the Supreme Court interpreted the second amendment in *United States v. Miller*, 307 U.S. 174 (1939), the only Supreme Court case specifically addressing that amendment's scope. There the Court held that the right to keep and bear arms extends only to those arms which are necessary to maintain a well regulated militia.

In an attempt to avoid the *Miller* holding that the right to keep and bear arms exists only as it relates to protecting the public security, appellants argue that "[t]he fact that the right to keep and bear arms is joined with language expressing one of its purposes in no way permits a construction which limits or confines the exercise of that right." Reichert br. at 35. They offer no explanation for how they have arrived at this conclusion. Alternatively, they argue that handguns are military weapons. Stengl's br. at 11-13. Our reading of *Miller* convinces us that it does not support either of these theories. As the Village correctly notes, appellants are essentially arguing that *Miller* was wrongly decided and should be overruled. Such arguments have no place before this court. Under the controlling authority of *Miller* we conclude that the right to keep and bear handguns is not guaranteed by the second amendment.

Because the second amendment is not applicable to Morton Grove and possession of handguns by individuals is not part of the right to keep and bear arms, Ordinance No. 81–11 does not violate the second amendment.

IV

Finally, we consider whether Ordinance No. 81–11 violates the ninth amendment. Appellants argue that, although the right to use commonly-owned arms for self-defense is not explicitly listed in the Bill of Rights, it is a fundamental right protected by the ninth amendment. Citing no authority which directly supports their contention, they rely on the debates in the First Congress and the writings of legal philosophers to establish that the right of an individual to own and possess firearms for self-defense is an absolute and inalienable right which cannot be impinged.

Since appellants do not cite, and our research has not revealed, any Supreme Court case holding that any specific right is protected by the ninth amendment, appellants' argument has no legal significance. Appellants may believe the ninth amendment should be read to recognize an unwritten, fundamental, individual right to own or possess firearms; the fact remains that the Supreme Court has never embraced this theory.

Reasonable people may differ about the wisdom of Ordinance No. 81–11. History may prove that the Ordinance cannot effectively promote peace and security for Morton Grove's citizens. Such issues, however, are not before the court. We simply hold the Ordinance No. 81–11 is a proper exercise of Morton Grove's police power and does not violate art. 1, section 22 of the Illinois Constitution or the second, ninth, or fourteenth amendments of the United States Constitution. Accordingly, the decision of the district court is

AFFIRMED.

SOURCE: http://www.cs.cmu.edu/afs/cs/usr/wbardwel/public/nfalist/quilici_v_morton_grove.txt

ANALYSIS

In 1981, the village of Morton Grove, Illinois, passed a local ordinance banning the possession of working handguns, with exceptions for police officers, security guards, and licensed gun collectors. Residents were not actually denied their handguns, however, as they could keep them in licensed gun clubs.

DID YOU KNOW?

Gun Banning Comes to Illinois

Three months after the assassination attempt against President Ronald Reagan by John Hinckley on March 30, 1981, the Chicago suburban community of Morton Grove enacted a law banning handguns. Unlike long guns (rifles and shotguns), which had hunting and sporting purposes, handguns had little sporting use, and were the guns of choice for criminals: even though there are twice as many long guns as handguns in America, and long guns are usually easier to obtain, 80 percent of all gun crimes are committed with handguns.

The local law was the product of a local initiative, not of any nationwide campaign by gun control supporters. But gun rights supporters viewed the law with great alarm. To them, it was the leading wedge of what they claimed was a nationwide effort to ban all guns, a fear that seemed confirmed when two nearby Illinois towns, Evanston and Oak Park, enacted similar laws. With the National Rifle Association leading the way, gun owners were mobilized around the country to fight similar laws elsewhere. But rather than try to halt ban efforts town by town, the NRA settled on a different strategy—to lobby state governments around the country to enact "pre-emption" laws barring localities from enacting local laws that were stricter than existing state laws. This strategy proved successful for two reasons. First, once state governments adopted laws barring new, tougher gun laws, they could halt local gun control efforts in one fell swoop. Second, state governments were generally more conservative and therefore more receptive to gun rights lobbying efforts. In addition, few citizens pay much attention to state policymaking, so gun rights groups could function in a low visibility manner through low-key pressure politics. By 2005, 45 states had some kind of gun preemption law on the books.

Source: Kristin A. Goss, *Disarmed: The Missing Movement for Gun Control in America*. Princeton: Princeton University Press, 2006.

Gun control opponents filed suit against the local law—one of the strictest in the nation—claiming that the law violated the Second, Fifth, Ninth, and Fourteenth Amendments, as well as Article I, Section 22 of the Illinois State Constitution. A federal court for the Northern District of Illinois ruled in favor of the local law. On appeal, the Seventh Circuit of the U.S. Court of Appeals also upheld the law. In its ruling, the court swept aside the argument that the Second Amendment protected an individual right to bear arms. Citing Supreme Court rulings in *Presser* (see Chapter 3) and *U.S. v. Miller* (see Chapter 5), the court said that the Second Amendment applied only to maintenance of a well-regulated militia: "it seems clear that the right to bear arms is inextricably connected to the preservation of a militia." The court also concluded that there was no basis for asserting that the Bill or Rights enshrined a right of personal self-defense (the right is well recognized, but is found in criminal law and the common-law tradition), nor was there any basis for saying that the entire Bill of Rights had been "implicitly incorporated" (that is, applied to the states, and not just the federal government), as only parts of the Bill of Rights had been incorporated, but not the Second Amendment. Those opposing the Morton Grove law also argued that the nineteenth-century *Presser* case was, in effect, obsolete. Yet this claim was also rebuffed because it was based on the false assumption that cases somehow may expire simply by virtue of their age. *Presser*, however, has never been overturned, and it has been cited as good law in recent decades.

The *Morton Grove* ruling was appealed to the Supreme Court, but it refused to hear the case, letting the ruling stand. Among gun control cases, this one vindicated the comment of two

Supreme Court justices in 1972 (see *Adams v. Williams*, Chapter 5) when they said that the Second Amendment posed no obstacle to strict gun laws, even including the banning of guns popular with criminals.

FURTHER READING

Goss, Kristen A. *Disarmed: The Missing Movement for Gun Control in America*. Princeton: Princeton University Press, 2006.

States May Enact Strict Laws Regarding the Carrying of Concealed Weapons

- **Document:** U.S. Court of Appeals for the Ninth Circuit, case of *Hickman v. Block*, cert. denied, 519 U.S. 912 (1996)
- **Date:** April 5, 1996
- **Where:** San Francisco, California
- **Significance:** This federal case upheld California's strict standard for who may be granted a permit to carry a concealed weapon.

DOCUMENT

Hickman v. Block, 81 F.3d 168 (9th Cir. 1996)

Appeal from the United States District Court for the Central District of California
Robert M. Takasugi, District Judge, Presiding
Argued and Submitted November 13, 1995—Pasadena, California
Filed April 5, 1996
Before: Cynthia Holcomb Hall and John T. Noonan, Jr., Circuit Judges, and William B. Shubb, District Judge. . . .
Opinion by Judge Hall
HALL, Circuit Judge:
Douglas Ray Hickman appeals from an order granting summary judgment in favor of the appellees, who denied Hickman a concealed weapons permit. He complains, among other things, that the appellees' permit issuance policy violated his Second Amendment right to bear arms. We have jurisdiction over his timely appeal pursuant to 28 U.S.C. section 1291, and affirm on the basis that Hickman lacks standing to sue for a violation of the Second Amendment.

I

Hickman owns and operates a responding security alarm company. He is also a federally licensed arms dealer. Wishing to break into the lucrative field of "executive protection," Hickman submitted a string of applications for a concealed firearms permit to the appellee municipal authorities. When the authorities denied Hickman's applications, he filed this suit for damages and injunctive relief, arguing several theories of liability under 42 U.S.C. sections 1983 and 1985(3). We considered and rejected in a unpublished memorandum disposition all of Hickman's various arguments save one: his claim for relief under section 1983 based on a violation of the Second Amendment. This issue we now address. . . .

The appellees issue concealed firearms permits under the authority of a California statute which provides, in relevant part:

The sheriff of a county or the chief or other head of a municipal police department of any city or city and county, upon proof that the person applying is of good moral character, that good cause exists for the issuance, and that the person applying is a resident of the county, may issue to that person a license to carry a pistol, revolver, or other firearm capable of being concealed upon the person. . . .

Cal. Penal Code S 12050(a)(1). The County and San Fernando share in common a policy concerning the requirements of "good cause." Under the policy, good cause is shown by: convincing evidence of a clear and present danger to life . . . which cannot be adequately dealt with by existing law enforcement resources, and which danger cannot be reasonably avoided by alternative measures, and which danger would be significantly mitigated by the applicant's carrying of a concealed firearm.

The policy also requires some proof of firearms training. Finally, the policy provides that "[n]o position or job classification in itself should constitute good cause for the issuance or denial of a license." Each application is to be reviewed individually for cause.

Hickman first applied for a permit in 1988. He applied to each of the appellees in turn, stating that he required a permit in order to work as a private bodyguard. The County and San Fernando denied his applications on the grounds that Hickman, having cited no "clear and present danger" to personal safety, had failed to show good cause. Hickman next attempted to obtain a permit in 1989 by joining a reserves unit for the San Fernando police department. For reasons not clear in the record, San Fernando denied him admission to the reserves and blocked this approach to a permit.

Hickman submitted his final round of permit applications in 1991, following two incidents which, he felt, amounted to a showing of good cause. First, Hickman reported being "approached" by two "Hispanic men" while he loaded ammunition into his car. He frightened them away by raising an unloaded pistol. Second, Hickman recited an isolated threat by a disgruntled ex-employee, who allegedly said: "I know where you live;" "You will have to look over your shoulder for the rest of your life;" and "I will get you and it won't even be me." On the force of these incidents Hickman reapplied to the County and San Fernando. The County denied Hickman's application for failure to show cause and San Fernando apparently failed to respond.

Hickman next went to court; he filed this lawsuit in October 1991. In March 1992 the district court granted the County's motion to dismiss Hickman's action to the extent that it was based upon a violation of the Second Amendment. It also denied his section 1985(3) conspiracy claim. The City of Los Angeles, having been a party only to the conspiracy claim, was then dismissed as a party to the suit. In July 1992 the County moved for summary judgment on the remaining claims. Discovery ensued. San Fernando joined in the County's motion. In May 1994 the district court entered its final order granting summary judgment for the remaining appellees: the County, San Fernando and their respective municipal officers.

II

The Second Amendment to the United States Constitution states: "A well regulated Militia, being necessary to the security of a free State, the right of the people to keep and bear Arms, shall not be infringed." U.S. Const. amend. II. Hickman argues that the Second Amendment requires the states to regulate gun ownership and use in a "reasonable" manner. The question presented at the threshold of Hickman's appeal is whether the Second Amendment confers upon individual citizens standing to enforce the right to keep and bear arms. We follow our sister circuits in holding that the Second Amendment is a right held by the states, and does not protect the possession of a weapon by a private citizen. We conclude that Hickman can show no legal injury, and therefore lacks standing to bring this action. . . .

This case turns on the first constitutional standing element: whether Hickman has shown injury to an interest protected by the Second Amendment. We note at the outset that no individual has ever succeeded in demonstrating such injury in federal court. The seminal authority in this area continues to be *United States v. Miller*, 307 U.S. 174 (1939), in which the Supreme Court upheld a conviction under the National Firearms Act, 26 U.S.C. S 1132 (1934), for transporting a sawed-off shotgun in interstate commerce. The Court rejected the appellant's hypothesis that the Second Amendment protected his possession of that weapon. Consulting the text and history of the amendment, the Court found that the right to keep and bear arms is meant solely to protect the right of the states to keep and maintain armed militia. In a famous passage, the Court held that

[i]n the absence of any evidence tending to show that the possession or use of a "shotgun having a barrel of less than eighteen inches in length" at this time has some reasonable relationship to the preservation or efficiency of a well-regulated militia, we cannot say that the Second Amendment guarantees the right to keep and bear such an instrument.

307 U.S. at 178. The Court's understanding follows a plain reading of the Amendment's text. The Amendment's second clause declares that the goal is to preserve the security of "a free state;" its first clause establishes the premise that well regulated militia are necessary to this end. Thus it is only in furtherance of state security that "the right of the people to keep and bear arms" is finally proclaimed.

Following Miller, "[i]t is clear that the Second Amendment guarantees a collective rather than an individual right." *United States v. Warin*, 530 F.2d 103, 106 (6th Cir.), cert. denied 96 S.Ct. 3168 (1976); see also *Thomas v. Members of City Council of Portland*, 730 F.2d 41, 42 (1st Cir. 1984) (same, citing *Warin*); *United States v. Johnson*, 497 F.2d 548, 550 (4th Cir. 1974) (cited with approval in *Lewis*, 445 U.S. at 65 n.8) (same). Because the Second Amendment guarantees the right of the states to maintain armed militia, the states alone stand in the position to show legal injury when this right is infringed.

Nevertheless, Hickman argues that under the Second Amendment, individuals have the right to complain about the manner in which a state arms its citizens. We fail to see the logic in this argument. The Second Amendment creates a right, not a duty. It does not oblige the states to keep an armed militia, or to arm their citizens generally, although some states do preserve, nominally at least, a broad individual right to bear arms as a foundation for their state militia. See, e.g., *People v. Blue*, 54 P.2d 385 (Colo. 1975) (en banc) (citing Colo. Const. art. II, S 13) (recognizing individual right to bear arms under state constitution); *State v. Amos*, 343 So.2d 166, 168 (La. 1977) (citing La. Const. art I, S 11) (same proposition); *State v. Krantz*, 164 P.2d 453 (Wash. 1945) (citing Wash. Const. art I, S 24) (same proposition); *Akron v. Williams*, 177 N.E.2d 802 (Ohio Ct. App. 1966) (citing Ohio Const. art. I, S 4) (same proposition). Even in states which profess to maintain a citizen militia, an individual may not rely on this fact to manipulate the Constitution's legal injury requirement by arguing that a particular weapon of his admits some military use, or that he himself is a member of the armed citizenry from which the state draws its militia. *United States v. Oakes*, 564 F.2d 384, 387 (10th Cir. 1977), cert. denied, 435 U.S. 926 (1978) (technical membership in state militia insufficient to show legal injury under Second Amendment); *Warin*, 530 F.2d at 106 (same with respect to individual "subject to enrollment" in state militia); *United States v. Hale*, 978 F.2d 1016, 1019 (8th Cir. 1982) (same, citing *Warin*); *United States v. Graves*, 554 F.2d 65, 66 n.2 (3rd. Cir. 1977) (en banc) (narrowly construing the Second Amendment "to guarantee the right to bear arms as a member of a militia").

Hickman's claim amounts to a "generalized grievance" regarding the organization and training of a state militia. See *Lujan*, 112 S.Ct. at 2144. We do not involve ourselves in such matters. As the Supreme Court has observed, "decisions as to the composition, training, equipping, and control of a military force are essentially professional military judgments," and as such are nonjusticiable. *Gilligan*, 413 U.S. at 10. "[I]t is difficult to conceive of an area of governmental activity in which the courts have less competence." Id. For this reason, among others, we leave military matters to the elected branches of government. See id.

III

Because Hickman has not sued to defend the state's right to keep an armed militia, he has failed to show "injury" as required by constitutional standing doctrine. Accordingly we have no jurisdiction to hear his appeal.

The judgment is AFFIRMED.

ANALYSIS

Douglas Ray Hickman was denied on several occasions a permit to carry a concealed weapon by the state of California. California's standard for granting a permit was a tough one, in that an applicant needed to show "convincing evidence of a clear and present danger to life . . . which cannot be adequately dealt with by existing law enforcement resources. . . . " Hickman filed suit against the start, partly on Second Amendment grounds.

In *Hickman*, the court rejected the man's claim, concluding that, "We follow our sister circuits in holding that the Second Amendment is a right held by the states, and does not protect the possession of a weapon by a private citizen." *Hickman* based its ruling largely on the Supreme Court's 1939 *Miller* ruling. *Hickman* found *Miller* to be clear-cut in its militia-based view of the Second Amendment, as it was based on a "plain reading" of the amendment. As the *Hickman* court said, "Consulting the text and history of the amendment, the [*Miller*] Court found that the right to keep and bear arms is meant solely to protect the right of the states to keep and maintain armed militia." As the court also said, "it is only in furtherance of state

Ruger Mini-14 .223-caliber rifle. Photo by Dawn Van Hall.

security that 'the right of the people to keep and bear arms' is finally proclaimed." Some later federal court rulings would claim that *Miller* was less than clear in its meaning.

FURTHER READING

Foster, Carol D., Mark A. Siegel, and Nancy R. Jacobs, eds. *Gun Control—Restricting Rights or Protecting People?* Wylie, TX: Information Plus, 1993.

A Federal Court Declares, for the First Time, That the Second Amendment Protects an Individual Right

- **Document:** U.S. Court of Appeals for the Fifth Circuit, case of *U.S. v. Emerson*, 270 F.3d 203 (2001), cert. denied 536 U.S. 907 (2002)
- **Date:** October 18, 2001
- **Where:** New Orleans, Louisiana
- **Significance:** For the first time, a federal court concludes that the Second Amendment protects an individual right to own guns, even though that conclusion proves of no help to the man whose claim to the right gave rise to this case.

DOCUMENT

U.S. v. Emerson, 270 F.3d 203 (5th Cir. 2001)

REVISED October 18, 2001

Before GARWOOD, DeMOSS and PARKER, Circuit Judges.

GARWOOD, Circuit Judge:

The United States appeals the district court's dismissal of the indictment of Defendant-Appellee Dr. Timothy Joe Emerson (Emerson) for violating 18 U.S.C. § 922(g)(8)(C)(ii). The district court held that section 922(g)(8)(C)(ii) was unconstitutional on its face under the Second Amendment and as applied to Emerson under the Due Process Clause of the Fifth Amendment. We reverse and remand.

Facts and proceedings below.

On August 28, 1998, Sacha Emerson, Emerson's wife, filed a petition for divorce in the 119th District Court of Tom Green County, Texas. The petition also requested, *inter alia*, a temporary injunction enjoining Emerson from engaging in any of twenty-nine enumerated acts. . . .

On September 14, 1998, Judge Sutton issued a temporary order that included a "Temporary Injunction" which stated that Emerson "is enjoined from" engaging in any of twenty-two enumerated acts, including the following:

"2. Threatening Petitioner in person, by telephone, or in writing to take unlawful action against any person."

"4. Intentionally, knowingly, or recklessly causing bodily injury to Petitioner or to a child of either party."

"5. Threatening Petitioner or a child of either party with imminent bodily injury."

The order provides that it "shall continue in force until the signing of the final decree of divorce or until further order of this court." The September 14, 1998 order did not include any express finding that Emerson posed a future danger to Sacha or to his daughter Logan. There is nothing to indicate that Emerson ever sought to modify or challenge any of the provisions of the September 14, 1998 order.

On December 8, 1998, the grand jury for the Northern District of Texas, San Angelo division, returned a five-count indictment against Emerson. . . . Count 1, the only remaining count and the count here at issue, alleged that Emerson on November 16, 1998, unlawfully possessed "in and affecting interstate commerce" a firearm, a Beretta pistol, while subject to the above mentioned September 14, 1998 order, in violation of 18 U.S.C. § 922(g)(8). . . .

Emerson moved pretrial to dismiss the indictment, asserting that section 922(g)(8), facially and as applied to him, violates the Second Amendment and the Due Process Clause of the Fifth Amendment. He also moved to dismiss on the basis that section 922(g)(8) was an improper exertion of federal power under the Commerce Clause and that, in any case, the law unconstitutionally usurps powers reserved to the states by the Tenth Amendment. An evidentiary hearing was held on Emerson's motion to dismiss.

The district court granted Emerson's motions to dismiss. Subsequently, the district court issued an amended memorandum opinion reported at 46 F.Supp.2d 598 (N.D. Tex. 1999). The district court held that dismissal of the indictment was proper on Second or Fifth Amendment grounds, but rejected Emerson's Tenth Amendment and Commerce Clause arguments.

The government appealed. Emerson filed a notice of cross-appeal, which was dismissed by this Court. The government challenges the district court's dismissal on Second and Fifth Amendment grounds. Emerson defends the district court's dismissal on those grounds and also urges that dismissal was in any event proper under the Commerce Clause and on statutory grounds. . . .

V. SECOND AMENDMENT

The Second Amendment provides:

"A well regulated Militia, being necessary to the security of a free State, the right of the people to keep and bear arms, shall not be infringed." . . .

In the last few decades, courts and commentators have offered what may fairly be characterized as three different basic interpretations of the Second Amendment. The first is that the Second Amendment does not apply to individuals; rather, it merely recognizes the right of a state to arm its militia. This "states' rights" or "collective rights" interpretation of the Second Amendment has been embraced by several of our sister circuits. The government commended the states' rights view of the Second Amendment to the district court, urging that the Second Amendment does not apply to individual citizens.

Proponents of the next model admit that the Second Amendment recognizes some limited species of individual right. However, this supposedly "individual" right to *bear* arms can only be exercised by members of a functioning, organized state militia who bear the arms while and as a part of actively participating in the organized militia's activities. The "individual" right to *keep* arms only applies to members of such a militia, and then only if the federal and state governments fail to provide the firearms necessary for such militia service. At present, virtually the only such organized and actively functioning militia is the National Guard, and this has been the case for many years. Currently, the federal government provides the necessary implements of warfare, including firearms, to the National Guard, and this likewise has long been the case. Thus, under this model, the Second Amendment poses no obstacle to the wholesale disarmament of the American people. A number of our sister circuits have accepted this model, sometimes referred to by commentators as the sophisticated collective rights model. On appeal the government has abandoned the states' rights model and now advocates the sophisticated collective rights model.

The third model is simply that the Second Amendment recognizes the right of individuals to keep and bear arms. This is the view advanced by Emerson and adopted by the district court. None of our sister circuits has subscribed to this model, known by commentators as the individual rights model or the standard model. The individual rights view has enjoyed considerable academic endorsement, especially in the last two decades.

We now turn to the question of whether the district court erred in adopting an individual rights or standard model as the basis of its construction of the Second Amendment.

B. Stare Decisis and *United States v. Miller*

The government steadfastly maintains that the Supreme Court's decision in *United States v. Miller*, 59 S.Ct. 816 (1939), mandated acceptance of the collective rights or sophisticated collective rights model, and rejection of the individual rights or standard model, as a basis for construction of the Second Amendment. We disagree.

Only in *United States v. Miller* has the Supreme Court rendered any holding respecting the Second Amendment as applied to the federal government. There, the indictment charged the defendants with transporting in interstate commerce, from Oklahoma to Arkansas, an unregistered "Stevens shotgun having a barrel less than 18 inches in length" without having the required stamped written order, contrary to the National Firearms Act. The defendants filed a demurrer challenging the facial validity of the indictment on the ground that "[t]he National Firearms Act . . . offends the inhibition of the Second Amendment," and "[t]he District Court held that section 11 of the Act [proscribing interstate transportation of a firearm, as therein defined, that lacked registration or a stamped order] violates the Second Amendment. It accordingly sustained the demurrer and quashed the indictment." *Id.* at 817–18. The government appealed, and we have examined a copy of its brief. The *Miller* defendants neither filed any brief nor made any appearance in the Supreme Court. . . .

The government's brief thereafter makes essentially *two* legal arguments.

First, it contends that the right secured by the Second Amendment is "only one which exists where the arms are borne in the militia or some other military organization provided for by law and intended for the protection of the state." *Id.* at 15. This, in essence, is the sophisticated collective rights model.

The *second* of the government's two arguments in *Miller* is reflected by the following passage from its brief:

"While some courts have said that the right to bear arms includes the right of the individual to have them for the protection of his person and property as well as the right of the people to bear them collectively (*People v. Brown,* 253 Mich. 537; *State v. Duke,* 42 Tex. 455), the cases are unanimous in holding that the term "arms" as used in constitutional provisions refers only to those weapons which are ordinarily used for military or public defense purposes and does not relate to those weapons which are commonly used by criminals. Thus in *Aymette v. State* [2 Humph., Tenn. 154 (1840)], *supra,* it was said (p. 158):

'As the object for which the right to keep and bear arms is secured, is of general and public nature, to be exercised by the people in a body, for their *common defence,* so the *arms,* the right to keep which is secured, are such as are usually employed in civilized warfare, and that constitute the ordinary military equipment. If the citizens have these arms in their hands, they are prepared in the best possible manner to repel any encroachments upon their rights by those in authority. They need not, for such a purpose, the use of those weapons which are usually employed in private broils, and which are efficient only in the hands of the robber and the assassin. These weapons would be useless in war. They could not be employed advantageously in the common defence of the citizens. The right to keep and bear them, is not, therefore, secured by the constitution.'" (*Id.* at 18–19).

The government's *Miller* brief then proceeds (at pp. 19–20) to cite various other state cases, and *Robertson v. Baldwin,* 17 S.Ct. 326, 329 (1897), in support of its *second* argument, and states:

"That the foregoing cases conclusively establish that the Second Amendment has relation only to the right of the people to keep and bear arms for lawful purposes and does not conceivably relate to weapons of the type referred to in the National Firearms Act cannot be doubted. Sawed-off shotguns, sawed-off rifles and machine guns are clearly weapons which can have no legitimate use in the hands of private individuals."

Thereafter, the government's brief in its "conclusion" states: " . . . we respectfully submit that Section 11 of the National Firearms Act does not infringe 'the right of the people to keep and bear arms' secured by the Second Amendment."

Miller reversed the decision of the district court and "remanded for further proceedings." *Id.* at 820. We believe it is entirely clear that the Supreme Court decided *Miller* on the basis of the government's *second* argument–that a "shotgun having a barrel of less than eighteen inches in length" as stated in the National Firearms Act is not (or cannot merely be assumed to be) one of the "Arms" which the Second Amendment prohibits infringement of the right of the people to keep and bear–and *not* on the basis of the government's *first* argument (that the Second Amendment protects the right of the people to keep and bear *no* character of "arms" when not borne in actual, active service in the militia or some other military organization provided for by law"). *Miller* expresses its holding, as follows:

> "In the absence of any evidence tending to show that possession or use of a 'shotgun having a barrel of less than eighteen inches in length' at this time has some reasonable relationship to the preservation or efficiency of a well regulated militia, we cannot say that the Second Amendment guarantees the right to keep and bear *such an* instrument. Certainly it is not within judicial notice that this weapon is any part of the ordinary military equipment or that its use could contribute to the common defense. *Aymette v. State of Tennessee*, 2 Humph., Tenn. 154, 158." *Id.* at 818 (emphasis added).

Note that the cited page of *Aymette* (p. 158) is the page from which the government's brief quoted in support of its *second* argument (see text at call for n.16 *supra*).

Nowhere in the Court's *Miller* opinion is there any reference to the fact that the indictment does not remotely suggest that either of the two defendants was ever a member of any organized, active militia, such as the National Guard, much less that either was engaged (or about to be engaged) in any actual military service or training of such a militia unit when transporting the sawed-off shotgun from Oklahoma into Arkansas. Had the lack of such membership or engagement been a ground of the decision in *Miller*, the Court's opinion would obviously have made mention of it. But it did not.

Nor do we believe that any other portion of the *Miller* opinion supports the sophisticated collective rights model.

Just after the above quoted portion of its opinion, the *Miller* court continued in a separate paragraph initially quoting the militia clauses of article 1, § 8 (clauses 15 and 16) and concluding:

> "With obvious purpose to assure the continuation and render possible the effectiveness of such forces [militia] the declaration and guarantee of the Second Amendment were made. It must be interpreted and applied with that end in view." *Id.* at 818.

Miller then proceeds to discuss what was meant by the term "militia," stating in part:

> "The signification attributed to the term Militia appears from the debates in the Convention, the history and legislation of Colonies and States, and the writings of approved commentators. These show plainly enough that *the Militia comprised all males physically capable of acting in concert for the common defense. . . .* ordinarily

when called for service these men were expected to appear *bearing arms supplied by themselves* and of the kind in common use at the time.

"The American Colonies In the 17th Century," Osgood, Vol. 1, ch. XIII, affirms in reference to the early system of defense in New England—

"In all the colonies, as in England, the militia system was based on the principle of the assize of arms. This implied the *general obligation of all adult male inhabitants to possess arms*, and, with certain exceptions, to cooperate in the work of defence.'" *Id.* at 818 (emphasis added).

"The General Court of Massachusetts, January Session 1784 (Laws and Resolves 1784, c. 55, pp. 140, 142), provided for the organization and government of the Militia. It directed that the Train Band should 'contain *all able bodied men*, from *sixteen to forty* years of age, and the Alarm List, *all other men under sixty* years of age, * * *.'" *Id.* at 819 (emphasis added).

These passages from *Miller* suggest that the militia, the assurance of whose continuation and the rendering possible of whose effectiveness *Miller* says were purposes of the Second Amendment, referred to the generality of the civilian male inhabitants throughout their lives from teenage years until old age and to their personally keeping their own arms, and not merely to individuals during the time (if any) they might be actively engaged in actual military service or only to those who were members of special or select units.

We conclude that *Miller* does not support the government's collective rights or sophisticated collective rights approach to the Second Amendment. Indeed, to the extent that *Miller* sheds light on the matter it cuts against the government's position. Nor does the government cite any other authority binding on this panel which mandates acceptance of its position in this respect. However, we do not proceed on the assumption that *Miller* actually accepted an individual rights, as opposed to a collective or sophisticated collective rights, interpretation of the Second Amendment. Thus, *Miller* itself does not resolve that issue. We turn, therefore, to an analysis of history and wording of the Second Amendment for guidance. In undertaking this analysis, we are mindful that almost all of our sister circuits have rejected any individual rights view of the Second Amendment. However, it respectfully appears to us that all or almost all of these opinions seem to have done so either on the erroneous assumption that *Miller* resolved that issue or without sufficient articulated examination of the history and text of the Second Amendment. . . .

E. Second Amendment Protects Individual Rights

We reject the collective rights and sophisticated collective rights models for interpreting the Second Amendment. We hold, consistent with *Miller*, that it protects the right of individuals, including those not then actually a member of any militia or engaged in active military service or training, to privately possess and bear their own firearms, such as the pistol involved here, that are suitable as personal, individual weapons and are not of the general kind or type excluded by *Miller*. However, because of our holding that section 922(g)(8), as applied to Emerson, does not infringe his individual rights under the Second Amendment we will not now further elaborate as to the exact scope of all Second Amendment rights.

VI. APPLICATION TO EMERSON

The district court held that section 922(g)(8) was unconstitutionally overbroad because it allows second amendment rights to be infringed absent any express judicial finding that the person subject to the order posed a future danger. In other words, the section 922(g)(8) threshold for deprivation of the fundamental right to keep and bear arms is too low.

Although, as we have held, the Second Amendment *does* protect individual rights, that does not mean that those rights may never be made subject to any limited, narrowly tailored specific exceptions or restrictions for particular cases that are reasonable and not inconsistent with the right of Americans generally to individually keep and bear their private arms as historically understood in this country. Indeed, Emerson does not contend, and the district court did not hold, otherwise. As we have previously noted, it is clear that felons, infants and those of unsound mind may be prohibited from possessing firearms. . . . Emerson's argument that his Second Amendment rights have been violated is grounded on the propositions that the September 14, 1998 order contains no express finding that he represents a credible threat to the physical safety of his wife (or child), that the evidence before the court issuing the order would not sustain such a finding and that the provisions of the order bringing it within clause (C)(ii) of section 922(g)(8) were no more than uncontested boiler-plate. In essence, Emerson, and the district court, concede that had the order contained an express finding, on the basis of adequate evidence, that Emerson actually posed a credible threat to the physical safety of his wife, and had that been a genuinely contested matter at the hearing, with the parties and the court aware of section 922(g)(8), then Emerson could, consistent with the Second Amendment, be precluded from possessing a firearm while he remained subject to the order.

Though we are concerned with the lack of express findings in the order, and with the absence of any requirement for same in clause (C)(ii) of section 922(g)(8), we are ultimately unpersuaded by Emerson's argument. . . .

In such a case, we conclude that the nexus between firearm possession by the party so enjoined and the threat of lawless violence, is sufficient, though likely barely so, to support the deprivation, while the order remains in effect, of the enjoined party's Second Amendment right to keep and bear arms, and that this is so even though the party enjoined may not collaterally attack the particular predicate order in the section 922(g)(8) prosecution, at least so long as the order, as here, is not so transparently invalid as to have only a frivolous pretense to validity.

VII. CONCLUSION

Error has not been demonstrated in the district court's refusal to dismiss the indictment on commerce clause grounds.

For the reasons stated, we reverse the district court's order granting the motion to dismiss the indictment under the Fifth Amendment. We agree with the district court that the Second Amendment protects the right of individuals to privately keep and bear their own firearms that are suitable as individual, personal weapons and are not of the general kind or type excluded by *Miller*, regardless of whether the particular individual is then actually a member of a militia. However, for the reasons stated, we also conclude that the predicate order in question here is sufficient, albeit likely minimally so, to support the deprivation, while it remains in effect, of the defendant's Second Amendment rights. Accordingly, we reverse the district court's dismissal of the indictment on Second Amendment grounds.

We remand the cause for further proceedings not inconsistent herewith.

Reversed and Remanded

ROBERT M. PARKER, Circuit Judge, specially concurring:

I concur in the opinion except for Section V. I choose not to join Section V, which concludes that the right to keep and bear arms under the Second Amendment is an individual right, because it is dicta and is therefore not binding on us or on any other court. The determination whether the rights bestowed by the Second Amendment are collective or individual is entirely unnecessary to resolve this case and has no bearing on the judgment we dictate by this opinion. The fact that the 84 pages of dicta contained in Section V are interesting, scholarly, and well written does not change the fact that they are dicta and amount to at best an advisory treatise on this long-running debate. . . .

No doubt the special interests and academics on both sides of this debate will take great interest in the fact that at long last some court has determined (albeit in dicta) that the Second Amendment bestows an individual right. The real issue, however, is the fact that whatever the nature or parameters of the Second Amendment right, be it collective or individual, it is a right subject to reasonable regulation. The debate, therefore, over the nature of the right is misplaced. In the final analysis, whether the right to keep and bear arms is collective or individual is of no legal consequence. It is, as duly noted by the majority opinion, a right subject to reasonable regulation. If determining that Emerson had an individual Second Amendment right that could have been successfully asserted as a defense against the charge of violating § 922(g)(8), then the issue would be cloaked with legal significance. As it stands, it makes no difference. Section 922(g)(8) is simply another example of a reasonable restriction on whatever right is contained in the Second Amendment.

And whatever the scope of the claimed Second Amendment right, no responsible individual or organization would suggest that it would protect Emerson's possession of the other guns found in his military-style arsenal the day the federal indictment was handed down. In addition to the Beretta nine millimeter pistol at issue here, Emerson had a second Beretta like the first, a semi-automatic M-1 carbine, an SKS assault rifle with bayonet, and a semi-automatic M-14 assault rifle. Nor would anyone suggest that Emerson's claimed right to keep and bear arms supercedes that of his wife, their daughter, and of others to be free from bodily harm or threats of harm. Though I see no mention of it in the majority's opinion, the evidence shows that Emerson pointed the Beretta at his wife and daughter when the two went to his office to retrieve an insurance payment. When his wife moved to retrieve her shoes, Emerson cocked the hammer and made ready to fire. Emerson's instability and threatening conduct also manifested itself in comments to his office staff and the police. Emerson told an employee that he had an AK-47 and in the same breath that he planned to pay a visit to his wife's boyfriend. To a police officer he said that if any of his wife's friends were to set foot on his property they would "be found dead in the parking lot." . . .

SOURCE: http://caselaw.lp.findlaw.com/cgi-bin/getcase.pl?court=5th&navby=case&no=9910331cr0

ANALYSIS

Timothy Joe Emerson was a Texas doctor indicted for illegally carrying a handgun while subject to a restraining order issued at the behest of his estranged wife. This put him in violation of a federal law that made it a crime for persons subject to domestic violence restraining orders to possess a firearm. In a ruling that departed from every other federal court case on the subject up until then, a federal district court judge voided the gun possession ban as a violation of Emerson's Second Amendment rights. That ruling was appealed to the Fifth Circuit, which unanimously reversed the lower court decision. The case was eventually sent back to Texas state court, where Emerson was convicted of violating the federal law.

But a two-member majority of this court went on to agree with the lower court that the Second Amendment did, in fact, protect an individual right of citizens to own guns apart from militia service. In this unprecedented federal decision, the majority examined the history of the Second Amendment in great detail, wading into the burgeoning academic debate between the "collective" or militia-based view of the amendment, and the "individualist" view, which had gained prominence, mostly in law journal articles, starting in the 1980s.

The decision focused particular attention on the Supreme Court's 1939 *U.S. v. Miller* case (see Chapter 5). The *Emerson* court's analysis of *Miller* departed from that of other courts by claiming that, in actuality, the *Miller* court did not endorse the militia-based view of the Second Amendment at all, but instead focused on the narrow question of whether possession of the illegal sawed-off gun in *Miller* was in violation of the 1934 federal law because it was not a weapon that would be used in a militia. It based this argument on its interpretation of the federal government's *Miller* brief. Therefore, the *Emerson* court concluded, the Supreme Court's view was, in fact, consistent with the individualist view adopted in *Emerson* (this allowed the Fifth Circuit to endorse a view that seemingly contradicted existing Supreme Court case doctrine, which it could not otherwise do).

Ironically, after concluding that the *Miller* case supported the individualist view, the court declined to use this conclusion to buttress its own ruling: "we do not proceed on the assumption that *Miller* actually accepted an individual rights . . . interpretation of the Second Amendment." In another irony, the individualist-based interpretation did not help Emerson, as the court said that the federal law was allowable even under its individualist view. This prompted the third judge in the *Emerson* case, Judge Parker, to write a separate opinion concluding that the majority's foray into Second Amendment interpretation was meaningless "dicta" (side comments that do not bear on the outcome of the case, and that therefore carry no legal weight).

Nevertheless, the *Emerson* ruling gave hope to those pressing the courts to accept the individualist view, and it helped pave the way for the 2008 ruling in *D.C. v. Heller* (see Chapter 5). It also prompted a kind of rebuttal from the Ninth Circuit the next year in the case of *Silveira v. Lockyer*.

FURTHER READING

Spitzer, Robert J. "The Second Amendment 'Right to Bear Arms' and *United States v. Emerson*." *St. John's Law Review* 77(Winter 2003): 1–28.

DID YOU KNOW?

The Individualist View of the Second Amendment Gains Traction

Changes in the law and in judicial interpretation can come from many places. Regarding the Second Amendment, more than 40 federal court decisions accepted the militia-based view of the Second Amendment, an interpretation held consistently by the Supreme Court from the nineteenth century through its 1939 *Miller* decision. This view was also accepted in 13 law journal articles published from the nineteenth century through the middle of the twentieth century. But in 1960, a law journal article appeared in a prominent law journal, the *William and Mary Law Review,* that argued for the first time that the Second Amendment protected an individual or personal right to own guns, and that the amendment also gave citizens the right to overthrow their own government—a so-called "right of revolution." Written by a law student at the law school, the article inspired the publication of two more articles in the 1960s making the same claims. In the 1970s, six more articles accepting the "individualist" view were published in law reviews. In these two decades, the militia-based view was defended in a total of 19 law journal articles. In the 1980s, 21 articles took the individualist view (many of the articles in the 1970s and 1980s were written by authors with attachments to gun rights organizations), with 58 published in the 1990s (compared with a total of 46 supporting the militia view in these two decades); by now, some of the authors were prominent law school faculty. By the end of the twentieth century, the individualist view had gained legitimacy in the legal community, thanks largely to this burgeoning law journal writing. That, plus the appointment of conservative judges to the federal bench by Presidents Ronald Reagan, George H. W. Bush, and George W. Bush set the stage for federal rulings more sympathetic to the individualist view.

Source: Robert J. Spitzer, "Lost and Found: Researching the Second Amendment," *Chicago-Kent Law Review* 76(2000): 349–401.

The Ninth Circuit Rebuts
the Fifth Circuit

- *Document:* U.S. Court of Appeals for the Ninth Circuit, case of *Silveira v. Lockyer*, 312 F.3d 1052 (2002), cert. denied 540 U.S. 1046 (2004)
- *Date:* December 5, 2002
- *Where:* San Francisco, California
- *Significance:* This case sustained the militia-based or "collective" interpretation of the Second Amendment held by other courts and provided a detailed historical analysis of the amendment to support its view, and to refute the historical analysis offered in the *Emerson* case.

DOCUMENT

Silveira v. Lockyer, 312 F.3d 1052 (9th Cir. 2002)

February 15, 2002, Argued and Submitted, San Francisco, California
December 5, 2002, Filed

PRIOR HISTORY: Appeal from the United States District Court for the Eastern District of California. D.C. No. CV-00–00411-WBS. William B. Shubb, District Judge, Presiding.

DISPOSITION: AFFIRMED in part, REVERSED in part, and REMANDED.

OPINION:

REINHARDT, Circuit Judge:

In 1999, the State of California enacted amendments to its gun control laws that significantly strengthened the state's restrictions on the possession, use, and transfer of the semi-automatic weapons popularly known as "assault weapons." Plaintiffs, California residents who either own assault weapons, seek to acquire such weapons, or both, brought this challenge to the gun control statute, asserting that the law, as amended, violates the Second Amendment, the Equal Protection Clause, and a host of other constitutional provisions. The district court dismissed all of the plaintiffs' claims. Because the Second Amendment does not confer an individual right to own or possess arms, we affirm the dismissal of all claims brought pursuant to that constitutional provision. As to the Equal Protection claims, we conclude that there is no constitutional infirmity in the statute's provisions regarding active peace officers. We find, however, no rational basis for the establishment of a statutory exception with respect to retired peace officers, and hold that the retired officers' exception fails even the most deferential level of scrutiny under the Equal Protection Clause. Finally, we conclude that each of the three additional constitutional claims asserted by plaintiffs on appeal is without merit.

I. INTRODUCTION

In response to a proliferation of shootings involving semi-automatic weapons, the California Legislature passed the Roberti-Roos Assault Weapons Control Act ("the AWCA") in 1989. . . . The AWCA renders it a felony offense to manufacture in California any of the semi-automatic weapons specified in the statute, or to possess, sell, transfer, or import into the state such weapons without a permit. CAL. PENAL CODE § 12280. The statute contains a grandfather clause that permits the ownership of assault weapons by individuals who lawfully purchased them before the statute's enactment, so long as the owners register the weapons with the state Department of Justice. *Id.* The grandfather clause, however, imposes significant restrictions on the use of weapons that are registered pursuant to its provisions. *Id.* § 12285(c) . . .

In 1999, the legislature amended the AWCA in order to broaden its coverage and to render it more flexible in response to technological developments in the manufacture of semiautomatic weapons. The amended AWCA retains both the original list of models of restricted weapons, and the judicial declaration procedure by which models may be added to the list. The 1999 amendments to the AWCA statute add a third method of defining the class of restricted weapons: The amendments provide that a weapon constitutes a restricted assault weapon if it possesses certain generic characteristics listed in the statute. *Id.* § 12276.1. Examples of the types of weapons restricted by the revised AWCA include a "semiautomatic, center-fire rifle that has a fixed magazine with the capacity to accept more than 10 rounds," § 12276.1(a)(2), and a semiautomatic, centerfire rifle that has the capacity to accept a detachable magazine and also features a flash suppressor, a grenade launcher, or a flare launcher. § 12276.1(a)(1)(A)-(E). The amended AWCA also restricts assault weapons equipped with "barrel shrouds," which protect the user's hands from the intense heat created by the rapid firing of the weapon, as well as semiautomatic weapons equipped with silencers. *Id.* . . .

Plaintiffs in this case are nine individuals, some of whom lawfully acquired weapons that were subsequently classified as assault weapons under the amended AWCA. They filed this action in February, 2000, one month after the 1999 AWCA amendments took effect. Plaintiffs who own assault weapons challenge the AWCA requirements that they either register, relinquish, or render inoperable their assault weapons as violative of their Second Amendment rights. Plaintiffs who seek to purchase weapons that may no longer lawfully be purchased in California also attack the ban on assault weapon sales as being contrary to their rights under that Amendment. Additionally, plaintiffs who are not active or retired California peace officers challenge on Fourteenth Amendment Equal Protection grounds two provisions of the AWCA: one that allows active peace officers to possess assault weapons while off-duty, and one that permits retired peace officers to possess assault weapons they acquire from their department at the time of their retirement. The State of California immediately moved to dismiss the action pursuant to Federal Rule of Civil Procedure 12(b)(6), contending that all the claims were barred as a matter of law. After a hearing, the district judge granted the defendants' motion in all respects, and dismissed the case. Plaintiffs appeal, and we affirm on all claims but one.

II. DISCUSSION

A. Background and Precedent

. . . There are three principal schools of thought that form the basis for the debate. The first, which we will refer to as the "traditional individual rights" model, holds that the Second Amendment guarantees to individual private citizens a fundamental right to possess and use firearms for any purpose at all, subject only to limited government regulation. This view, urged by the NRA and other firearms enthusiasts, as well as by a prolific cadre of fervent supporters in the legal academy, had never been adopted by any court until the recent Fifth Circuit decision in *United States v. Emerson*, 270 F.3d 203, 227 (5th Cir. 2001), *cert. denied*, 153 L. Ed. 2d 184, 122 S. Ct. 2362 (2002). The second view, a variant of the first, we will refer to as the "limited individual rights" model. Under that view, individuals maintain a constitutional right to possess firearms insofar as such possession bears a reasonable relationship to militia service. The third, a wholly contrary view, commonly called the "collective rights" model, asserts that the Second Amendment right to "bear arms" guarantees the right of the people to maintain effective state militias, but does not provide any type of individual right to own or possess weapons. Under this theory of the amendment, the federal and state governments have the full authority to enact prohibitions and restrictions on the use and possession of firearms, subject only to generally applicable constitutional constraints, such as due process, equal protection, and the like. Long the dominant view of the Second Amendment, and widely accepted by the federal courts, the collective rights model has recently come under strong criticism from individual rights advocates. After conducting a full analysis of the amendment, its history, and its purpose, we reaffirm our conclusion in *Hickman v. Block*, 81 F.3d 98 (9th Cir. 1996), that it is this collective rights model which provides the best interpretation of the Second Amendment.

Despite the increased attention by commentators and political interest groups to the question of what exactly the Second Amendment protects, with the sole exception of the Fifth Circuit's *Emerson* decision there exists no thorough judicial examination of the amendment's meaning. The Supreme Court's most extensive treatment of the amendment is a somewhat cryptic discussion in *United States v. Miller*, 307 U.S. 174, 83 L. Ed. 1206, 59 S. Ct. 816 (1939). . . . in *Miller* the Supreme Court decided that because a weapon was not suitable for use in the militia, its possession was not protected by the Second Amendment. As a result of its phrasing of its holding in the negative, however, the *Miller* Court's opinion stands only for the proposition that the possession of certain weapons is not protected, and offers little guidance as to what rights the Second Amendment does protect. . . .

Some thirty-odd years after *Miller*, two Justices of the Court pithily expressed their views on the question whether the Second Amendment limits the power of the federal or state governments to enact gun control laws. Justice Douglas, joined by Justice Thurgood Marshall, stated in dissent in *Adams v. Williams*, that in his view, the problem of police fearing that suspects they apprehend are armed:

"is an acute one not because of the Fourth Amendment, but because of the ease with which anyone can acquire a pistol. A powerful lobby dins into the ears of our citizenry that these gun purchases are constitutional rights protected by the Second Amendment. . . . There is under our decisions no reason why stiff state laws governing the purchase and possession of pistols may not be enacted. There is no reason why pistols may not be barred from anyone with a police record. There is no reason why a State may not require a purchaser of a pistol to pass a psychiatric test. There is no reason why all pistols should not be barred to everyone except the police."

. . . Our court, like every other federal court of appeals to reach the issue except for the Fifth Circuit, has interpreted *Miller* as rejecting the traditional individual rights view. In *Hickman v. Block*, we held that "the Second Amendment guarantees a collective rather than an individual right." 81 F.3d at 102 (citation and quotation marks omitted). Like the other courts, we reached our conclusion regarding the Second Amendment's scope largely on the basis of the rather cursory discussion in *Miller*, and touched only briefly on the merits of the debate over the force of the amendment. *See id*.

Appellants contend that we misread *Miller* in *Hickman*. They point out that, as we have already noted, *Miller*, like most other cases that address the Second Amendment, fails to provide much reasoning in support of its conclusion. We agree that our determination in *Hickman* that *Miller* endorsed the collective rights position is open to serious debate. We also agree that the entire subject of the meaning of the Second Amendment deserves more consideration than we, or the Supreme Court, have thus far been able (or willing) to give it. This is particularly so because, since *Hickman* was decided, there have been a number of important developments with respect to the interpretation of the highly controversial provision: First, as we have noted, there is the recent *Emerson* decision in which the Fifth Circuit, after analyzing the opinion at length, concluded that the Supreme Court's decision in *Miller* does not resolve the issue of the Amendment's meaning. The *Emerson* court then canvassed the pertinent scholarship and historical materials, and held that the Second Amendment does establish an individual right to possess arms—the first federal court of appeals ever to have so decided. Second, the current leadership of the United States Department of

Justice recently reversed the decades-old position of the government on the Second Amendment, and adopted the view of the Fifth Circuit. Now, for the first time, the United States government contends that the Second Amendment establishes an individual right to possess arms. The Solicitor General has advised the Supreme Court that "the current position of the United States . . . is that the Second Amendment more broadly protects the rights of individuals, including persons who are not members of any militia or engaged in active military service or training, to possess and bear their own firearms, subject to reasonable restrictions. . . . " Opposition to Petition for Certiorari in *United States v. Emerson*, No. 01–8780, at 19 n.3. In doing so, the Solicitor General transmitted to the Court a memorandum from Attorney General John Ashcroft to all United States Attorneys adopting the Fifth Circuit's view and emphasizing that the *Emerson* court "undertook a scholarly and comprehensive review of the pertinent legal materials . . . ," although the Attorney General was as vague as the Fifth Circuit with respect both to the types of weapons that he believes to be protected by the Second Amendment, and the basis for making such determinations. *Id.*, app. A. . . .

In light of the United States government's recent change in position on the meaning of the amendment, the resultant flood of Second Amendment challenges in the district courts, the Fifth Circuit's extensive study and analysis of the amendment and its conclusion that *Miller* does not mean what we and other courts have assumed it to mean, the proliferation of gun control statutes both state and federal, and the active scholarly debate that is being waged across this nation, we believe it prudent to explore Appellants' Second Amendment arguments in some depth, and to address the merits of the issue, even though this circuit's position on the scope and effect of the amendment was established in *Hickman*. Having engaged in that exploration, we determine that the conclusion we reached in *Hickman* was correct. . . .

> *1. The Text and Structure of the Second Amendment Demonstrate that the Amendment's Purpose is to Preserve Effective State Militias; That Purpose Helps Shape the Content of the Amendment.*

The Second Amendment states in its entirety: "A well regulated Militia being necessary to the security of a free State, the right of the people to keep and bear Arms, shall not be infringed." U.S. CONST. amend. II. As commentators on all sides of the debate regarding the amendment's meaning have acknowledged, the language of the amendment alone does not conclusively resolve the question of its scope. . . . What renders the language and structure of the amendment particularly striking is the existence of a prefatory clause, a syntactical device that is absent from all other provisions of the Constitution, including the nine other provisions of the Bill of Rights. Our analysis thus must address not only the meaning of each of the two clauses of the amendment but the unique relationship that exists between them.

> *a. The Meaning of the Amendment's First Clause: "A Well-Regulated Militia Being Necessary to the Security of A Free State."*

The first or prefatory clause of the Second Amendment sets forth the amendment's purpose and intent. An important aspect of ascertaining that purpose and intent is determining the import of the term "militia." Many advocates of the traditional individual rights model, including the Fifth Circuit, have taken the position that the term "militia" was meant to refer to all citizens, and, therefore, that the first clause simply restates the second in more specific terms. . . . We agree with the Fifth Circuit in a very limited respect. We agree that the interpretation of the first clause and the extent to which that clause shapes the content of the second depends in large part on the meaning of the term "militia." If militia refers, as the Fifth Circuit suggests, to all persons in a state, rather than to the state military entity, the first clause would have one meaning—a meaning that would support the concept of traditional individual rights. If the term refers instead, as we believe, to the entity ordinarily identified by that designation, the state-created and -organized military force, it would likely be necessary to attribute a considerably different meaning to the first clause of the Second Amendment and ultimately to the amendment as a whole.

We believe the answer to the definitional question is the one that most persons would expect: "militia" refers to a state military force. We reach our conclusion not only because that is the ordinary meaning of the word, but because contemporaneously enacted provisions of the Constitution that contain the word "militia" consistently use the term to refer to a state military entity, not to the people of the state as a whole. We look to such contemporaneously enacted provisions for an understanding of words used in the Second Amendment in part because this is an interpretive principle recently explicated by the Supreme Court in a case involving another word that appears in that amendment—the word "people." That same interpretive principle is unquestionably applicable when we construe the word "militia."

"Militia" appears repeatedly in the first and second Articles of the Constitution. From its use in those sections, it is apparent that the drafters were referring in the Constitution to the second of two government-established and -controlled military forces. Those forces were, first, the national army and navy, which were subject to civilian control shared by the president and Congress, and, second, the *state militias*, which were to be "essentially organized and under control of the states, but subject to regulation by Congress and to 'federalization' at the command of the president." Paul Finkelman, *"A Well Regulated Militia": The Second Amendment in Historical Perspective*, 76 CHI.-KENT L. REV. 195, 204 (2000). . . .

After examining each of the significant words or phrases in the Second Amendment's first clause, we conclude that the clause declares the importance of state militias to the security of the various free states within the confines of their newly structured constitutional relationship. With that understanding, the reason for and purpose of the Second Amendment becomes clearer.

> b. *The Meaning of the Amendment's Second Clause: "The Right of the People to Keep and Bear Arms, Shall Not Be Infringed."*

Having determined that the first clause of the Second Amendment declares the importance of state militias to the proper functioning of the new constitutional system, we now turn to the meaning of the second clause, the effect the first clause has on the second, and the meaning of the amendment as a whole. The second clause—"the right of the people to keep and bear Arms, shall not be infringed"—is not free from ambiguity. We consider it highly significant, however, that the second clause does not purport to protect the right to "possess" or "own" arms, but rather to "keep and bear" arms. This choice of words is important because the phrase "bear arms" is a phrase that customarily relates to a military function.

Historical research shows that the use of the term "bear arms" generally referred to the carrying of arms in military service—not the private use of arms for personal purposes. For instance, Professor Dorf, after canvassing documents from the founding era, concluded that "overwhelmingly, the term had a military connotation." Dorf, *supra,* at 314. Our own review of historical documents confirms the professor's report. . . .

   c. *The Relationship Between the Two Clauses.*

Our next step is to consider the relationship between the two clauses, and the meaning of the amendment as a whole. As we have noted, and as is evident from the structure of the Second Amendment, the first clause explains the purpose of the more substantive clause that follows, or, to put it differently, it explains the reason necessitating or warranting the enactment of the substantive provision. Moreover, in this case, the first clause does more than simply state the amendment's purpose or justification: it also helps shape and define the meaning of the substantive provision contained in the second clause, and thus of the amendment itself. . . .

When the second clause is read in light of the first, so as to implement the policy set forth in the preamble, we believe that the most plausible construction of the Second Amendment is that it seeks to ensure the existence of effective state militias in which the people may exercise their right to bear arms, and forbids the federal government to interfere with such exercise. This conclusion is based in part on the premise, explicitly set forth in the text of the amendment, that the maintenance of effective state militias is essential to the preservation of a free State, and in part on the historical meaning of the right that the operative clause protects—the right to bear arms. In contrast, it seems reasonably clear that any fair reading of the "bear Arms" clause with the end in view of "assuring . . . the effectiveness of" the state militias cannot lead to the conclusion that the Second Amendment guarantees an individual right to own or possess weapons for personal and other purposes. . . .

In the end, however, given the history and vigor of the dispute over the meaning of the Second Amendment's language, we would be reluctant to say that the text and structure alone establish with certainty which of the various views is correct. Fortunately, we have available a number of other important sources that can help us determine whether ours is the proper understanding. These include records that reflect the historical context in which the amendment was adopted, and documents that contain significant portions of the contemporary debates relating to the adoption and ratification of the Constitution and the Bill of Rights. . . .

In sum, our review of the historical record regarding the enactment of the Second Amendment reveals that the amendment was adopted to ensure that effective state militias would be maintained, thus preserving the people's right to bear arms. The militias, in turn, were viewed as critical to preserving the integrity of the states within the newly structured national government as well as to ensuring the freedom of the people from federal tyranny. Properly read, the historical record relating to the Second Amendment leaves little doubt as to its intended scope and effect.

3. *Text, History, and Precedent All Support the Collective Rights View of the Amendment. . . .*

After conducting our analysis of the meaning of the words employed in the amendment's two clauses, and the effect of their relationship to each other, we concluded that the language and structure of the amendment strongly support the collective rights view. The preamble establishes that the amendment's purpose was to ensure the maintenance of effective state militias, and the amendment's operative clause establishes that this objective was to be attained by preserving the right of the people to "bear arms"—to carry weapons in conjunction with their service in the militia. . . .

IV. CONCLUSION

Because the Second Amendment affords only a collective right to own or possess guns or other firearms, the district court's dismissal of plaintiffs' Second Amendment claims is AFFIRMED. . . . The constitutional challenges to the validity of the California Assault Weapons Control Act are all rejected, with the exception of the claim relating to the retired officers provision.

AFFIRMED in part, REVERSED in part, and REMANDED.

SOURCE: http://www.ux1.eiu.edu/~cfib/courses/silveira.htm

ANALYSIS

Sean Silveira and several others challenged California's ban on assault weapons, the Assault Weapons Control Act (AWCA), arguing in part that it violated their Second Amendment rights. The court upheld the state law and dismissed the Second Amendment-based challenge. Ruling that "the Second Amendment does not confer an individual right to own or possess arms," the court examined the Second Amendment in great detail, comparable to, but different in conclusion from, the detailed analysis in the *Emerson* case (see previously). Indeed, the *Silveira* decision was taken in part to be a rebuttal of *Emerson*.

The decision referenced its earlier Ninth Circuit *Hickman* decision (see previously), which also endorsed the collective, militia-based view of the Second Amendment, and noted that this view has also been accepted in every other federal court decision on the Second Amendment, with the exception of *Emerson* in 2001. Both *Emerson* and *Silveira* refer to three schools of thought on the meaning of the Second Amendment: the "traditional" individualist view, which posits that the amendment provides for an individual right to own guns aside and apart from militia service; a "limited individual rights" view that identifies a right of individuals to own guns "insofar as such possession bears a reasonable relationship to militia service," and the collective rights view which pertains to "the right of the people to maintain effective state militias, but does not provide any type of individual right to own or possess weapons." *Emerson* supported the first view, whereas *Silveira* endorsed the third. In its analysis, *Silveira* judges that the first part of the Second Amendment references government-controlled militias, and that the second half of the sentence is also military in orientation, as the phrase "keep and bear arms" has long had a military, rather than civilian, reference. One conclusion both cases share (a criticism not offered until recent years) is that the 1939 *Miller* Supreme Court case provided an inadequate or incomplete interpretation of the Second Amendment.

Silveira also mentions a change in Justice Department policy that occurred in 2001, when then Attorney General John Ashcroft announced that his department was changing the government's view of the Second Amendment to embrace the individualist view. This change sparked much controversy, because it reversed the Justice Department's consistent stand on the subject, held by Republican and Democratic administrations going back at least to the 1950s that accepted the collective view. Ashcroft had formerly served in the U.S. Senate and was strongly supported by the National Rifle Association throughout his political career. In fact, Ashcroft announced his department's position in an unorthodox way—in a letter to an NRA officer.

FURTHER READING

Nosanchuk, Mathew S. "The Embarrassing Interpretation of the Second Amendment," *Northern Kentucky Law Review* 29(2002): 705–800.

7

MODERN GUN LAWS

The Old-Style Militias Become the National Guard

- *Document:* The Militia Act of 1903; also known as the Dick Act
- *Date:* January 21, 1903
- *Where:* Washington, D.C.
- *Significance:* This law finally modernized the old and mostly obsolete federal militia laws.

DOCUMENT

CHAP. 196—An act to promote the efficiency of the militia, and for other purposes.

Public Law No. 33; 32 Stat. 775

Be it enacted by the Senate and House of Representatives of the United States of America in Congress assembled, That the militia shall consist of every able-bodied male citizen Of the respective States Territories, and the District of Columbia, and every able-bodied male of foreign birth who has declared his intention to become a citizen, who is more than eighteen and less than forty-five years of age, and shall be divided into two classes—the organized militia, to be known as the National Guard of the State, Territory, or District of Columbia, or by such other designations as may be given them by the laws of the respective States or Territories, and the remainder to be known as the Reserve Militia.

SEC. 2. That the Vice-President of the United States, the officers, judicial and executive, of the Government of the United States, the members and officers of each House of Congress, persons in the military or naval service of the United States, all custom-house officers with their clerks, postmasters and persons employed by the United States in the transmission of the Militia. ferrymen employed at any ferry on a post road, artificers and workmen employed in the armories and arsenals of the

United States, pilots, mariners actually employed in the sea service of any citizen or merchant within the United States, and all persons who are exempted by the laws of the respective States or Territories shall be exempted from militia duty, without regard to age: *Provided,* That nothing in this Act shall be construed to require or compel any member of any well-recognized religious sect or organization at present organized and existing whose creed forbids its members to participate in war in any form, and whose religious convictions are against war or participation therein, in accordance with the creed of said religious organization, to serve in the militia or any other armed or volunteer force under the jurisdiction and authority of the United States.

SEC. 3. That the regularly enlisted, organized, and uniformed active militia in the several States and Territories and the District of Columbia who have heretofore participated or shall hereafter participate in the apportionment of the annual appropriation provided by section sixteen hundred and sixty-one of the Revised Statutes of the United States, as amended, whether known and designated as National Guard, militia, or otherwise, shall constitute the organized militia. The organization, armament, and discipline of the organized militia in the several States and Territories and in the District of Columbia shall be the same as that which is now or may hereafter be prescribed for the Regular and Volunteer Armies of the United States, within five years from the date of the approval of this Act: *Provided,* That the President of the United States, in time of peace, may by order fix the minimum number of enlisted men in each company, troop, battery, signal corps, engineer corps, and hospital corps: *And provided further,* That any corps of artillery, cavalry and infantry existing in any of the States at the passage of the Act of May eighth, seventeen hundred and ninety-two, which, by the laws, customs or usages of the said States have been in continuous existence since the passage of said Act under its provisions and under the provisions of Section two hundred and thirty-two and Sections sixteen hundred and twenty-five to sixteen hundred and sixty, both inclusive, of Title sixteen of the Revised Statutes of the United States relating to the Militia, shall be allowed to retain their accustomed privileges, subject, nevertheless, to all other duties required by law in like manner as the other Militia.

SEC. 4. That whenever the United States is invaded, or in danger of invasion from any foreign nation or of rebellion against the authority of the Government of the United States, or the President is unable, with the other forces at his command, to execute the laws of the Union in any part thereof, it shall be lawful for the President to call forth, for a period not exceeding nine months, such number of the militia of the State or of the States or Territories or of the District of Columbia as he may deem necessary to repel such invasion, suppress such rebellion, or to enable him to execute such laws, and to issue his orders for that purpose to such officers of the militia as he may think proper.

SEC. 5. That whenever the President calls forth the militia, of any State or Territory or of the District of Columbia to be employed in the service of the United States, he may specify in his call the period for which such service is required, not exceeding nine months, and the militia so called shall continue to serve during the term so specified, unless sooner discharged by order of the President.

SEC. 6. That when the militia of more than one State is called into the actual service of the United States by the President he may, in his discretion apportion them among such States or Territories or to the District of Columbia according to representative population.

SEC. 7. That every officer and enlisted man of the militia who shall be called forth in the manner hereinbefore prescribed and shall be found fit for military service shall be mustered or accepted into the United States service by a duly authorized mustering officer of the United States: *Provided, however,* That any officer or enlisted man of the militia who shall refuse or neglect to present himself to such mustering officer upon being called forth as herein prescribed shall be subject to trial by court-martial, and shall be punished as such court-martial may direct.

SEC. 8. That courts-martial for the trial of officers or men of the militia, when in the service of the United States, shall be composed of militia officers only.

SEC. 9. That the militia, when called into the actual service of the United States, shall be subject to the same Rules and Articles of War as the regular troops of the United States.

SEC. 10. That the militia, when called into the actual service of the United States, shall, during their time of service, be entitled to the same pay and allowances as are or may be provided by law for the Regular Army.

SEC. 11. That when the militia is called into the actual service of the United States, or any portion of the militia is accepted under the provisions of this Act, their pay shall commence from the day of their appearing at the place of company rendezvous. But this provision shall not be construed to authorize any species of expenditure previous to arriving at such places of rendezvous which is not provided by existing laws to be paid after their arrival at such places of rendezvous.

SEC. 12. That there shall be appointed in each State, Territory and District of Columbia, an Adjutant-General, who shall perform such duties as may be prescribed by the laws of such State, territory, and District, respectively and make returns to the Secretary of War, at such times and in such form as he shall from time to time prescribe, of the strength of the organized militia, and also make such reports as may from time to time be required by the Secretary of War. That the Secretary of War shall, with his annual report of each year, transmit to Congress an abstract of the returns and reports of the adjutants-general of the States, Territories, and the District of Columbia with such observations thereon as he may deem necessary for the information of Congress.

SEC. 13. That the Secretary of War is hereby authorized to issue, on the requisitions of the governors of the several States and Territories, or of the commanding general of the militia of the District of Columbia, such number of the United States standard service magazine arms, with bayonets, bayonet scabbards, gun slings, belts, and such other necessary accouterments and equipments as are required for the Army of the United States, for arming all of the organized militia in said States and Territories and District of Columbia, without charging the cost or value thereof, or any which have been issued since December first, nineteen hundred and one, or any expense connected therewith, against the allotment to said State, Territory, or District of Columbia, out of the annual appropriation provided by section sixteen hundred and sixty-one of the Revised Statutes, as amended, or requiring payment therefor, and to exchange, without receiving any money credit therefor, ammunition, or parts thereof, suitable to the new arms, round for round, for corresponding ammunition suitable to the old arms theretofore issued to said State, Territory, or District by the United States: *Provided,* That said rifles and carbines and other property shall be receipted for and shall remain the property of the United States and be annually accounted for by the governors of the States and Territories as now required by law, and that each State, Territory, and District shall, on receipt of the new arms, turn in to the Ordnance Department of the United States Army, without receiving any money credit therefor, and without expense for transportation, all United States rifles and carbines now in its possession.

To provide means to carry into effect the provisions of this section, the necessary money to cover the cost of exchanging or issuing the new arms, accouterments, equipments, and ammunition to be exchanged or issued hereunder is hereby appropriated out of any moneys in the Treasury not otherwise appropriated.

SEC. 14. That whenever it shall appear by the report of inspections, which it shall be the duty of the Secretary of War to cause to be made at least once in each year by officers detailed by him for that purpose, that the organized militia of a State or Territory or of the District of Columbia is sufficiently armed, uniformed, and equipped for active duty in the field, the Secretary of War is authorized, on the requisition of the governor of such State or Territory, to pay to the quartermaster-general thereof, or to such other officer of the militia of said State as the said governor may designate and appoint for the purpose, so much of its allotment out of the said annual appropriation under section sixteen hundred and sixty-one of the Revised Statutes as amended as shall be necessary for the payment, subsistence, and transportation of such portion of said organized militia as shall engage in actual field or camp service for instruction, and the officers and enlisted men of such militia while so engaged shall be entitled to the same pay, subsistence, and transportation or travel allowances as officers and enlisted men of corresponding grades of the Regular Army are or may hereafter be entitled by law, and the officer so designated and appointed shall be regarded as a disbursing officer of the United States, and shall render his accounts through the War Department to the proper accounting officers of the Treasury for settlement, and he shall be required to give good and sufficient bonds to the United States, in such sums as the Secretary of War may direct, faithfully to account for the safe- keeping and payment of the public moneys so intrusted to him for disbursement.

SEC. 15. That the Secretary of War is hereby authorized to provide for participation by any part of the organized militia of any State or Territory on the request of the governor thereof in the encampment, maneuvers, and field instruction of any part of the Regular Army at or near any military post or camp or lake or seacoast defenses of the United States. In such case the organized militia so participating shall receive the same pay, subsistence, and transportation as is provided by law for the officers and men of the Regular Army, to be paid out of the appropriation for the pay, subsistence, and transportation of the Army: *Provided,* That the command of such military post or camp and of the officers and troops of the United States there stationed shall remain with the regular commander of the post without regard to the rank of the commanding or other officers of the militia temporarily so encamped within its limits or in its vicinity.

SEC. 16. That whenever any officer of the organized militia shall, upon recommendation of the governor of any State, Territory, or general commanding the

District of Columbia, and when authorized by the President, attend and pursue a regular course of study at any military school or college of the United States such officer shall receive from the annual appropriation for the support of the Army the same travel allowances, and quarters, or commutation of quarters, to which an officer of the Regular Army would be entitled if attending such school or college under orders from proper military authority, and shall also receive commutation of subsistence at the rate of one dollar per day while in actual attendance upon the course of instruction.

SEC. 17. That the annual appropriation made by section sixteen hundred and sixty-one, Revised Statutes, as amended, shall be available for the purpose of providing for issue to the organized militia any stores and supplies or publications which are supplied to the Army by any department. Any State Territory, or the District of Columbia may, with the approval of the Secretary of War, purchase for cash from the War Department, for the use of its militia, stores, supplies, material of war, or military publications, such as are furnished to the Army, in addition to those issued under the provisions of this Act, at the price at which they are listed for issue to the Army, with the cost of transportation added, and funds received from such sales shall be credited to the appropriations to which they belong and shall not be covered into the Treasury, but shall be available until expended to replace therewith the supplies sold to the States and Territories and to the District of Columbia in the manner herein provided.

SEC. 18. That each State or Territory furnished with material of war under the provisions of this or former Acts of Congress shall, during the year next preceding each annual allotment of funds, in accordance with section sixteen hundred and sixty-one of the Revised Statutes as amended, have required every company, troop, and battery in its organized militia not excused by the governor of such State or Territory to participate in practice marches or go into camp of instruction at least five consecutive days, and to assemble for drill and instruction at company, battalion, or regimental armories or rendezvous or for target practice not less than twenty-four times, and shall also have required during such year an inspection of each such company, troop, and battery to be made by an officer of such militia or an officer of the Regular Army.

SEC. 19. That upon the application of the governor of any State or Territory furnished with material of war under the provisions of this Act or former laws of Congress, the Secretary of War may detail one or more officers of the Army to attend any encampment of the organized militia, and to give such instruction and information to the officers and men assembled in such camp as may be requested by the governor. Such officer or officers shall immediately make a report of such encampment to the Secretary of War, who shall furnish a copy thereof to the governor of the State or Territory.

SEC. 20. That upon application of the governor of any State or Territory furnished with material of war under the provisions of this Act or former laws of Congress, the Secretary of War may, in his discretion, detail one or more officers of the Army to report to the governor of such State or Territory for duty in connection with the organized militia. All such assignments may be revoked at the request of the governor of such State or Territory or at the pleasure of the Secretary of War.

SEC. 21. That the troops of the militia encamped at any military post or camp of the United States may be furnished such amounts of ammunition for instruction in firing and target practice as may be prescribed by the Secretary of War, and such instruction in firing shall be carried on under the direction of an officer selected for that purpose by the proper military commander.

SEC. 22. That when any officer, noncommissioned officer, or private of the militia is disabled by reason of wounds or disabilities received or incurred in the service of the United States he shall be entitled to all the benefits of the pension laws existing at the time of his service, and in case such officer noncommissioned officer, or private dies in the service of the United States or in returning to his place of residence after being mustered out of such service, or at any time, in consequence of wounds or disabilities received in such service, his widow and children, if any, shall be entitled to all the benefits of such pension laws.

SEC. 23. That for the purpose of securing a list of persons specially qualified to hold commissions in any volunteer force which may hereafter be called for and organized under the authority of Congress, other than a force composed of organized militia, the Secretary of War is authorized from time to time to convene boards of officers at suitable and convenient army posts in different parts of the United States, who shall examine as to their qualifications for the command of troops or for the performance of staff duties all applicants who shall have served in the Regular Army of the United States, in any of the volunteer forces of the United States, or in the organized militia of any State or Territory or District of Columbia, or who, being a citizen of the United States, shall have attended or pursued a regular course of instruction in any military school or college of the United States Army, or shall have graduated from any educational institution to which an officer of the Army or Navy has been detailed as superintendent or professor pursuant to law after having creditably pursued the course of military instruction therein provided. Such examinations shall be under rules and regulations prescribed by the Secretary of War, and shall be especially directed to ascertain the practical capacity of the applicant. The record of previous service of the applicant shall be considered as a part of the examination. Upon the conclusion of each examination the board shall certify to the War Department its judgment as to the fitness of the applicant, stating the office, if any, which it deems him qualified to fill, and, upon approval by the President, the names of the persons certified to be qualified shall be inscribed in a register to be kept in the War Department for that purpose. The persons so certified and registered shall, subject to a physical examination at the time, constitute an eligible class for commissions pursuant to such certificates in any volunteer force hereafter called for and organized under the authority of Congress, other than a force composed of organized militia, and the President may authorize persons from this class, to attend and pursue a regular course of study at any military school or college of the United States other than the Military Academy at West Point and to receive from the annual appropriation for the support of the Army the same allowances and commutations as provided in this Act for officers of the organized militia: *Provided*, That no person shall be entitled to receive a Commission as a second lieutenant after be shall have passed the age of thirty; as first lieutenant after he shall have passed the age of thirty-five; as captain after he shall have passed the age of forty; as major after he shall have passed the age of forty-five; as lieutenant colonel after be shall have passed the age of fifty, or as colonel after be shall have passed the age of fifty-five: *And provided further*, That such appointments shall be distributed proportionately, as near as may be, among the various States contributing such volunteer force: *And provided,* That the appointments in this section provided for shall not be deemed to include appointments to any office in any company, troop, battery, battalion, or regiment of the organized militia which volunteers as a body or the officers of which are appointed by the governor of a State or Territory.

SEC. 24. That all the volunteer forces of the United States called for by authority of Congress shall, except as hereinbefore provided, be organized in the manner provided by the Act entitled "An Act to provide for temporarily increasing the military establishment of the United States in time of war, and for other purposes," approved April twenty-second, eighteen hundred and ninety-eight.

SEC. 25. That sections sixteen hundred and twenty-five to sixteen hundred and sixty, both included, of title sixteen of the Revised Statutes, and section two hundred and thirty-two thereof, relating to the militia, are hereby repealed.

SEC. 26. That this Act shall take effect upon the date of its approval.

Approved, January 21, 1903.

SOURCE: Statutes at Large

ANALYSIS

From the end of the Civil War until the start of the twentieth century, pressures to revamp and modernize the old-style militia system accelerated in the United States. Since colonial times, there had been two types of militias in America: the general or unorganized militias, consisting of all able-bodied men roughly from ages 18 to 45 (although most of these men never served, even when called to do so), and the organized or select or volunteer militias, consisting of more elite, self-organized units that sought to professionalize themselves through more extensive training, better armaments, uniforms, and the development of unit *esprit de corps*. These latter units consisted of about 10 percent of all militia participants. The old militia system was organized under the Uniform Militia Act of 1792 (see Chapter 2), and that law, amended periodically, continued to serve as the legal basis for militia organization throughout the nineteenth century, even though the system it prescribed was all but abandoned as the century wore on.

As the general militias gave way to the military draft in times of national military emergency (that is, placing drafted men into the regular army instead of forming state militia units), the organized militia units remained, and in the latter part of the nineteenth century, these units clamored to be recognized under law as "national guards" in order to gain greater legitimacy and greater financial backing from the government. The manifold problems of military mobilization during the Spanish-American War of 1898 finally tipped the scales in favor of reform, including the elevation of guard units. Federal recognition and reorganization came to fruition in 1903 with the passage of the Militia Act of 1903 (also called the Dick Act, after bill sponsor Rep. Charles Dick (R-Ohio)), a measure strongly backed by President Theodore Roosevelt, who referred to the old militia system as "obsolete and worthless." This

Assassination of William McKinley. Leon Czolgosz shoots President McKinley with a concealed revolver, at Pan-American Exposition reception, Buffalo, New York, September 6, 1901. Library of Congress.

new law distinguished between the organized militias, which henceforth would be "known as the National Guard," and the "reserve militia," a synonym for the general militias. Aside from reserving to Congress the option of calling up the reserve militia should the need arise (it never has), no other provision was made for the latter. Most of the rest of this law provided for federal arming, training, and drilling of the National Guard, requiring these units to conform to federal military standards and organization, sweeping aside eighteenth-century requirements that militiamen arm themselves. Federal funding for Guards also increased dramatically. Note that the language in Section 4 of the law borrows from the Constitution's wording that says militias are to be used "to execute the Laws of the Union, suppress Insurrections and repel invasions" (Article I, Section 8) and in Sections 4–6 of the law, referencing the Constitution's Article II, Section 2, saying that the President is commander-in-chief "of the Militia of the several States."

For some gun rights activists, this and subsequent laws violated the idea that militia units could somehow serve as a check against the federal government. Yet the system was federalized, underscoring the broader idea that militias in America could exist only when formed by, not against, the government.

DID YOU KNOW?

The First Modern Gun Law

In the late 1800s and early 1900s, handgun ownership proliferated in Eastern cities as cheap guns were marketed more heavily to the public, and fears of crime spread. On August 9, 1910, New York City Mayor William J. Gaynor was shot and wounded by a disgruntled former city employee. Gaynor recovered, but the assassination attempt fanned reformist flames in the city and state, as newspapers continued to report cases of shootings in the city, including a pitched revolver battle on an excursion boat, a series of tong war shootings in Chinatown, and various shootings attributed to anarchists. Crime statistics from 1910 supported public perceptions: firearm homicides rose 50 percent compared to 1909. From 1907–1910, city police confiscated 10,567 revolvers in the course of making routine arrests.

In 1911, at the urging of various citizen groups, State Senator Timothy Sullivan introduced a bill to establish state-wide regulations regarding the purchase, possession, and carrying of concealed weapons—including, but not limited to, guns. During legislative hearings, witnesses reported handguns sold from New York City street pushcarts; medical and law enforcement representatives, along with clergy, among others, urged strongly that the state take decisive action. On May 29, Governor John A. Dix signed what came to be known as the Sullivan Law. Exceeding past gun measures, this law regulated not only the carrying of dangerous weapons, but also their possession and sale. Citizens wanting to own a handgun now had to obtain a permit. The initial public reaction to the law was confusion, but vigorous enforcement drove down the number of guns in the city.

Source: Kennett, Lee, and James LaVerne Anderson. *The Gun in America*. Westport, CT: Greenwood Press, 1975.

FURTHER READING

Mahon, John K. *History of the Militia and the National Guard*. New York: Macmillan, 1983.

The Depression-Era Crime Wave Prompts New Gun Law

- *Document:* The National Firearms Act of 1934
- *Date:* June 26, 1934
- *Where:* Washington, D.C.
- *Significance:* This was the first significant modern national gun control law.

DOCUMENT

The National Firearms Act of 1934

PL 73–474; 48 Stat. 1236

To provide for the taxation of manufacturers, importers, and dealers in certain firearms and machine guns, to tax the sale or other disposal of such weapons, and to restrict importation and regulate interstate transportation thereof.

Be it enacted by the Senate and House of Representatives of the United States of America in Congress assembled, That for the purposes of this Act—

(a) The term "firearm" means a shotgun or rifle having a barrel of less than eighteen inches in length, or any other weapon, except a pistol or revolver, from which a shot is discharged by an explosive if such weapon is capable of being concealed on the person, or a machine gun, and includes a muffler or silencer for any firearm whether or not such firearm is included within the foregoing definition.

(b) The term "machine gun" means any weapon which shoots, or is designed to shoot, automatically or semi automatically, more than one shot, without manual reloading, by a single function of the trigger.

(c) The term "person" includes a partnership, company, association, or corporation, as well as a natural person.

(d) The term "continental United States" means the States of the United States and the District of Columbia.

(e) The term "importer" means any person who imports or brings firearms into the continental United States for sale.

(f) The term "manufacturer" means any person who is engaged within the continental United States in the manufacture of firearms, or who otherwise produces therein any firearm for sale or disposition.

(g) The term "dealer" means any person not a manufacturer or importer engaged within the continental United States in the business of selling firearms. The term "dealer" shall include wholesalers, pawnbrokers, and dealers in used firearms.

(h) The term "interstate commerce" means transportation from any State or Territory or District, or any insular possession of the United States (including the Philippine Islands), to any other State or to the District of Columbia.

(i) The term "Commissioner" means the Commissioner of Internal Revenue.

(j) The term "Secretary" means the Secretary of the Treasury.

(k) The term "to transfer" or "transferred" shall include to sell, assign pledge, lease, loan, give away, or otherwise dispose of.

SEC 2. (a) Within fifteen days after the effective date of this Act, or upon first engaging in business, and thereafter on or before the 1st day of July of each year, every importer, manufacturer, and dealer in firearms shall register with the collector of internal revenue for each district in which such business is to be carried on his name or style, principal place of business, and places of business in such district, and pay a special tax at the following rates: Importers or manufacturers, $500 a year; dealers, other than pawnbrokers, $200 a year; pawnbrokers, $300 a year. Where the tax is payable on the 1st day of July in any year it shall be computed for one year; where the tax is payable on any other day it shall be computed proportionately from the 1st day of the month in which the liability to the tax accrued to the 1st day of July following.

(b) It shall be unlawful for any person required to register under the provisions of this section to import, manufacture, or deal in firearms without having registered and paid the tax imposed by this section.

SEC. 3. (a) There shall be levied, collected, and paid upon firearms transferred in the continental United States a tax at the rate of $200 for each firearm, such tax; to be paid by the transferor, and to be represented by appropriate stamps to be provided by the Commissioner, with the approval of the secretary; and the stamps herein provided shall be affixed to the order for such firearm, hereinafter provided for. The tax imposed by this section shall be in addition to any import duty imposed on such firearm.

(b) All provisions of law (including those relating to special taxes, to the assessment, collection, remission, and refund of internal revenue taxes, to the engraving, issuance, sale, accountability, cancellation, and distribution of tax-paid stamps provided for in the internal-revenue laws, and to penalties) applicable with respect to the taxes imposed by section 1 of the Act of December 17, 1914, as amended (U.S.C., Supp. VII, title 26, secs. 1040 and 1383), and all other provisions of the internal-revenue laws shall, insofar as not inconsistent with the provisions of this Act, be applicable with respect to the taxes imposed by this Act.

(c) Under such rules and regulations as the Commissioner, with the approval of the Secretary, may prescribe, and upon proof of the exportation of and firearm to any foreign country (whether exported as part of another article or not) with respect to which the transfer tax under this section has been paid by the manufacturer, the Commissioner shall refund to the manufacturer the amount of the tax so paid, or, if the manufacturer waives all claim for the amount to be refunded, the refund shall be made to the exporter.

SEC. 4. (a) It shall be unlawful for any person to transfer a firearm except in pursuance of a written order from the person seeking to obtain such article, on an application form issued in blank in duplicate for that purpose by the Commissioner. Such order shall identify the applicant by such means of identification as may be prescribed by regulations under this Act: Provided, That, if the applicant is an individual, such identification shall include fingerprints and a photograph thereof.

(b) The Commissioner, with the approval of the Secretary, shall cause suitable forms to be prepared for the purposes above mentioned, and shall cause the same to be distributed to collectors of internal revenue.

(c) Every person so transferring a firearm shall set forth in each copy of such order the manufacturer's number or other mark identifying such firearm, and shall forward a copy of such order to the Commissioner. The original thereof with stamps affixed, shall be returned to the applicant.

(d) No person shall transfer a firearm which has previously been transferred on or after the effective date of this Act, unless such person, in addition to complying with subsection (c), transfers therewith the stamp-affixed order provided for in this section for each such prior transfer, in compliance with such regulations as may be prescribed under this act for proof of payment of all taxes on such firearms.

(e) If the transfer of a firearm is exempted from the provisions of this Act as provided in section 13 hereof, the person transferring such firearm shall notify the Commissioner of the name and address of the applicant, the number or other mark identifying such firearm, and the date of its transfer, and shall file with the Commissioner such documents in proof thereof as the Commissioner may by regulations prescribe.

(f) Importers, manufacturers, and dealers who have registered and paid the tax as provided for in section 2(a) of this Act shall not be required to conform to the provisions of this section with respect to transactions in firearms with dealers or manufacturers if such dealers or manufacturers have registered and have paid such tax, but shall keep such records and make such reports regarding such transactions as may be prescribed by regulations under this Act.

SEC. 5. (a) within sixty days after the effective date of this act every person possessing a firearm shall register, with the collector of the district in which he resides, the number or other mark identifying such firearm, together with his name address, place where such firearm is usually kept, and place of business or employment, and, if such person is other than a natural person, the name and home address of an executive officer thereof: Provided, That no person shall be required to register under this section with respect to any firearm acquired after the effective date of, and in conformity with the provisions of, this Act.

(b) Whenever on trial for a violation of section 6 hereof the defendant is shown to have or to have had possession of such firearm at any time after such period of sixty days without having registered as required by this section such possession shall create a presumption that such firearm came into the possession of the defendant subsequent to the effective date of this act, but this presumption shall not be conclusive.

SEC. 6. It shall be unlawful for any person to receive or possess any firearm which has at any time been transferred in violation of section 3 or 4 of this Act.

SEC. 7. (a) Any firearm which has at any time been transferred in violation of the provisions of this act shall be subject to seizure and forfeiture, and (except as provided in subsection (b)) all the provisions of internal-revenue laws relating to searches, seizures, and forfeiture of unstamped articles are extended to and made to apply to the articles taxed under this Act, and the persons to whom this Act applies.

(b) In the case of the forfeiture of any firearm by reason of a violation of this Act: No notice of public sale shall be required; no such firearm shall be sold at public sale; if such firearm is in the possession of any officer of the United States except the Secretary, such officer shall deliver the firearm to the Secretary; and the Secretary may order such firearm destroyed or may sell such firearm to any State, Territory, or possession (including the Philippine Islands), or political subdivision thereof, or the District of Columbia, or retain it for the use of the Treasury department or transfer it without charge to any Executive department or independent establishment of the Government for use by it.

SEC. 8. (a) Each manufacturer and importer of a firearm shall identify it with a number or other identification mark approved by the Commissioner, such number or mark to be stamped or other placed thereon in a manner approved by the Commissioner.

(b) It shall be unlawful for anyone to obliterate, remove, change, or alter such number or other identification mark. Whenever on trial for a violation of this subsection the defendant is shown to have or to have had possession of any firearm upon which such number or mark shall have been obliterated, removed, changed, or altered, such possession shall be deemed sufficient evidence to authorize conviction unless the defendant explains such possession to the satisfaction of the jury.

SEC. 9. Importers, manufacturers, and dealers shall keep such books and records and render such returns in relation to the transactions in firearms specified in this Act as the Commissioner, with the approval of the Secretary, may by regulations require.

SEC. 10. (a) No firearm shall be imported or brought into the United States or any territory under its control or jurisdiction (including the Philippine Islands) except that, under regulations prescribed by the Secretary, any firearm may be so imported or brought in when (1) the purpose thereof is shown to be lawful and (2) such firearm is unique or of a type which cannot be obtained within the United States or such territory.

(b) It shall be unlawful (1) fraudulently or knowingly to import or bring any firearm into the United States or any territory under its control or jurisdiction (including the Philippine Islands), in violation of the provisions of this Act; or (2) knowingly to assist in so doing; or (3) to receive, conceal, buy, sell, or in any manner facilitate the transportation, concealment or sale of any such firearm after being imported or brought in, knowing the same to have been imported or brought in contrary to law. Whenever on trial for a violation of this section the defendant is shown to have or to have had possession of such firearm, such possession shall be deemed sufficient evidence to authorize conviction unless the defendant explains such possession to the satisfaction of the jury.

SEC. 11. It shall be unlawful for any person who is required to register as provided in section 5 hereof and who shall not have so registered, or any other person who has not in his possession a stamp-affixed order as provided in section 4 hereof, to ship, carry, or deliver any firearm in interstate commerce.

SEC. 12. The Commissioner with the approval of the Secretary, shall prescribe such rules and regulations as may be necessary for carrying the provisions of this Act into effect.

SEC. 13. This Act shall not apply to the transfer of firearms (1) to the United States Government, any State, Territory, or possession of the United States, or to any political subdivision thereof, or to the District of Columbia; (2) to any peace officer or any Federal officer designated by regulations of the Commissioner; (3) to the transfer of any firearm which is unserviceable and which is transferred as a curiosity or ornament.

SEC. 14. Any person who violates or fails to comply with any of the requirement of this Act shall, upon conviction, be fined not more than $2,000 or be imprisoned for not more than five years, or both, in the discretion of the court.

SEC. 15. The taxes imposed by paragraph (a) of section 600 of the Revenue Act of 1926 (U.S.C., Supp. VII, title 26, sec. 1120) and by section 610 of the Revenue Act of 1932 (47 Stat. 169, 264), shall not apply to any firearm on which the tax provided by section 3 of this Act has been paid.

SEC. 16. If any provision of this Act, or the application thereof to any person or circumstance, is held invalid, the remainder of the Act, and the application of such provision to other persons or circumstances shall not be affected thereby.

SEC. 17. This Act shall take effect on the thirtieth day after the date of its enactment.

SEC. 18. This Act may be cited as the "National Firearms Act."

Approved, June 26, 1934.

SOURCE: U.S. Code Congressional and Administrative News

ANALYSIS

A tide of gangster violence and crime swept the country as the Great Depression stretched from months into years. Crime seemed to escalate in early 1934, most notably as law enforcement pursued and eventually gunned down the notorious gangster John Dillinger in the summer of 1934, an event that made nationwide headlines. In response, President Franklin D. Roosevelt pushed for stronger gun control legislation. (Until this time, the only notable national gun law, the Mailing of Firearms Act of 1927, barred the sale of handguns through the mails—a measure easily circumvented by using a delivery company other than the U.S. mail.)

The National Firearms Act barred gangster-type weapons, including sawed-off shotguns (the possession of which by two men led to the 1939 Supreme Court case of *U.S. v. Miller*; see Chapter 5), machine guns, and silencers. It also required that new guns be stamped with unique, identifying serial numbers, a practice that would be a boon to law enforcement efforts to track guns used in crimes. The law used the federal government's power to tax these weapons in order to restrict them, as there was concern that the courts might reject a regulatory effort based on Congress's power to regulate interstate commerce. In implementation, the steep fees imposed by the law proved effective. Aside from a few thousand licensed dealers, the law has successfully kept weapons like machine guns out of civilian hands. The terms of this law are administered by the Bureau of Alcohol, Tobacco, Firearms, and Explosives.

FURTHER READING

Frye, Brian L. "The Peculiar Story of *United States v. Miller*." *N.Y.U. Journal of Law & Liberty* 3(2008): 48–82.

Gun Dealers Now Licensed, and Trafficking Regulated

- *Document:* The Federal Firearms Act of 1938
- *Date:* June 30, 1938
- *Where:* Washington, D.C.
- *Significance:* This law increased control over gun sales by establishing a system of gun dealer licensing.

DOCUMENT

[Chapter 850; PL 75–785; 52 Stat. 1250]

AN ACT

To regulate commerce in firearms.

Be it enacted by the Senate and House of Representatives of the United States of America in Congress assembled, That as used in this Act—

(1) The term "person" includes an individual, partnership, association, or corporation.

(2) The term "interstate or foreign commerce" means commerce between any State, Territory, or possession (including the Philippine Islands but not including the Canal Zone), or the District of Columbia, and any place outside thereof; or between points within the same State, Territory, or possession (including the Philippine Islands but not including the Canal Zone), or the District of Columbia, but through any place outside thereof; or within any Territory or possession or the District of Columbia.

(3) The term "firearm" means any weapon, by whatever name known, which is designed to expel a projectile or projectiles by the action of an explosive and a firearm muffler or firearm silencer, or any part or parts of such weapon.

(4) The term "manufacturer" means any person engaged in the manufacture or importation of firearms, or ammunition or cartridge cases, primers, bullets, or propellent powder for purposes of sale or distribution; and the term "licensed manufacturer" means any such person licensed under the provisions of this Act.

(5) The term "dealer" means any person engaged in the business of selling firearms or ammunition or cartridge cases, primers, bullets or propellent powder, at wholesale or retail, or any person engaged in the business of repairing such firearms or of manufacturing or fitting special barrels, stocks, trigger mechanisms, or breach mechanisms to firearms, and the term "licensed dealer" means any such person licensed under the provisions of this Act.

(6) The term "crime of violence" means murder, manslaughter, rape, mayhem, kidnapping, burglary, housebreaking; assault with intent to kill, commit rape, or rob; assault with a dangerous weapon, or assault with intent to commit any offense punishable by imprisonment for more than one year.

(7) The term "fugitive from justice" means any person who has fled from any State, Territory, the District of Columbia, or possession of the United States to avoid prosecution for a crime of violence or to avoid giving testimony in any criminal proceeding.

(8) The term "ammunition" shall include all pistol or revolver ammunition except .22-caliber rim-fire ammunition.

SEC. 2. (a) It shall be unlawful for any manufacturer or dealer, except a manufacturer or dealer having a license issued under the provisions of this Act, to transport, ship, or receive any firearm or ammunition in interstate or foreign commerce.

(b) It shall be unlawful for any person to receive any firearm or ammunition transported or shipped in interstate or foreign commerce in violation of subdivision (a) of this section, knowing or having reasonable cause to believe such firearms or ammunition to have been transported or shipped in violation of subdivision (a) of this section.

(c) It shall be unlawful for any licensed manufacturer or dealer to transport or ship any firearm in interstate or foreign commerce to any person other than a licensed manufacturer or dealer in any State the laws of which require that a license be obtained for the purchase of such firearm, unless such license is exhibited to such manufacturer or dealer by the prospective purchaser.

(d) It shall be unlawful for any person to ship, transport, or cause to be shipped or transported in interstate or foreign commerce any firearm or ammunition to any person knowing or having reasonable cause to believe that such person is under indictment or has been convicted in any court of the United States, the several States, Territories, possessions (including the Philippine Islands), or the District of Columbia of a crime of violence or is a fugitive from justice.

(e) It shall be unlawful for any person who is under indictment or who has been convicted of a crime of violence or who is a fugitive from justice to ship, transport, or cause to be shipped or transported in interstate or foreign commerce any firearm or ammunition.

(f) It shall ho unlawful for any person who has been convicted of a crime of violence or is a fugitive from justice to receive any firearm or ammunition which has been shipped or transported in interstate or foreign commerce, and the possession of a firearm or ammunition by any such person shall be presumptive evidence that such firearm or ammunition was shipped or transported or received, as the case may be, by such person in violation of this Act.

(g) It shall be unlawful for any person to transport or ship or cause to be transported or shipped in interstate or foreign commerce any stolen firearm or ammunition, knowing, or having reasonable cause to believe, same to have been stolen.

(h) It shall be unlawful for any person to receive, conceal, store, barter, sell, or dispose of any firearm or ammunition or to pledge or accept as security for a loan any firearm or ammunition moving in or which is a part of interstate or foreign commerce, and which while so moving or constituting such part has been stolen, knowing, or having reasonable cause to believe the same to have been stolen.

(i) It shall be unlawful for any person to transport, ship, or knowingly receive in interstate or foreign commerce any firearm from which the manufacturer's serial number has been removed, obliterated, or altered, and the possession of any such firearm shall be presumptive evidence that such firearm was transported, shipped, or received, as the case may be, by the possessor in violation of this Act.

SEC. 3. (a) Any manufacturer or dealer desiring a license to transport, ship, or receive firearms or ammunition in interstate or foreign commerce shall make application to the Secretary of the Treasury, who shall prescribe by rules and regulations the information to be contained in such application. The applicant shall, if a manufacturer, pay a fee of $25 per annum and, if a dealer, shall pay a fee of $1 per annum.

(b) Upon payment of the prescribed, fee, the Secretary of the Treasury shall Issue to such applicant a license which shall entitle the licensee to transport, ship, and receive firearms and ammunition in interstate and foreign commerce unless and until the license is suspended or revoked in accordance with the provisions of this Act: *Provided,* That no license shall be issued to any applicant within two years after the revocation of a previous license.

(c) Whenever any licensee is convicted of a violation of any of the provisions of this Act, it shall be the duty of the clerk of the court to notify the Secretary of the Treasury within forty-eight hours after such conviction and said Secretary shall revoke such license: *Provided,* That in the case of appeal from such conviction the licensee may furnish a bond in the amount of $1,000, and upon receipt of such bond acceptable to the Secretary of the Treasury he may permit the licensee to continue business during the period of the appeal, or should the licensee refuse or neglect to furnish such bond, the Secretary of the Treasury shall suspend such license until he is notified by the clerk of the court of last appeal as to the final disposition of the case.

(d) Licensed dealers shall maintain such permanent records of importation, shipment, and other disposal of firearms and ammunition as the Secretary of the Treasury shall prescribe.

SEC. 4. The provisions of this Act shall not apply with respect to the transportation, shipment, receipt, or importation of any firearm, or ammunition, sold or shipped to, or issued for the use of, (1) the United States or any department, independent establishment or agency thereof; (2) any State, Territory, or possession, or the District of Columbia, or any department, independent establishment, agency, or any political subdivision thereof; (3) any duly commissioned officer or agent of the United States, a

State, Territory, or possession, or the District of Columbia, or any political subdivision thereof; (4) or to any bank, public carrier, express, or armored-truck company organized and operating in good faith for the transportation of money and valuables; (5) or to any research laboratory designated by the Secretary of the Treasury: *Provided,* That such bank, public carriers, express, and armored-truck companies are granted exemption by the Secretary of the Treasury; nor to the transportation, shipment, or receipt of any antique or unserviceable firearms, or ammunition, possessed and held as curios or museum pieces: *Provided,* That nothing herein contained shall be construed to prevent shipments of firearms and ammunition to institutions, organizations, or persons to whom such firearms and ammunition may be lawfully delivered by the Secretary of War, nor to prevent the transportation of such firearms and ammunition so delivered by their lawful possessors while they are engaged in military training or in competitions.

SEC. 5. Any person violating any of the provisions of this Act or any rules and regulations promulgated hereunder, or who makes any statement in applying for the license or exemption provided for in this Act knowing such statement to be false, shall, upon conviction thereof, be fined not more than $2,000, or imprisoned for not more than five years, or both.

SEC. 6. This Act shall take effect thirty days after its enactment.

SEC. 7. The Secretary of the Treasury may prescribe such rules and regulations as he deems necessary to carry out the provisions of this Act.

SEC. 8. Should any section or subsection of this Act be declared unconstitutional, the remaining portion of the Act shall remain in full force and effect.

SEC. 9. This Act may be cited as the Federal Firearms Act.

Approved, June 30, 1938.

SOURCE: U.S. Code Congressional and Administrative News

ANALYSIS

The Federal Firearms Act relied on Congress's power to regulate interstate commerce by requiring gun manufacturers, dealers, and importers to first acquire a federal license from the secretary of the treasury, and to keep permanent records of transactions. The law barred those with criminal records from transporting or receiving guns or ammunition

Efforts to enact a tougher law failed when gun groups succeeded in weakening the measure's language in Congress by setting a high bar for successful prosecution: prosecutors had to prove that gun dealers sold guns in violation of the law knowingly ("knowing or having reasonable cause to believe" that firearms or ammunition had been shipped in violation of the law), a standard the Justice Department could rarely meet. From the 1930s to the 1960s, fewer than 100 arrests were made under the terms of this law. In addition, the low licensing fee encouraged private citizens to acquire dealer licenses to obtain dealer benefits, such as lower prices. When dealer license fees were raised in the 1990s by the Brady Law, the number of dealers dropped precipitously. This was the last significant national gun law enacted until the 1960s.

Lyndon Johnson taking the oath of office on Air Force One after the assassination of John F. Kennedy in Dallas, Texas, November 22, 1963. Lyndon Baines Johnson Library.

FURTHER READING

Leff, Carol Skalnik, and Mark H. Leff. "The Politics of Ineffectiveness: Federal Firearms Legislation, 1919–38." *Annals of the American Academy of Political and Social Sciences* 455(May, 1981): 48–62.

Assassinations and Violence Spark New Gun Measures

- *Document:* Gun Control Act of 1968
- *Date:* October 22, 1968
- *Where:* Washington, D.C.
- *Significance:* The first significant gun law enacted in 30 years, this law restricted interstate gun shipments and strengthened licensing and regulations over explosives.

DOCUMENT

The Gun Control Act of 1968

Public Law 90–618; 82 Stat. 1213

An Act to amend title 18, United States Code, to provide for better control of the interstate traffic in firearms.

Be it enacted by the Senate and House of Representatives of the United States of America in Congress assembled, That: This Act may be cited as the "Gun Control Act of 1968."

Title I—State Firearms Control Assistance

PURPOSE

Sec. 101. The Congress hereby declares that the purpose of this title is to provide support to Federal, State, and local law enforcement officials in their fight against crime and violence, and it is not the purpose of this title to place any undue or unnecessary Federal restrictions or burdens on law-abiding citizens with respect to the acquisition, possession, or use of firearms appropriate to the purpose of hunting, trapshooting, target shooting, personal protection, or any other lawful activity, and that this title is not intended to discourage or eliminate the private ownership or use of firearms by law-abiding citizens for lawful purposes, or provide for the imposition by Federal regulations of any procedures or requirements other than those reasonably necessary to implement and effectuate the provisions of this title. . . .

§ 922. UNLAWFUL ACTS

(a) It shall be unlawful—

(1) for any person, except a licensed importer, licensed manufacturer, or licensed dealer, to engage in the business of importing, manufacturing, or dealing in firearms, or in the course of such business to ship, transport, or receive any firearm in interstate or foreign commerce;

(2) for any importer, manufacturer, dealer, or collector licensed under the provisions of this chapter to ship or transport in interstate or foreign commerce any firearm or ammunition to any person other than a licensed importer, licensed manufacturer, licensed dealer, or licensed collector, except that—

(A) this paragraph and subsection (b)(3) shall not be held to preclude a licensed importer, licensed manufacturer, licensed dealer, or licensed collector from returning a firearm or replacement firearm of the same kind and type to a person from whom it was received; and this paragraph shall not be held to preclude an individual from mailing a firearm owned in compliance with Federal, State, and local law to a licensed importer, licensed manufacturer, or licensed dealer for the sole purpose of repair or customizing;

(B) this paragraph shall not be held to preclude a licensed importer, licensed manufacturer, or licensed dealer from depositing a firearm for conveyance in the mails to any officer, employee, agent, or watchman who, pursuant to the provisions of section 1715 of this title, is eligible to receive through the mails pistols, revolvers, and other firearms capable of being concealed on the person, for use in connection with his official duty; and

(C) nothing in this paragraph shall be construed as applying in any manner in the District of Columbia, the Commonwealth of Puerto Rico, or any possession of the United States differently than it would apply if the District of Columbia, the Commonwealth of Puerto Rico, or the possession were in fact a State of the United States;

(3) for any person, other than a licensed importer, licensed manufacturer, licensed dealer, or licensed collector to transport into or receive in the State where he resides (or if the person is a corporation or other business entity, the State where it maintains a place of business) any firearm purchased or otherwise obtained by such person outside that State, except that this paragraph (A) shall not preclude any person who lawfully acquires a firearm by bequest or intestate succession in a State other than his State of residence from transporting the firearm into or receiving it in that State, if it is lawful for such person to purchase or possess such firearm in that State, (B) shall not apply to the transportation or receipt of a firearm obtained in conformity with subsection (b)(3) of this section, and (C) shall not apply to the transportation of any firearm acquired in any State prior to the effective date of this chapter;

(4) for any person, other than a licensed importer, licensed manufacturer, licensed dealer, or licensed collector, to transport in interstate or foreign commerce

any destructive device, machinegun (as defined in section 5845 of the Internal Revenue Code of 1954), short-barreled shotgun, or short-barreled shotgun, or short-barreled rifle, except as specifically authorized by the Secretary consistent with public safety and necessity;

(5) for any person (other than a licensed importer, licensed manufacturer, licensed dealer, or licensed collector) to transfer, sell, trade, give, transport, or deliver any firearm to any person (other than a licensed importer, licensed manufacturer, licensed dealer, or licensed collector) who the transferor knows or has reasonable cause to believe resides in any State other than that in which the transferor resides (or other than that in which its place of business is located if the transferor is a corporation or other business entity); except that this paragraph shall not apply to (A) the transfer, transportation, or delivery of a firearm made to carry out a bequest of a firearm to, or an acquisition by intestate succession of a firearm by, a person who is permitted to acquire or possess a firearm under the laws of the State of his residence, and (B) the loan or rental of a firearm to any person for temporary use for lawful sporting purposes; and

(6) for any person in connection with the acquisition or attempted acquisition of any firearm or ammunition from a licensed importer, licensed manufacturer, licensed dealer, or licensed collector, knowingly to make any false or fictitious oral or written statement or to furnish or exhibit any false, fictitious, or misrepresented identification, intended or likely to deceive such importer, manufacturer, dealer, or collector with respect to any fact material to the lawfulness of the sale or other disposition of such firearm or ammunition under the provisions of this chapter.

(b) It shall be unlawful for any licensed importer, licensed manufacturer, licensed dealer, or licensed collector to sell or deliver—

(1) any firearm or ammunition to any individual who the licensee knows or has reasonable cause to believe is less than eighteen years of age, and, if the firearm, or ammunition is other than a shotgun or rifle, or ammunition for a shotgun or rifle, to any individual who the licensee knows or has reasonable cause to believe is less than twenty-one years of age.

(2) any firearm or ammunition to any person in any State where the purchase or possession by such person of such firearm or ammunition would be in violation of any State law or any published ordinance applicable at the place of sale, delivery or other disposition, unless the licensee knows or has reasonable cause to believe that the purchase or possession would not be in violation of such State law or such published ordinance;

(3) any firearm to any person who the licensee knows or has reasonable cause to believe does not reside in (or if the person is a corporation or other business entity, does not maintain a place of business in) the State in which the licensee's place of business is located, except that this paragraph (A) shall not apply to the sale or delivery of any rifle or shotgun to a resident of a State other than a State in which the licensee's place of business is located if the transferee meets in person with the transferor to accomplish the transfer, and the sale, delivery, and receipt fully comply with the legal conditions of sale in both such States (and any licensed manufacturer, importer or dealer shall be presumed, for purposes of this subparagraph, in the absence of evidence to the contrary, to have had actual knowledge of the State laws and published ordinances of

both States), and (B) shall not apply to the loan or rental of a firearm to any person for temporary use for lawful sporting purposes. . . .

(4) to any person any destructive device, machinegun (as defined in section 5845 of the Internal Revenue Code of 1954), short-barreled shotgun, or short-barreled rifle, except as specifically authorized by the Secretary consistent with public safety and necessity; and

(5) any firearm or ammunition to any person unless the licensee notes in his records, required to be kept pursuant to section 923 of this chapter, the name, age, and place of residence of such person if the person is an individual, or the identity and principal and local places of business of such person if the person is a corporation or other business entity.

Paragraphs (1), (2), (3), and (4) of this subsection shall not apply to transactions between licensed importers, licensed manufacturers, licensed dealers, and licensed collectors. Paragraph (4) of this subsection shall not apply to a sale or delivery to any research organization designated by the Secretary. . . .

(d) It shall be unlawful for any licensed importer, licensed manufacturer, licensed dealer, or licensed collector to sell or otherwise dispose of any firearm or ammunition to any person knowing or having reasonable cause to believe that such person—

(1) is under indictment for, or has been convicted in any court of, a crime punishable by imprisonment for a term exceeding one year;

(2) is a fugitive from justice;

(3) is an unlawful user of or addicted to marihuana or any depressant or stimulant drug (as defined in section 201(v) of the Federal Food, Drug, and Cosmetic Act) or narcotic drug (as defined in section 4731(a) of the Internal Revenue Code of 1954); or

(4) has been adjudicated as a mental defective or has been committed to any mental institution. . . .

§ 923. Licensing

(a) No person shall engage in business as a firearms or ammunition importer, manufacturer, or dealer until he has filed an application with, and received a license to do so from, the Secretary. The application shall be in such form and contain such information as the Secretary shall by regulation prescribe. Each applicant shall pay a fee for obtaining such a license, a separate fee being required for each place in which the applicant is to do business, as follows:

(1) If the applicant is a manufacturer—

(A) of destructive devices or ammunition for destructive devices, a fee of $1,000 per year;

(B) of firearms other than destructive devices, a fee of $50 per year; or

(C) of ammunition for firearms other than destructive devices, a fee of $10 per year.

(2) If the applicant is an importer—

(A) of destructive devices or ammunition for destructive devices, a fee of $1,000 per year; or

(B) of firearms other than destructive devices or ammunition for firearms other than destructive devices, a fee of $50 per year.

(3) If the applicant is a dealer—

(A) in destructive devices or ammunition for destructive devices, a fee of $1,000 per year;

(B) who is a pawnbroker dealing in firearms other than destructive devices or ammunition for firearms other than destructive devices, a fee of $25 per year; or

(C) who is not a dealer in destructive or a pawnbroker, a fee of $10 per year. . . .

§ 924. PENALTIES

(a) Whoever violates any provision of this chapter or knowingly makes any false statement or representation with respect to the information required by the provisions of this chapter to be kept in the records of a person licensed under this chapter, or in applying for any license or exemption or relief from disability under the provisions of this chapter, shall be fined not more than $5000, or imprisoned not more than five years, or both, and shall become eligible for parole as the Board of Parole shall determine.

(b) Whoever, with intent to commit therewith an offense punishable by imprisonment for a term exceeding one year, or with knowledge or reasonable cause to believe that an offense punishable by imprisonment for a term exceeding one year is to be committed therewith, ships, transports, or receives a firearm or any ammunition in interstate or foreign commerce shall be fined not more than $10,000, or imprisoned not more than ten years, or both. . . .

SOURCE: U.S. Code Congressional and Administrative News

ANALYSIS

In the late 1960s, civil disorder, unrest, and violence escalated, especially in many of America's cities. And in 1968, two of America's most prominent leaders were gunned down—civil rights leader Dr. Martin Luther King, Jr., and presidential candidate Senator Robert F. Kennedy (D-NY). These developments accelerated the push for the enactment of new federal gun laws, a process that had begun with the assassination of President John F. Kennedy in 1963, who had been killed with a rifle purchased through interstate mail.

The end result, the Gun Control Act of 1968, fell short of the goals set by bill supporters, which had originally included national firearms registration. As enacted by Congress, the law barred the interstate shipment of firearms and ammunition to private individuals; barred gun sales to minors, drug addicts, mental incompetents, fugitives, and felons; strengthened licensing and record-keeping requirements for gun dealers and collectors; extended federal regulation and taxation to "destructive devices" including land mines, bombs, mortars, and hand grenades; increased penalties for those who used guns in the commission of federal crimes; and restricted the import of foreign-made nonsporting firearms. Part of the 1968 law revised the National Firearms Act of 1934, which first regulated gangster weapons (see previous).

The law had several effects. The number of gun dealers increased, as the definition of who was a dealer under the law was broadened, yet the dealer fee (now $10) was still small. Rifle and handgun importation declined, but shotgun imports increased. And because the law regulated gun imports, but not the import of gun parts, the latter increased. Despite the fairly limited nature of these new regulations, gun control opponents considered the law an excessive burden, and began efforts to roll back its provisions. That effort succeeded partially in 1986.

FURTHER READING

Zimring, Franklin E. "Firearms and Federal Law: The Gun Control Act of 1968." *Journal of Legal Studies* 4(January 1975): 133–143.

Congress Enacts the First Significant Rollback of National Gun Laws

- **Document:** Firearms Owners' Protection Act of 1986, also known as the McClure-Volkmer bill
- **Date:** May 19, 1986
- **Where:** Washington, D.C.
- **Significance:** This law reduced or restricted federal regulations on gun sales and dealer inspections.

DOCUMENT

Firearms Owners' Protection Act

Public Law 99–308; 100 Stat. 449

An Act to amend chapter 44 (relating to firearms) of title 18, United States Code, and for other purposes.

Be it enacted by the Senate and House of Representatives of the United States of America in Congress assembled,

Section 1. Short Title and Congressional Findings

(a) Short Title—This Act may be cited as the "Firearms Owners' Protection Act."

(b) Congressional Findings.—The Congress finds that—

(1) the rights of citizens—

(A) to keep and bear arms under the second amendment to the United States Constitution;

(B) to security against illegal and unreasonable searches and seizures under the fourth amendment;

(C) against uncompensated taking of property, double jeopardy, and assurance of due process of law under the fifth amendment; and

(D) against unconstitutional exercise of authority under the ninth and tenth amendments;

require additional legislation to correct existing firearms statutes and enforcement policies; and

(2) additional legislation is required to reaffirm the intent of the Congress, as expressed in section 101 of the Gun Control Act of 1968, that 'it is not the purpose of this title to place any undue or unnecessary Federal restrictions or burdens on law-abiding citizens with respect to the acquisition, possession, or use of firearms appropriate to the purpose of hunting, trapshooting, target shooting, personal protection, or any other lawful activity, and that this title is not intended to discourage or eliminate the private ownership or use of firearms by law-abiding citizens for lawful purposes.' . . .

(21) The term "engaged in the business" means—

(A) as applied to a manufacturer of firearms, a person who devotes time, attention, and labor to manufacturing firearms as a regular course of trade or business with the principal objective of livelihood and profit through the sale or distribution of the firearms manufactured;

(B) as applied to a manufacturer of ammunition, a person who devotes time, attention, and labor to manufacturing ammunition as a regular course of trade or business with the principal objective of livelihood and profit through the sale or distribution of the ammunition manufactured;

(C) as applied to a dealer in firearms, as defined in section 921(a)(11)(A) [18 USCS § 921(a)(11)(A)], a person who devotes time, attention, and labor to dealing in firearms as a regular course of trade or business with the principal objective of livelihood and profit through the repetitive purchase and resale of firearms, but such term shall not include a person who makes occasional sales, exchanges, or purchases of firearms for the enhancement of a personal collection or for a hobby, or who sells all or part of his personal collection of firearms;

(D) as applied to a dealer in firearms, as defined in section 921(a)(11)(B) [18 USCS § 921(a)(11)(B)], a person who devotes time, attention, and labor to engaging in such activity as a regular course of trade or business with the principal objective of livelihood and profit, but such term shall not include a person who makes occasional repairs of firearms, or who occasionally fits special barrels, stocks, or trigger mechanisms to firearms;

(E) as applied to an importer of firearms, a person who devotes time, attention, and labor to importing firearms as a regular course of trade or business with the principal objective of livelihood and profit through the sale or distribution of the firearms imported; and

(F) as applied to an importer of ammunition, a person who devotes time, attention, and labor to importing ammunition as a regular course of trade or business with the principal objective of livelihood and profit through the sale or distribution of the ammunition imported.

(22) The term "with the principal objective of livelihood and profit" means that the intent underlying the sale or disposition of firearms is predominantly one of obtaining livelihood and pecuniary gain, as opposed to other intents, such as improving or liquidating a personal firearms collection.

(23) The term "machinegun" has the meaning given such term in section 5845(b) of the National Firearms Act (26 U.S.C. 5845(b)).

(24) The terms "firearm silencer" and "firearm muffler" mean any device for silencing, muffling, or diminishing the report of a portable firearm, including any combination of parts, designed or redesigned, and intended for use in assembling or fabricating a firearm silencer or firearm muffler, and any part intended only for use in such assembly or fabrication. . . .

(a) In General.—The amendments made by this Act shall become effective one hundred and eighty days after the date of the enactment of this Act. Upon their becoming effective, the Secretary shall publish and provide to all licensees a compilation of the State laws and published ordinances of which licensees are presumed to have knowledge pursuant to chapter 44 of title 18, United States Code, as amended by this Act. All amendments to such State laws and published ordinances as contained in the aforementioned compilation shall be published in the Federal Register, revised annually, and furnished to each person licensed under chapter 44 of title 18, United States Code, as amended by this Act.

(b) Pending Actions, Petitions, and Appellate Proceedings.—The amendments made by sections 103(6)(B), 105, and 107 of this Act shall be applicable to any action, petition, or appellate proceeding pending on the date of the enactment of this Act.

(c) Machinegun Prohibition.—Section 102(9) shall take effect on the date of the enactment of this Act.

Approved May 19, 1986.

SOURCE: U.S. Code Congressional and Administrative News

ANALYSIS

The Firearms Owners' Protection Act was the culmination of an effort dating to the 1970s to roll back provisions of the 1968 Gun Control Act. Because this measure took the form of a series of amendments to the earlier law, it is difficult to grasp its effects from the text provided here. Nicknamed the McClure-Volkmer bill, after bill sponsors Senator James McClure (R-Ida.) and Rep. Harold Volkmer (R-Mo.), the efforts to repeal the 1968 law coincided with the country's more conservative turn, as seen in the election of Ronald Reagan as president in 1980 and 1984, the election of more conservative congresses during this time, and the rising power and politicization of the nation's largest gun group, the National Rifle Association (NRA).

The 1986 law contracted the definition of gun dealer to exclude those who did not sell guns "regularly," eliminated record-keeping for ammunition dealers, legalized the interstate sale of rifles and shotguns (as long as the sale was legal in the states of the buyer and seller), reduced requirements for gun dealers, made it more difficult for the government to revoke a gun seller's license and to inspect gun dealer records, made it easier for licensees to do business at "temporary" locations such as gun shows, raised the prosecutorial bar by requiring that prosecutors must prove that those charged with violations did so "willfully" or "knowingly," restricted the transfer of gun records to other government agencies, restricted the Bureau of Alcohol, Tobacco and Firearms to one unannounced inspection of gun dealers per year, and barred any system of firearms registration.

The law did increase some gun regulations. It now barred the sale of guns and ammunition to illegal aliens, those dishonorably discharged from the military, and those who renounced U.S. citizenship. It also retained the ban on civilian possession of machine guns, increased penalties for those who commit certain crimes with guns, and increased restrictions on the import of gun parts that would be illegal in the United States if the weapon as assembled were already illegal.

FURTHER READING

Spitzer, Robert J. *The Politics of Gun Control.* Washington, D.C.: CQ Press, 2007.

Congress Enacts Waiting Period and Background Checks for Handgun Purchases

- *Document:* The Brady Handgun Violence Prevention Act of 1993
- *Date:* November 30, 1993
- *Where:* Washington, D.C.
- *Significance:* In a small shift back toward greater national gun controls, this law required nationwide background checks for handgun purchasers and for a time also required a waiting period for prospective purchasers.

DOCUMENT

The Brady Law of 1993

PL 103–159; 107 Stat. 1536

An Act to provide for a waiting period before the purchase of a handgun, and for the establishment of a national instant criminal background check system to be contacted by firearms dealers before the transfer of any firearm.

Be it enacted by the Senate and House of Representatives of the United States of America in Congress assembled,

Title I—Brady Handgun Control

SEC. 101. SHORT TITLE.

This title may be cited as the 'Brady Handgun Violence Prevention Act'.

INTERIM PROVISION—IN GENERAL—Section 922 of title 18, United States Code, is amended by adding at the end the following: '(s)(1) Beginning on the date that is 90 days after the date of enactment of this subsection and ending on the day before the date that is 60 months after such date of enactment, it shall be unlawful for any licensed importer, licensed manufacturer, or licensed dealer to sell, deliver, or transfer a handgun to an individual who is not licensed under section 923, unless—'(A) after the most recent proposal of such transfer by the transferee—'(i) the transferor has—'(I) received from the transferee a statement of the transferee containing the information described in paragraph (3); '(II) verified the identity of the transferee by examining the identification document presented; '(III) within 1 day after the transferee furnishes the statement, provided notice of the contents of the statement to the chief law enforcement officer of the place of residence of the transferee; and '(IV) within 1 day after the transferee furnishes the statement, transmitted a copy of the statement to the chief law enforcement officer of the place of residence of the transferee; and '(ii)(I) 5 business days (meaning days on which State offices are open) have elapsed from the date the transferor furnished notice of the contents of the statement to the chief law enforcement officer, during which period the transferor has not received information from the chief law enforcement officer that receipt or possession of the handgun by the transferee would be in violation of Federal, State, or local law; or' (II) the transferor has received notice from the chief law enforcement officer that the officer has no information indicating that receipt or possession of the handgun by the transferee would violate Federal, State, or local law; '(B) the transferee has presented to the transferor a written statement, issued by the chief law enforcement officer of the place of residence of the transferee during the 10-day period ending on the date of the most recent proposal of such transfer by the transferee, stating that the transferee requires access to a handgun because of a threat to the life of the transferee or of any member of the household of the transferee; '(C)(i) the transferee has presented to the transferor a permit that—' (I) allows the transferee to possess or acquire a handgun; and' (II) was issued not more than 5 years earlier by the State in which the transfer is to take place; and '(ii) the law of the State provides that such a permit is to be issued only after an authorized government official has verified that the information available to such official does not indicate that possession of a handgun by the transferee would be in violation of the law; '(D) the law of the State requires that, before any licensed importer, licensed manufacturer, or licensed dealer completes the transfer of a handgun to an individual who is not licensed under section 923, an authorized government official verify that the information available to such official does not indicate that possession of a handgun by the transferee would be in violation of law; '(E) the Secretary has approved the transfer under section 5812 of the Internal Revenue Code of 1986; or '(F) on application of the transferor, the Secretary has certified that compliance with subparagraph (A)(i)(III) is impracticable because—' (i) the ratio of the number of law enforcement officers of the State in which the transfer is to occur to the number of square miles of land area of the State does not exceed 0.0025;' (ii) the business premises of the transferor at which the transfer is to occur are extremely remote in relation to the chief law enforcement officer; and' (iii) there is an absence of telecommunications facilities in the geographical area in which the business premises are located.' (2) A chief law enforcement officer to whom a transferor has provided notice pursuant to paragraph (1)(A)(i)(III) shall make a reasonable effort to ascertain within 5 business days whether receipt or possession would be in violation of the law, including research in whatever State and local recordkeeping systems are available and in a national system designated by the Attorney General.' (3) The statement referred to in paragraph (1)(A)(i)(I) shall contain only—'(A) the name, address, and date of birth appearing on a valid identification document (as defined in section 1028(d)(1)) of the transferee containing a photograph of the transferee and a description of the identification used;' (B) a statement that the transferee—' (i) is not under indictment for, and has not been convicted in any court of, a crime punishable by imprisonment for a term exceeding 1 year;' (ii) is not a fugitive from justice;' (iii) is not an unlawful user of or addicted to any controlled substance (as defined in section 102 of the Controlled Substances Act);' (iv) has not been adjudicated as a mental defective or been committed to a mental institution; '(v) is not an alien who is illegally or unlawfully in the United States;' (vi) has not been discharged from the Armed Forces under dishonorable conditions; and' (vii) is not a person who, having been a citizen of the United States, has renounced such citizenship; '(C) the date the statement is made; and' (D) notice that the transferee intends to obtain a handgun from the transferor.' (4) Any transferor of a handgun who, after such transfer, receives a report from a chief law enforcement officer containing information that receipt or possession of the handgun by the transferee violates Federal, State, or local law shall, within 1 business day after receipt of such request, communicate any information related to the transfer that the transferor has about the transfer and the transferee to—

'(A) the chief law enforcement officer of the place of business of the transferor; and

'(B) the chief law enforcement officer of the place of residence of the transferee.

'(5) Any transferor who receives information, not otherwise available to the public, in a report under this subsection shall not disclose such information except to the transferee, to law enforcement authorities, or pursuant to the direction of a court of law.

'(6)(A) Any transferor who sells, delivers, or otherwise transfers a handgun to a transferee shall retain the copy of the statement of the transferee with respect to the handgun transaction, and shall retain evidence that the transferor has complied with subclauses (III) and (IV) of paragraph (1)(A)(i) with respect to the statement.

'(B) Unless the chief law enforcement officer to whom a statement is transmitted under paragraph (1)(A)(i)(IV) determines that a transaction would violate Federal, State, or local law—

'(i) the officer shall, within 20 business days after the date the transferee made the statement on the basis of which the notice was provided, destroy the statement, any record containing information derived from the statement, and any record created as a result of the notice required by paragraph (1)(A)(i)(III);

'(ii) the information contained in the statement shall not be conveyed to any person except a person who has a need to know in order to carry out this subsection; and

'(iii) the information contained in the statement shall not be used for any purpose other than to carry out this subsection.

'(C) If a chief law enforcement officer determines that an individual is ineligible to receive a handgun and the individual requests the officer to provide the reason for such determination, the officer shall provide such reasons to the individual in writing within 20 business days after receipt of the request.

'(7) A chief law enforcement officer or other person responsible for providing criminal history background information pursuant to this subsection shall not be liable in an action at law for damages—

'(A) for failure to prevent the sale or transfer of a handgun to a person whose receipt or possession of the handgun is unlawful under this section; or

'(B) for preventing such a sale or transfer to a person who may lawfully receive or possess a handgun.

'(8) For purposes of this subsection, the term 'chief law enforcement officer' means the chief of police, the sheriff, or an equivalent officer or the designee of any such individual.

'(9) The Secretary shall take necessary actions to ensure that the provisions of this subsection are published and disseminated to licensed dealers, law enforcement officials, and the public.'

HANDGUN DEFINED—Section 921(a) of title 18, United States Code, is amended by adding at the end the following:

'(29) The term 'handgun' means—

'(A) a firearm which has a short stock and is designed to be held and fired by the use of a single hand; and

'(B) any combination of parts from which a firearm described in subparagraph (A) can be assembled.'

PERMANENT PROVISION—Section 922 of title 18, United States Code, as amended by subsection (a)(1), is amended by adding at the end the following:

'(t)(1) Beginning on the date that is 30 days after the Attorney General notifies licensees under section 103(d) of the Brady Handgun Violence Prevention Act that the national instant criminal background check system is established, a licensed importer, licensed manufacturer, or licensed dealer shall not transfer a firearm to any other person who is not licensed under this chapter, unless—

'(A) before the completion of the transfer, the licensee contacts the national instant criminal background check system established under section 103 of that Act;

'(B) (i) the system provides the licensee with a unique identification number; or

'(ii) 3 business days (meaning a day on which State offices are open) have elapsed since the licensee contacted the system, and the system has not notified the licensee that the receipt of a firearm by such other person would violate subsection (g) or (n) of this section; and

'(C) the transferor has verified the identity of the transferee by examining a valid identification document (as defined in section 1028(d)(1) of this title) of the transferee containing a photograph of the transferee.

'(2) If receipt of a firearm would not violate section 922 (g) or (n) or State law, the system shall—

'(A) assign a unique identification number to the transfer;

'(B) provide the licensee with the number; and

'(C) destroy all records of the system with respect to the call (other than the identifying number and the date the number was assigned) and all records of the system relating to the person or the transfer.

'(3) Paragraph (1) shall not apply to a firearm transfer between a licensee and another person if—

'(A) (i) such other person has presented to the licensee a permit that—

'(I) allows such other person to possess or acquire a firearm; and

'(II) was issued not more than 5 years earlier by the State in which the transfer is to take place; and'(ii) the law of the State provides that such a permit is to be issued only after an authorized government official has verified that the information available to such official does not indicate that possession of a firearm by such other person would be in violation of law;

'(B) the Secretary has approved the transfer under section 5812 of the Internal Revenue Code of 1986; or

'(C) on application of the transferor, the Secretary has certified that compliance with paragraph (1)(A) is impracticable because—

'(i) the ratio of the number of law enforcement officers of the State in which the transfer is to occur to the number of square miles of land area of the State does not exceed 0.0025;

'(ii) the business premises of the licensee at which the transfer is to occur are extremely remote in relation to the chief law enforcement officer (as defined in subsection (s)(8)); and

'(iii) there is an absence of telecommunications facilities in the geographical area in which the business premises are located.

'(4) If the national instant criminal background check system notifies the licensee that the information available to the system does not demonstrate that the receipt of a firearm by such other person would violate subsection (g) or (n) or State law, and the licensee transfers a firearm to such other person, the licensee shall include in the record of the transfer the unique identification number provided by the system with respect to the transfer.

'(5) If the licensee knowingly transfers a firearm to such other person and knowingly fails to comply with paragraph (1) of this subsection with respect to the transfer and, at the time such other person most recently proposed the transfer, the national instant criminal background check system was operating and information was available to the system demonstrating that receipt of a firearm by such other person would violate subsection (g) or (n) of this section or State law, the Secretary may, after notice and opportunity for a hearing, suspend for not more than 6 months or revoke any license issued to the licensee under section 923, and may impose on the licensee a civil fine of not more than $5,000.

'(6) Neither a local government nor an employee of the Federal Government or of any State or local government, responsible for providing information to the national instant criminal background check system shall be liable in an action at law for damages—

'(A) for failure to prevent the sale or transfer of a firearm to a person whose receipt or possession of the firearm is unlawful under this section; or

'(B) for preventing such a sale or transfer to a person who may lawfully receive or possess a firearm.'

PENALTY—Section 924(a) of title 18, United States Code, is amended—in paragraph (1), by striking 'paragraph (2) or (3) of'; and by adding at the end the following:

'(5) Whoever knowingly violates subsection (s) or (t) of section 922 shall be fined not more than $1,000, imprisoned for not more than 1 year, or both.'

DETERMINATION OF TIMETABLES—Not later than 6 months after the date of enactment of this Act, the Attorney General shall—

determine the type of computer hardware and software that will be used to operate the national instant criminal background check system and the means by which State criminal records systems and the telephone or electronic device of licensees will communicate with the national system; investigate the criminal records system of each State and determine for each State a timetable by which the State should be able to provide criminal records on an on-line capacity basis to the national system; and notify each State of the determinations made pursuant to paragraphs (1) and (2).

ESTABLISHMENT OF SYSTEM—Not later than 60 months after the date of the enactment of this Act, the Attorney General shall establish a national instant criminal background check system that any licensee may contact, by telephone or by other electronic means in addition to the telephone, for information, to be supplied immediately, on whether receipt of a firearm by a prospective transferee would violate section 922 of title 18, United States Code, or State law.

EXPEDITED ACTION BY THE ATTORNEY GENERAL—The Attorney General shall expedite—

the upgrading and indexing of State criminal history records in the Federal criminal records system maintained by the Federal Bureau of Investigation;

the development of hardware and software systems to link State criminal history check systems into the national instant criminal background check system established by the Attorney General pursuant to this section; and

the current revitalization initiatives by the Federal Bureau of Investigation for technologically advanced fingerprint and criminal records identification.

NOTIFICATION OF LICENSEES—On establishment of the system under this section, the Attorney General shall notify each licensee and the chief law enforcement officer of each State of the existence and purpose of the system and the means to be used to contact the system.

Administrative Provisions

AUTHORITY TO OBTAIN OFFICIAL INFORMATION—

Notwithstanding any other law, the Attorney General may secure directly from any department or agency of the United States such information on persons for whom receipt of a firearm would violate subsection (g) or (n) of section 922 of title 18, United States Code or State law, as is necessary to enable the system to operate in accordance with this section. On request of the

Attorney General, the head of such department or agency shall furnish such information to the system.

OTHER AUTHORITY—The Attorney General shall develop such computer software, design and obtain such telecommunications and computer hardware, and employ such personnel, as are necessary to establish and operate the system in accordance with this section.

WRITTEN REASONS PROVIDED ON REQUEST—If the national instant criminal background check system determines that an individual is ineligible to receive a firearm and the individual requests the system to provide the reasons for the determination, the system shall provide such reasons to the individual, in writing, within 5 business days after the date of the request.

CORRECTION OF ERRONEOUS SYSTEM INFORMATION—If the system established under this section informs an individual contacting the system that receipt of a firearm by a prospective transferee would violate subsection (g) or (n) of section 922 of title 18, United States Code or State law, the prospective transferee may request the Attorney General to provide the prospective transferee with the reasons therefor. Upon receipt of such a request, the Attorney General shall immediately comply with the request. The prospective transferee may submit to the Attorney General information to correct, clarify, or supplement records of the system with respect to the prospective transferee. After receipt of such information, the Attorney General shall immediately consider the information, investigate the matter further, and correct all erroneous Federal records relating to the prospective transferee and give notice of the error to any Federal department or agency or any State that was the source of such erroneous records.

REGULATIONS—After 90 days' notice to the public and an opportunity for hearing by interested parties, the Attorney General shall prescribe regulations to ensure the privacy and security of the information of the system established under this section.

Prohibition Relating to Establishment of Registration Systems

WITH RESPECT TO FIREARMS—No department, agency, officer, or employee of the United States may—

require that any record or portion thereof generated by the system established under this section be recorded at or transferred to a facility owned, managed, or controlled by the United States or any State or political subdivision thereof; or use the system established under this section to establish any system for the registration of firearms, firearm owners, or firearm transactions or dispositions, except with respect to persons, prohibited by section 922 (g) or (n) of title 18, United States Code or State law, from receiving a firearm.

DEFINITIONS—As used in this section:

LICENSEE—The term 'licensee' means a licensed importer (as defined in section 921(a)(9) of title 18, United States Code), a licensed manufacturer (as defined in section 921(a)(10) of that title), or a licensed dealer (as defined in section 921(a)(11) of that title).

OTHER TERMS—The terms 'firearm,' 'handgun,' 'licensed importer,' 'licensed manufacturer,' and 'licensed dealer' have the meanings stated in section 921(a) of title 18, United States Code, as amended by subsection (a)(2).

AUTHORIZATION OF APPROPRIATIONS—There are authorized to be appropriated, which may be appropriated from the Violent Crime Reduction Trust Fund established by section 1115 of title 31, United States Code, such sums as are necessary to enable the Attorney General to carry out this section.

Sec. 104. Remedy for Erroneous Denial of Firearm.

IN GENERAL—Chapter 44 of title 18, United States Code, is amended by inserting after section 925 the following new section:

'Sec. 925A. Remedy for erroneous denial of firearm 'Any person denied a firearm pursuant to subsection (s) or (t) of section 922—

'(1) due to the provision of erroneous information relating to the person by any State or political subdivision thereof, or by the national instant criminal background check system established under section 103 of the Brady Handgun Violence Prevention Act; or

'(2) who was not prohibited from receipt of a firearm pursuant to subsection (g) or (n) of section 922, may bring an action against the State or political subdivision responsible for providing the erroneous information, or responsible for denying the transfer, or against the United States, as the case may be, for an order directing that the erroneous information be corrected or that the transfer be approved, as the case may be. In any action under this section, the court, in its discretion, may allow the prevailing party a reasonable attorney's fee as part of the costs.'. . . .

Sec. 105. Rule of Construction.

This Act and the amendments made by this Act shall not be construed to alter or impair any right or remedy under section 552a of title 5, United States Code.

Sec. 106. Funding for Improvement of Criminal Records.

USE OF FORMULA GRANTS—Section 509(b) of title I of the Omnibus Crime Control and Safe Streets Act of 1968 (42 U.S.C. 3759(b)) is amended—

in paragraph (2) by striking 'and' after the semicolon;

in paragraph (3) by striking the period and inserting '; and'; and by adding at the end the following new paragraph:

'(4) the improvement of State record systems and the sharing with the Attorney General of all of the records described in paragraphs (1), (2), and (3) of this subsection and the records required by the Attorney General under section 103 of the Brady Handgun Violence Prevention Act, for the purpose of implementing that Act.'

Additional Funding—

Grants for the Improvement of Criminal Records

The Attorney General, through the Bureau of Justice Statistics, shall, subject to appropriations and with preference to States that as of the date of enactment of this Act have the lowest percent currency of case dispositions in computerized criminal history files, make a grant to each State to be used—

for the creation of a computerized criminal history record system or improvement of an existing system; to improve accessibility to the national instant criminal background system; and upon establishment of the national system, to assist the State in the transmittal of criminal records to the national system.

AUTHORIZATION OF APPROPRIATIONS—There are authorized to be appropriated for grants under paragraph (1), which may be appropriated from the Violent Crime Reduction Trust Fund established by section 1115 of title 31, United States Code, a total of $200,000,000 for fiscal year 1994 and all fiscal years thereafter.

Title II—Multiple Firearm Purchases to State and Local Police

SEC. 201. REPORTING REQUIREMENT.

Section 923(g)(3) of title 18, United States Code, is amended—

in the second sentence by inserting after 'thereon,' the following: 'and to the department of State police or State law enforcement agency of the State or local law enforcement agency of the local jurisdiction in which the sale or other disposition took place,'; by inserting '(A)' after '(3)'; and by adding at the end thereof the following: '(B) Except in the case of forms and contents thereof regarding a purchaser who is prohibited by subsection (g) or (n) of section 922 of this title from receipt of a firearm, the department of State police or State law enforcement agency or local law enforcement agency of the local jurisdiction shall not disclose any such form or the contents thereof to any person or entity, and shall destroy each such form and any record of the contents thereof no more than 20 days from the date such form is received. No later than the date that is 6 months after the effective date of this subparagraph, and at the end of each 6-month period thereafter, the department of State police or State law enforcement agency or local law enforcement agency of the local jurisdiction shall certify to the Attorney General of the United States that no disclosure contrary to this subparagraph has been made and that all forms and any record of the contents thereof have been destroyed as provided in this subparagraph.'. . . .

SOURCE: sinfo.state.gov/usa/infousa/laws/majorlaw/h1025_en.htm

---

ANALYSIS

The enactment of the Brady Law in 1993 was the culmination of seven years of effort to impose a national standard for handgun purchases. The aim was twofold: first, to prevent felons, those judged mentally incompetent or others otherwise unqualified to own handguns to make such a purchase; and second, to provide for a waiting period between the time of the purchase and the customer's actual acquisition of a handgun in order to provide a "cooling off" period for those who might seek a handgun in a fit of temper or rage. Even though this legislative effort was a modest one supported by large majorities of Americans, the protracted political struggle that ensued was typical for that of gun policy.

Named for James Brady, President Ronald Reagan's press secretary who was shot and wounded in the 1981 assassination attempt against Reagan, this measure enacted a five-day waiting period for handgun purchases. Yet that waiting period was eliminated in 1998, under the terms of the law, and was replaced by a national instant background check (NICS) system that now allows nearly all handgun purchases to be completed within minutes of sale. The other major provision of the law, the background check provision, was to be carried out by local law enforcement. In a legal challenge to the law, the Supreme Court ruled in *Printz v. U.S.* (see Chapter 5) that the federal government could not require such actions by local law enforcement, but the rest of the law remained in force, and the electronic check system has generally functioned effectively.

In addition, the Brady Law authorized funding to assist states to improve and upgrade their computerization of criminal records, increased federal firearms license fees to $200 for the first three years and $90 for renewals, made it a federal crime to steal firearms from licensed dealers, barred package labeling for guns being shipped to deter theft, and required that law enforcement be informed of multiple handgun sales. The increase in federal firearms license fees had the effect of reducing the number of licensed dealers nationwide from about 300,000 to about 100,000, eliminating so-called kitchen table dealers—people who were not really gun dealers, but who got the formerly cheap licenses to obtain discounts and other advantages. In its first decade of implementation, the Brady Law stopped about a million handgun purchases. In 2007, the federal government enacted a new measure to improve state record-keeping relating to those with mental problems, as many states still did not keep proper records or report them to the national database. This problem was brought to the nation's attention when a student with a history of mental problems was nevertheless able to legally purchase two handguns in Virginia that he used to kill 32 people on the campus of Virginia Tech University in 2007, even though a judge had ruled him mentally incompetent—information that never made it to the state and national database.

FURTHER READING

DeFrances, Carol J., and Steven K. Smith. "Federal-State Relations in Gun Control: The 1993 Brady Handgun Violence Prevention Act," *Publius* 24(Summer 1994): 68–82.

Ludwig, Jens, and Philip Cook. "Homicide and Suicide Rates Associated With Implementation of the Brady Handgun Violence Prevention Act." *Journal of the American Medical Association* 284(August 2, 2000): 585–591.

DID YOU KNOW?

Brady

Early in the afternoon of March 30, 1981, President Ronald Reagan was leaving the Washington Hilton hotel after giving a speech there and preparing to enter his limousine when several shots rang out. In a bizarre effort to impress the actress Jodie Foster, John Hinckley attempted to assassinate the president of the United States using a handgun. Several people were wounded, including Reagan and his press secretary, James Brady. All survived, but Brady's injury—a bullet to the head—left him permanently disabled.

The incident inspired Brady's wife, Sarah, to become involved in the gun control movement. The daughter of an FBI agent who had been trained in the use of guns, Sarah Brady joined and eventually became the leader of the nation's largest pro-gun control group, then called Handgun Control, Inc (HCI). Her husband joined in the effort, and the couple came to represent the face of efforts to enact what they considered "sensible" gun laws that imposed some restrictions but that also preserved legitimate gun practices and uses. Chief among their goals was enactment of a nationwide system of background checks for handgun purchases, an effort that came to fruition in 1993. As the political campaign for what became known as the Brady bill escalated, James Brady's former boss, President Reagan, initially opposed the measure. After leaving the White House in 1989, however, Reagan reversed his position and endorsed the Brady bill, as well as the assault weapons ban enacted in 1994. In 2001, HCI was renamed the Brady Campaign to Prevent Gun Violence. Both Bradys continued to be active in gun law reform efforts.

Assault Weapons Banned for Ten Years

- **Document:** Violent Crime Control and Law Enforcement Act of 1994, Title XI, also known as the Assault Weapons Ban
- **Date:** September 13, 1994
- **Where:** Washington, D.C.
- **Significance:** This law barred military-style assault weapons to the civilian population for 10 years.

DOCUMENT

Violent Crime Control and Law Enforcement Act of 1994

PL 103–322; 108 Stat. 1796
TITLE XI—FIREARMS
Subtitle A—Assault Weapons
SEC. 110101. SHORT TITLE.

This subtitle may be cited as the 'Public Safety and Recreational Firearms Use Protection Act'.

SEC. 110102. RESTRICTION ON MANUFACTURE, TRANSFER, AND POSSESSION OF CERTAIN SEMIAUTOMATIC ASSAULT WEAPONS.

(a) RESTRICTION—Section 922 of title 18, United States Code, is amended by adding at the end the following new subsection:

'(v)(1) It shall be unlawful for a person to manufacture, transfer, or possess a semi-automatic assault weapon.

'(2) Paragraph (1) shall not apply to the possession or transfer of any semiautomatic assault weapon otherwise lawfully possessed under Federal law on the date of the enactment of this subsection.

'(3) Paragraph (1) shall not apply to—

'(A) any of the firearms, or replicas or duplicates of the firearms, specified in Appendix A to this section, as such firearms were manufactured on October 1, 1993;

'(B) any firearm that—

'(i) is manually operated by bolt, pump, lever, or slide action;

'(ii) has been rendered permanently inoperable; or

'(iii) is an antique firearm;

'(C) any semiautomatic rifle that cannot accept a detachable magazine that holds more than 5 rounds of ammunition; or

'(D) any semiautomatic shotgun that cannot hold more than 5 rounds of ammunition in a fixed or detachable magazine.

The fact that a firearm is not listed in Appendix A shall not be construed to mean that paragraph (1) applies to such firearm. No firearm exempted by this subsection may be deleted from Appendix A so long as this subsection is in effect.

'(4) Paragraph (1) shall not apply to—

'(A) the manufacture for, transfer to, or possession by the United States or a department or agency of the United States or a State or a department, agency, or political subdivision of a State, or a transfer to or possession by a law enforcement officer employed by such an entity for purposes of law enforcement (whether on or off duty);

'(B) the transfer to a licensee under title I of the Atomic Energy Act of 1954 for purposes of establishing and maintaining an on-site physical protection system and security organization required by Federal law, or possession by an employee or contractor of such licensee on-site for such purposes or off-site for purposes of licensee-authorized training or transportation of nuclear materials;

'(C) the possession, by an individual who is retired from service with a law enforcement agency and is not otherwise prohibited from receiving a firearm, of a semiautomatic assault weapon transferred to the individual by the agency upon such retirement; or

'(D) the manufacture, transfer, or possession of a semiautomatic assault weapon by a licensed manufacturer or licensed importer for the purposes of testing or experimentation authorized by the Secretary.'

(b) DEFINITION OF SEMIAUTOMATIC ASSAULT WEAPON- Section 921(a) of title 18, United States Code, is amended by adding at the end the following new paragraph:

'(30) The term 'semiautomatic assault weapon' means—

'(A) any of the firearms, or copies or duplicates of the firearms in any caliber, known as—

'(i) Norinco, Mitchell, and Poly Technologies Avtomat Kalashnikovs (all models);

'(ii) Action Arms Israeli Military Industries UZI and Galil;

'(iii) Beretta Ar70 (SC-70);

'(iv) Colt AR-15;

'(v) Fabrique National FN/FAL, FN/LAR, and FNC;

'(vi) SWD M-10, M-11, M-11/9, and M-12;

'(vii) Steyr AUG;

'(viii) INTRATEC TEC-9, TEC-DC9 and TEC-22; and

'(ix) revolving cylinder shotguns, such as (or similar to) the Street Sweeper and Striker 12;

'(B) a semiautomatic rifle that has an ability to accept a detachable magazine and has at least 2 of—

'(i) a folding or telescoping stock;

'(ii) a pistol grip that protrudes conspicuously beneath the action of the weapon;

'(iii) a bayonet mount;

'(iv) a flash suppressor or threaded barrel designed to accommodate a flash suppressor; and

'(v) a grenade launcher;

'(C) a semiautomatic pistol that has an ability to accept a detachable magazine and has at least 2 of—

'(i) an ammunition magazine that attaches to the pistol outside of the pistol grip;

'(ii) a threaded barrel capable of accepting a barrel extender, flash suppressor, forward handgrip, or silencer;

'(iii) a shroud that is attached to, or partially or completely encircles, the barrel and that permits the shooter to hold the firearm with the nontrigger hand without being burned;

'(iv) a manufactured weight of 50 ounces or more when the pistol is unloaded; and

'(v) a semiautomatic version of an automatic firearm; and

'(D) a semiautomatic shotgun that has at least 2 of—

'(i) a folding or telescoping stock;

'(ii) a pistol grip that protrudes conspicuously beneath the action of the weapon;

'(iii) a fixed magazine capacity in excess of 5 rounds; and

'(iv) an ability to accept a detachable magazine.'

(c) PENALTIES—

(1) VIOLATION OF SECTION 922(v)—Section 924(a)(1)(B) of such title is amended by striking 'or (q) of section 922' and inserting '(r), or (v) of section 922'.

(2) USE OR POSSESSION DURING CRIME OF VIOLENCE OR DRUG TRAFFICKING CRIME- Section 924(c)(1) of such title is amended in the first sentence by inserting ', or semiautomatic assault weapon,' after 'short-barreled shotgun,'

(d) IDENTIFICATION MARKINGS FOR SEMIAUTOMATIC ASSAULT WEAPONS—Section 923(i) of such title is amended by adding at the end the following: 'The serial number of any semiautomatic assault weapon manufactured after the date of the enactment of this sentence shall clearly show the date on which the weapon was manufactured.'

Sec. 110103. Ban of Large Capacity Ammunition Feeding Devices.

(a) PROHIBITION—Section 922 of title 18, United States Code, as amended by section 110102(a), is amended by adding at the end the following new subsection:

'(w)(1) Except as provided in paragraph (2), it shall be unlawful for a person to transfer or possess a large capacity ammunition feeding device.

'(2) Paragraph (1) shall not apply to the possession or transfer of any large capacity ammunition feeding device otherwise lawfully possessed on or before the date of the enactment of this subsection.

'(3) This subsection shall not apply to—

'(A) the manufacture for, transfer to, or possession by the United States or a department or agency of the United States or a State or a department, agency, or political subdivision of a State, or a transfer to or possession by a law enforcement officer employed by such an entity for purposes of law enforcement (whether on or off duty);

'(B) the transfer to a licensee under title I of the Atomic Energy Act of 1954 for purposes of establishing and maintaining an on-site physical protection system and security organization required by Federal law, or possession by an employee or contractor of such licensee on-site for such purposes or off-site for purposes of licensee-authorized training or transportation of nuclear materials;

'(C) the possession, by an individual who is retired from service with a law enforcement agency and is not otherwise prohibited from receiving ammunition, of a large capacity ammunition feeding device transferred to the individual by the agency upon such retirement; or

'(D) the manufacture, transfer, or possession of any large capacity ammunition feeding device by a licensed manufacturer or licensed importer for the purposes of testing or experimentation authorized by the Secretary.'

'(4) If a person charged with violating paragraph (1) asserts that paragraph (1) does not apply to such person because of paragraph (2) or (3), the Government shall have the burden of proof to show that such paragraph (1) applies to such person. The lack of a serial number as described in section 923(i) of title 18, United States Code, shall be a presumption that the large capacity ammunition feeding device is not subject to the prohibition of possession in paragraph (1).'

(b) DEFINITION OF LARGE CAPACITY AMMUNITION FEEDING DEVICE—Section 921(a) of title 18, United States Code, as amended by section 110102(b), is amended by adding at the end the following new paragraph:

'(31) The term 'large capacity ammunition feeding device'—

'(A) means a magazine, belt, drum, feed strip, or similar device manufactured after the date of enactment of the Violent Crime Control and Law Enforcement Act of 1994 that has a capacity of, or that can be readily restored or converted to accept, more than 10 rounds of ammunition; but

'(B) does not include an attached tubular device designed to accept, and capable of operating only with, .22 caliber rimfire ammunition.'

(c) PENALTY—Section 924(a)(1)(B) of title 18, United States Code, as amended by section 110102(c)(1), is amended by striking 'or (v)' and inserting '(v), or (w)'.

(d) IDENTIFICATION MARKINGS FOR LARGE CAPACITY AMMUNITION FEEDING DEVICES—Section 923(i) of title 18, United States Code, as amended by section 110102(d) of this Act, is amended by adding at the end the following: 'A large capacity ammunition feeding device manufactured after the date of the enactment of this sentence shall be identified by a serial number that clearly shows that the device was manufactured or imported after the effective date of this subsection, and such other identification as the Secretary may by regulation prescribe.' . . .

Sec. 110105. Effective Date.

This subtitle and the amendments made by this subtitle—
(1) shall take effect on the date of the enactment of this Act; and
(2) are repealed effective as of the date that is 10 years after that date. . . .

Subtitle B—Youth Handgun Safety

SEC. 110201. PROHIBITION OF THE POSSESSION OF A HANDGUN OR AMMUNITION BY, OR THE PRIVATE TRANSFER OF A HANDGUN OR AMMUNITION TO, A JUVENILE.

(a) OFFENSE—Section 922 of title 18, United States Code, as amended by section 110103(a), is amended by adding at the end the following new subsection:

'(x)(1) It shall be unlawful for a person to sell, deliver, or otherwise transfer to a person who the transferor knows or has reasonable cause to believe is a juvenile—

'(A) a handgun; or

'(B) ammunition that is suitable for use only in a handgun.

'(2) It shall be unlawful for any person who is a juvenile to knowingly possess—

'(A) a handgun; or

'(B) ammunition that is suitable for use only in a handgun.

'(3) This subsection does not apply to—

'(A) a temporary transfer of a handgun or ammunition to a juvenile or to the possession or use of a handgun or ammunition by a juvenile if the handgun and ammunition are possessed and used by the juvenile—

'(i) in the course of employment, in the course of ranching or farming related to activities at the residence of the juvenile (or on property used for ranching or farming at which the juvenile, with the permission of the property owner or lessee, is performing activities related to the operation of the farm or ranch), target practice, hunting, or a course of instruction in the safe and lawful use of a handgun;

'(ii) with the prior written consent of the juvenile's parent or guardian who is not prohibited by Federal, State, or local law from possessing a firearm, except—

'(I) during transportation by the juvenile of an unloaded handgun in a locked container directly from the place of transfer to a place at which an activity described in clause (i) is to take place and transportation by the juvenile of that handgun, unloaded and in a locked container, directly from the place at which such an activity took place to the transferor; or

'(II) with respect to ranching or farming activities as described in clause (i), a juvenile may possess and use a handgun or ammunition with the prior written approval of the juvenile's parent or legal guardian and at the direction of an adult who is not prohibited by Federal, State or local law from possessing a firearm;

'(iii) the juvenile has the prior written consent in the juvenile's possession at all times when a handgun is in the possession of the juvenile; and

'(iv) in accordance with State and local law;

'(B) a juvenile who is a member of the Armed Forces of the United States or the National Guard who possesses or is armed with a handgun in the line of duty;

'(C) a transfer by inheritance of title (but not possession) of a handgun or ammunition to a juvenile; or

'(D) the possession of a handgun or ammunition by a juvenile taken in defense of the juvenile or other persons against an intruder into the residence of the juvenile or a residence in which the juvenile is an invited guest.

'(4) A handgun or ammunition, the possession of which is transferred to a juvenile in circumstances in which the transferor is not in violation of this subsection shall not be subject to permanent confiscation by the Government if its possession by the juvenile subsequently becomes unlawful because of the conduct of the juvenile, but shall be returned to the lawful owner when such handgun or ammunition is no longer required by the Government for the purposes of investigation or prosecution.

'(5) For purposes of this subsection, the term 'juvenile' means a person who is less than 18 years of age.

'(6)(A) In a prosecution of a violation of this subsection, the court shall require the presence of a juvenile defendant's parent or legal guardian at all proceedings.

'(B) The court may use the contempt power to enforce subparagraph (A).

'(C) The court may excuse attendance of a parent or legal guardian of a juvenile defendant at a proceeding in a prosecution of a violation of this subsection for good cause shown.'

(b) PENALTIES—Section 924(a) of title 18, United States Code, is amended—

(1) in paragraph (1) by striking 'paragraph (2) or (3) of'; and

(2) by adding at the end the following new paragraph:

'(5)(A) (i) A juvenile who violates section 922(x) shall be fined under this title, imprisoned not more than 1 year, or both, except that a juvenile described in clause (ii) shall be sentenced to probation on appropriate conditions and shall not be incarcerated unless the juvenile fails to comply with a condition of probation.

'(ii) A juvenile is described in this clause if—

'(I) the offense of which the juvenile is charged is possession of a handgun or ammunition in violation of section 922(x)(2); and

'(II) the juvenile has not been convicted in any court of an offense (including an offense under section 922(x) or a similar State law, but not including any other offense consisting of conduct that if engaged in by an adult would not constitute an offense) or adjudicated as a juvenile delinquent for conduct that if engaged in by an adult would constitute an offense.

'(B) A person other than a juvenile who knowingly violates section 922(x)—

'(i) shall be fined under this title, imprisoned not more than 1 year, or both; and

'(ii) if the person sold, delivered, or otherwise transferred a handgun or ammunition to a juvenile knowing or having reasonable cause to know that the juvenile intended to carry or otherwise possess or discharge or otherwise use the handgun or ammunition in the commission of a crime of violence, shall be fined under this title, imprisoned not more than 10 years, or both.'

(c) TECHNICAL AMENDMENT OF JUVENILE DELINQUENCY PROVISIONS IN TITLE 18, UNITED STATES CODE—

(1) SECTION 5031—Section 5031 of title 18, United States Code, is amended by inserting 'or a violation by such a person of section 922(x)' before the period at the end.

(2) SECTION 5032—Section 5032 of title 18, United States Code, is amended—

(A) in the first undesignated paragraph by inserting 'or (x)' after '922(p)'; and

(B) in the fourth undesignated paragraph by inserting 'or section 922(x) of this title,' before 'criminal prosecution on the basis'.

(d) TECHNICAL AMENDMENT OF THE JUVENILE JUSTICE AND DELINQUENCY PREVENTION ACT OF 1974—Section 223(a)(12)(A) of the Juvenile

Justice and Delinquency Prevention Act of 1974 (42 U.S.C. 5633(a)(12)(A)) is amended by striking 'which do not constitute violations of valid court orders' and inserting '(other than an offense that constitutes a violation of a valid court order or a violation of section 922(x) of title 18, United States Code, or a similar State law).'

(e) MODEL LAW—The Attorney General, acting through the Director of the National Institute for Juvenile Justice and Delinquency Prevention, shall—

(1) evaluate existing and proposed juvenile handgun legislation in each State;

(2) develop model juvenile handgun legislation that is constitutional and enforceable;

(3) prepare and disseminate to State authorities the findings made as the result of the evaluation; and

(4) report to Congress by December 31, 1995, findings and recommendations concerning the need or appropriateness of further action by the Federal Government. . . .

SOURCE: http://thomas.loc.gov/cgi-bin/query/F?c103:1:./temp/~c103aPpvIc:e643897

ANALYSIS

Enacted a year after the Brady Law, the Assault Weapons Ban of 1994 barred sale or possession of 19 named types of assault weapons, plus several dozen copycat models, for a 10-year period. The measure, enacted as part of a larger crime bill, did not include assault weapons already in circulation before the law went into effect. The impetus for such a measure arose partly because of several high-profile shootings in the years preceding the law's enactment, especially a shooting in a California schoolyard in 1989 by a man who killed 5 children and wounded 29 others using an AK-47.

In addition to banning assault weapons (incorporating assault rifles, semiautomatic shotguns, and certain semiautomatic pistols), the measure also barred large-capacity ammunition clips (those holding more than 10 bullets), excluding those in circulation before 1994. An appendix to the bill specifically excluded from regulation 661 named types of guns. The law also barred handguns and its ammunition to those below the age of 18.

Like the Brady Law, this measure provoked sharp controversy. Critics of the bill noted that most standard hunting and sporting rifles were also semiautomatic in their firing mechanism—that is, they fired a bullet with each pull of the trigger (fully automatic weapons, which fire a constant stream of bullets when the trigger is depressed, were already strictly regulated by the National Firearms Act of 1934; see previously). Thus, they argued, there was no real difference between banned assault weapons and legal guns, and that the public was merely responding to the menacing appearance of these weapons. But bill supporters noted key differences, in that assault weapons were designed specifically for military use: as defined in the bill, assault weapons are shorter in length (their barrels are less than 20 inches long), lighter weight, can receive large-capacity ammunition clips, are made from lightweight stampings and plastics, and also have features like pistol grips or thumbhole stocks, folding or telescoping stocks, have grenade launcher or bayonet fittings, and are designed to lay down "spray fire." According to the law, assault weapons possess at least two of these characteristics.

The limited scope of the law meant that millions of pre-1994 weapons and clips remained in circulation, but bill supporters cited studies showing that the use of these weapons in crime declined during this period (assault weapons accounted for only a small proportion of gun crimes both before and after the ban). Despite the public's support for continuation of the ban, Congress failed to reenact it in 2004.

FURTHER READING

Koper, Christopher S. "An Updated Assessment of the Federal Assault Weapons Ban." Report to the National Institute of Justice, U.S. Department of Justice. June 2004.

Roth, Jeffrey A., and Christopher S. Koper. Impact Evaluation of the Public Safety and Recreational Firearms Use Protection Act of 1994. Washington, D.C.: Urban Institute.

The Gun Lobby Wins Unique Legal Protection for the Gun Industry

- **Document:** Protection of Lawful Commerce in Arms Act of 2005
- **Date:** October 26, 2005
- **Where:** Washington, D.C.
- **Significance:** Congress extends special lawsuit protection to the gun industry.

DOCUMENT

Protection of Lawful Commerce in Arms Act of 2005

PL 109–92; 119 Stat. 2095

An Act

To prohibit civil liability actions from being brought or continued against manufacturers, distributors, dealers, or importers of firearms or ammunition for damages, injunctive or other relief resulting from the misuse of their products by others.

Be it enacted by the Senate and House of Representatives of the United States of America in Congress assembled,

Section 1. Short Title.

This Act may be cited as the 'Protection of Lawful Commerce in Arms Act'.

Sec. 2. Findings; Purposes.

(a) Findings—Congress finds the following:

(1) The Second Amendment to the United States Constitution provides that the right of the people to keep and bear arms shall not be infringed.

(2) The Second Amendment to the United States Constitution protects the rights of individuals, including those who are not members of a militia or engaged in military service or training, to keep and bear arms.

(3) Lawsuits have been commenced against manufacturers, distributors, dealers, and importers of firearms that operate as designed and intended, which seek money damages and other relief for the harm caused by the misuse of firearms by third parties, including criminals.

(4) The manufacture, importation, possession, sale, and use of firearms and ammunition in the United States are heavily regulated by Federal, State, and local laws. Such Federal laws include the Gun Control Act of 1968, the National Firearms Act, and the Arms Export Control Act.

(5) Businesses in the United States that are engaged in interstate and foreign commerce through the lawful design, manufacture, marketing, distribution, importation, or sale to the public of firearms or ammunition products that have been shipped or transported in interstate or foreign commerce are not, and should not, be liable for the harm caused by those who criminally or unlawfully misuse firearm products or ammunition products that function as designed and intended.

(6) The possibility of imposing liability on an entire industry for harm that is solely caused by others is an abuse of the legal system, erodes public confidence in our Nation's laws, threatens the diminution of a basic constitutional right and civil liberty, invites the disassembly and destabilization of other industries and economic sectors lawfully competing in the free enterprise system of the United States, and constitutes an unreasonable burden on interstate and foreign commerce of the United States.

(7) The liability actions commenced or contemplated by the Federal Government, States, municipalities, and private interest groups and others are based on theories without foundation in hundreds of years of the common law and jurisprudence of the United States and do not represent a bona fide expansion of the common law. The possible sustaining of these actions by a maverick judicial officer or petit jury would expand civil liability in a manner never contemplated by the framers of the Constitution, by Congress, or by the legislatures of the several States. Such an expansion of liability would constitute a deprivation of the rights, privileges, and immunities guaranteed to a citizen of the United States under the Fourteenth Amendment to the United States Constitution.

(8) The liability actions commenced or contemplated by the Federal Government, States, municipalities, private interest groups and others attempt to use the judicial branch to circumvent the Legislative branch of government to regulate interstate and foreign commerce through judgments and judicial decrees thereby threatening the Separation of Powers doctrine and weakening and undermining important principles of federalism, State sovereignty and comity between the sister States.

(b) Purposes—The purposes of this Act are as follows:

(1) To prohibit causes of action against manufacturers, distributors, dealers, and importers of firearms or ammunition products, and their trade associations, for the harm solely caused by the criminal or unlawful misuse of firearm products or ammunition products by others when the product functioned as designed and intended.

(2) To preserve a citizen's access to a supply of firearms and ammunition for all lawful purposes, including hunting, self-defense, collecting, and competitive or recreational shooting.

(3) To guarantee a citizen's rights, privileges, and immunities, as applied to the States, under the Fourteenth Amendment to the United States Constitution, pursuant to section 5 of that Amendment.

(4) To prevent the use of such lawsuits to impose unreasonable burdens on interstate and foreign commerce.

(5) To protect the right, under the First Amendment to the Constitution, of manufacturers, distributors, dealers, and importers of firearms or ammunition products, and trade associations, to speak freely, to assemble peaceably, and to petition the Government for a redress of their grievances.

(6) To preserve and protect the Separation of Powers doctrine and important principles of federalism, State sovereignty and comity between sister States.

(7) To exercise congressional power under article IV, section 1 (the Full Faith and Credit Clause) of the United States Constitution.

Sec. 3. Prohibition on Bringing of Qualified Civil Liability Actions in Federal or State Court.

(a) In General—A qualified civil liability action may not be brought in any Federal or State court.

(b) Dismissal of Pending Actions—A qualified civil liability action that is pending on the date of enactment of this Act shall be immediately dismissed by the court in which the action was brought or is currently pending.

Sec. 4. Definitions.

In this Act:

(1) ENGAGED IN THE BUSINESS—The term 'engaged in the business' has the meaning given that term in section 921(a)(21) of title 18, United States Code, and, as applied to a seller of ammunition, means a person who devotes time, attention, and labor to the sale of ammunition as a regular course of trade or business with the principal objective of livelihood and profit through the sale or distribution of ammunition.

(2) MANUFACTURER—The term 'manufacturer' means, with respect to a qualified product, a person who is engaged in the business of manufacturing the product in interstate or foreign commerce and who is licensed to engage in business as such a manufacturer under chapter 44 of title 18, United States Code.

(3) PERSON—The term 'person' means any individual, corporation, company, association, firm, partnership, society, joint stock company, or any other entity, including any governmental entity.

(4) QUALIFIED PRODUCT—The term 'qualified product' means a firearm (as defined in subparagraph (A) or (B) of section 921(a)(3) of title 18, United States Code), including any antique firearm (as defined in section 921(a)(16) of such title), or ammunition (as defined in section 921(a)(17)(A) of such title), or a component part of a firearm or ammunition, that has been shipped or transported in interstate or foreign commerce.

(5) QUALIFIED CIVIL LIABILITY ACTION—

(A) IN GENERAL—The term 'qualified civil liability action' means a civil action or proceeding or an administrative proceeding brought by any person against a manufacturer or seller of a qualified product, or a trade association, for damages, punitive damages, injunctive or declaratory relief, abatement, restitution, fines, or penalties, or other relief, resulting from the criminal or unlawful misuse of a qualified product by the person or a third party, but shall not include—

(i) an action brought against a transferor convicted under section 924(h) of title 18, United States Code, or a comparable or identical State felony law, by a party directly harmed by the conduct of which the transferee is so convicted;

(ii) an action brought against a seller for negligent entrustment or negligence per se;

(iii) an action in which a manufacturer or seller of a qualified product knowingly violated a State or Federal statute applicable to the sale or marketing of the product, and the violation was a proximate cause of the harm for which relief is sought, including—

(I) any case in which the manufacturer or seller knowingly made any false entry in, or failed to make appropriate entry in, any record required to be kept under Federal or State law with respect to the qualified product, or aided, abetted, or conspired with any person in making any false or fictitious oral or written statement with respect to any fact material to the lawfulness of the sale or other disposition of a qualified product; or

(II) any case in which the manufacturer or seller aided, abetted, or conspired with any other person to sell or otherwise dispose of a qualified product, knowing, or having reasonable cause to believe, that the actual buyer of the qualified product was prohibited from possessing or receiving a firearm or ammunition under subsection (g) or (n) of section 922 of title 18, United States Code;

(iv) an action for breach of contract or warranty in connection with the purchase of the product;

(v) an action for death, physical injuries or property damage resulting directly from a defect in design or manufacture of the product, when used as intended or in a reasonably foreseeable manner, except that where the discharge of the product was caused by a volitional act that constituted a criminal offense, then such act shall be considered the sole proximate cause of any resulting death, personal injuries or property damage; or

(vi) an action or proceeding commenced by the Attorney General to enforce the provisions of chapter 44 of title 18 or chapter 53 of title 26, United States Code.

(B) NEGLIGENT ENTRUSTMENT—As used in subparagraph (A)(ii), the term 'negligent entrustment' means the supplying of a qualified product by a seller for use by another person when the seller knows, or reasonably should know, the person to whom the product is supplied is likely to, and does, use the product in a manner involving unreasonable risk of physical injury to the person or others.

(C) RULE OF CONSTRUCTION—The exceptions enumerated under clauses (i) through (v) of subparagraph (A) shall be construed so as not to be in conflict, and no provision of this Act shall be construed to create a public or private cause of action or remedy.

(D) MINOR CHILD EXCEPTION—Nothing in this Act shall be construed to limit the right of a person under 17 years of age to recover damages authorized under Federal or State law in a civil action that meets 1 of the requirements under clauses (i) through (v) of subparagraph (A).

(6) SELLER—The term 'seller' means, with respect to a qualified product—

(A) an importer (as defined in section 921(a)(9) of title 18, United States Code) who is engaged in the business as such an importer in interstate or foreign commerce and who is licensed to engage in business as such an importer under chapter 44 of title 18, United States Code;

(B) a dealer (as defined in section 921(a)(11) of title 18, United States Code) who is engaged in the business as such a dealer in interstate or foreign commerce and who is licensed to engage in business as such a dealer under chapter 44 of title 18, United States Code; or

(C) a person engaged in the business of selling ammunition (as defined in section 921(a)(17)(A) of title 18, United States Code) in interstate or foreign commerce at the wholesale or retail level.

(7) STATE—The term 'State' includes each of the several States of the United States, the District of Columbia, the Commonwealth of Puerto Rico, the Virgin Islands, Guam, American Samoa, and the Commonwealth of the Northern Mariana Islands, and any other territory or possession of the United States, and any political subdivision of any such place.

(8) TRADE ASSOCIATION—The term 'trade association' means—

(A) any corporation, unincorporated association, federation, business league, professional or business organization not organized or operated for profit and no part of the net earnings of which inures to the benefit of any private shareholder or individual;

(B) that is an organization described in section 501(c)(6) of the Internal Revenue Code of 1986 and exempt from tax under section 501(a) of such Code; and

(C) 2 or more members of which are manufacturers or sellers of a qualified product.

(9) UNLAWFUL MISUSE—The term 'unlawful misuse' means conduct that violates a statute, ordinance, or regulation as it relates to the use of a qualified product.

Sec. 5. Child Safety Locks.

(a) SHORT TITLE—This section may be cited as the 'Child Safety Lock Act of 2005'.

(b) PURPOSES—The purposes of this section are—

(1) to promote the safe storage and use of handguns by consumers;

(2) to prevent unauthorized persons from gaining access to or use of a handgun, including children who may not be in possession of a handgun; and

(3) to avoid hindering industry from supplying firearms to law abiding citizens for all lawful purposes, including hunting, self-defense, collecting, and competitive or recreational shooting.

(c) FIREARMS SAFETY—

(1) MANDATORY TRANSFER OF SECURE GUN STORAGE OR SAFETY DEVICE—Section 922 of title 18, United States Code, is amended by inserting at the end the following:

'(z) SECURE GUN STORAGE OR SAFETY DEVICE—

'(1) IN GENERAL—Except as provided under paragraph (2), it shall be unlawful for any licensed importer, licensed manufacturer, or licensed dealer to sell, deliver, or transfer any handgun to any person other than any person licensed under this chapter, unless the transferee is provided with a secure gun storage or safety device (as defined in section 921(a)(34)) for that handgun.

'(2) EXCEPTIONS—Paragraph (1) shall not apply to—

'(A)(i) the manufacture for, transfer to, or possession by, the United States, a department or agency of the United States, a State, or a department, agency, or political subdivision of a State, of a handgun; or

'(ii) the transfer to, or possession by, a law enforcement officer employed by an entity referred to in clause (i) of a handgun for law enforcement purposes (whether on or off duty); or

'(B) the transfer to, or possession by, a rail police officer employed by a rail carrier and certified or commissioned as a police officer under the laws of a State of a handgun for purposes of law enforcement (whether on or off duty);

'(C) the transfer to any person of a handgun listed as a curio or relic by the Secretary pursuant to section 921(a)(13); or

'(D) the transfer to any person of a handgun for which a secure gun storage or safety device is temporarily unavailable for the reasons described in the exceptions stated in section 923(e), if the licensed manufacturer, licensed importer, or licensed dealer delivers to the transferee within 10 calendar days from the date of the delivery of the handgun to the transferee a secure gun storage or safety device for the handgun.

'(3) LIABILITY FOR USE—

'(A) IN GENERAL—Notwithstanding any other provision of law, a person who has lawful possession and control of a handgun, and who uses a secure gun storage or safety device with the handgun, shall be entitled to immunity from a qualified civil liability action.

'(B) PROSPECTIVE ACTIONS—A qualified civil liability action may not be brought in any Federal or State court.

'(C) DEFINED TERM—As used in this paragraph, the term 'qualified civil liability action'—

'(i) means a civil action brought by any person against a person described in subparagraph (A) for damages resulting from the criminal or unlawful misuse of the handgun by a third party, if—

'(I) the handgun was accessed by another person who did not have the permission or authorization of the person having lawful possession and control of the handgun to have access to it; and

'(II) at the time access was gained by the person not so authorized, the handgun had been made inoperable by use of a secure gun storage or safety device; and

'(ii) shall not include an action brought against the person having lawful possession and control of the handgun for negligent entrustment or negligence per se.'

(2) CIVIL PENALTIES—Section 924 of title 18, United States Code, is amended—

(A) in subsection (a)(1), by striking 'or (f)' and inserting '(f), or (p)'; and

(B) by adding at the end the following:

'(p) PENALTIES RELATING TO SECURE GUN STORAGE OR SAFETY DEVICE—

'(1) IN GENERAL—

'(A) SUSPENSION OR REVOCATION OF LICENSE; CIVIL PENALTIES— With respect to each violation of section 922(z)(1) by a licensed manufacturer, licensed importer, or licensed dealer, the Secretary may, after notice and opportunity for hearing—

'(i) suspend for not more than 6 months, or revoke, the license issued to the licensee under this chapter that was used to conduct the firearms transfer; or

'(ii) subject the licensee to a civil penalty in an amount equal to not more than $2,500.

'(B) REVIEW—An action of the Secretary under this paragraph may be reviewed only as provided under section 923(f).

'(2) ADMINISTRATIVE REMEDIES—The suspension or revocation of a license or the imposition of a civil penalty under paragraph (1) shall not preclude any administrative remedy that is otherwise available to the Secretary.'

(3) LIABILITY; EVIDENCE—

(A) LIABILITY—Nothing in this section shall be construed to—

(i) create a cause of action against any Federal firearms licensee or any other person for any civil liability; or

(ii) establish any standard of care.

(B) EVIDENCE—Notwithstanding any other provision of law, evidence regarding compliance or noncompliance with the amendments made by this section shall not be admissible as evidence in any proceeding of any court, agency, board, or other entity, except with respect to an action relating to section 922(z) of title 18, United States Code, as added by this subsection.

(C) RULE OF CONSTRUCTION—Nothing in this paragraph shall be construed to bar a governmental action to impose a penalty under section 924(p) of title 18, United States Code, for a failure to comply with section 922(z) of that title.

(d) EFFECTIVE DATE—This section and the amendments made by this section shall take effect 180 days after the date of enactment of this Act.

Sec. 6. Armor Piercing Ammunition.

(a) Unlawful Acts—Section 922(a) of title 18, United States Code, is amended by striking paragraphs (7) and (8) and inserting the following:

'(7) for any person to manufacture or import armor piercing ammunition, unless—

'(A) the manufacture of such ammunition is for the use of the United States, any department or agency of the United States, any State, or any department, agency, or political subdivision of a State;

'(B) the manufacture of such ammunition is for the purpose of exportation; or

'(C) the manufacture or importation of such ammunition is for the purpose of testing or experimentation and has been authorized by the Attorney General;

'(8) for any manufacturer or importer to sell or deliver armor piercing ammunition, unless such sale or delivery—

'(A) is for the use of the United States, any department or agency of the United States, any State, or any department, agency, or political subdivision of a State;

'(B) is for the purpose of exportation; or

'(C) is for the purpose of testing or experimentation and has been authorized by the Attorney General;'.

(b) Penalties—Section 924(c) of title 18, United States Code, is amended by adding at the end the following:

'(5) Except to the extent that a greater minimum sentence is otherwise provided under this subsection, or by any other provision of law, any person who, during and in relation to any crime of violence or drug trafficking crime (including a crime of violence or drug trafficking crime that provides for an enhanced punishment if committed by the use of a deadly or dangerous weapon or device) for which the person may be prosecuted in a court of the United States, uses or carries armor piercing ammunition, or who, in furtherance of any such crime, possesses armor piercing ammunition, shall, in addition to the punishment provided for such crime of violence or drug trafficking crime or conviction under this section—

'(A) be sentenced to a term of imprisonment of not less than 15 years; and

'(B) if death results from the use of such ammunition—

'(i) if the killing is murder (as defined in section 1111), be punished by death or sentenced to a term of imprisonment for any term of years or for life; and

'(ii) if the killing is manslaughter (as defined in section 1112), be punished as provided in section 1112.'

(c) Study and Report—

(1) STUDY—The Attorney General shall conduct a study to determine whether a uniform standard for the testing of projectiles against Body Armor is feasible.

(2) ISSUES TO BE STUDIED—The study conducted under paragraph (1) shall include—

(A) variations in performance that are related to the length of the barrel of the handgun or center-fire rifle from which the projectile is fired; and

(B) the amount of powder used to propel the projectile.

(3) REPORT—Not later than 2 years after the date of enactment of this Act, the Attorney General shall submit a report containing the results of the study conducted under this subsection to—

(A) the chairman and ranking member of the Committee on the Judiciary of the Senate; and

(B) the chairman and ranking member of the Committee on the Judiciary of the House of Representatives. . . .

SOURCE: http://www.govtrack.us/congress/billtext.xpd?bill=s109-397&show-changes=0\

ANALYSIS

The presidency of George W. Bush represented a high-water mark for the influence of gun rights groups. At the top of the National Rifle Association's (NRA) agenda in the first decade of the twenty-first century was the enactment of federal legislation to protect gun manufacturers and dealers from a rising tide of lawsuits filed against them by several cities, states, and individuals who held the industry at least partly responsible for gun violence.

For a number of years, plaintiffs had brought legal actions against gun manufacturers and dealers based on the tort law principle that individuals or companies can be held legally liable for selling products that, while legal, needlessly or willfully expose others to great risk or harm. Such legal actions had long been used against automobile companies, for example, for marketing cars they knew to be unsafe, and against the tobacco industry, among others. In gun lawsuits, litigants argued that some gun manufacturers and dealers knew that, because of their sales and distribution practices, a disproportionate number of their guns wound up in the hands of criminals. Some companies failed to install simple and cheap safety devices for their guns to, for example, prevent them from being fired when their clips were removed.

After nearly five years of effort, Congress enacted the Protection of Lawful Commerce in Arms Act, which barred civil suits against gun and ammunition manufacturers, distributors, dealers, trade associations, and importers, making narrow exception for cases involving defective guns or expressly criminal behavior by those otherwise protected, as, for example, when a gun is knowingly sold to someone not legally eligible. The law stopped over a dozen then-pending lawsuits around the country. In addition, the law required that handguns be sold with locks, and barred the manufacture or import of armor-piercing bullets. This unprecedented legal immunity for the gun industry prompted other businesses to lobby Congress for similar protection.

Supporters of the bill claimed that these lawsuits represented back-door gun control, in that successful civil suits could force gun manufacturers or dealers to pay millions of dollars in damages which could force them out of business, and which could also reduce the nation's supply of guns. Opponents claimed that there was no basis for extending such unusual protection to a single industry, and that those in the gun business should be subject to the kind of legal action that could be brought against any industry.

FURTHER READING

Lytton, Timothy D., ed. *Suing the Gun Industry: A Battle at the Crossroads of Gun Control and Mass Torts*. Ann Arbor: University of Michigan Press, 2005.

McIntosh, Wayne V., and Cynthia Cates. "Cigarettes, Firearms, and the New Litigation Wars." *The Interest Group Connection*, ed. Paul S. Herrnson, Ronald G. Shaiko, and Clyde Wilcox. Washington, D.C.: CQ Press, 2005, 341–364.

8

GUN CONTROL, THE
STATES, AND POLITICS

Most States Have Right-to-Bear-Arms-Type Provisions in Their State Constitutions

- **Document:** Right-to-bear-arms-type provisions in 44 state constitutions
- **Date:** various
- **Where:** state constitutions
- **Significance:** Most states have included right-to-bear-arms-type provisions in their constitutions, but they have not been a deterrent to state gun laws (the years noted after each provision date the first appearance of right-to-bear-arms-type language in the state documents; in many instances, the language was amended or altered later, and it is this current language that appears here).

DOCUMENT

Alabama Constitution Article I, Section 26

That the great, general and essential principles of liberty and free government may be recognized and established, we declare. . . . That every citizen has a right to bear arms in defense of himself and the state. (1819)

Alaska Constitution Article I, Section 19

A well-regulated militia being necessary to the security of a free state, the right of the people to keep and bear arms shall not be infringed. The individual right to keep and bear arms shall not be denied or infringed by the State or a political subdivision of the State. (1959)

Arizona Constitution, Article 2, Section 26

The right of the individual citizen to bear arms in defense of himself or the State shall not be impaired, but nothing in this section shall be construed as authorizing individuals or corporations to organize, maintain, or employ an armed body of men. (1912)

Arkansas Constitution Article II, Section 5

The citizens of this State shall have the right to keep and bear arms for their common defense. (1836)

Colorado Constitution Article II, Section 13

The right of no person to keep and bear arms in defense of his home, person and property, or in aid of the civil power when thereto legally summoned, shall be called in question; but nothing herein contained shall be construed to justify the practice of carrying concealed weapons. (1876)

Connecticut Constitution Article I, Section 15

Every citizen has a right to bear arms in defense of himself and the state. (1818)

Delaware Constitution Article I, Section 20

A person has the right to keep and bear arms for the defense of self, family, home and State, and for hunting and recreational use. (1987)

Florida Constitution Article I, Section 8(a)

The right of the people to keep and bear arms in defense of themselves and of the lawful authority of the state shall not be infringed, except that the manner of bearing arms may be regulated by law. (1838)

Georgia Constitution Article I, Section 1, Paragraph VIII.

The right of the people to keep and bear arms shall not be infringed, but the General Assembly shall have power to prescribe the manner in which arms may be borne. (1865)

Hawaii Constitution Article I, Section 17

A well regulated militia being necessary to the security of a free state, the right of the people to keep and bear arms shall not be infringed. (1959)

Idaho Constitution Article I, Section 11

The people have the right to keep and bear arms, which right shall not be abridged; but this provision shall not prevent the passage of laws to govern the carrying of weapons concealed on the person nor prevent passage of legislation providing minimum sentences for crimes committed while in possession of a firearm, nor prevent the passage of legislation providing penalties for the possession of firearms by a convicted felon, nor prevent the passage of any legislation punishing the use of a firearm. No law shall impose licensure, registration or special taxation on the ownership or possession of firearms or ammunition. Nor shall any law permit the confiscation of firearms, except those actually used in the commission of a felony. (1889)

Illinois Constitution Article I, Section 22

Subject only to the police power, the right of the individual citizen to keep and bear arms shall not be infringed. (1970)

Indiana Constitution Article I, Section 32

The people shall have a right to bear arms, for the defense of themselves and the State. (1816)

Kansas Constitution Bill of Rights 4

The people have the right to bear arms for their defense and security; but standing armies, in time of peace, are dangerous to liberty, and shall not be tolerated, and the military shall be in strict subordination to the civil power. (1859)

Kentucky Constitution Section 1

All men are, by nature, free and equal, and have certain inherent and inalienable rights, among which may be reckoned: . . . Seventh: The right to bear arms in defense of themselves and of the State, subject to the power of the General Assembly to enact laws to prevent persons from carrying concealed weapons. (1792)

Louisiana Constitution Article I, Section 11

The right of each citizen to keep and bear arms shall not be abridged, but this provision shall not prevent the passage of laws to prohibit the carrying of weapons concealed on the person. (1879)

Maine Constitution Article 1, Section 16

Every citizen has a right to keep and bear arms and this right shall never be questioned. (1819)

Massachusetts Constitution Part The First, Article XVII

The people have a right to keep and to bear arms for the common defence. And as, in time of peace, armies are dangerous to liberty, they ought not to be maintained without the consent of the legislature; and the military power shall always be held in an exact subordination to the civil authority, and be governed by it. (1780)

Michigan Constitution Article I, Section 6

Every person has a right to keep and bear arms for the defense of himself and the state. (1835)

Mississippi Constitution Article III, Section 12

The right of every citizen to keep and bear arms in defense of his home, person, or property, or in aid of the civil power when thereto legally summoned, shall not be called in question, but the legislature may regulate or forbid carrying concealed weapons. (1817)

Missouri Constitution Article I, Section 23

That the right of every citizen to keep and bear arms in defense of his home, person and property, or when lawfully summoned in aid of the civil power, shall not be questioned; but this shall not justify the wearing of concealed weapons. (1820)

Montana Constitution Article II, Section 12

The right of any person to keep or bear arms in defense of his own home, person, and property, or in aid of the civil power when thereto legally summoned, shall not be called in question, but nothing herein contained shall be held to permit the carrying of concealed weapons.

Article VI, Section 13(2)

The militia forces shall consist of all able-bodied citizens of the state except those exempted by law. (1889)

Nebraska Constitution Article I, Section 1

All persons are by nature free and independent, and have certain inherent and inalienable rights; among these are life, liberty, the pursuit of happiness, and the right to keep and bear arms for security or defense of self, family, home, and others, and for lawful common defense, hunting, recreational use, and all other lawful purposes, and such rights shall not be denied or infringed by the state or any subdivision thereof. To secure these rights, and the protection of property, governments are instituted among people, deriving their just powers from the consent of the governed. (1988)

Nevada Constitution Article 1, Section 11, [1.]

Every citizen has the right to keep and bear arms for security and defense, for lawful hunting and recreational use and for other lawful purposes. (1982)

New Hampshire Constitution Part First, Article 2-a

All persons have the right to keep and bear arms in defense of themselves, their families, their property and the state.

Part First, Article 13

No person, who is conscientiously scrupulous about the lawfulness of bearing arms, shall be compelled thereto. (1982)

New Mexico Constitution Article II, Section 6

No law shall abridge the right of the citizen to keep and bear arms for security and defense, for lawful hunting and recreational use and for other lawful purposes, but nothing herein shall be held to permit the carrying of concealed weapons. No municipality or county shall regulate, in any way, an incident of the right to keep and bear arms. (1912)

North Carolina Constitution Article I, Section 30

A well regulated militia being necessary to the security of a free State, the right of the people to keep and bear arms shall not be infringed; and, as standing armies in time of peace are dangerous to liberty, they shall not be maintained, and the military shall be kept under strict subordination to, and governed by, the civil power. Nothing herein shall justify the practice of carrying concealed weapons, or prevent the General Assembly from enacting penal statutes against that practice. (1776)

North Dakota Constitution Article I, Section 1

All individuals are by nature equally free and independent and have certain inalienable rights, among which are those of enjoying and defending life and liberty; acquiring, possessing and protecting property and reputation; pursuing and obtaining safety and happiness; and to keep and bear arms for the defense of their person, family, property, and the state, and for lawful hunting, recreational and other lawful purposes, which shall not be infringed. (1984)

Ohio Constitution Article I, Section 4

The people have the right to bear arms for their defense and security; but standing armies, in time of peace, are dangerous to liberty, and shall not be kept up; and the military shall be in strict subordination to the civil power. (1802)

Oklahoma Constitution Article II, Section 26

The right of a citizen to keep and bear arms in defense of his home, person, or property, or in aid of the civil power, when thereunto legally summoned, shall never be prohibited; but nothing herein contained shall prevent the Legislature from regulating the carrying of weapons. (1907)

Oregon Constitution Article I, Section 27

The people shall have the right to bear arms for the defence of themselves, and the State, but the Military shall be kept in strict subordination to the civil power. (1857)

Pennsylvania Constitution Article I, Section 21

The right of the citizens to bear arms in defense of themselves and the State shall not be questioned. (1790)

Rhode Island Constitution Article I, Section 22

The right of the people to keep and bear arms shall not be infringed. (1842)

South Carolina Constitution Article I, Section 20

A well regulated militia being necessary to the security of a free State, the right of the people to keep and bear arms shall not be infringed. As, in times of peace, armies are dangerous to liberty, they shall not be maintained without the consent of the General Assembly. The military power of the State shall always be held in subordination to the civil authority and be governed by it. No soldier shall in time of peace be quartered in any house without the consent of the owner nor in time of war but in the manner prescribed by law. (1895)

South Dakota Constitution Article VI, Section 24

The right of the citizens to bear arms in defense of themselves and the state shall not be denied. (1889)

Tennessee Constitution Article I, Section 26

That the citizens of this State have a right to keep and to bear arms for their common defense; but the Legislature shall have power, by law, to regulate the wearing of arms with a view to prevent crime. (1796)

Texas Constitution Article I, Section 23

Every citizen shall have the right to keep and bear arms in the lawful defense of himself or the State; but the Legislature shall have power, by law, to regulate the wearing of arms, with a view to prevent crime. (1836)

Utah Constitution Article I, Section 6

The individual right of the people to keep and bear arms for security and defense of self, family, others, property, or the state, as well as for other lawful purposes shall not be infringed; but nothing herein shall prevent the Legislature from defining the lawful use of arms. (1896)

Vermont Constitution Chapter 1, Article 16

That the people have a right to bear arms for the defence of themselves and the State—and as standing armies in time of peace are dangerous to liberty, they ought not to be kept up; and that the military should be kept under strict subordination to and governed by the civil power. (1777)

Virginia Constitution Article I, Section 13

That a well regulated militia, composed of the body of the people, trained to arms, is the proper, natural, and safe defense of a free state, therefore, the right of the people to keep and bear arms shall not be infringed; that standing armies, in time of peace, should be avoided as dangerous to liberty; and that in all cases the military should be under strict subordination to, and governed by, the civil power. (1971)

Washington State Constitution Article I, Section 24

The right of the individual citizen to bear arms in defense of himself, or the state, shall not be impaired, but nothing in this section shall be construed as authorizing individuals or corporations to organize, maintain or employ an armed body of men. (1889)

West Virginia Constitution Article III, Section 22

A person has the right to keep and bear arms for the defense of self, family, home and state, and for lawful hunting and recreational use. (1986)

Wisconsin Constitution Article I, Section 25

The people have the right to keep and bear arms for security, defense, hunting, recreation or any other lawful purpose. (1998)

Wyoming Constitution Article I, Section 24

The right of citizens to bear arms in defense of themselves and of the state shall not be denied. (1889)

States with no such provisions: California, Iowa, Maryland, Minnesota, New Jersey, New York.

SOURCE: http://www.saf.org/Constitutions.html#With

ANALYSIS

Under the American system of federalism, where governing power is divided between the national government and the states, each state establishes its own system of governance through its unique constitution. Although state constitutions were inspired by the federal document, each is different, responding to the history, traditions, preferences, and needs of particular states.

In the case of right-to-bear-arms provisions, 44 of the 50 states have some kind of analogous provision. Some states, like Alaska, Hawaii, North Carolina, and South Carolina borrow exactly from the U.S. Constitution's Second Amendment, although Alaska's added language referring to an "individual right to keep and bear arms" in addition to the militia-based Second Amendment wording, and the Carolinas added language about the danger of standing armies. Thirty-four state provisions reference a collective or militia-based right, referencing some version of defense of the state. Twenty-eight states reference a personal or individual right (more than half of these state provisions reference both personal and collective rights). Delaware's provision, for example, says that a "person has the right to keep and bear arms for the defense of self, family, home," as well as "state." Seven states simply refer to a generic "right to keep and bear arms," and six states also include protections for hunting and recreational activities. In this way, states embraced their own version of a bearing-arms right. Note also that some of these provisions predate the adoption of the federal Bill of Rights. The most recent such language was that added to Wisconsin's state constitution in 1998. In a majority of instances, states adopted this language around the time that the states joined the Union (note that the years given after each provision refer to the first time that right-to-bear-arms-type language appeared in state constitutions; many of these states altered or amended this language at a later time. The versions that appear here reflect contemporary wording, not earlier or historical versions).

Obviously, the wording in some of these states provides a more expansive right than that found in the U.S. Constitution's Second Amendment. Yet even in these instances, state gun control laws have almost invariably withstood legal and constitutional scrutiny. In one of the more dramatic examples, a local law barring the possession of handguns in Illinois successfully withstood state and federal court challenges (see Chapter 4), even though the Illinois provision has expansive wording saying that "the right of the individual citizen to keep and bear arms shall not be infringed."

FURTHER READING

Ridberg, Michael D. "The Impact of State Constitutional Right to Bear Arms Provisions on State Gun Control Legislation." *University of Chicago Law Review* 38(Autumn 1970): 185–210.

Volokh, Eugene. "State Constitutional Rights to Bear Arms." *Texas Review of Law & Politics* 11(2006): 191–217.

Powerline Airstrike BB gun. Photo by Dawn Van Hall.

DID YOU KNOW?

The Gun Issue and the Bush Administration

The gun issue played a prominent role in the 2000 presidential elections, as Democratic presidential nominee Al Gore touted his support for "common-sense gun laws," while his opponent, Republican George W. Bush, argued for stronger law enforcement measures instead of tougher gun laws. After winning the historically close election with key support from the National Rifle Association, Bush proceeded as president to embrace the NRA's political agenda. In 2001, Bush's Attorney General, John Ashcroft, reversed decades of Justice Department policy spanning Democratic and Republican administrations that defined the amendment's right as militia based, and instead endorsed the "individualist" view of the Second Amendment, claiming that it protected a personal right of citizens to own guns aside from militia service. The administration also enacted a new rule to destroy gun background check data after 24 hours instead of holding it for 90 days. It also changed policy to now bar law enforcement agencies from examining gun background check data, even in the case of terrorist investigations: a month after the 9/11 terrorist attack, two terrorist "hits" were found among 186 individuals suspected of terrorist ties whose names were found in gun background check data. Even so, that practice was halted in October 2001. The Bush administration also worked behind the scenes to prevent the reenactment of the assault weapons ban (it lapsed in 2004) and pushed aggressively to enact the NRA's top legislative goal, passage of a bill to grant legal liability protection to the gun industry, enacted in 2005 (see Chapter 7). In all, the second Bush administration proved to be the most gun-friendly presidency in modern times.

Democratic Party Platform Statements on Gun Control and Gun Rights

- *Document:* excerpts from Democratic party platforms
- *Date:* 1864–2008
- *Where:* various
- *Significance:* Democratic party platform statements on the gun issue emphasize the link between guns, crime, and crime control.

DOCUMENT

Democratic Party Platform Statements on Gun Control

1864

Resolved, That the aim and object of the Democratic Party is to preserve the Federal Union and the rights of the States unimpaired, and they hereby declare that they consider that the administrative usurpation of extraordinary and dangerous powers not granted by the Constitution—the subversion of the civil by the military law in States not in insurrection; the arbitrary military arrest, imprisonment, trial, and sentence of American citizens in States where civil law exists in full force; the suppression of freedom of speech and of the press; the denial of the right of asylum; the open and avowed disregard of State rights; the employment of unusual test-oaths; and the interference with and denial of the right of the people to bear arms in their defence is calculated to prevent a restoration of the Union and the perpetuation of a Government deriving its just powers from the consent of the governed.

SOURCE: http://www.adena.com/adena/usa/cw/cw114.htm

1968

Under Democratic leadership, furthermore, the Juvenile Delinquency Prevention and Control Act was passed to aid states and communities to plan and carry out comprehensive programs to prevent and combat youth crime. We have added more personnel to strengthen the Federal Bureau of Investigation and the enforcement of narcotics laws, and have intensified the campaign against organized crime. The federal government has to come swiftly to the aid of cities needing help to bring major disturbances under control, and Democratic leadership secured the enactment of a new gun control law as a step toward putting the weapons of wanton violence beyond the reach of criminal and irresponsible hands. . . .

Promote the passage and enforcement of effective federal, state and local gun control legislation.

SOURCE: http://patriotpost.us/histdocs/platforms/democratic/dem.968.html

---

1972

VI. CRIME, LAW AND JUSTICE

So that Americans can again live without fear of each other the Democratic Party believes. . . .

- There must be laws to control the improper use of hand guns. Four years ago a candidate for the presidency was slain by a hand gun. Two months ago, another candidate for that office was gravely wounded. Three out of four police officers killed in the line of duty are slain with hand guns. Effective legislation must include a ban on sale of hand guns known as Saturday night specials which are unsuitable for sporting purposes.

SOURCE: http://patriotpost.us/histdocs/platforms/democratic/dem.972.html

---

1976

LAW ENFORCEMENT AND LAW OBSERVANCE

We support a major reform of the criminal justice system, but we oppose any legislative effort to introduce repressive and anti-civil libertarian measures in the guise of reform of the criminal code.

Handguns simplify and intensify violent crime. Ways must be found to curtail the availability of these weapons. The Democratic Party must provide the leadership for a coordinated federal and state effort to strengthen the presently inadequate controls over the manufacture, assembly, distribution and possession of handguns and to ban Saturday night specials.

Furthermore, since people and not guns commit crimes, we support mandatory sentencing for individuals convicted of committing a felony with a gun.

The Democratic Party, however, affirms the right of sportsmen to possess guns for purely hunting and target-shooting purposes.

SOURCE: http://patriotpost.us/histdocs/platforms/democratic/dem.976.html

---

1980

LAW ENFORCEMENT

The Democratic Party affirms the right of sportsmen to possess guns for purely hunting and target-shooting purposes. However, handguns simplify and intensify violent crime. Ways must be found to curtail the availability of these weapons. The Democratic Party supports enactment of federal legislation to strengthen the presently inadequate regulations over the manufacture, assembly, distribution, and possession of handguns and to ban "Saturday night specials."

SOURCE: http://patriotpost.us/histdocs/platforms/democratic/dem.980.html

---

Remington 700P Tactical .308-caliber rifle. Photo by Dawn Van Hall.

1984

CRIME

We support tough restraints on the manufacture, transportation, and sale of snub nosed handguns, which have no legitimate sporting use and are used in a high proportion of violent crimes.

SOURCE: http://patriotpost.us/histdocs/platforms/democratic/dem.984.html

1988

WE BELIEVE that the federal government should provide increased assistance to local criminal justice agencies, enforce a ban on "cop killer" bullets that have no purpose other than the killing and maiming of law enforcement officers, reinforce our commitment to help crime victims, and assume a leadership role in securing the safety of our neighborhoods and homes. We further believe that the repeated toleration in Washington of unethical and unlawful greed among too many of those who have been governing our nation, procuring our weapons and polluting our environment has made far more difficult the daily work of the local policemen, teachers and parents who must convey to our children respect for justice and authority.

SOURCE: http://www.presidency.ucsb.edu/ws/index.php?pid=29609

1992

Combating Crime and Drugs. None suffer more than the poor: an explosive mixture of blighted prospects, drugs and exotic weaponry has turned many of our inner city communities into combat zones. As a result, crime is not only a symptom but also a major cause of the worsening poverty and demoralization that afflicts inner city communities.

To empower America's communities, Democrats pledge to restore government as the upholder of basic law and order for crime-ravaged communities. The simplest and most direct way to restore order in our cities is to put more police on the streets.

Neighborhoods and police should be partners in the war on crime. Democrats support more community policing, which uses foot patrols and storefront offices to make police officers visible fixtures in urban neighborhoods. We will combat street violence and emphasize building trust and solving the problems that breed crime.

Firearms. It is time to shut down the weapons bazaars in our cities. We support a reasonable waiting period to permit background checks for purchases of handguns, as well as assault weapons controls to ban the possession, sale, importation and manufacture of the most deadly assault weapons. We do not support efforts to restrict weapons used for legitimate hunting and sporting purposes. We will work for swift and certain punishment of all people who violate the country's gun laws and for stronger sentences for criminals who use guns. We will also seek to shut down the black market for guns and impose severe penalties on people who sell guns to children.

SOURCE: http://www.presidency.ucsb.edu/ws/index.php?pid=29610

1996

Fighting crime. Today's Democratic Party believes the first responsibility of government is law and order. Four years ago, crime in America seemed intractable. The violent crime rate and the murder rate had climbed for seven straight years. Drugs seemed to flow freely across our borders and into our neighborhoods. Convicted felons could walk into any gun shop and buy a handgun. Military-style assault weapons were sold freely. Our people didn't feel safe in their homes, walking their streets, or even sending their children to school. Under the thumb of special interests like the gun lobby, Republicans talked tough about crime but did nothing to fight it.

Bill Clinton promised to turn things around, and that is exactly what he did. After a long hard fight, President Clinton beat back fierce Republican opposition, led by Senator Dole and Speaker Gingrich, to answer the call of America's police officers and pass the toughest Crime Bill in history. The Democratic Party under President Clinton is putting more police on the streets and tougher penalties on the books; we are taking guns off the streets and working to steer young people away from crime and gangs and drugs in the first place. And it is making a difference. In city after city and town after town, crime rates are finally coming down.

RE: *Brady Bill*

Protecting our children, our neighborhoods, and our police from criminals with guns. Bob Dole, Newt Gingrich, and George Bush were able to hold the Brady Bill hostage for the gun lobby until Bill Clinton became President. With his leadership, we made the Brady Bill the law of the land. And because we did, more than 60,000 felons, fugitives, and stalkers have been stopped from buying guns.

RE: *Assault Weapons Ban*

President Clinton led the fight to ban 19 deadly assault weapons, designed for one purpose only—to kill human beings. We oppose efforts to restrict weapons used for legitimate sporting purposes, and we are proud that not one hunter or sportsman was forced to change guns because of the assault weapons ban. But we know that the military-style guns we banned have no place on America's streets, and we are proud of the courageous Democrats who defied the gun lobby and sacrificed their seats in Congress to make America safer.

RE: *"Cop Killer" Bullets*

Today's Democratic Party stands with America's police officers. We are proud to tell them that as long as Bill Clinton and Al Gore are in the White House, any attempt to repeal the Brady Bill or assault weapons ban will be met with a veto. We must do everything we can to stand behind our police officers, and the first thing we should do is pass a ban on cop-killer bullets. Any bullet that can rip through a bulletproof vest should be against the law; that is the least we can do to protect the brave police officers who risk their lives to protect us.

RE: *Youth Prevention Programs*

The Democratic Party understands what the police have been saying for years: The best way to fight crime is to prevent it. That is why we fought for drug-education and gang-prevention programs in our schools. We support well thought out, well organized, highly supervised youth programs to provide young people with a safe and healthy alternative to hanging out on the streets. We made it a federal crime for any person under the age of 18 to possess a handgun except when supervised by an adult. Democrats fought to pass, and President Clinton ordered states to impose, zero tolerance for guns in school, requiring schools to expel for one year any student who brings a gun to school.

SOURCE: http://www.presidency.ucsb.edu/ws/index.php?pid=29611

2000

Fighting Crime

Bill Clinton and Al Gore. . . . stood up to the gun lobby, to pass the Brady Bill and ban deadly assault weapons and stopped nearly half a million felons, fugitives, and stalkers from buying guns. . . . serious crime is down seven years in a row, to its lowest level in a quarter-century. Violent crime is down by 24 percent. The number of juveniles committing homicides with guns is down by nearly 60 percent. . . . We can't surrender to the right-wing Republicans who threatened funding for new police, who tried to gut crime prevention, and who would invite the NRA into the Oval Office. Nor will we go back to the old approach which was tough on the causes of crime, but not tough enough on crime itself. . . . A shocking level of gun violence on our streets and in our schools has shown America that the need to keep guns away from those who shouldn't have them—in ways that respect the rights of hunters, sportsmen, and legitimate gun owners. The Columbine tragedy struck America's heart, but in its wake Republicans have done nothing to keep guns away from those who should not have them.

Democrats believe that we should fight gun crime on all fronts—with stronger laws and stronger enforcement. That's why Democrats fought and passed the Brady Law and the Assault Weapons Ban. We increased federal, state, and local gun crime prosecution by 22 percent since 1992. Now gun crime is down by 35 percent.

Now we must do even more. We need mandatory child safety locks, to protect our children. We should require a photo license I.D., a full background check, and a gun safety test to buy a new handgun in America. We support more federal gun prosecutors, ATF agents and inspectors, and giving states and communities another 10,000 prosecutors to fight gun crime. . . .

Strong and Sensible Gun Laws. A shocking level of gun violence on our streets and in our schools has shown America the need to keep guns away from those who shouldn't have them—in ways that respect the rights of hunters, sportsmen, and legitimate gun owners. The Columbine tragedy struck America's heart, but in its wake Republicans have done nothing to keep guns away from those who should not have them.

Democrats believe that we should fight gun crime on all fronts—with stronger laws and stronger enforcement. That's why Democrats fought and passed the Brady Law and the Assault Weapons Ban. We increased federal, state, and local gun crime prosecution by 22 percent since 1992. Now gun crime is down by 35 percent.

Now we must do even more. We need mandatory child safety locks, to protect our children. We should require a photo license I.D., a full background check, and a gun safety test to buy a new handgun in America. We support more federal gun prosecutors, ATF agents and inspectors, and giving states and communities another 10,000 prosecutors to fight gun crime.

SOURCE: http://a9.g.akamai.net/7/9/8082/v001/www.democrats.org/pdfs/2000platform.pdf

---

2004

Crime and violence. While terrorism poses an especially menacing threat to our nation, a strong America must remain vigilant against the scourge of homegrown crime as well. We are proud that Democrats led the fight to put more than 100,000 cops on the beat through the COPS program, and we will continue our steadfast support for COPS and community policing. To keep our streets safe for our families, we support tough punishment of violent crime and smart efforts to reintegrate former prisoners into our communities as productive citizens. We will crack down on the gang violence and drug crime that devastate so many communities, and we will increase drug treatment, including mandatory drug courts and mandatory drug testing for parolees and probationers, so fewer crimes are committed in the first place. We support the rights of victims to be respected, to be heard, and to be compensated. We will help break the cycle of domestic violence by punishing offenders and standing with victims. We will protect Americans' Second Amendment right to own firearms, and we will keep guns out of the hands of criminals and terrorists by fighting gun crime, reauthorizing the assault weapons ban, and closing the gun show loophole, as President Bush proposed and failed to do.

SOURCE: http://www.presidency.ucsb.edu/ws/index.php?pid=29613

2008

Firearms. We recognize that the right to bear arms is an important part of the American tradition, and we will preserve Americans' Second Amendment right to own and use firearms. We believe that the right to own firearms is subject to reasonable regulation, but we know that what works in Chicago may not work in Cheyenne. We can work together to enact and enforce commonsense laws and improvements—like closing the gun show loopholes, improving our background check system, and reinstating the assault weapons ban, so that guns do not fall into the hands of terrorists or criminals. Acting responsibly and with respect for differing views on this issue, we can both protect the constitutional right to bear arms and keep our communities and our children safe.

SOURCE: http://www.demconvention.com/assets/downloads/2008-Democratic-Platform-by-Cmte-08-13-08.pdf

---

ANALYSIS

National political party platforms are more than window-dressing for a political party. Drawn up every four years at the presidential nominating conventions by party leaders, the platforms reflect the politics and ideology of both the party and the presidential nominee. They also reflect the manner in which the party plans to present itself to the electorate for the fall election.

The major parties first addressed the issue of gun control in 1968, but both also mentioned the right to bear arms around the time of the Civil War. The Democratic Party in 1864 had grave misgivings about Republican President Abraham Lincoln's vigorous and uncompromising prosecution of the war against the rebellious southern states. Thus, its platform was harshly critical of the Lincoln administration's suspension of rights, which extended to the administration of military governance over rebellious territories instead of yielding to local control, including local militias, prompting the reference to the "denial of the right of the people to bear arms in their defence."

In the modern era, Democratic platform statements on the gun issue generally emphasize the connection between crime and guns, leading to an emphasis on various gun control proposals, a move endorsed by Democratic-leaning gun control interest groups. Starting in the 1990s, however, the presidential nominees—especially Clinton and Kerry in 2004—shifted the platforms' emphasis toward gun rights, while keeping some endorsements of limited gun control measures. This shift represented a conscious effort by the Democrats to court more conservative, pro-gun constituencies.

By the tumultuous year of 1968, the country had been rocked with rioting in large cities and had recently been shocked by the assassinations of two political leaders earlier that year—civil rights leader Dr. Martin Luther King, Jr., and presidential candidate Robert F. Kennedy. Thus, the emphasis in the platform was on the link between crime control and gun control, echoing Congress's recent enactment of the Gun Control Act (see Chapter 7).

The 1972 platform statement again linked gun control to crime, focusing specifically on controlling "the improper use of hand guns." Invoking the assassinations of Robert Kennedy and the attempt against 1972 Democratic presidential candidate George Wallace (who survived the attempt, but was permanently paralyzed), the platform of the party that nominated Senator George McGovern for the presidency urged a ban on small, cheap handguns, referred to as "Saturday night specials." The 1976 platform also recommended handgun controls, but reflecting the views of the more conservative nominee, former Georgia Governor Jimmy Carter, added language for the first time that affirmed "the right of sportsmen to possess guns for purely hunting and target-shooting purposes." The 1980 platform kept the same language, but inverted the order so as to elevate the reference to protecting the rights of sportspeople.

Perhaps reflecting the views of the more liberal nominee, Walter Mondale, the 1984 platform dropped direct reference to hunting, emphasizing the need to control "snub nosed handguns." Despite former Massachusetts Governor Michael Dukakis's early support for tougher gun laws, the 1988 platform retreated on former tough language. Its only specific gun regulation proposal was a call for enforcement of the ban on armor-piercing, so-called "cop killer" bullets enacted two years earlier—a proposal that was both uncontroversial and inconsequential, as the law was already on the books. This wording back-pedaling might be attributable to the party's desire to paint Dukakis as less liberal and more tough on crime, in response to attacks by his opponent, George H. W. Bush.

The party that nominated Arkansas Governor Bill Clinton adopted a stronger and more specific position on the issue. After asserting that it was "time to shut down the weapons bazaars," it endorsed a waiting period for handgun purchases (what became the Brady Law in 1993; see Chapter 7), and a ban on "the most deadly assault weapons" (enacted in 1994; see Chapter 7). Both measures had languished in Congress since the late 1980s. It also called for tougher penalties for gun-related criminal activities. Returning to, and amplifying, language from the Carter era, the platform also stated its opposition to measures that would restrict the activities of hunters and sportspeople (Clinton was a hunter). The 1996 platform claimed credit for enactment of the Brady Law and assault weapons ban, and repeated themes from four years earlier.

The platform of the party that nominated Vice President Al Gore extolled his record of standing up to the "gun lobby," cited past successes of the Clinton-Gore administration, and also promised to continue a tough approach to gun-related crime.

DID YOU KNOW?

Gun Mayhem Comes to College

On the morning of April 16, 2007, a graduate student with a history of mental problems used two handguns to shoot and kill, in an apparently random fashion, 32 students and faculty on the campus of Virginia Polytechnic Institute and State University, also known as Virginia Tech. As police closed in on him, the student, Seung Hui Cho, killed himself with a final shot.

Cho purchased the two handguns legally, even though he had a history of emotional problems dating to junior high school, and a judge had ruled him mentally ill and a danger to himself. Yet his name did not appear on the federal list of those barred from purchasing a handgun because of an inconsistency in how Virginia reported such data to the national government (because he had been ordered to obtain counseling but was not committed, his name was not sent on). In fact, even though the federal Brady Law (see Chapter 7) called for states to report such data to the National Instant Criminal Background Check System, in 2007 only 22 states did so, as there was then no penalty for states that failed to comply, and some states said they could not afford to fund necessary recordkeeping improvements. In the months after the shooting, Virginia enacted new legislation to correct its recordkeeping and reporting practices, and in early 2008 Congress enacted legislation to impel all states to comply with federal requirements.

The platform's detailed treatment of the gun issue reflected its emphatic injection in the 2000 elections in the aftermath of the 1999 Columbine High School massacre and the "Million Mom March" on Washington, D.C. in the spring of 2000. The 2004 convention that nominated Massachusetts Senator John Kerry called, for the first time, for protecting "Americans' Second Amendment right to own firearms," and to push for other anti-gun-crime measures, including renewal of the assault weapons ban (it lapsed in 2004; see Chapter 7). The first-time reference in a Democratic platform was significant, as it was a talismanic invocation in Republican platforms that generally emphasized gun rights over gun control. It was also symptomatic of the Democratic Party's belief that its pursuit of strong gun laws was no longer a politically effective strategy. Similarly, the 2008 Democratic platform for Democratic nominee Barack Obama also referenced protecting citizens' right to bear arms, but it also supported closing the gun show loophole, improving background checks, and reinstituting the assault weapons ban that lapsed in 2004 (see Chapter 7).

FURTHER READING

Goss, Kristin A. *Disarmed: The Missing Movement for Gun Control in America*. Princeton, NJ: Princeton University Press, 2006.

Spitzer, Robert J. *The Politics of Gun Control*. Washington, D.C.: CQ Press, 2007.

Republican Party Platform Statements on Gun Control and Gun Rights

- *Document:* excerpts from Republican Party platforms
- *Date:* 1856–2008
- *Where:* various
- *Significance:* Republican Party platform statements on the gun issue emphasize gun rights and crime control.

DOCUMENT

Republican Party Platform Statements on Gun Control

1856

Resolved: That while the Constitution of the United States was ordained and established by the people, in order to "form a more perfect union, establish justice, ensure domestic tranquility, provide for the common defense, promote the general welfare, and secure the blessings of liberty," and contain ample provision for the protection of the life, liberty, and property of every citizen, the dearest Constitutional rights of the people of Kansas have been fraudulently and violently taken from them.

Their Territory has been invaded by an armed force. . . .

The right of the people to keep and bear arms has been infringed.

SOURCE: http://members.aol.com/jfepperson/r1856.html

1968

Total commitment to a federal program to deter, apprehend, prosecute, convict and punish the overlords of organized crime in America, including full implementation of the Congressional mandate that court-supervised wiretapping and electronic surveillance tools be used against the mobsters and racketeers;

Enactment of legislation to control indiscriminate availability of firearms, safeguarding the right of responsible citizens to collect, own and use firearms for legitimate purposes, retaining primary responsibility at the state level, with such federal laws as necessary to better enable the states to meet their responsibilities.

SOURCE; HTTP://patriotpost.us/histdocs/platforms/republican/rep.968.html

1972

LAW ENFORCEMENT

Our goal is justice for everyone.

We pledge a tireless campaign against crime to restore safety to our streets, and security to law-abiding citizens who have a right to enjoy their homes and communities free from fear.

We pledge to:

- Intensify efforts to prevent criminal access to all weapons, including special emphasis on cheap, readily-obtainable handguns, retaining primary responsibility at the State level, with such Federal law as necessary to enable the States to meet their responsibilities.
- Safeguard the right of responsible citizens to collect, own and use firearms for legitimate purposes, including hunting, target shooting and self-defense. We will strongly support efforts of all law enforcement agencies to apprehend and prosecute to the limit of the law all those who use firearms in the commission of crimes.

SOURCE: http://patriotpost.us/histdocs/platforms/republican/rep.972.html

1976

A SAFE AND JUST SOCIETY

The federal criminal code should include automatic and mandatory minimum sentences for persons committing offenses under federal jurisdiction that involve the use of a dangerous weapon; that involve exceptionally serious crimes, such as trafficking in hard drugs, kidnapping and aircraft hijacking; and that involve injuries committed by repeat offenders.

We support the right of citizens to keep and bear arms. We oppose federal registration of firearms. Mandatory sentences for crimes committed with a lethal weapon are the only effective solution to this problem.

SOURCE: http://patriotpost.us/histdocs/platforms/republican/rep.976.html

1980

CRIME

We believe the right of citizens to keep and bear arms must be preserved. Accordingly, we oppose federal registration of firearms. Mandatory sentences for commission of armed felonies are the most effective means to deter abuse of this right. We therefore support Congressional initiatives to remove those provisions of the Gun Control Act of 1968 that do not significantly impact on crime but serve rather to restrain the law-abiding citizen in his legitimate use of firearms.

SOURCE: http://patriotpost.us/histdocs/platforms/republican/rep.980.html

1984

CRIME

Republicans will continue to defend the constitutional right to keep and bear arms. When this right is abused and armed felonies are committed, we believe in stiff, mandatory sentencing. Law-abiding citizens exercising their constitutional rights must not be blamed for crime. Republicans will continue to seek repeal of legislation that restrains innocent citizens' more than violent criminals.

SOURCE: http://patriotpost.us/histdocs/platforms/republican/rep.984.html

1988

THE RIGHT OF GUN OWNERSHIP

Republicans defend the constitutional right to keep and bear arms. When this right is abused by an individual who uses a gun in the commission of a crime, we call for stiff, mandatory penalties.

SOURCE: http://patriotpost.us/histdocs/platforms/republican/rep.988.html

1992

Safe Homes and Streets

Violent crime is the gravest domestic threat to our way of life. It has turned our communities into battlegrounds, playgrounds into grave yards. It threatens everyone, but especially the very young, the elderly, the weak. It destroys business and suffocates economic opportunity in struggling communities. It is a travesty that some American children have to sleep in bathtubs for protection from stray bullets. The poverty of values that justifies drive-by shootings and random violence holds us hostage and insecure, even in our own homes. We must work to develop community-help projects designed to instill a sense of responsibility and pride.

Individual Rights. The protection of individual rights is the foundation for opportunity and security.

The Republican Party is unique in this regard. Since its inception, it has respected every person, even when that proposition was not universally popular. Today, as in the day of Lincoln, we insist that no American's rights are negotiable.

Republicans defend the constitutional right to keep and bear arms. We call for stiff mandatory sentences for those who use firearms in a crime. We note that those who seek to disarm citizens in their homes are the same liberals who tried to disarm our Nation during the Cold War and are today seeking to cut our national defense below safe levels. We applaud congressional Republicans for overturning the District of Columbia's law blaming firearm manufacturers for street crime.

SOURCE: http://www.presidency.ucsb.edu/ws/index.php?pid=25847

1996

We defend the constitutional right to keep and bear arms. We will promote training in the safe usage of firearms, especially in programs for women and the elderly. We strongly support Bob Dole's National Instant Check Initiative, which will help keep all guns out of the hands of convicted felons. The point-of-purchase instant check has worked well in many states and now it is time to extend this system all across America. We applaud Bob Dole's commitment to have the national instant check system operational by the end of 1997. In one of the strangest actions of his tenure, Bill Clinton abolished Operation Triggerlock, the Republican initiative to jail any felon caught with a gun. We will restore that effort and will set by law minimum mandatory penalties for the use of guns in committing a crime: 5 years for possession, 10 years for brandishing, and 20 for discharge.

SOURCE: http://www.cnn.com/ALLPOLITICS/1996/conventions/san.diego/facts/gop.plat form/platform.all.shtml

2000

We defend the constitutional right to keep and bear arms, and we affirm the individual responsibility to safely use and store firearms. Because self-defense is a basic human right, we will promote training in their safe usage, especially in federal programs for women and the elderly. A Republican administration will vigorously enforce current gun laws, neglected by the Democrats, especially by prosecuting dangerous offenders identified as felons in instant background checks. Although we support background checks to ensure that guns do not fall into the hands of criminals, we oppose federal licensing of law-abiding gun owners and national gun registration as a violation of the Second Amendment and an invasion of privacy of honest citizens. Through programs like Project Exile, we will hold criminals individually accountable for their actions by strong enforcement of federal and state firearm laws, especially when guns are used in violent or drug-related crimes. With a special emphasis upon school safety, we propose the crackdown on youth violence explained elsewhere in this platform.

Any juvenile who commits any crime while carrying a gun should automatically be detained, not released to someone's custody.

SOURCE: http://www.presidency.ucsb.edu/showplatforms.php?platindex=R2000

2004

Protecting Our Rights, Fighting Criminals, and Supporting Victims

Republicans and President Bush strongly support an individual right to own guns, which is explicitly protected by the Constitution's Second Amendment. Our Party honors the great American tradition of hunting and we applaud efforts by the Bush Administration to make more public lands available to hunters, to increase access to hunting clinics and safety programs for children and adults, and to improve opportunities for hunting for Americans with disabilities.

We believe the Second Amendment and all of the rights guaranteed by it should enable law-abiding citizens throughout the country to own firearms in their homes for self-defense. To protect the rights and safety of law-abiding citizens, the Congress passed and President Bush signed the Law Enforcement Officers Safety Act, which allows active and retired law enforcement officers to carry concealed guns in public while off-duty. We support efforts by the Administration and Congress to enhance the instant background check system for gun purchases and to ensure that records of lawful transactions are destroyed in a timely manner. We applaud Congressional Republicans for seeking to stop frivolous lawsuits against firearms manufacturers, which is a transparent attempt to deprive citizens of their Second Amendment rights. We oppose federal licensing of law-abiding gun owners and national gun registration as a violation of the Second Amendment and an invasion of privacy of honest citizens.

We agree that the best way to deter crime is to enforce existing laws and hand down tough penalties against anyone who commits a crime with a gun. This approach is working. Since Project Safe Neighborhoods was instituted in 2001, hundreds of new federal, state, and local prosecutors have been hired to target criminals who use guns.

Prosecutions are up 68 percent, and the violent crime victimization rate is down 21 percent. The Republican Party and President Bush support a federal Constitutional amendment for victims of violent crime that would provide specific rights for victims protected under the U.S. Constitution. We support courts having the option to impose the death penalty in capital murder cases. We praise President Bush and Republicans in Congress for the measures they have taken to protect pregnant women from violent crime by passing Laci and Conner's law, which recognizes the common-sense proposition that when a crime of violence against a pregnant woman kills or injures her unborn child, there are two victims and two offenses that should be punished.

SOURCE: http://www.gop.com/media/2004platform.pdf

2008

Upholding the Constitutional Right to Keep and Bear Arms

We uphold the right of individual Americans to own firearms, a right which antedated the Constitution and was solemnly confirmed by the Second Amendment. We applaud the Supreme Court's decision in *Heller* affirming that right, and we assert the individual responsibility to safely use and store firearms. We call on the next president to appoint judges who will similarly respect the Constitution. Gun ownership is responsible citizenship, enabling Americans to defend themselves, their property, and communities.

We call for education in constitutional rights in schools, and we support the option of firearms training in federal programs serving senior citizens and women. We urge immediate action to review the automatic denial of gun ownership to returning members of the Armed Forces who have suffered trauma during service to their country. We condemn frivolous lawsuits against firearms manufacturers, which are transparent attempts to deprive citizens of their rights. We oppose federal licensing of law-abiding gun owners and national gun registration as violations of the Second Amendment. We recognize that gun control only affects and penalizes law-abiding citizens, and that such proposals are ineffective at reducing violent crime.

SOURCE: http://www.gop.com/pdf/PlatformFINAL_WithCover.pdf

ANALYSIS

National political party platforms are more than window-dressing for a political party. Drawn up every four years at the presidential nominating conventions by party leaders, the platforms reflect the politics and ideology of both the party and the presidential nominee. They also reflect the manner in which the party plans to present itself to the electorate for the fall election.

The major parties first addressed the issue of gun control in 1968, but both also mentioned the right to bear arms around the time of the Civil War. The newly formed

Republican Party, holding its first convention in 1856, referenced the ongoing tumult and bloodshed in the Kansas territory—"bloody Kansas," as it was called—where Congress had decided that the issue of slavery would be decided by the people of the territory. This led to an influx of proslavery and antislavery forces, which often fought pitched battles and massacred civilians. In their platform, the antislavery Republicans called for a restoration of a right to bear arms.

In the modern era, Republican platform statements on the gun issue generally emphasize gun rights, reflecting a close allegiance to the views of gun rights groups, especially the NRA (beginning with the 2000 Republican convention, the NRA was a cosponsor of the convention). More moderate Republican presidential nominees, such as Nixon, Ford, and Dole, emphasized other issues, including crime control, whereas more conservative nominees, including Reagan and the second Bush, emphasized gun rights more strongly. The politicization of the gun rights movement in the 1970s and its rightward tilt into the 1990s is reflected in Republican platforms.

The 1968 Republican Party platform, supporting nominee Richard Nixon, urged "control [of] indiscriminate availability of firearms" but also "safeguarding the right of responsible citizens to collect, own and use firearms . . . retaining primary responsibility at the state level." The 1972 platform, supporting Nixon's renomination, again endorsed citizen rights to firearms, but also included "self-defense" as a purpose and emphasized efforts "to prevent criminal access to all weapons," especially cheap handguns, while relying mainly on state enforcement. The 1976 platform took a turn to the right; it simply stated: "We support the right of citizens to keep and bear arms." The platform also stated its opposition to federal registration of firearms and advocated harsher sentences for crimes committed with guns. If the previous GOP platforms contained at least a nod to gun regulation, the 1976 document, produced by the convention that nominated Gerald Ford, conformed closely to NRA policy.

In 1980, the Republican platform wording was duplicated from 1976, with an added phrase urging removal of "those provisions of the Gun Control Act of 1968" that serve "to restrain the law-abiding citizen in his legitimate use of firearms." This sentence foreshadowed the original purpose behind the Firearms Owners' Protection Act of 1986 (see Chapter 7). Reflecting the conservative views of party nominee Ronald Reagan, this platform language reflected the agenda of gun rights groups.

The 1984 convention that renominated Reagan adopted a platform that dropped any reference to the Gun Control Act or to the lifting of gun regulations and said instead that citizens ought not to be blamed for "exercising their constitutional rights." The 1988 platform of the convention that nominated George H. W. Bush also indicated the party's support for "the constitutional right to keep and bear arms" and called for "stiff, mandatory penalties" for those who used guns in the commission of crimes. This wording was kept in the 1992 platform (although the NRA refused to endorse Bush) along with additional wording tying gun ownership to national defense, and criticizing efforts at "blaming firearm manufacturers for street crime."

The 1996 platform again invoked the Second Amendment but added wording about the need for training programs for safe firearms use. It also supported presidential candidate Robert Dole's support for an instant background check system for handgun purchases (implemented as part of the Brady Law in 1998; see Chapter 7). The platform also called for mandatory penalties for gun crimes. The 2000 platform for nominee George W. Bush paralleled that of 1996, invoking the Second Amendment, citing the importance of self-defense, and also promising vigorous enforcement of existing gun laws. It further stated express opposition to gun licensing and registration. The 2004 platform for President Bush's reelection again contained an emphatic Second Amendment gun rights statement, applauding the hunting tradition, the use of guns for self-protection, and administration efforts to open federal lands to hunting. It also supported quick destruction of gun purchase documentation and the ongoing effort to protect the gun industry from lawsuits (enacted in 2005), and opposed any gun licensing or registration. The 2008 platform accompanying the nomination of John McCain extolled the pro-gun rights decision in *D.C. v. Heller* (see Chapter 5), announced in June 2008, and argued for the appointment of judges who would support this controversial ruling. In a new twist, the platform called for "firearms training in federal programs serving senior citizens and women." There was no explanation for who would conduct such training, how it would be funded, its purpose, or why it would be aimed at, or connected with, senior citizens and women.

FURTHER READING

Spitzer, Robert J. *The Politics of Gun Control*. Washington, D.C.: CQ Press. 2007.

Vizzard, William J. *Shots in the Dark: The Policy, Politics, and Symbolism of Gun Control*. Lanham, MD: Rowman & Littlefield, 2000.

GUN CONTROL RESOURCES

WEB SITES

Many groups and organizations are active in the gun control issue, covering the broad spectrum of positions. Here are a few of the most prominent on both sides of the issue, followed by research and government sites. Each of these organizations provides considerable information and information links.

Gun Rights Groups

Citizens Committee for the Right to Keep and Bear Arms
http://www.ccrkba.org/

Gun Owners of America
http://www.gunowners.org/

The National Rifle Association
http://www.nra.org/

National Shooting Sports Foundation
http://www.nssf.org/

The Second Amendment Foundation (affiliated with the CCRKBA)
http://www.saf.org/

Gun Control Groups

The Brady Campaign to Prevent Gun Violence
http://www.bradycampaign.org/

The Brady Center to Prevent Gun Violence
http://www.bradycenter.org/

Coalition to Stop Gun Violence
http://www.csgv.org/site/c.pmL5JnO7KzE/b.3509205/

The Violence Policy Center
http://www.vpc.org/

Research and Information Sites

Firearm and Injury Center at Penn, the University of Pennsylvania
http://www.uphs.upenn.edu/ficap/

Gundebate.com
http://www.gundebate.com/

Harvard Injury Control Research Center, Harvard School of Public Health
http://www.hsph.harvard.edu/research/hicrc/

Johns Hopkins Center for Gun Policy and Research, the Johns Hopkins University
http://www.jhsph.edu/gunpolicy

The Second Amendment Center at the John Glenn Institute for Public Service and Public Policy at Ohio State University
http://www.secondamendmentcenter.org/

Government Agencies

Bureau of Alcohol, Tobacco, Firearms, and Explosives
http://www.atf.gov/

Bureau of Justice Statistics, Office of Justice Programs, U.S. Department of Justice
http://www.ojp.usdoj.gov/bjs/

National Center for Injury Prevention and Control, Centers for Disease Control and Prevention, Department of Health and Human Services
http://www.cdc.gov/ncipc/

National Institute of Justice, U.S. Department of Justice
http://www.ojp.usdoj.gov/nij/

BIBLIOGRAPHY

Anderson, Jack. *Inside the NRA*. Beverly Hills, CA: Dove Books, 1996.

Athearn, Robert J. *The Mythic West*. Lawrence: University Press of Kansas, 1986.

Bogus, Carl T., ed. *The Second Amendment in Law and History*. New York: New Press, 2002.

Brown, Peter Harry, and Daniel G. Abel. *Outgunned: Up Against the NRA*. New York: The Free Press 2003.

Bruce, John M., and Clyde Wilcox, eds. *The Changing Politics of Gun Control*. Lanham, MD: Rowman and Littlefield,1998.

Burbick, Joan. *Gun Show Nation*. New York: The New Press, 2006.

Carlson, Andrew. *The Antiquated Right*. New York: Peter Lang, 2002.

Carter, Gregg Lee. *The Gun Control Movement*. New York: Twayne, 1997.

Carter, Gregg Lee, ed. *Encyclopedia of Guns in American Society*. 2 vols. Santa Barbara, CA: ABC-CLIO, 2003.

Cook, Philip, and Jens Ludwig. *Gun Violence: The Real Costs*. New York: Oxford University Press, 2000.

Cooper, Jerry. *The Rise of the National Guard*. Lincoln: University of Nebraska Press, 1997.

Cornell, Saul. *A Well-Regulated Militia*. New York: Oxford University Press, 2006.

Cornell, Saul, ed. *Whose Right to Bear Arms Did the Second Amendment Protect?* New York: St. Martin's, 2000.

Cottrol, Robert J., ed. *Gun Control and the Constitution*. New York: Garland Publishers, 1994.

Cress, Lawrence D. *Citizens in Arms: The Army and the Militia in American Society to the War of 1812*. Chapel Hill: University of North Carolina Press, 1982.

Davidson, Osha Gray. *Under Fire*. New York: Henry Holt, 1993.

DeConde, Alexander. *Gun Violence in America*. Boston: Northeastern University Press, 2001.

Diaz, Tom. *Making a Killing: The Business of Guns in America*. New York: The New Press, 1999.

Edel, Wilbur. *Gun Control: Threat to Liberty or Defense Against Anarchy?* Westport, CT: Praeger, 1995.

Feldman, Richard, *Ricochet: Confessions of a Gun Lobbyist*. New York: Wiley, 2007.

Goss, Kristin A. *Disarmed: The Missing Movement for Gun Control in America*. Princeton: Princeton University Press, 2006.

Halbrook, Stephen P. *That Every Man Be Armed*. Oakland, CA: The Independent Institute 1984.

Harcourt, Bernard E. *Language of the Gun: Youth, Crime, and Public Policy*. Chicago: University of Chicago Press, 2006.

Harcourt, Bernard E., ed. *Guns, Crime, and Punishment in America*. New York: New York University Press, 2003.

Hemenway, David. *Private Guns, Public Health*. Ann Arbor: University of Michigan Press 2004.

Henderson, Harry. *Gun Control*. New York: Facts on File, Inc., 2000.

Henigan, Dennis A., E. Bruce Nicholson, and David Hemenway. *Guns and the Constitution*. Northampton, MA: Aletheia Press, 1995.

Homsher, Deborah. *Women and Guns: Politics and the Culture of Firearms in America*. Armonk, NY: M.E. Sharpe, 2001.

Jacobs, James B. *Can Gun Control Work?* New York: Oxford University Press, 2004.

Karl, Jonathan. *The Right to Bear Arms*. New York: HarperCollins, 1995.

Kelly, Caitlin. *Blown Away: American Women and Guns*. New York: Pocket Books, 2004.

Kennett, Lee, and James LaVerne Anderson. *The Gun in America*. Westport, CT: Greenwood, 1975.

Kleck. Gary. *Targeting Guns*. New York: Aldine DeGruyter, 1997.

LaPierre, Wayne. *Guns, Crime, and Freedom*. Washington, D.C.: Regnery, 1994.

LaPierre, Wayne, and James Jay Baker. *Shooting Straight: Telling the Truth About Guns in America*. Washington, D.C.: Regnery, 2002.

Larson, Erik. *Lethal Passage: The Story of a Gun*. New York: Vintage, 1995.

Lott, John R. *The Bias Against Guns*. Washington, D.C.: Regnery, 2003.

Ludwig, Jens, and Philip Cook, eds. *Evaluating Gun Policy*. Washington, D.C.: Brookings, 2003.

Malcolm, Joyce Lee. *Guns and Violence*. Cambridge, MA: Harvard University Press, 2002.

McClurg, Andrew J., David B. Kopel and Brannon P. Denning, eds. *Gun Control and Gun Rights*. New York: New York University Press, 2002.

Moore, James. *Very Special Agents*. Urbana: University of Illinois Press, 2001.

National Research Council. *Firearms and Violence: A Critical Review*. Washington, D.C.: The National Academies Press, 2005.

Roleff, Tamara L. *Gun Control*. Farmington Hills, MI: Greenhaven Press, 2007.

Sherrill, Robert. *The Saturday Night Special*. New York: Charterhouse, 1973.

Shields, Pete. *Guns Don't Die—People Do*. New York: Arbor House, 1981.

Shy, John. *A People Numerous and Armed*. Ann Arbor: University of Michigan Press, 1990.

Spitzer, Robert J. *The Right to Bear Arms*. Santa Barbara, CA: ABC-CLIO, 2001.

Spitzer, Robert J. *The Politics of Gun Control*, 4th ed. Washington, D.C.: CQ Press, 2007.

Stern, Kenneth S. *A Force Upon the Plain*. New York: Simon and Schuster, 1996.

Sugarmann, Josh. *Every Handgun Is Aimed At You: The Case for Banning Handguns*. New York: The New Press, 2001.

Tita, George, et al. *Reducing Gun Violence*. Santa Monica, CA: RAND Corporation, 2003.

Utley, Robert M. *High Noon in Lincoln: Violence on the Western Frontier*. Albuquerque: University of New Mexico Press, 1990.

Utter, Glenn H. *Encyclopedia of Gun Control and Gun Rights*. Phoenix, AZ: Oryx Press, 1999.

Uviller, H. Richard, and William G. Merkel. *The Militia and the Right to Arms*. Durham, NC: Duke University Press, 2002.

Vinzant, Carol. *Lawyers, Guns and Money: One Man's Battle with the Gun Industry*. New York: Palgrave Macmillan, 2005.

Vizzard, William J. *In the Crossfire: A Political History of the Bureau of Alcohol, Tobacco, and Firearms*. Boulder, CO: Lynne Rienner, 1997.

Vizzard, William J. *Shots in the Dark: The Policy, Politics, and Symbolism of Gun Control*. Lanham, MD: Rowman and Littlefield, 2000.

Williams, David C. *Mythic Meanings of the Second Amendment*. New Haven, CT: Yale University Press, 2003.

Wills, Garry. *A Necessary Evil*. New York: Simon and Schuster, 1999.

Windlesham, Lord. *Politics, Punishment, and Populism*. New York: Oxford University Press, 1998.

Young, Mitchell, ed. *Gun Control*. Farmington, Hills, MI: Greenhaven Press, 2007.

INDEX

About the Author

ROBERT J. SPITZER is Distinguished Service Professor of Political Science at the State University of New York, College at Cortland. His books include *The Presidency and Public Policy* (1983), *The Right to Life Movement and Third Party Politics* (1987), *The Presidential Veto* (1988), *The Bicentennial of the U.S. Constitution* (1990), *President and Congress* (1993), *Media and Public Policy* (1993), *The Politics of Gun Control* (1995; 2nd ed. 1998; 3rd ed. 2004; 4th ed. 2007), *Politics and Constitutionalism* (2000), *The Right to Bear Arms* (2001), *Essentials of American Politics* (co-authored, 2002; 2nd ed. 2006; 3rd ed. 2009), *The Presidency and the Constitution* (co-authored, 2005), and *Saving the Constitution from Lawyers: How Legal Training and Law Reviews Distort Constitutional Meaning* (2008). He is also Series Editor for the book series *American Constitutionalism* for SUNY Press. In 2003, he received the SUNY Chancellor's Award for Excellence in Scholarship. Spitzer is the author of over 300 articles and papers appearing in many journals and books on a variety of American political subjects. He served as President of the Presidency Research Group of the American Political Science Association from 2001–2003. He also served as a member of the New York State Commission on the Bicentennial of the U.S. Constitution, and has testified before Congress on several occasions. Spitzer has appeared on NBC's *Today Show*, ABC's *Good Morning America*, and *Network Nightly News*, PBS's *News Hour With Jim Lehrer*, CNN, CNBC, the PBS documentary film *Guns and Mothers*, and has been quoted in or by such media outlets as the *New York Times*, the *Washington Post*, *Time* magazine, *Newsweek*, the *Los Angeles Times*, *USA Today*, the *Wall Street Journal*, the *Christian Science Monitor*, the BBC (Britain), CBC (Canada), NHK (Japan), National Public Radio, and CBS Radio, among others. His op-ed articles on gun control and other subjects have appeared in many newspapers around the country. He is also a regular panelist on the weekly public affairs program, *The Ivory Tower Half Hour*, broadcast on WCNY-TV, Syracuse, New York.